TRANSNATIONAL REPRESSION
IN THE AGE OF GLOBALISATION

Edinburgh Studies on Diasporas and Transnationalism

Series Editors: Bahar Baser and Mari Toivanen

Bringing together high-quality academic works written by diaspora and transnationalism scholars, this series adopts an interdisciplinary approach and is open to empirical and theoretical submissions alike, making meaningful contributions to contemporary debates in the field. While focusing on economic, political, social and cultural factors that shape and maintain transnational identities and diasporic attachments to the country of origin and residence, the series is also open to submissions on different aspects of transnational interactions from an arts and humanities perspective.

Published and forthcoming titles

Diasporic Futures: Cypriot Diaspora, Temporality and the Politics of Hope
Evropi Chatzipanagiotidou

Second-Generation 'Return' Migration: The Turkish-German Experience
Nilay Kılınç and Russell King

Transnational Repression in the Age of Globalisation
Dana M. Moss and Saipira Furstenberg

Kurdish Diaspora Mobilisation in Denmark: Supporting the Struggle in Syria
Anne-Sofie Schøtt

Transnational Culture in the Iranian Armenian Diaspora
Claudia Yaghoobi

edinburghuniversitypress.com/series/esdt

TRANSNATIONAL REPRESSION IN THE AGE OF GLOBALISATION

Edited by Dana M. Moss and
Saipira Furstenberg

EDINBURGH
University Press

To those who shared their stories, struggles and hardships,
we thank you and honour your courage.

For Kate Picard (1944–2023), always the indefatigable investigator.
– DMM

For my children, Emma and Mario.
– SF

Edinburgh University Press is one of the leading university presses in the UK. We publish academic books and journals in our selected subject areas across the humanities and social sciences, combining cutting-edge scholarship with high editorial and production values to produce academic works of lasting importance. For more information visit our website: edinburghuniversitypress.com

Edinburgh University Press Ltd
13 Infirmary Street
Edinburgh EH1 1LT

First published in hardback by Edinburgh University Press 2024

Typeset in 11/15 EB Garamond by
IDSUK (DataConnection) Ltd

A CIP record for this book is available from the British Library

ISBN 978 1 3995 0606 9 (hardback)
ISBN 978 1 3995 0607 6 (paperback)
ISBN 978 1 3995 0608 3 (webready PDF)
ISBN 978 1 3995 0609 0 (epub)

This work has been supported by H2020-MSCA-COFUND-2019-Marie Skłodowska-Curie COFUND 'GLOBAL_AT_VENICE – Research training for Global Challenges', acronym G@V GA 945361, CUP H74I20000430002.

CONTENTS

FIGURES AND TABLES

ABOUT THE CONTRIBUTORS

Fiona B. Adamson is Professor of International Relations in the Department of Politics and International Studies at SOAS, University of London. Her research interests are in the international politics of migration, mobility and diaspora, with a focus on conflict, peace and security. She is an Associate Editor of *Security Studies* and serves as an adjunct faculty member of the Queen Elizabeth II Academy for Leadership in International Affairs at Chatham House. Her published works have appeared in *International Security, International Studies Quarterly, International Affairs, European Journal of International Relations, International Migration Review, International Migration, International Studies Review, International Studies Perspectives, Current History, Political Science Quarterly, Cambridge Review of International Affairs* and *Journal of Ethnic and Migration Studies*, among others.

Bahar Baser is Associate Professor in Middle East Politics, at Durham University. Previously, she was Associate Professor at the Centre for Trust, Peace and Social Relations, Coventry. She is also an associate research fellow at the Security Institute for Governance and Leadership in Africa at Stellenbosch University, South Africa, and a visiting fellow at Tampere Peace Research Institute in Tampere University, Finland. She is author of the book *Diasporas and Homeland Conflicts: A Comparative Perspective* (2015) and has published numerous articles on ethnic and migration studies with a focus on Middle

Eastern diasporas. Dr Baser holds a PhD from the European University Institute in Florence, Italy. She is a series editor of Kurdish Societies, Politics, and International Relations and the Edinburgh University Press series Studies on Diasporas and Transnationalism.

Gözde Böcü is a PhD Candidate in the Department of Political Science at the University of Toronto, Canada, specialising in comparative politics and international relations. Her research interests include transnationalism, migration and authoritarianism. Her PhD research, based on multisite fieldwork in Europe, explores Turkey's authoritarian diaspora policies and their effects on diasporas from a comparative perspective. Her work has been published in a variety of outlets, including *Ethnopolitics*, *Social Forces* and *Middle East Critique*, among others. Currently, she is a Doctoral Fellow at the Citizen Lab, where she conducts research at the intersection of human rights and cybersecurity with a specific focus on the digital dimension of transnational repression.

Alexander Dukalskis is Associate Professor at University College Dublin, Ireland and director of the UCD Centre for Asia-Pacific Research. His research focuses on authoritarian states, Asian politics and international human rights. His work has been published in several leading journals, including the *Journal of Peace Research*, *China Quarterly*, *International Studies Review*, *Journal of Democracy*, *Review of International Studies* and *Democratization*. He is the author of two books: *The Authoritarian Public Sphere*: *Legitimation and Autocratic Power in North Korea, Burma, and China* (2017) and *Making the World Safe for Dictatorship* (2021).

Saipira Furstenberg is a Marie Skłodowska-Curie Cofund Research Fellow, at Ca' Foscari, University of Venice. Her project examines host states' responses to transnational repression. She gained her PhD in Political Science from the University of Bremen in 2017. Prior to joining the University of Venice, she was a Postdoctoral Researcher at the University of Portsmouth and a Research Associate at the University of Exeter. Her research examines international dimensions of authoritarian regimes, state repression, and human rights. Her work on transnational repression has been published in several leading journals, including *European Journal of International Security*, *Journal of Conflict Resolution* and *The International Journal of Human Rights*.

Marlies Glasius is Professor in International Relations at the Department of Politics, University of Amsterdam. Her research interests include authoritarian practices, global civil society, international criminal justice and taxation of the super-rich. She was the Principal Investigator of the ERC-funded project Authoritarianism in a Global Age (2013–18). Her work has been published in venues such as *International Studies Quarterly, Human Rights Quarterly* and *International Affairs*. Her monographs include *The International Criminal Court: A Global Civil Society Achievement* (2006) and *Authoritarian Practices in a Global Age* (2023).

Sandra Grossman is a founding partner of Grossman Young & Hammond, a full-service immigration and international human rights law firm. She has developed a unique practice representing clients before Interpol. In 2019 she testified before a Congressional committee as a national expert on how to curb abuse of Interpol by autocratic nations. She also represents clients before US consulates worldwide, both in immigrant and non-immigrant visa applications, administrative processing and waivers of inadmissibility. She is actively involved in litigation, advocating before the immigration courts, the Board of Immigration Appeals and in Federal District Courts. She also represents clients in deportation defence, the immigration consequences of criminal convictions, asylum, and naturalisation applications. *Washingtonian* has repeatedly recognised her as one of 'Washington's Top Lawyers'.

Nicole Hirt is a political scientist and associate of the German Institute for Global and Area Studies (GIGA), based in Hamburg, Germany. Her research focuses on the persistence of authoritarian regimes, militarisation, diaspora positionalities and transnational repression with a focus on the Horn of Africa, especially Eritrea. She is also interested in memory politics and European migration policies. Her work has been published in journals such as *African Affairs, Africa Spectrum, Journal of Modern African Studies, Current History and Globalizations*. She contributed chapters to the *Routledge Handbook on the Horn of Africa* (2022) and the *Routledge Handbook on Middle Eastern Diasporas* (2023).

Meg Hobbins is Partner at Grossman Young & Hammond, LLC, based in Bethesda, MD (USA). She has extensive experience in US immigration and international human rights law, with a focus on complex US immigration matters and Interpol defence. She has represented clients seeking permanent residence, the full spectrum of humanitarian immigration benefits, and relief from removal proceedings.

Gillian Kennedy is a Lecturer in Politics and International Relations at the University of Southampton, UK. Her research focuses on diaspora networks among British-Egyptians, exploring the connection between diaspora mobilisation and political engagement before and after the Arab Spring. From 2017 to 2020, she was a Leverhulme Early Career Fellow in the Department of Middle Eastern Studies at King's College London. Her first book, *From Independence to Revolution: Egypt's Islamists and the Contest for Power*, was published in 2017.

Edward Lemon is a Research Assistant Professor at the Bush School of Government and Public Service of Texas A&M University, based in Washington, DC. His research focuses on the transnational dimensions of authoritarianism, including transnational repression and authoritarian regional organisations, with a focus on post-Soviet Central Asia, Russia and China. He has also conducted extensive research on security issues, including violent extremism and political violence. He has spent over three years conducting research in Tajikistan, Russia, Kyrgyzstan and Kazakhstan, and speaks Russian and Tajik. He is editor of the book *Critical Approaches to Security in Central Asia* (2018), and has published his research in peer-reviewed venues that include *Democratization*, *Central Asian Affairs*, *Caucasus Survey*, *Journal of Democracy*, *Foreign Affairs*, *Central Asian Survey*, *Review of Middle Eastern Studies* and *The RUSI Journal*.

Marcus Michaelsen is a researcher studying digital technologies, human rights activism and authoritarian politics. He works as a Senior Researcher at the Citizen Lab (University of Toronto), focusing on digital transnational repression. Previously he was a Marie-Skłodowska-Curie Fellow in the Law, Science, Technology and Society (LSTS) research group of Vrije Universiteit Brussel and a Senior Information Controls Fellow with the Open Technology Fund. From 2014 until 2018 he was a post-doctoral researcher in the project Authoritarianism in a Global Age, directed by Marlies Glasius at the University of Amsterdam. His work on transnational repression has been published in *Globalizations, Global Networks, European Journal of International Security* and *Surveillance & Society*.

Abdulkader Saleh Mohammad is a sociologist with extensive experience in teaching and research. He has served as a professor at the universities of Sebha, Libya and Asmara, Eritrea. He worked as a researcher for GIGA Hamburg and the University of Hamburg. He was a visiting professor at the University of Oslo and a senior advisor to the International Law and Policy Institute in Oslo. He authored the book *The Saho of Eritrea: Ethnic Identity and National Consciousness*. He conducted extensive research on diasporas, refugees, transnationalism, national identity formation and traditional mediation systems, and his work has been published in peer-reviewed journals such as *Africa Spectrum, Globalizations, Journal of Modern Africa Studies* and *Remittances Review*. He currently works as an independent country expert.

Dana M. Moss is Associate Professor in the Department of Sociology at the University of Notre Dame, USA and a Faculty Fellow at Notre Dame's Kroc Institute for International Peace Studies. To date, her research focuses primarily on collective action, state repression, authoritarianism, transnationalism, diasporas and the Middle Eastern region. Her award-winning book, *The Arab Spring Abroad: Diaspora Activism Against Authoritarian Regimes* (2022), investigates how and to what extent anti-regime diaspora activists in the US and Britain mobilised to support the 2011 uprisings in Libya, Syria and Yemen. Her work has been published in a variety of venues, including *American Sociological Review, Social Forces, Social Problems, Mobilization: An International Journal* and *Comparative Migration Studies*.

Ahmet Erdi Öztürk is Associate Professor in Politics and International Relations at London Metropolitan University. He was Marie Skłodowska-Curie Research Fellow at Coventry University in the UK and GIGA in Germany (2021–3). He is also an associate researcher (*Chercheur Associé*) at the Institut Français d'Études Anatoliennes and Non-Residence Scholar at ELIAMEP's Turkey Programme. He is the author, co-author and editor of six books, more than 40 peer-reviewed articles and numerous book chapters, policy reports and op-eds. He is the winner of of ISA's ENMISA Section Distinguished

Emerging Scholar Award 2022, the Exceptional Performance Award of Coventry University 2022 and the Outstanding Early Career Researcher Award of London Metropolitan University 2021.

Don Picard is a partner in the Washington, DC-based law firm Picard, Kentz & Rowe, whose practice focuses on disputes and agreements between and among sovereign states. He has represented clients before the United Nations Compensation Commission, the Eritrea-Ethiopia Claims Commission and before international tribunals ruling on boundary and maritime disputes between states. With extensive experience working across the Horn of Africa and Yemen, he was a board member of The Yemen Peace Project (2010–19), a non-profit organisation dedicated to educating Americans about Yemeni politics and the arts.

Sharon M. Quinsaat is Associate Professor in the Department of Sociology at Grinnell College, USA. She studies social movements and revolutions, migrant and diaspora politics, race and ethnicity, and media discourse from a global and transnational perspective. She has published her research in edited volumes and peer-reviewed journals such as *Journal of Ethnic and Migration Studies*, *Mobilization: An International Quarterly*, *Ethnic and Racial Studies*, *Mass Communication and Society*, *Sociology Compass* and *Asian Survey*. Her first book, *Insurgent Communities: How Protests Create a Filipino Diaspora* (2024), explains the dynamic process of diaspora formation through transnational protests using the case of Filipinos in the United States and the Netherlands.

Sean R. Roberts is the Director of the International Development Studies programme at Elliott School of International Affairs at Georgetown University, USA. He is a cultural anthropologist with extensive applied experience in international development work. Having conducted ethnographic fieldwork among the Uyghur people of Central Asia and China during the 1990s, he has published extensively on this community in scholarly journals and collected volumes. In addition, he produced a documentary film on the community entitled *Waiting for Uighurstan* (1996). His first book, *The War on the Uyghurs: China's Internal Campaign against a Muslim Minority*, was published in the US in 2020. It is also available in the UK under the title *The War on the Uyghurs: China's Campaign against Xinjiang's Muslims*.

Alessandra Russo is Assistant Professor in International Relations and Security Studies at the University of Trento, Italy. She held postdoctoral research positions in Italy, France and Belgium, and has been awarded grants for multiyear research projects, respectively titled 'International Determinants in the Production of Regional Counter-crime Norms, Policies and Practices' and 'Countering Terrorism, Radicalisation, Extremism: EU's Schemes and Local Responses'. Her research activities are positioned in the fields of comparative regionalism, security studies and, more recently, critical approaches to security issues in EU external governance.

Redmond Scales is a PhD student at University College Dublin, Ireland. He was awarded the Iseult Honohan PhD Scholarship by the Department of Politics and International Relations at UCD. His research interests lie in authoritarian politics, aid and development, and international relations. His PhD thesis (dissertation) explores the variations in the control of authoritarian regimes and the impact of foreign aid on subnational regime control.

Gerasimos Tsourapas is Professor of International Relations at the University of Glasgow and the Chair of the Ethnicity, Nationalism and Migration Studies Section of the International Studies Association. He is the Principal Investigator of a five-year European Research Council Starting Grant project on migration diplomacy. His first book, *The Politics of Migration in Modern Egypt: Strategies for Regime Survival in Autocracies* (Cambridge University Press), received the 2020 ENMISA Distinguished Book Award from the International Studies Association, while his research on migration interdependence was recognised with the 2017 Martin O. Heisler Award. Currently he works on the logic of migration and refugee rent-seeking strategies across the Global South. His latest book, *Migration Diplomacy in the Middle East and North Africa: Power, Mobility, and the State*, was published by Manchester University Press.

INTRODUCTION
TRANSNATIONAL REPRESSION AS A GROWING GLOBAL THREAT

Dana M. Moss and Saipira Furstenberg

On 23 May 2021, an activist couple – Roman Protasevich, an exiled activist and media blogger from Belarus, and Sofia Sapega, a Russian law student and rights advocate – boarded Ryanair Flight 4978 in Greece bound for Lithuania. After it entered his airspace, Belarusian President Alexander Lukashenko deployed a fighter jet to intercept the aircraft. Following a forced landing in Minsk, state security whisked Protasevich and Sapega into detention. Despite widespread international condemnation of Lukashenko's actions, the two activists were charged separately as threats to Belarusian security and found guilty of inciting 'mass unrest'. Protasevich was sentenced to eight years in prison and served two. It is widely believed that he was subjected to physical abuse and coerced into making apologetic confessions on state television.[1] In 2022, Sapega was sentenced to six years, where she remains a political prisoner at the time of writing (in 2023).

The arrest of the Belarusian blogger and his girlfriend resonated with another multinational plot involving the murder of journalist Jamal Khashoggi a few years earlier. Khashoggi had been forced into exile in 2017 for criticising the monarchy in his home country of Saudi Arabia. After settling in the US, he and Canada-based student activist Omar Abdulaziz planned to counter regime

---

[1] On 22 May 2023, Protasevich was granted a Presidential pardon.

propaganda on social media. Unbeknown to either of them, however, Saudi agents had remotely implanted spyware on Abdulaziz's phone and uncovered their plans. Soon after, in October 2018, officials lured Khashoggi to the Saudi consulate in Istanbul, Turkey. Once inside, agents of a hit squad strangled him to death, dismembered him with a bone saw, and smuggled his body out of the building in a suitcase. Multinational investigations revealed that the heinous assassination of this mild-mannered journalist with a warm smile had been orchestrated by the highest authorities in Saudi Arabia, implicating Crown Prince Mohammed bin Salman directly.[2]

These shocking incidents are just two examples of what we call *transnational repression*: the border-crossing practices used by authoritarian regimes and non-state actors to control, coerce and punish exiles and diaspora members abroad.[3] Incidents of transnational repression are not new, as illustrated by Leon Trotsky's gruesome assassination in Mexico City by an axe-wielding agent of Joseph Stalin in 1940 (Brand 2006; Miller 1981; Quinsaat 2013; Shain 1989/2005, 2005). Yet, today, incidents of transnational violence against human rights defenders, political exiles, migrants, international students and diaspora communities are on the rise worldwide (Gorokhovskaia and Linzer 2022). According to Freedom House, there were '854 direct, physical incidents of transnational repression committed by 38 governments in 91 countries' between 2014 and 2022. In 2021 alone, researchers counted seventy-nine documented acts of transnational repression committed by twenty different governments (Gorokhovskaia et al. 2023).

The transnational repression toolkit includes assassinations, surveillance, unlawful renditions and detentions, extortion, the withdrawal of student

---

[2] International condemnation over the Khashoggi murder did little to dissuade Saudi authorities from pursuing other wanted defectors that same year. In 2018, the Saudi regime sent the same Tiger Squad hit team to murder a defector named Saad AlJabri in Canada, but failed in their attempt. Regime officials also confronted Abdulaziz, Khashoggi's former activist-partner, forcing him to a meeting in person on Canadian soil, to issue threats against him and his family.

[3] Although authoritarian regimes are the most common perpetrators of transnational repression, other types of illiberal political actors, such as loyalist trolls and insurgent movement groups, also control, threaten and extort diaspora members; see Adamson's contribution, Chapter 4, this volume and Moss (2018).

scholarships, blacklisting and slander, harassment online and in-person, and coercion. Regimes also use coercion-and-punishment by *proxy*, which occurs when diaspora members' family and friends in the home country become targets of repression as punishment for activism undertaken abroad (Adamson and Tsourapas 2020; Moss et al. 2022).[4] In 2022, Freedom House found that China, Turkey, Russia, Egypt and Tajikistan were the top offenders (Gorokhovskaia et al. 2023), although transnational repression stems from every major world region. Transnational repression also appears to be expanding with the rapid development of globalised technologies, such as social media and privately marketed spyware. These tools make it easier and cheaper for regimes to track their critics across borders (Gorokhovskaia et al. 2023, Gorokhovskaia and Linzer 2022, Michaelsen 2018).

Transnational repression poses a growing global threat to human rights, democratic principles, and the rule of law across host states. However, while domestic repression taking place within authoritarian states has been studied extensively (e.g. Davenport 2007, Escribà-Folch 2013; Frantz and Kendall-Taylor 2014; Linz 2000; Svolik 2012), the transnational dimensions of authoritarian social control and cross-border repression have received far less attention. In order to address this oversight, scholars and practitioners in social sciences and legal fields have recently begun to document the extent of the problem and its varied effects on diaspora voice. Host-country governments have only recently begun to collect data on transnational repression and implement policies to better protect affected groups. As the chapters of this volume illustrate, far more proactive strategies are needed to curtail its practice.

In bringing together scholars working across sectors that are all too often disconnected in practice, this volume addresses several important questions: What are the different tactics that regimes and non-state actors use to repress their opponents across borders? What are the effects of transnational repression on activists and diaspora communities? How does its operation vary over time and by home and host country? How have the rise of social media and Internet communication technologies influenced this phenomenon? How can international institutions and host-country governments better protect

---

[4] Many types of transnational repression, such as hacking and online threats, are harder to detect and count, and therefore remain under-represented in data collected by researchers.

these communities? And what are the theoretical and practical implications for understanding state power, geographical space and democracy in the twenty-first century? The end result is the compilation of scholarship from top researchers in different fields and world regions, providing a comprehensive, comparative picture of the problem and potential solutions.[5]

The Importance of Safe Spaces for Diaspora Activism

As both history and scholarship demonstrate, mobilised diasporas are important global actors who contribute in significant ways to social, political and economic changes in their countries of origin (Adamson 2016; Shain 2005 [1989]). Exiles and activists from countries experiencing anti-democracy crackdowns, such as Hong Kong, mainland China and Russia, are often well positioned to speak about human rights abuses underway at home. By engaging in actions such as filing lawsuits, testifying at the United Nations, lobbying host-country governments to sanction regimes, protesting visiting officials, spreading awareness about atrocities and sending remittances to humanitarian relief and rebellions, diaspora advocates mobilise to undermine authoritarian regime legitimacy, control and longevity from afar.[6]

Using the heuristic theoretical framework of 'exit, voice, and loyalty' developed by Albert Hirschman (1970, 1978), emigrants who gain 'voice' after 'exit' use it to demonstrate 'loyalty' to the people and causes left behind at home. While some diaspora members do indeed mobilise to *support* home-country

---

[5] All research populating this book's findings has been conducted in accordance with the protocols and 'human subjects' protections' at the authors' respective universities. For practitioners, all cases are discussed in accordance with the professional standards and ethics of legal writings. See Moss (2016) on the 'coming out' process during times of conflict and crisis in the home country. See also Moss (2018) and Moss et al. (2022) on self-censorship and other adaptive strategies to the threats posed by transnational repression.

[6] In the phrasing of Benedict Anderson (1992, 1998), 'home' in this case may be autobiographical (i.e. the country where a person is born, raised and retains official membership) or perceived (i.e. a foreign-born child of a parent who was exiled from their homeland, but who retains a strong hybrid identity). The unifying characteristic is that diaspora members attribute their origins to a common home country or territory (which is almost always claimed or circumscribed by a state power) or ethnic group with roots spread across territories (i.e. the Kurdish diaspora).

dictatorships (see Hirt and Mohammed, this volume), they also use voice after exit to advocate for democracy, human rights, development and humanitarian aid in the home country (Amarasingam 2015; Ayoub 2016; Brinkerhoff 2009; Horst 2008; Fair 2005; Glasius 2018; Koinova 2012; Lainer-Vos 2013; Orjuela 2008; Moss 2022; Quinsaat 2019, 2024; Shain 2005 [1989]). Diaspora communities also sustain opposition movements that have been crushed by state repression at home, keeping them alive and in 'abeyance' until a time when new opportunities for mass action emerge (Taylor 1989). Although not all diaspora members promote democracy from a distance (e.g. Adamson 2013, Smith and Stares 2007), many of them do capitalise on their newfound 'political opportunities' (Tarrow 2005) to mobilise for anti-authoritarian causes, as well as to present alternative facts and opinions to the official party lines of homeland regimes.

At the same time, the targets of transnational repression do not have to be politically active or overtly vocal against regimes to face threats. This is because authoritarian leaders and institutions perceive diasporas as a real and potential collective threat to their domestic monopolies over political power and information. In other words, even when diasporas renounce home-country politics, autocrats often view diasporas as 'their' subjects who are required to demonstrate loyalty, no matter where they live. This may even apply to members of the second generation who have citizenship abroad, as in the case of second-generation Eritreans or Syrians (Moss 2016; see also Hirt and Mohammad, Chapter 7, this volume). This puts exiles at risk of repression even after they have 'retired' from anti-regime mobilisation (Hilsum 2012).

In viewing diaspora control as a strategic and ideological imperative, regimes dedicate a significant amount of attention and resources to enforcing 'loyalty' abroad. Their capacity to do so varies widely (Shain 2005 [1989]), with resource-rich states like China leading in the range of deployed tactics and quantifiable incidents of transnational repression enacted against diaspora members (Gorokhovskaia and Linzer 2022; Schenkkan and Linzer 2021). Nevertheless, Protasevich's kidnapping and Khashoggi's murder are only two examples of the lengths that regimes will go to silence their critics abroad. The related plight of Khashoggi's colleague Omar Abdulaziz illustrates how violence overlaps with covert forms of transnational repression, including the use of hacking and spyware, the proxy punishment of relatives at home (Adamson and Tsourapas 2020; Moss 2016) and the use of third-party countries as hunting grounds. Countries like Turkey both experience transnational repression within their territory *and* perpetuate it against ethnic minorities and political opponents living in foreign states (Böcü et al., Chapter 10, this volume).

Democratic state governments have also played a role in enabling, facilitating and collaborating in acts of transnational repression. As Francesca Lessa (2022) describes in her groundbreaking research on Operation Condor in Latin America, the US Government collaborated with a network of autocratic regimes to engage in transnational repression. This led to kidnappings, detentions and murders of anti-authoritarian activists, students and communists over the course of the Cold War, as well as to the disappearing and displacement of their children (ibid.) in the name of anti-communism.

So too have democracies engaged in acts of transnational repression under the pretence of the more recent War on Terror, and in efforts to block asylum seekers and irregular migrants from obtaining sanctuary abroad (Chaudhary and Moss 2019; FitzGerald 2019). The geopolitical climate in which transnational repression takes place, therefore, leads to strategic bilateral and multilateral co-operation over security enforcement. Unfortunately, these agreements often place law-abiding exiles, civil society activists, journalists *and* their family members in danger. Accordingly, while authoritarian regimes take the lead in practising transnational repression, democracies are also guilty of facilitating it as a means to advance strategic and ideological imperatives.

Although transnational repression is most obviously and frequently perpetuated by authoritarian regimes (Gorokhovskaia and Linzer 2022; Schenkkan and Linzer 2021), it is also facilitated by supposedly politically neutral international organisations. For instance, Interpol, the international organisation dedicated to helping law enforcement agencies share information about wanted persons, has been increasingly used as a tool by authoritarian regimes to persecute innocent individuals and suppress dissent across borders (Appuzo 2019; Bromund 2021; Dhillon and Bromund 2022; Grossman and Hobbins, this volume; Lemon 2019, this volume). Interpol's Red Notice system is just one means by which states like Russia and China use *foreign* security services to capture *their* wanted exiles and render them home on invented charges of terrorism and corruption (Fair Trials 2018; Furstenberg et al. 2021). This abuse reflects a broader effort of dictators to weaponise international organisations for the purposes of political and ethnic persecution.

Acts of violence abroad take place in tandem with what Freedom House calls 'everyday' tactics of transnational repression, such as in-person and online surveillance of diaspora members and their organisations (Schenkkan et al. 2020). These methods are more common and low-cost for regimes to use, while also posing the challenge of being difficult for researchers to track and quantify. They are also often co-ordinated by embassies and consulate staff with diplomatic protections (Moss 2016). Furthermore, regime agents issue threats by using relatives in the home country as involuntary messengers of regime demands, or by locking them up as punishment for activism abroad (Moss et al. 2022). Regimes also monitor the actions of student groups, diaspora associations and opposition media abroad (Allen-Ebrahimian 2018; Del Sordi 2018). As a result, a sense of threat often hangs over these communities. Mistrust based on the widespread understanding that surveillance is potentially ever-present and must be treated as so also discourages citizens from exercising their rights to speak out against authoritarianism at home (Moss 2016). Unfortunately, such threats – while an enduring fact of life for members in many diaspora communities – rarely make newspaper headlines.

Transnational Repression in the Twenty-first Century

What is new about transnational repression in the twenty-first century? The spillover of struggles from local contexts onto foreign lands is likely as old as politics itself. Revolutionaries, reformers and peaceful reformers facing repression are often forced to flee, or exit, after using their voice to demand change against authorities (Hirschman 1978; Moss 2022; Moore 1978). The fascist Italian Mussolini regime and the authoritarian Kuomintang (KMT) from Taiwan sent spies abroad to monitor immigrant communities in the United States. Opponents of autocratic regimes, such as Libya's Muammar al-Gaddafi (1969–2011), Syria's Assad dynasty (1970–present) and the Ayatollah Khomeini (1979–89), have been shot, blown up and injured by regime agents across the Middle East and Europe since at least the 1970s. Such brazen attacks have even taken place in broad daylight on the streets of major cities such as Paris, London and Washington, DC. In a 1976 case of the latter, agents of Chilean dictator Augusto Pinochet killed refugee-dissident Orlando Letier and his American colleague, Ronni Moffitt, by car bomb, on a bustling avenue in broad daylight.

At the same time, the profound changes produced by globalisation have had an indelible impact on the exercise of political power, diffusing it across different sets of actors and institutions. As the speed of information and cross-border flows of ideas, people and capital have increased (Held 1995; Hudson 1998), so too has governance diffused beyond the borders of the nation-state to include international and supra-national non-governmental organisations (e.g. the United Nations), which attempt to govern state policies and practices (Sassen 2003; Smith 2008). The globalisation of organisations and institutions dedicated to overseeing the behaviour of state governments has produced new modes of governance that are not nested within a neat hierarchy. Rather, they coexist along more traditional forms of state sovereignty, which – in its ideal type formation – involves a centralised authority exerting a monopoly over decision-making and the exercise of power, both directly and indirectly, over populations residing within its territory (Weber 1978). These sources of governance also influence one another as intertwined, co-constitutive forces of power, pressure and social change (Jessop et al. 2008).

In light of these changes, globalisation has created a paradox. On the one hand, the power grounded in the territorialised nation-state has been challenged as political authority has become decentralised and internationalised across multilateral institutions and organisations. But on the other hand, globalisation has also simultaneously strengthened the sovereignty and importance of the nation-state. This is because states typically comprise the membership of international organisations (IOs) that set the 'rules' governing world society, as in the case of the United Nations. From within IOs, regimes notoriously take advantage of weak or lacking enforcement mechanisms to violate human rights, all while appearing as legitimate co-operative members of the international community.[7] As scholars of political science and international relations have pointed out, such practices are expanding in light of the wider global shift towards illiberalism, whereby autocracies challenge liberal norms and human rights by co-opting the institutions designed to enforce them (Bettiza and Lewis 2020; Tsourapas 2020).

---

[7] The leadership of Saudi Arabia, which is currently governed by a repressive monarchy that is a major offender of human rights, in the UN Human Rights Committee is a case in point (as is the fact that the Interpol president is a UAE general accused of participating in torture) (BBC 2021).

Such dynamics have also allowed democratic states to acquire 'extra-territorial means what they could not, or would not, attempt in domestic territory' (D'Arcus 2014: 79). Internationalised governance structures, including multilateral co-operation agreements and security arrangements, are often culpable in this process. The policy on extraordinary rendition pursued in the so-called War on Terror has enabled the US and other states to circumvent both domestic and international human rights laws in the name of counterterrorism (D'Arcus 2014). Under the guise of increasing security, they also share information, technologies and strategies, and control migration with and for authoritarian states (FitzGerald 2019). In this context, as argued by Adamson and Greenhill (2021), we need to view the current global security environment as *entangled* and *interconnected*, rather than *discrete* and *delimited* by official borders. In this context, state power diffuses and operates across multiple spaces and involves the co-operation and collaboration of different actors and agencies (Furstenberg et al. 2021). Scholars of repression, therefore, need to attend not only to states, but to the networks, actors and geographies of security that span territorial boundaries and include cross-border relationships between them.

Furthermore, processes of globalisation have had an unprecedented impact on populations in the nation-state, who may become increasingly transnational in their identities and practices (Czaika and de Haas 2014). Many diaspora members profess cosmopolitan and hybrid identities (Appiah 1997) and openly celebrate their origins in a home state in community gatherings and in their political organising. Furthermore, as millions of people move across state borders each year in search of opportunities abroad, so too do their ways of 'being and belonging' transcend territorial boundaries (Basch et al. 1994; Levitt 2001; Levitt and Glick Schiller 2004; Wimmer and Glick Schiller 2002). By propping up home-country economies with their remittances and serving as both a source of 'brain drain' *and* 'brain gain', diasporas are increasingly recognised as a transnational force for political change in their places of origin and resettlement alike (Adamson 2016; Bauböck 2003; Dustmann et al. 2011; Shain 2005; Vertovec 2004).

In light of these trends, *state-led transnationalism* has become an important influence in the contemporary world. Having recognised the positive potential of their diasporas to channel political and economic support back home, sending states are increasingly exercising 'governmentality' over their nationals in the diaspora through the regulation of their political, social and economic life (Gamlen 2014; Goldring 2002). As a part of exercising soft power over their populations abroad (Adamson and Tsourapas 2019; Tsourapas 2018), states grant their citizens extraterritorial voting rights, foster their allegiance to the homeland, co-sponsor development projects and campaign for their votes, among other policies (Abramson 2017, 2019; Brand 2010, 2014; Délano and Gamlen 2014; Fitzgerald 2009; Duquette-Rury 2020; Gamlen 2014; Goldring 2002; Kapur 2010; Koinova and Tsourapas 2020b; Ragazzi 2014; Pearlman 2014). In contrast to Albert Hirschman's (1970) classic formulation that 'exit' in the form of emigration *precludes* 'voice', the relations between sending states and diasporas can actively *facilitate* political engagement across borders.

It is precisely for this reason that regimes seek to exercise control over voice *after* exit (Moss 2022). Exiles and dissidents often form networks and organisations dedicated to addressing regime abuses and neglect (Betts and Jones 2016; Lainer-Vos 2013; Moss 2022). When they resettle in states that are friendly to their interests and ensure the rights to free speech, diaspora activists spread information about state-sanctioned violence, establish independent social media and cable news channels, lobby for international intervention, and channel resources to political causes at home. As demonstrated in the Chinese revolution of 1911 and more recently during the Arab uprisings of 2011, diasporas who mobilise against their home-country governments can become powerful instigators of change, both for good and for ill (Moss 2022). As in the case of Iraqi exile Ahmed Chalabi, who helped to legitimise the US's invasion and occupation of Iraq in 2003, émigrés can also threaten dictatorships' legitimacy and survival (Roston 2009; Vanderbush 2014). In this sense, migrants and diasporas are not only seen as economic actors who remit money to their countries of origin, but also as important agents of sociopolitical change (Kleist 2008; Koinova 2018; Kennedy 2019). It is in this context that we seek to unpack the dynamics of transnational repression, highlight emergent trends using the best data available, and present potential policy solutions to these damaging acts.

The Contents of this Book

This edited volume builds on the painstaking efforts by Freedom House, the Oxus Society, Citizen Lab based at the University of Toronto, media and NGO reporting, researchers responsible for compiling the Central Asian Political Exiles (CAPE) Database, the Authoritarian Actions Abroad Database (AAAD) and the work of legal advocates to analyse transnational repression across different contexts (Dukalskis et al. 2022). After initiating this project just before the onset of the Covid-19 pandemic in 2020, our authors participated in a two-day multinational workshop online to exchange insights and provide developmental feedback. We benefited tremendously from the insights of invited discussant-experts Laurie Brand, Yossi Shain, Fiona Adamson and Marlies Glasius: thank you for your encouragement of this project along the way.

Much of the data upon which this research is based would not have been possible without the bravery of exiles and diaspora members themselves. Many have broken a normative code of silence to testify about their experiences and endured traumas. Because many of our respective participants and clients remain in danger, most of the testimonials that inform this book have been anonymised. Exceptions have been made in cases where activists have testified publicly and in the media about transnational repression, or are well-known regime opponents who made the principled decision to 'come out' prior to engaging with the authors of this volume.[8] Some contributors to this volume are members of persecuted diaspora groups themselves, who have detailed insider knowledge of these phenomena, and whose families are or may be at risk. To our knowledge, this is the first book that brings together this diverse array of authors to address transnational repression in a comparative, comprehensive and truly globalised fashion.

Part I opens our discussion by addressing how transnational repression should be understood from a conceptual and theoretical perspective. In Chapter 1, Marlies Glasius offers a compelling theoretical framework for understanding the different ways that regimes treat their extraterritorial subjects and how varied state–diaspora relations impact voice after exit differently. Chapter 2, by Gerasimos Tsourapas, provides a theoretical discussion of the 'illiberal paradox' facing

[8]   See note 5.

authoritarian regimes. As argued by the author, in the age of migration and trans-nationalism, autocracies seek to reap the material and economic benefits generated by liberal migration flows, while at the same time ensuring that the population abroad pose little threat to their regime survival. The chapter illustrates some of the most pervasive tactics using a range of sources and rich case histories. In Chapter 3, Marcus Michaelsen expounds upon regimes' increasing authoritarian learning and adaptation of Internet-based communication technologies, showing how digital transnational repression poses a major challenge for diaspora activists. Chapter 4, by Fiona Adamson, adds a critical dimension to our discussion by showing how transnational repression can be perpetuated by illiberal social movements and *non-state* actors. Building on the opening discussion by Glasius in Chapter 1, Adamson shows how transnational repression is not just the purview of the state, but an authoritarian *practice* that can be deployed by a range of political players keen to extract resources and loyalty from their diasporas.

Part II examines the conditions and mechanisms that facilitate transnational repression and its escalation over time. The chapters in this section feature case studies with broad and comparative implications. Chapter 5, by Alexander Dukalskis and Redmond Scales, uses extensive comparative data to illustrate changes in transnational repression in East and Southeast Asia. Taking up Cambodia and Thailand as case studies, they demonstrate how increasing autocratisation of the region has led to an increase in transnational repression incidents and cross-country collaborations under China's leadership. This has reduced the spaces where activists can find sanctuary, and puts them at increased risk for rendition, kidnappings and murder across the region. Chapter 6, by Sean R. Roberts, adds to this discussion by showing how changes within the People's Republic of China over the past three decades have led to the globalisation and racialisation of state repression from the Chinese Communist Party (CCP). Fuelled by geopolitical conditions such as the US-led War on Terror, the CCP is increasingly persecuting its racial, ethnic and religious minorities using new technologies, couching its global campaign against Uyghurs, Tibetans, Falun Gong members and others within a legitimising frame of 'anti-terrorism'. Chapter 7, by Nicole Hirt and Abdulkader Saleh Mohammad, closes this section by presenting a fascinating historical analysis of Eritrea's transnational reach. Building on original research, they show how the Eritrean state perpetuates its stability and legitimacy through a two-pronged global campaign targeting diasporas. On the one hand, the regime of Afwerki survives in part by *exploiting* diaspora loyalty, or 'long-distance nationalism' (Anderson 1998; Glick Schiller and Fouron 2001), as well as by *forcing* its diaspora into performing and enacting loyalty. Taken together, these chapters demonstrate how transnational repression bolsters authoritarian legitimacy and stability in both strong states (like China) and weak states (like Eritrea), as well as how it reflects the *globalised* expansion of state-led terror, taxation and cultural genocide.

Part III brings the role of host countries into the discussion. As we note above, this not only includes authoritarian states as perpetrators of transnational repression, such as Turkey and Thailand, but democratic states as well. Chapter 8, by Sharon Quinsaat, discusses the shameful history of the US Government in repressing Filipino activists critical of the Marcos regime during the Cold War. The chapter also demonstrates how US-based advocates of the rule of law helped to put a stop to this practice, illustrating how host-country policymakers can make a difference in combating transnational repression.

Following this, Chapter 9, authored by legal experts and practising attorneys Sandra Grossman and Meg Hobbins, examines how US Immigration and Customs Enforcement officials act as pawns of authoritarian regimes by arresting, detaining and deporting persons targeted by regimes via Interpol's 'Red Notice' system. These disturbing cases not only illustrate how regimes abuse Interpol to target exiles and dissidents, but how democracies like the US enable this practice by doing the dirty work for illiberal regimes from Russia, Guatemala, Venezuela and elsewhere. Like the chapters by Roberts and Quinsaat, their contributions include how transnational repression intersects with xenophobia and racism in the host country, making racial and ethnic minorities vulnerable to repression by foreign actors in democratic states.

Chapter 10, by Gözde Böcü, Bahar Baser and Ahmet Erdi Öztürk, looks at how internal political turmoil in Turkey and the increasing authoritarianism of President Erdoğan have impacted transnational repression across Europe. Their study shows that this has not affected diasporas in a uniform manner, but rather placed Kurds and Gülen Movement members in highly vulnerable positions compared to other Turkish regime critics. They also describe promising efforts by some European countries to increase asylum protections and civil society protections for individuals affected by transnational repression.

Conversely, Saipira Furstenberg, Alessandra Russo and Gillian Kennedy show in Chapter 11 that the strengthening of Italy's ties with Egypt has put international students and asylum seekers from Egypt at an increased risk of transnational repression should they reside in, or attempt to travel to, Italy. Tightened bilateral ties have not only coincided with Italy accepting fewer asylum seekers from Egypt, but international students from Egypt remain at risk of detention, incarceration and torture upon returning home for conducting independent, rights-related research. As emphasised in the chapters by Quinsaat and Grossman and Hobbins, this brings us again to a crucial point: host countries often become complicit enablers of transnational repression when they place so-called national security concerns ahead of residents' and asylum seekers' fundamental rights.

The final section, Part IV, is devoted to exploring the role of international institutions and international law in transnational repression. Chapter 12, by Edward Lemon, builds on the discussion of Interpol presented in Chapter 9 (by Grossman and Hobbins), explaining how international regional organisations, such as the Shanghai Cooperation Organisation and Commonwealth of Independent States, increase interstate participation and co-operation in enacting transnational repression. His analysis demonstrates how organisations formed to diffuse and facilitate authoritarian practices are escalating the threat of transnational repression by facilitating what we might call 'worst practices' and cross-national collaborations to kidnap, rendition, extradite and incarcerate regime opponents across Asia.

Lastly, attorney Don Picard and sociologist Dana Moss suggest ways that existing international law, including human rights provisions and laws governing state-to-state relations, can provide a means for countering transnational repression. Not only can individual victims, survivors and legal advocates use these legal tools to pursue claims, but so too can host-country governments sue for reparations when acts of transnational repression are committed on their soil. The authors argue that it is imperative for states to uphold the rule of law in their territories, as well as to fulfil their internationally mandated duty to protect their residents' fundamental rights, regardless of their citizenship status.

The book concludes by summarising the major themes and conclusions of the chapters and outlines key lines of inquiry for future scholarship and practice. These include the need for further historical, comparative investigation into both high- and low-profile incidents of transnational repression, such as online harassment and proxy punishment; improved efforts by host states to protect refugees and diasporas from transnational repression; and new policies and lawsuits designed to facilitate protections and impose costs on states for perpetuating transnational repression. In doing so, the book urges those with the capacity to act – host-country governments, international institutions, civil society advocates and community leaders – to increase their efforts to counter these threats to diaspora members' basic rights and democracy writ large.

References

Abramson, Y. 2017. 'Making a homeland, constructing a diaspora: The case of Taglit-Birthright Israel'. *Political Geography* 58: 14–23.

——. 2019. 'Securing the diasporic "self" by travelling abroad: Taglit-Birthright and ontological security'. *Journal of Ethnic and Migration Studies* 45(4): 656–73.

Allen-Ebrahimian, B. 2018. 'China's Long Arm Reaches Into American Campuses'. *Foreign Policy*. 7 March. https://foreignpolicy.com/2018/03/07/chinas-long-arm-reaches-into-american-campuses-chinese-students-scholars-association-university-communist-party/

Adamson, F. and Tsourapas, G. 2019. 'Migration diplomacy in world politics'. *International Studies Perspectives* 20(2): 113–28.

Adamson, F. and Tsourapas, G. 2020. 'At home and abroad: Coercion-by-proxy as a tool of transnational repression'. *Freedom House Special Report 2020*. 15 December. https://freedomhouse.org/report/special-report/2020/home-and-abroad-coercion-proxy-tool-transnational-repression

Adamson, F. and Greenhill, K. 2021. 'Globality and entangled security: Rethinking the post-1945 order'. *New Global Studies* 15(2/3): 165–80.

Adamson, F. 2016. 'The growing importance of diaspora politics'. *Current History* 784(115): 291–7.

——. 2019a. 'Non-state authoritarianism and diaspora politics'. *Global Networks* 20(1): 150–69.

——. 2019b. 'Sending states and the making of intra-diasporic politics: Turkey and its diaspora(s)'. *International Migration Review* 53(1): 210–36.

Amarsaringham, A. 2015. *Pain, Pride, and Politics: Social Movement Activism and the Sri Lankan Diaspora in Canada*. Athens: University of Georgia Press.

Anderson, B. 1998. *The Spectre of Comparisons: Nationalism, Southeast Asia, and the World*. New York: Verso.

——. 2006 [1983]. *Imagined Communities*, 2nd edn. New York: Verso.

Appiah, K. 1997. 'Cosmopolitan patriots'. *Critical Inquiry* 23(3): 617–39.

Appuzo, M. 2019. 'How strongmen turned Interpol into their personal weapon'. *The New York Times*, https://www.nytimes.com/2019/03/22/world/europe/interpol-most-wanted-red-notices.html. Last accessed 9 June 2023.

Ayoub, P. M. 2016. *When States Come Out: Europe's Sexual Minorities and the Politics of Visibility*. New York: Cambridge University Press.

Basch, L., Glick Schiller, N. and Szanton Blanc, C. 1994. *Nations Unbound: Transnational Projects, Postcolonial Predicaments, and Deterritorialized Nation States*. New York: Gordon & Breach.

Baser, B. 2015. *Diasporas and Homeland Conflicts: A Comparative Perspective*. New York: Routledge.

Baser, B. and Öztürk, A. 2020. 'Positive and negative diaspora governance in context: From public diplomacy to transnational authoritarianism'. *Middle East Critique* 29(3): 1–16.

Bauböck, R. 2003. 'Towards a political theory of migrant transnationalism'. *International Migration Review* 37(3): 700–23.

Bettiza, G. and Lewis, D. 2020. 'Authoritarian powers and norm contestation in the liberal international order: Theorizing the power politics of ideas and identity'. *Journal of Global Security Studies* 5(4), October 2020: 559–77, https://doi.org/10.1093/jogss/ogz075

Betts, A. and Jones, W. 2016. *Mobilising the Diaspora: How Refugees Challenge Authoritarianism*. Cambridge: Cambridge University Press.

Brand, L. 2006. *Citizens Abroad: Emigration and the State in the Middle East and North Africa*. New York: Cambridge University Press.

——. 2010. 'Authoritarian states and voting from abroad: North African experiences'. *Comparative Politics* 43(1): 81–99.

——. 2014. 'Arab uprisings and the changing frontiers of transnational citizenship: Voting from abroad in political transitions'. *Political Geography* 41: 54–63.

Brinkerhoff, J. M. 2009. *Digital Diasporas: Identity and Transnational Engagement*. Cambridge: Cambridge University Press.

Bromund, Ted R. 2019. 'Key goals for the US at the 2019 Meeting of the Interpol General Assembly'. The Heritage Foundation Issue Brief No. 5002, 18 September. https://www.heritage.org/sites/default/files/2019-09/IB5002_NEW.pdf. Last accessed 9 June 2023.

——. 2020. 'The US must promote democratic leadership in Interpol'. The Heritage Foundation Issue Brief No. 6025, 10 November. https://www.heritage.org/sites/default/files/2020-11/IB6025.pdf. Last accessed 9 June 2023.

Chaudhary, A. and Moss, D. 2019. 'Suppressing transnationalism: Bringing constraints into the study of transnational political action'. *Comparative Migration Studies* 7(9): 1–22.

Clifford, J. 1994. 'Diasporas'. *Cultural Anthropology* 9(3): 302–38.

Cooley, A. and Heathershaw, J. 2017. *Dictators without Borders: Power and Money in Central Asia*. New Haven, CT: Yale University Press.

Czaika, M. and de Haas, H. 2014. 'The globalization of migration: Has the world become more migratory?' *International Migration Review* 48(2): 283–323.

D'Arcus, B. 2014. 'Extraordinary rendition, law and the spatial architecture of rights'. *ACME: An International Journal for Critical Geographies* 13(1): 79–99.

Dalmasso, E., Del Sordi, A., Glasius, M., Hirt, N., Michaelsen, M., Mohammad, A. and Moss, D. 2017. 'Intervention: Extraterritorial authoritarian power'. *Political Geography* 64: 95–104.

Davenport, C. 2007. 'State repression and political order'. *Annual Review of Political Science* 10: 1–23. doi: 10.1146/annurev.polisci.10.101405.143216

Délano, A. and Gamlen, A. 2014. 'Comparing and theorizing state–diaspora relations'. *Political Geography* 41: 43–53.

Duquette-Rury, L. 2020. *Exit and Voice: The Paradox of Cross-Border Politics in Mexico*. Los Angeles: University of California Press.

Dhillon, U. and Ted R. Bromund. 2022. 'Interpol accountability'. *International Enforcement Law Reporter* 38(3): 124–6.

Dukalskis, A., Furstenberg, S., Gorokhovskaia, Y., Heathershaw, J., Lemon, E. and Schenkkan, N. 2022. 'Transnational repression: Data advances, comparisons, and challenges'. *Political Research Exchange* 4(1): 1–17.

Dustmann, C., Itzhak F. and Weiss, Y. 2011. 'Return migration, human capital accumulation and the brain drain'. *Journal of Development Economics* 95(1): 58–67.

Fair, C. 2005. 'Diaspora involvement in insurgencies: Insights from the Khalistan and Tamil Eelam movements'. *Nationalism and Ethnic Politics* 11(1): 125–56.

Fair Trials. 2018. 'Dismantling the tools of oppression: Ending the misuse of Interpol'. [Online]. Available at: https://atlas-of-torture.org/api/files/1578408433587zu88 6744x9n.pdf

FitzGerald, D. 2009. *A Nation of Emigrants: How Mexico Manages its Migration*. Berkeley: University of California Press.

——. 2019. *Refuge beyond Reach: How Rich Democracies Repel Asylum Seekers*. New York: Oxford University Press.

Frantz, E. and Kendall-Taylor, A. 2014. 'A dictator's toolkit: Understanding how co-optation affects repression in autocracies'. *Journal of Peace Research* 51(3): 332–46.

Furstenberg, S., Lemon, E. and Heathershaw, J. 2021. 'Spatialising state practices through transnational repression'. *European Journal of International Security* 6(3): 358–78.

Gamlen, A. (2014). 'Diaspora institutions and diaspora governance'. *International Migration Review* 48(1): 180–217.

Glasius, M. 2018. 'Extraterritorial authoritarian practices: A framework'. *Globalizations* 15(2): 179–97.

Glick Schiller, N. and Fouron, G. E. 2001. *Georges Woke Up Laughing: Long Distance Nationalism and the Search for Home*. Durham, NC: Duke University Press.

Goldring, L. 2004. 'Family and collective remittances to Mexico: A multi-dimensional typology'. *Development and Change* 35(4): 799–840.

Gorokhovskaia, Y. and Linzer, S. 2022. *Defending Democracy in Exile: Policy Responses to Transnational Repression*. Washington, DC: Freedom House, June 2022.

Gorokhovskaia, Y., Schenkkan, N. and Vaughan, G. 2023. *Still Not Safe: Transnational Repression in 2022*. Washington, DC: Freedom House, April 2023.

Held, D. 1995. 'Cosmopolitan democracy and the global order: Reflections on the 200th anniversary of Kant's "Perpetual Peace"'. *Alternatives: Global, Local, Political* 20(4): 415–29.

Hirschman, A. 1970. *Exit, Voice, and Loyalty: Responses to Decline in Firms, Organizations, and States*. Cambridge, MA: Harvard University Press.

——. 1978. 'Exit, voice and the state'. *World Politics* 31(1): 90–107.

Horst, C. 2008. 'The transnational political engagements of refugees: Remittance sending practices amongst Somalis in Norway'. *Conflict, Security & Development* 8(3): 317–39.

Hudson, A. 1998. 'Beyond the borders: Globalisation, sovereignty and extra-territoriality'. *Geopolitics* 3(1): 89–105.

Jessop, B., Brenner, N. and Jones, M. 2008. 'Theorizing sociospatial relations'. *Environment and Planning D: Society and Space* 26(3): 389–401.

Jörum, E. 2015. 'Repression across borders: Homeland response to anti-regime mobilization among Syrians in Sweden'. *Diaspora Studies* 8(2): 104–19

Kapur, D. 2010. *Diaspora, Development, and Democracy: The Domestic Impact of International Migration from India*. Princeton: Princeton University Press.

Kennedy, G. 2019. 'Diaspora incorporation mechanisms: Sustained and episodic mobilisation among the British-Egyptian diaspora after the Arab Spring'. *Journal of Ethnic and Migration Studies*. https://doi.org/10.1080/1369183X.2019.1693887

Kleist, N. (2008). 'Mobilising "The Diaspora": Somali Transnational political engagement'. *Journal of Ethnic and Migration Studies* 34(2): 307–23.

Koinova, M. and Tsourapas, G. 2018. 'How do countries of origin engage migrants and diasporas? Multiple actors and comparative perspectives'. *International Political Science Review* 39(3): 311–21.

Koinova, M. 2012. 'Autonomy and positionality in diaspora politics'. *International Political Sociology* 6(1): 99–103.

——. 2018. 'Critical junctures and transformative events in diaspora mobilisation for Kosovo and Palestinian statehood'. *Journal of Ethnic and Migration Studies* 44(8): 1289–308.

Lainer-Vos, D. 2013. *Sinews of the Nation: Constructing Irish and Zionist Bonds in the United States*. Malden, MA: Polity Press.

Lemon, E. (2019). 'Weaponizing Interpol'. *Journal of Democracy* 30(2): 15–29.

Lessa, F. 2022. *The Condor Trials: Transnational Repression and Human Rights in South America*. New Haven, CT: Yale University Press.

Levitt, P. and Glick Schiller, N. 2004. 'Conceptualizing simultaneity: A transnational social field perspective on society'. *International Migration Review* 38(3): 1002–39.

Levitt, P. 2001. *The Transnational Villagers*. Berkeley: University of California Press.

Lewis, D. 2015. '"Illiberal spaces": Uzbekistan's extraterritorial security practices and the spatial politics of contemporary authoritarianism'. *Nationalities Papers* 43(1): 140–59.

Linz, J. J. 2000. *Totalitarian and Authoritarian Regimes*. Boulder, CO: Lynne Rienner Publishers.

Michaelsen, M. 2017. 'Far away, so close: Transnational activism, digital surveillance and authoritarian control in Iran'. *Surveillance & Society* 15(3/4): 465–70.

——. 2018. 'Exit and voice in a digital age: Iran's exiled activists and the authoritarian state'. *Globalizations* 15(2): 248–64.

——. 2020. 'Resisting transnational repression: The digital security practices of diaspora and exiled human rights defenders'. *AoIR Selected Papers of Internet Research, 2020*. https://doi.org/10.5210/spir.v2020i0.11280/. Michigan Press/ Migration, Policy and Society. Oxford: University of Oxford.

Miller, M. 1981. *Foreign Workers in Western Europe: An Emerging Political Force*. New York: Praeger.

Moss, D. M. 2016. 'Transnational repression, diaspora mobilization, and the case of the Arab Spring'. *Social Problems* 63(4): 480–98.

——. 2018. 'The ties that bind: Internet communication technologies, networked authoritarianism, and "voice" in the Syrian diaspora'. *Globalizations* 15(2): 265–82.

——. 2019. 'The promises and perils of diaspora mobilization against authoritarian regimes'. *Brown J. World Affairs* 26(1): 1–19.

——. 2020. 'Voice after exit: Explaining diaspora mobilization for the Arab Spring'. *Social Forces* 98(4): 1669–94.

——. 2022. *The Arab Spring Abroad: Diaspora Activism Against Authoritarian Regimes*. New York: Cambridge University Press.

Moss, D. M., Michaelsen, M. and Kennedy, G. 2022. 'Going after the family: Transnational repression and the proxy punishment of Middle Eastern diasporas'. *Global Networks* 22(4): 735–51.

Olar, R.-G. 2019. 'Do they know something we don't? Diffusion of repression in authoritarian regimes'. *Journal of Peace Research* 56(5): 667–81.

Orjuela, C. 2008. 'Distant warriors, distant peace workers? Multiple diaspora roles in Sri Lanka's violent conflict'. *Global Networks* 8(4): 436–52.

Kose, O. 2018. TOPSHOT-TURKEY-CHINA-UIGHUR-DEMO. AFP via Getty Images. [Online]. Available at: https://www.gettyimages.co.uk/detail/news-photo/demonstrator-wearing-a-mask-painted-with-the-colours-of-the-news-photo/992174444. Accessed 17 July 2023.

Pearlman, W. 2014. 'Competing for Lebanon's diaspora: Transnationalism and domestic struggles in a weak state'. *International Migration Review* 48(1): 34–75.

Prelect, T., Furstenberg, S., Heathershaw, J. and Thomson, C. 2022. 'Academic freedom and internationalisation in higher education'. *The International Journal of Human Rights* 26(10): 1698–722.

Quinsaat, S. 2013. 'Migrant mobilization for homeland politics: A social movement approach'. *Sociology Compass* 7(11): 952–64.

——. 2019. 'Linkages and strategies in Filipino diaspora mobilization for regime change'. *Mobilization: An International Quarterly* 24(2): 221–39.

——. 2024. *Insurgent Communities: How Protests Create A Filipino Diaspora*. Chicago: University of Chicago Press.

Ragazzi, F. 2014. 'A comparative analysis of diaspora policies'. *Political Geography* 41: 74–89. Roston, A. 2008. *The Man Who Pushed America to War: The Extraordinary Life, Adventures, and Obsessions of Ahmad Chalabi*. New York: Nation Books.

Sassen. S. 2003. 'Globalization or denationalization?'. *Review of International Political Economy* 10(1): 1–22.

Schenkkan, N. and Linzer, I. 2021. 'Out of sight, not out of reach: The global scale and scope of transnational repression'. Freedom House, February 2021. https://freedomhouse.org/report/transnational-repression

Schenkkan, N., Linzer, I., Furstenberg, S. and Heathershaw, J. 2020. *Perspectives on 'Everyday' Transnational Repression in an Age of Globalization*. Freedom House, July 2020.

Shain, Y. 2005 [1989]. *The Frontier of Loyalty: Political Exiles in the Age of the Nation-State*. Ann Arbor: University of Michigan Press.

——. 2007. *Kinship and Diasporas in International Affairs*. Ann Arbor: University of Michigan Press.

Smith, J. 2008. *Social Movements for Global Democracy*. Baltimore, MD: Johns Hopkins University Press.

Svolik, M. W. 2012. 'The politics of authoritarian rule'. New York: Cambridge University Press.

Tarrow, S. 2005. *The New Transnational Activism*. New York: Cambridge University Press.

Tsourapas, G. 2018. 'Authoritarian emigration states: Soft power and cross-border mobility in the Middle East'. *International Political Science Review* 39(3): 400–16. doi: 10.1177/0192512118759902

——. 2020a. 'Global autocracies: Strategies of transnational repression, legitimation, and co-optation in world politics'. *International Studies Review*. https://doi .org/10.1093/isr/viaa061

——. 2020b. 'The long arm of the Arab state'. *Ethnic and Racial Studies* 43(2): 351–70.

Vanderbush, W. 2014. 'The Iraqi diaspora and the US invasion of Iraq'. In J. DeWind and R. Segura (eds), *Diaspora Lobbies and the US Government: Convergence and Divergence in Making Foreign Policy*. New York: New York University Press, pp. 211–35.

Von Soest, C. 2015. 'Democracy prevention: The international collaboration of authoritarian regimes'. *European Journal of Political Research* 54(4): 623–38.

Wimmer, A. and Glick Schiller, N. 2002. 'Methodological nationalism and beyond: Nation-state building, migration and the social sciences'. *Global Networks* 2(4): 301–34.

PART I

CONCEPTUALISING AND UNPACKING TRANSNATIONAL REPRESSION

PART 1

1

EXTRATERRITORIAL PRACTICES OF AUTHORITARIAN STATES: A TYPOLOGY AND MAPPING

Marlies Glasius

Introduction

The Berlin Wall was once a potent symbol of 'closed' authoritarian rule: it literally locked East German nationals in to prevent them from escaping to the West. Those who tried to scale the Wall or dig tunnels underneath could be shot on sight. Yet, even at the time, this wall represented an oversimplification of authoritarian rule of mobility, which did not consist only in imprisoning all nationals inside their borders. In fact, the German Democratic Republic actively facilitated the departure of its most vocal dissidents into exile, attempting to cut them off from political developments within (Hirschman 1993). It is but one example of an authoritarian regime *managing*, rather than preventing, mobility in order to stabilise its rule.

Yet in International Relations and Comparative Politics it has taken a long time to recognise the phenomena of authoritarian mobility management and transnational repression. Since the late 1990s, a burgeoning field of globalisation studies began to correct the ontological image of a world map made up of discrete territorial states, each with their own population inside. The migration literature did not lose sight of the state, but analysed its responses to increased mobility of populations. It critically examined uneven access and exclusionary mechanisms of liberal states (Hyndman 1997; Mountz 2011;

De Genova 2013). Recent work on bordering has also begun to focus on extraterritorial state power (Bialasiewicz 2012; Mountz 2011; Fitzgerald 2019), but the critical gaze of this work has typically been from the West outwards.

Some contributions have begun to examine the politics of so-called 'sending' states (Gamlen 2008; Collyer, ed. 2013) and the implications of extraterritorial voting (Collyer 2014; Caramani and Grotz, eds, 2015). But these works still do not fully equip us with the tools to observe and theorise authoritarian states as exerting physical, material and symbolic power beyond borders through extraterritorial practices.

The authoritarianism literature, on the other hand, has continued to leave its territorial assumptions largely unexamined. Since the 2000s, comparative politics scholars have shown a renewed interest in the endurance of authoritarianism (see, for instance, Gandhi 2007; Gerschewski 2013; McMann 2006; Schedler 2013), but the orientation has been overwhelmingly domestic and comparative. There is some focus in this new authoritarianism literature on how states influence each other (Bader et al. 2010; Levitsky and Way 2010; Brownlee 2012; Tansey 2016), but it has yet to give sustained attention to population mobility, and spatial approaches have been almost entirely absent.

These blind spots leave us with an 'extraterritorial gap': an inability to perceive and analyse extraterritorial state power in general, and extraterritorial or transnational authoritarian power in particular, which this edited volume seeks to redress. Theoretically, this extraterritorial gap can be considered as one consequence of the oft-cited 'territorial trap' (Agnew 1994) of 'methodological nationalism' (Gore 1996; Wimmer and Glick Schiller 2002) that leading theorists of globalisation have sought to transcend. This gap, which was left wide open by the early globalisation scholars, is only beginning to being filled by a host of case studies (Dalmasso 2018; Del Sordi 2018; Hirt and Mohamed 2018; Lewis 2015; Michaelsen 2018; Moss 2016; Sunier et al. 2016; To 2014; Tsourapas 2018; Yanasmayan and Kasli 2019) and now more systematically with this volume.

The point of departure of this chapter in attempting to fill the gap is that authoritarian rule should not be considered a territorially bounded regime type, but rather as a mode of governing people through a distinct set of practices. The chapter provides a typology of extraterritorial practices by authoritarian states, and a mapping of the configurations of actors that may be involved. 'Extraterritorial' as used here is a slightly narrower concept than 'transnational

repression', which also encompasses proxy punishment of domestic populations and repressive measures against return migrants. 'Extraterritorial practices' focuses on actions that actually take place or are felt outside the borders
of the authoritarian states, since an authoritarian regime's ability to project
its power over populations beyond its borders is still relatively unfamiliar to
political science and in need of investigation.

As shown in the chapter that follows by Tsourapas (Chapter 2, this volume), not all of the practices of authoritarian states towards their population can be considered as overtly repressive. However, the authoritarian state
can adapt to the specific assets and insecurities of populations abroad with
practices to include or exclude them: as subjects or outlaws, as patriots or
traitors, or as clients – but never as citizens. The chapter will first provide
examples of each of these categories. Second, the chapter disaggregates the
'authoritarian state' by introducing the idea of configurations of actors and
provides a mapping of which actors are involved in the extraterritorial practices of authoritarian states. After drawing on existing works to build a new
theoretical framework for conceptualising these practices, I illustrate the
mapping of actors on the basis of three different migrant groups' experiences
in the Netherlands. The typology and mapping, accompanied by empirical
examples, provide analytical tools and a vocabulary to open up the black box
of extraterritorial authoritarian governance. These tools enable scholars in the
field to systematically examine and compare the inner workings of transnational repression.

Extraterritorial Authoritarian Governance: A Typology

The immigration literature, casting relations between states and populations
in terms of inclusion and exclusion (Hyndman 1997; Torpey 1999; Isin and
Turner, eds 2002; Joppke 2005; Mountz 2011), has largely focused on the
exclusionary tendencies of formally democratic receiving states. As such, it
has introduced the idea of a 'politics of membership' (Brubaker 2010). As I
illustrate below, this concept and the mechanisms of inclusion and exclusion
it implies can also be usefully applied to extraterritorial authoritarian rule. But
the idea of 'inclusion' can be misleading if it is understood only in terms of
extension of citizenship and rights. Thus, Gamlen's seminal contributions
(e.g. Gamlen 2014, 2019) on the emigrant state devote much discussion to
state mechanisms to extend rights, political, civil and social, to diasporas.

However, Gamlen's work and related scholarship has much less to say about the extraction of obligations, which he deems 'more difficult than extending rights, because the coercive power of the origin state is severely restricted' outside of its borders (Gamlen 2008: 850). This chapter and the contributions in this volume demonstrate that, on the contrary, the authoritarian state has ample opportunities to extend its coercive power beyond borders. Hence, 'inclusion' by an authoritarian home state does not have the same benign tenor as it does when applied to democratic home or host states. Regardless of formal citizenship laws, the authoritarian state does not see its internal population as 'citizens' with 'rights'. When such regimes facilitate mobility, or recognise and 'include' populations abroad, this does not imply extension of citizenship rights, or even a balanced package of rights and obligations, to populations abroad. Inclusion in the authoritarian polity can take on repressive forms; even when inclusion comes with benefits, these are not rights-based, regulated or legally guaranteed.

In order to better understand how inclusion and exclusion function in extraterritorial authoritarian governance, I build on Gerschewski's classic typology of the ways in which authoritarian governments seek to stabilise their rule through repression, legitimation and co-optation. If we transpose this terminology to state–citizen relations, we can say that for stabilisation purposes, the authoritarian state includes its citizens as subjects (to be controlled and repressed), as patriots (getting them to buy into legitimation strategies) or as clients (with potential for co-optation). When populations resist being included in these ways, they may be excluded, treated as outlaws (denied any trappings of legal personality) and as traitors (castigated and scapegoated as enemies of the state). Gerschewski's typology takes the authoritarian regime's domestic setting to be its universe. I adapt this framework to the phenomenon of extraterritorial authoritarian governance by combining it with Collyer and King's identification of 'a number of ways in which transnational space can be said to be actively produced by attempts of state institutions to control the activities of individuals beyond the territory of the state' (2015: 187). What Collyer and King mean is that, against the classical conception of state power, state actions and policies actually create virtual territories, where their control may be different from inside the borders, but still acutely felt.

Collyer and King distinguish between direct control of physical space, symbolic control of transnational spaces and discursive control of imaginative space (2015: 194). The two typologies map onto each other, as illustrated in Table 1.1.

Table 1.1 Theorising extraterritorial practices of authoritarian states

Authoritarian pillars of stability (adapted from Gerschewski 2013)	repression		legitimation	co-optation
State controls of transnational space (adapted from Collyer and King 2015)	physical	symbolic	imaginative	
Extraterritorial practices of authoritarian states	*subjects* *outlaws*		*patriots* *traitors*	*clients*

Repression: Subjects and Outlaws

The first mode or strategy of authoritarian state control is what Gerschewski calls 'repression'. He uses Davenport's (2007: 2) definition, citing the 'actual or threatened use of physical sanctions against an individual or organisation, *within the territorial jurisdiction of the state*, for the purpose of imposing a cost on the target as well as deterring specific activities' (italics added). Take away the italics, and the definition maps neatly onto Collyer and King's definition of the 'direct', 'physical' state control of transnational space. Collyer and King (2015: 194, 199) are primarily concerned with receiving states' exclusionary use of repression, which takes the forms of immigrant 'expulsion and detention'. That said, they also include extraterritorial practices of authoritarian states, such as overseas assassinations of opposition figures, in their discussion of direct control.

As recent studies and the chapters in this volume demonstrate, states often go far afield to directly repress and undermine their emigrants and diasporas. These actions are often unhindered and even aided by host country and multilateral authorities. For instance, Lewis' (2015) study of Uzbekistan documents how authorities have controlled their populations abroad through surveillance, intelligence and informal control, extradition, and assassinations and attacks beyond their borders. These kinds of practices clearly rest on the authoritarian emigrant state's inclusion of its population abroad within its own imagined jurisdiction. Yet, inclusion in this sense can hardly be associated with the usual notion of citizenship. Instead, this category of practices is best referred to as inclusion as *subjects*: in a range of repressive policies, the authoritarian government asserts its authority *as if* the subject were still on its territory (see Wedeen 2015 [1999]).

The rise of Internet-based communications has further facilitated the extension of repressive threats. As writings by Michaelsen (2016, this volume) and Moss (2016) illuminate, the Internet has transformed interactions between authoritarian governments and dissidents abroad. Their research respectively demonstrates how Iran and Syria interfere with exiled dissidents' digital communications and send death threats, attempting – not always successfully – to make them feel as if they were still at home and act accordingly (see also Chapter 3 of this volume by Michaelsen).

Exclusive repression, or the exclusion of emigrants and diaspora members as outlaws, is equally at the repressive end of extraterritorial practices of authoritarian states, but it is a very different type of practice. Here, the authoritarian state tries to exclude populations abroad from participation in the polity even as subjects by disrupting or destroying their ties with the home country. Exclusion can take the form of cutting intimate ties by forcing friends or relatives at home to repudiate those abroad and sever connections. But it can also take a legal form by withdrawing citizenship, refusing routine consular services (such as passport renewal) and refusing re-entry. For Collyer and King, control over individuals' legal status falls under symbolic control, because it is 'neither imagined nor completely physically grounded' (2015: 195).

Hannah Arendt famously considered withdrawal of nationality a loss of 'the right to have rights'. Unless people made stateless are admitted into another polity, their 'plight is not that they are not equal before the law, but that no law exists for them; not that they are oppressed but that no one even wants to oppress them' (Arendt 1958: 298, 296). Withdrawal of nationality can either prevent those already abroad from returning, or precipitate their exile. On a dramatic scale directly reminiscent of Arendt's description, Myanmar's military regime stripped hundreds of thousands of Rohingya of Burmese citizenship in the 1980s, precipitating waves of violence and displacement and creating a situation of statelessness that persists to this day (Cheesman 2017). More recently, Gulf states such as Bahrain, Kuwait, Oman, Qatar and the United Arab Emirates have revoked the citizenship of political dissidents (Human rights in the Gulf 2014; Protest and lose your passport 2016), and Yemen's embassies and consulates have refused to renew the passports of refugees and exiles following the 2014 coup d'état, ensuing war and devastating humanitarian crisis (personal correspondence with Don Picard and Dana M. Moss 2022).

Legitimation: Patriots and Traitors

Legitimation, as defined by Gerschewski (2013: 18), 'seeks to guarantee active consent, compliance with the rule, passive obedience, or mere toleration within the population'. By defining legitimation in this manner, Gerschewski sidesteps normative debates about legitimacy and the empirical difficulties in measuring discursive success (i.e. identifying whether a government is genuinely experienced as legitimate) in authoritarian contexts. His definition simply refers to the state's legitimation practices, with intent to help stabilise the regime, without pronouncing on their degree of success. While Gerschewski distinguishes between performance legitimation (based on authorities' actual or perceived track record) and discursive legitimation, I focus purely on the discursive element to better distinguish this type of practice from co-optation.

Transported into the transnational realm, performance legitimation corresponds to symbolic and imaginative control, as conceptualised in Collyer and King's (2015) typology. Symbolic control is described as governments 'placing themselves in the symbolically powerful position of guardians of 'home' [which] can draw on loyalties of resident and nonresident citizens alike' (Collyer and King 2015: 194). Such control often finds its practical expression in the 'discursive control of imaginative space' (ibid.: 193), exerted particularly in cyberspace and through media representations. Such strategies fit the general trend of sending states' increasing discursive recognition of populations abroad as part of the nation-state, but again, this takes on a particularly threatening inflection in the authoritarian context. What authoritarian discourses aimed at populations abroad do may be termed 'loyalty conflation'. This means that they are adept at eliding the differences between people, nation, state and government, conflating these different loyalties in discourses of 'national loyalty' (Shain 2005: 165). Populations abroad are particularly susceptible to this rhetoric because their physical location has denaturalised their belonging. I refer to this set of practices as 'inclusion as patriots'.

As noted by Shain (2005: 165), inclusion as patriots is precarious because it depends both on the population's so-called good behaviour and on the regime's interests. Whenever it suits, populations abroad can be discursively excluded as traitors, that is, as agents of foreign governments, deserters, cultural degenerates or tax evaders. Just as loyalty to the nation is conflated with loyalty to the regime, actual or potential opposition to the regime is conflated with being unpatriotic.

The act of physical exit makes populations abroad more vulnerable to this type of critique than opponents within. An example of this is Eritrea. For decades, the regime of Isaias Afwerki (1991–) has perfected practices of 'loyalty conflation': the people, the nation and the leadership are one, and duty to the homeland is equated with duty to the home government. Through mandatory taxation, diaspora associations, festivals, seminars and satellite-television broadcasts, the regime keeps a tight grip on populations abroad by conflating loyalty to the nation with loyalty to the government. Moreover, there is always the threat of exclusion as traitors. If they are not outright opponents of the regime, Eritreans abroad may be particularly susceptible to fearing discursive exclusion because of the sense of betrayal (to family, community and the nation) they may feel. Not only does guilt arise from have having left their homeland and families behind, but the newly formed nation also emerged as a result of a brutal war with Ethiopia. Open critics of the regime abroad are therefore automatically labelled as traitors, as discussed further by Hirt and Mohammad in this volume.

Co-optation: Clients

Co-optation, in Gerschewski's framework, is 'the capacity to tie strategically-relevant actors (or a group of actors) to the regime elite' (2013: 22). The mechanism will be a familiar one to students of authoritarianism: personal perks are promised, and sometimes disbursed, to specific population groups in return for their support. It is, as it were, 'inclusion within inclusion': those targeted are made not just part of the *polity*, but also of its *elite*. While Gerschewski mentions business and military elites in his discussion, populations abroad may also be 'strategically relevant' to the regime, such that co-opting them may be mutually beneficial. The fortunes and careers of persons abroad are often tied not just to the host and home country, but more specifically to the home *regime*. Members of the regime dominate not only political affairs, but often exert monopolistic power over the private economy and welfare state alike. Again, this practice does not map neatly onto liberal ideas of inclusion as citizenship. In terms of its material benefits, such co-optation of nationals abroad is something more; but in its informality and precariousness, it is also something less. An appropriate term for these practices is inclusion as *clients*. This practice extends Collyer and King's (2015) characterisation of states' controls over transnational citizenship, which does not speak to the idea of binding populations abroad by means of material incentives. Yet, the practice of co-opting populations abroad as clients does just that.

This practice is probably deployed by regimes more widely than the current literature recognises. That said, case studies are informative: Dalmasso (2018) and Hirt and Mohammad (2018) have described how Moroccans and Eritreans abroad, respectively, have been given access to various services exclusive to the home-based elite. Morocco, moreover, has cultivated particular individuals to establish even closer ties with emigrants and diaspora groups. It targets individuals who hold political positions in host societies in order to deploy them as brokers of Moroccan interests in European politics. These clientelistic relations are, of course, much more advantageous to nationals abroad than their inclusion as subjects to be repressed, as they involve *quid pro quos*. Nevertheless, it is still a relation of dependency that takes place on uneven terms, and is therefore not to be equated with citizenship rights. The Kazakh study-abroad scheme Bolashak described by Del Sordi (2016), for instance, can be considered as a more official form of co-optation. As she describes, the regime invests in the loyalty of a young, educated elite to the regime by guaranteeing returnees access to superior jobs and career opportunities. Thus, their fortunes and careers are tied to the home government, and temporary residence abroad – and their loyalty – attain value as both individual and national assets.

By unpacking the practices of repression, legitimation and co-optation with the 'regime's demarcation' (Shain 2005: 165) and 'politics of membership' (Brubaker: 2010), I have derived five types of practices used by authoritarian states for ruling populations abroad. These are inclusion as (1) subjects, (2) patriots or (3) clients, versus exclusion as (4) outlaws or (5) traitors. These types are not mutually exclusive, and future studies may elaborate or extend these types; nevertheless, they provide a useful theoretical and heuristic foundation for future empirical studies. The following section discusses more concretely which actors are involved in extraterritorial authoritarian governance and how they matter in the exercise of extraterritorial power.

Extraterritorial Authoritarian Governance: A Configuration of Actors

When moving from a regime type to a practice-based approach to authoritarianism, it becomes conceptually possible to discern a more complex 'configuration of actors' (Elias 2012) behind extraterritorial authoritarian governance, rather than simply 'the state'. This allows researchers to shine a light on authoritarian governance more accurately, since state actions are not enacted by singular monoliths, but are instead 'performed by collectives' (Adler and Pouliot 2011: 8). Configurations are a flexible concept capable of capturing dynamic realities: they 'can be more or less complex, stable, durable, harmonic, and regulated' (Quintaneiro 2006; see also Glasius 2023, 24–6, on configurations and authoritarian practices). The only necessary condition involved is that collectively, the actors in question exert a degree of control over a population abroad.

Taking practices as our unit of analysis makes it possible to transcend the oversimplification of attributing all phenomena to singular monolithic regimes, their dictators and to official policy. Practices are, simply put, 'patterned actions that are embedded in particular organized contexts' (Adler and Pouliot 2011: 5). They include both normative, informal, unacknowledged actions, as well as the enactment and enforcement of formal policies. This leaves an empirical challenge, however. Given that a lack of transparency is a common feature of authoritarian rule (Ahram and Goode 2016) and that the sensitivities of host states may provide additional incentives for secretiveness, it is no surprise that less is known about exactly which agents are directly deployed to perpetuate extraterritorial authoritarian practice. Nevertheless, we can glean insights from dissident testimonials, journalistic investigations, legal cases and human rights reports, among other sources, to theorise which configurations are involved in enacting authoritarian governance abroad.

This section aims to provide a first exploratory mapping of the more obvious and many less-obvious actors who are actually and potentially involved in perpetuating extraterritorial authoritarian control. In order to be able to provide examples of who is 'doing' extraterritorial authoritarian governance, I will focus on three migrant communities with which I am familiar: people of Turkish, Iranian or Eritrean descent living in the Netherlands. The first two communities are subject to very different manifestations of authoritarian governance. Dutch Eritreans and Turks are both exposed to overt discursive practices, while Dutch Iranian dissidents are subjected to much more secretive forms of intimidation. Together, the examination of *who* exerts authoritarian power over these communities sheds light on a wide spectrum of actors, allowing for a first mapping of who is involved in extraterritorial authoritarian governance.

Configurations in Three Communities

What I propose here is that in cases of extraterritorial practices, we don't assume that the organised context is simply the home state. Instead, we must disaggregate and empirically examine who is involved. Doing so helps to discern the different configurations of actors involved, which are also dynamic. When observing the extraterritorial authoritarian governance of the Turkish, Iranian and Eritrean communities in the Netherlands, for instance, I have discerned three overlapping configurations: an *overt* configuration centred on the embassy and consulate; a *covert* configuration led by secret services (about which, necessarily, little is known, but we get glimpses), and an Internet-communication technological (ICT) configuration that does not rely on the physical presence of repressive agents in the host country, but on technical mechanisms and corporate ICT platforms. Of course, such ICT-based configurations may benefit from the actions of other actor configurations, and vice versa, since the information collected by one can be used in the service of the other.

The configurations described here are not intended to be exhaustive. Scholars such as Brand (2006) and Miller (1981) have also described labour-centred configurations, in which sending state agencies, middlemen and employers collaborate in the exploitation of migrant workers in order to repress migrant labour activism. In anti-terrorism practices, different intelligence and law-enforcement agencies collaborate with multilateral organisations at times, and across the democratic–authoritarian divide (see also Chapter 7 by Roberts and Chapter 12 by Lemon). The concept of configurations nevertheless provides a vocabulary for describing such shifting coalitions that help enable authoritarian governance in a globalised world.

Three Communities

Traditionally, fault lines within the Dutch Turkish community have existed between religious, secular state-dominated and leftist organisations. Furthermore, 'being careful in unfamiliar company has always been second nature' to Dutch Turks (Pinedo and Schravesande 2017), owing to rifts in the community. However, there was no suggestion that any Turkish authorities directed or stoked these mutual suspicions prior to the last decade. During this time, three important shifts in Turkish politics have impacted the lives of Dutch Turks vis-à-vis the home state. First, after the adoption of new electoral laws in 2008 and 2012, Turks living abroad were able to vote in national elections from their countries of residence (Yanasmayan and Kasli 2019), strengthening the role of Turkish politics in Dutch Turkish community life (Sterkenburg 2016). Second, in the succeeding years, Dutch Turks who criticised President Recep Tayyip Erdoğan or his party, the AKP, experienced increasing threats. Third, as discussed by Baser and Öztürk in this volume (Chapter 10), there has been the growing rift between Erdoğan and his erstwhile ally, the US-based Sunni Muslim religious leader Fethullah Gülen, since 2013. Before this split, many Sunni Turks knew Gülenists among their family and friends; afterwards Gülen supporters became targeted abroad as 'traitors' (see typology), to be shunned and combated by good patriots.

The 38,000 legal residents and citizens in the Netherlands with an Iranian migrant background (CBS 2018) stand out from most other migrant groups because many, perhaps most, arrived as political refugees during or after the 1979 Iranian revolution (Honari et al. 2017: 20). They include people who identify as Ahwazi, Armenian, Baha'i, Christian, Kurdish, secularist and/or members of the political Green Movement. Apart from very recent arrivals, they typically have Dutch as well as Iranian nationality, because according to Iranian law, all Iranians retain their nationality. This nationality is bestowed in a mandatory fashion even unto the second generation. Iranians in the Netherlands are described as a splintered community (Ghorashi 2009: 82–6; De Jong 2018). A recent survey even found that Iranians in Western Europe trust other Iranian migrants much less than they trust host country natives (Honari et al. 2017: 16, 22; see also interviews in Groen 2019), suggesting that community rifts and transnational repression cast a strong shadow over group dynamics.

Dutch Eritreans, who comprise an even smaller community, estimated at 21,000 (CBS 2020), are both notoriously and closely watched by state agents and unofficial spies. A first group arrived in the Netherlands as political refugees in the context of the war of independence in the 1990s, and bigger waves arrived in the 2000s as a result of the latter war against Ethiopia. Others have fled in order to avoid the time-unlimited public service and conscription, akin to forced labour, that the government has imposed since 2009 (Hirt and Mohammad 2018). The community, if that term can be used at all, is characterised by fear and distrust, caused in part by rifts between the pro-government stance of many in the first generation and anti-government sentiments in later generations, but in at least equal part by the government's considerable investment in overseas social control.

Overt Configurations Orchestrated by Embassies

Diplomats and consular staff are the most obvious actors within the configurations perpetuating extraterritorial authoritarian governance. Their official functions include maintaining relations with their host states, as well as rendering services to nationals abroad. As such, embassy staff of authoritarian states are involved in the legitimation aspect of extraterritorial authoritarian governance. This is manifested, for instance, in sponsored national festivals with food, music and dance put on for Eritrean migrants. These events are organised by the party in power, the PFDJ, and its youth wing, and embassy staff and itinerant ministers give political speeches at these events (DSP-group 2016: 43–6).

Religious institutions are also part of the embassy configuration: both Eritrea and Turkey support 'official' churches and mosques (DSP-group 2016: 10; Sunier et al. 2016), which operate alongside more independent places of worship. In both cases, embassies may monitor institutional practice and deploy them as an arm of the state. In so doing, places of worship not only encourage loyalty, but target so-called traitors. An example is the response of the Turkish representation in The Hague to German satirist Jan Böhmermann's televised insult of President Erdoğan in 2016. Soon afterwards, it sent an email to dozens of Dutch Turkish organisations, including mosques, requesting them to 'report to us insults against the Turkish president, Turkey and the Turkish community, on social media or elsewhere' (Kok et al. 2016; Van der Kooy 2016).

Both party representatives and religious leaders can also be part of this actor configuration on the hunt for 'enemies of the nation'. In a competitive authoritarian polity such as Turkey, diasporic votes have become increasingly important as a source of support for the ruling party. Hence, *party* officials, rather than just state agents, often get involved in encouraging votes for the party and intimidating its critics (Yanasmayan and Kasli 2019). In a remarkable case, a member of the AK party turned out to be behind a campaign to convince Dutch Turkish parents to take their children out of a 'Gülenist' primary school (Groen and Kuiper 2016). In 2016 it was revealed that the chair of the official mosque association of the Turkish Directorate of Religious Affairs (*Diyanet*) – who also worked for the Turkish embassy – had reported the names of Dutch Gülen supporters to the Turkish government (Polman 2016).

The Turkish case also stands out for the extent to which members of the Dutch Turkish community are mobilised in the persecution of the regime's appointed enemies, which include all Gülenists alongside other vocal critics of Erdoğan. For example, thousands of Dutch Turks were involved in issuing threats on social media and in real life on boycotting businesses, publications and schools that were branded 'Gülenist' (Glasius 2023: 47–9). It is clear that such threats were indirectly and directly encouraged or instigated by embassy staff and party members. Nonetheless, the passion with which ordinary people within the Dutch Turkish community quite voluntarily denounce, threaten and ostracise suspected Gülen supporters remains quite extraordinary.

Consular services can also be instrumentalised in order to intimidate and extort money from populations abroad, which is a clear case of treating populations abroad as subjects, rather than citizens. A notorious example is the so-called 2 per cent tax demanded from Eritreans abroad. Officially, this is a voluntary contribution to support victims of the Ethiopian–Eritrean war (DSP-group 2016: 14). In practice, it is often demanded from anyone who needs consular services or access to fiscal transactions with people back in Eritrea. Not paying the tax may mean having to give up all ties to the homeland – in effect, becoming an outlaw (DSP-group 2016: 88–9; Hirt and Mohammad 2018; see also Chapter 10 in this volume). In recognition of the problematic 2 per cent tax and considerable evidence of the embassy's transnational repression practices, Dutch authorities no longer require recent Eritrean arrivals to use consular services in asylum procedures (DSP-group 2016: 88).

What I have termed 'embassy configurations' are the most overt and visible among the overlapping sets of actors involved in extraterritorial authoritarian governance, but they are also complemented by other less visible and tangible configurations, such as the loyalist intimidations by the broader community mentioned above.

Covert Configurations Involving Secret Agents

Equally central are the covert deployments of authoritarian states' secret agents abroad. Sometimes agents operate from or in close collaboration with the sending-state embassy; at other times there may be friction, but this will typically be difficult for an outside researcher to know. What is clear is that secret agents gather information on and sometimes harass, threaten or even kidnap or kill their nationals abroad, specifically those who are openly critical of the regime. Agents are required to treat populations abroad as subjects and to conform to home-state rules.

Politically vocal Dutch Iranians of different generations and different groups have reported experiencing intimidation that they assume emanates from intelligence agents (Kooper 2011; De Jong 2018; Groen 2019; see also Michaelsen 2018). For instance, after the failure of Iran's Green Movement in 2009, the Dutch internal intelligence service, AIVD, reported for the first time that the 'activities of Iranian intelligence services are directed towards groups and individuals that are considered by the Iranian regime as a threat to its continued existence . . . both suspected members of the Mujahedin-e Khalq and supporters of the Iranian opposition are a target for these intelligence and influencing activities' (AIVD 2009). One particular category of secret agents that deserves closer scrutiny is interpreters. There have been egregious cases in the Dutch Eritrean community (as well as among Uyghurs in the Netherlands) where interpreters used by the Dutch immigration service in the asylum procedure were revealed to be home-government spies (Plaut 2016; Vluchtelingenwerk 2013: 5). They were eventually fired.

While actual intelligence service personnel may be assumed to be on the payroll of the Iranian state, the regime also recruits informants from among Iranians abroad. One secular dissident in the Netherlands, Afshin Ellian, has recalled the story of a poet who became addicted to heroin, and – as he later confessed to Ellian – agreed to inform on his friends (Groen 2019). An independence activist from the Arabic-speaking province of Ahvaz was also ostensibly 'turned' by the Iranian intelligence service and sent to the Netherlands to execute an Ahvazi activist named Ahmad Mola Nissi. Instead, he took the opportunity to seek asylum and warn the Dutch authorities of the intended execution (VPRO Argos 2021). Eritrean community members also widely believe there are many informants in their community, including among recent arrivals (DSP-group 2016: 80–3).

Secret services from different states may also collaborate in transnational repression. For instance, Syrian secret services facilitated the arrest and abduction of another Dutch Ahvazi activist, Abdullah Al-Mansouri, from Syria to Iran. He was eventually released seven years later (Hulshof 2014). Furthermore, there are two known cases in which Iranian intelligence is widely suspected to have paid Dutch criminal gangs with no political affiliations to assassinate regime opponents. In the first case, two Amsterdam hitmen confessed to the contract killing of former Mojahedin-e-Khalq (MEK) member Ali Motamed, killed in 2015, but claimed not to know who the commissioning party was (Vugts 2019). Ahmad Mola Nissi, mentioned above, was shot and killed in 2017. Police pointed to a Rotterdam-based gang, while Dutch politicians claimed to have 'strong indications' that Iranian intelligence was ultimately behind the murder (Ministerie van Buitenlandse Zaken 2019). The AIVD has refused to comment on this case at the time of writing.

While these examples are all known due to revelations by diaspora members themselves and research by journalists, these glimpses of informant networks, allied and hostile secret services, and criminal gangs likely only represent the tip of the iceberg in terms of the configurations of secret agents involved in extraterritorial authoritarian governance.

ICT-based Configurations

A third category of actors involved in extraterritorial authoritarian governance is not located in the host societies, but is instead involved in monitoring, propagandising, harassing and slandering populations abroad by means of satellite and Internet-communication technologies (ICTs). Both the Eritrean and the

Turkish media have state-controlled satellite television channels focused specifically on the diaspora that broadcast from the motherland. Media from the home country tell populations abroad not only what patriotism entails, but also specifically who among them are traitors. In August 2016, for instance, Turkish state press agency Anadolu Ajansi (AA) published a list of Dutch 'Gülenist' organisations, including Dutch schools, companies, non-profit organisations and a newspaper, so as to facilitate the community in boycotting them (Jonker 2016).

Digital surveillance and harassment has traditionally been the province of intelligence services, so there is an overlap between secret agent-led configurations and ICT configurations. For instance, Dutch television journalists, in collaboration with a cybersecurity company, recently discovered an Iranian command-and-control server used to spread malware near Haarlem in the Netherlands. Once again, the server appeared to be specifically aimed at Ahwazi activists living in the Netherlands and beyond, including in Iran itself (Delhaas and Davidson 2021). As for harassment on social media, Turkey's AKP has been involved in trolling its opponents (Akis 2022), but in the Netherlands, much of the harassment appears to have been emanating from members of the community directly. Likewise, repeated hacks of a Dutch-Turkish newspaper associated with Gülenism came from within the community itself ('Aangifte 2015; Bahara 2016; Chorus 2016).

Actors in ICT configurations can also be engaged in the production of 'outlaws' by cutting ties between critical voices abroad and their compatriots in the homeland, as well as by blocking their social media accounts. In the case of Dutch-Turkish newspaper editor Mehmet Cerit, his Twitter account in Turkey was blocked on the basis of a Turkish court order in collaboration with the Twitter corporation itself (Van Dedem 2016). Twitter later stated that it did not usually accede to legal requests 'to remove content posted by verified journalists or news outlets', but 'with limited exceptions in Germany and Turkey' ('Twitter Suspends' 2017).

ICT configurations have been the most dynamic in the past decade, involving a mix of state-owned media, corporate platforms, and human and non-human 'bot' actors involved in surveillance and trolling. Their combined impact on populations abroad can hardly be overestimated.

Conclusion

This chapter has shown that authoritarian governance is not territorially bounded. National governments, or sections within them, have the ability to repress, propagandise and co-opt their nationals (including those who would prefer to renounce their nationality) beyond their own borders. The slowness of social scientists to systematically come to grips with this long-standing phenomenon can be attributed in part to the theoretical 'extraterritorial gap' in the social sciences. Specifically, scholars of migration have largely neglected authoritarian host countries (with some exceptions, such as Brand 2006, for instance), and scholars of authoritarianism have been blinded to the transnational turn in migration studies. Another explanation lies in the double challenge of accessibility of the empirical field – both of doing research in and on authoritarian regimes *and* gaining the confidence of respondents in migrant and diaspora communities. Doing so is far more challenging than social science research undertaken in more open contexts. As a result, the literature has long been dominated by profound but hard-to-compare single-case studies on one country and one topic.

This chapter has sought to make two contributions to systematising our knowledge about the extraterritorial practices of authoritarian states. First, building on Glasius (2016), I have categorised the ways in which authoritarian regimes deploy mechanisms of inclusion and exclusion vis-à-vis their extraterritorial populations, distinguishing five roles in which migrants are cast: subjects, outlaws, patriots, traitors and clients. Second, it has shown that extraterritorial authoritarian governance is not exerted by state officials alone. A first mapping, which will undoubtedly be expanded in future work, has laid bare the involvement of different configurations of actors, including embassy personnel, members of the governing party abroad, secret agents, religious leaders, migrant community members and host-state criminal networks. Further research on the different, and dynamic, configurations of actors involved should provide a better purchase on the conditions that actually make room for authoritarian states to manoeuvre within this repertoire. Conversely, it should also help researchers and practitioners better understand the vulnerabilities of the targets of extraterritorial authoritarian practices. Providing conceptual models and empirical comparisons will therefore help shrink the abilities of foreign states to practise extraterritorial authoritarian governance, as well as strengthen the resilience of its target populations.

References

'Aangifte om hack Nederlands-Turkse nieuwssite'. 2015. *Algemeen Nederlands Persbureau* ANP, 10 November.

Adler, E. and Pouliot, V. 2011. 'International practices'. *International Theory* 3(1): 1–36.

Agnew, J. 1994. 'The territorial trap: The geographical assumptions of international relations theory'. *Review of International Political Economy*: 53–80.

Ahram, A. I. and Goode, J. P. 2016. 'Researching authoritarianism in the discipline of democracy'. *Social Science Quarterly* 97: 834–49.

AIVD [Algemene Inlichtingen en Veiligheidsdienst – General Intelligence and Security Service]. 2009. *Jaarverslag AIVD 2009*. The Hague: Ministry of Internal Affairs.

Akiş, F. A. 2022. 'Turkey's troll networks'. Brussels: Heinrich Boell Stiftung, https://eu.boell.org/en/2022/03/21/turkeys-troll-networks, 21 March.

Arendt, H. 1958. *The Origins of Totalitarianism*. New York: Harcourt Brace Jovanovich.

Bader, J., Grävingholt, J. and Kästner, A. 2010. 'Would autocracies promote autocracy? A political economy perspective on regime-type export in regional neighbourhoods'. *Contemporary Politics*: 81–100.

Bahara, H. 2016. 'We hebben nog maar een paar adverteerders over'. *De Volkskrant*, 1 September.

Bialasiewicz, L. 2012. 'Off-shoring and out-sourcing the borders of EUrope: Libya and EU border work in the Mediterranean'. *Geopolitics*: 843–66.

Brand, L. 2006. *Citizens Abroad: State and Emigration in the Middle East and North Africa*. Cambridge: Cambridge University Press.

Brownlee, J. 2012. *Democracy Prevention: The politics of the U.S.–Egyptian Alliance*. New York: Cambridge University Press.

Brubaker, R. 2010. 'Migration, membership, and the modern nation-state: Internal and external dimensions of the politics of belonging'. *Journal of Interdisciplinary History* 41(1): 61–78.

Caramani, D. and Grotz, F. (eds). 2015. 'Voting rights in the age of globalization'. Special Issue of *Democratization* 22(5).

Cats, R. 2016. 'We willen die lange arm van Ankara hier niet'. *Financieel Dagblad*, 16 September.

CBS [Centraal Bureau voor de Statistiek]. 2018. 'Population; sex, age, migration background and generation', 1 June.

CBS [Centraal Bureau voor de Statistiek]. 2020. 'Population; sex, age, migration background and generation', 1 June.

Cheesman, N. 2017. 'How in Myanmar "national races" came to surpass citizenship and exclude Rohingya'. *Journal of Contemporary Asia* 47(3): 461–83.

Chorus, J. 2016. 'Een dagje zenuwen op de Gülen-krant'. *NRC Next*, 24 August.

Collyer, M. (ed.). 2013. *Emigration Nations: Policies and Ideologies of Emigrant Engagement*. Houndmills: Palgrave.

Collyer, M. 2014. 'Inside out? Directly elected "special representation" of emigrants in national legislatures and the role of popular sovereignty'. *Political Geography* 41: 64–73.

Collyer, M. and King, R. 2015. 'Producing transnational space: International migration and the extra-territorial reach of state power'. *Progress in Human Geography* 39(2): 185–204.

Dalmasso, E. 2018. 'Participation without representation: Moroccans abroad at a time of unstable authoritarian rule'. *Globalizations* 15(2): 198–214.

Davenport, C. 2007. 'State repression and political order'. *Annual Review of Political Science* 10: 1–23.

De Genova, N. 2013. 'Spectacles of migrant "illegality": The scene of exclusion, the obscene of inclusion'. *Ethnic and Racial Studies*: 1180–98.

De Jong, L. 2018. 'Mensen zijn bang om voor de deur van hun huis neergeknald te worden', *De Volkskrant*, 13 November.

Del Sordi, A. 2018. 'Sponsoring student mobility as a source of authoritarian stability: The case of Kazakhstan'. *Globalizations*.

DSP-groep Amsterdam, Universiteit Tilburg. 2016. *Niets is Wat het Lijkt: Eritrese organisaties en integratie*, DSP-groep Amsterdam, Universiteit Tilburg.

Elias, N. 2012. *What is Sociology?* Dublin: University College of Dublin Press.

Gamlen, A. 2008. 'The emigration state and the modern geopolitical imagination'. *Political Geography* 27(8): 840–56.

Gandhi, J. 2008. *Political Institutions under Dictatorship*. New York: Cambridge University Press.

Gardner, Frank. 2020. 'Saudi Arabia: Just how deep are its troubles?', BBC, 13 May.

Gerschewski, J. 2013. 'The three pillars of stability: Legitimation, repression, and cooptation in autocratic regimes'. *Democratization* 20(1): 13–38.

Ghorashi, H. 2009. 'National identity and the sense of (non-)belonging: Iranians in the United States and the Netherlands'. In Sharam, A., Thomas H. E. and Ghorashi,

H. (eds), *Paradoxes of Cultural Recognition: Perspectives from Northern Europe*. Surrey: Ashgate.

Glasius, M. 2023. *Authoritarian Practices in a Global Age*. Oxford: Oxford University Press.

Gore, C. 1996. 'Methodological nationalism and the misunderstanding of East Asian industrialization'. *European Journal of Development Research*: 77–122.

Groen, J. 2019. 'Deze Iraanse Nederlanders zijn altijd alert op de wraak van Teheran', *De Volkskrant*, 22 January.

Groen, J. and Kuiper, R. 2016. 'Wie blijft, is een landverrader, krijg je bij de thee te horen', *De Volkskrant*, 10 September.

Hirschman, A. O. 1993. 'Exit, voice, and the fate of the German Democratic Republic: An essay in conceptual history'. *World politics* 45(2): 173–202.

Hirt, N. and Mohammad, A. S. 2018. 'By way of patriotism, coercion, or instrumentalization: How the Eritrean regime makes use of the diaspora to stabilize its rule'. *Globalizations* 15(2): 232–47.

Honari, A., van Besouw, M. and Namazie, P. 2017. *The Role and Impact of Iranian Migrants in Western Europe*. Vrije Universiteit Amsterdam/The Simorgh.

Hulshof, A. 2014. 'Abdullah al-Mansouri: 'Ze lieten me geloven dat mijn zoon in de cel naast me zat', Wordt Vervolgd, December.

'Human rights in the Gulf: the new unpeople'. 2014. *The Economist*, 15 November.

Hyndman, J. 1997. 'BorderCrossings'. *Antipode* 29(2): 149–76.

Isin, E. and Turner, B. (eds). 2002. *Handbook of Citizenship Studies*. Thousand Oaks: Sage.

Joppke, C. 2005. 'Exclusion in the liberal state: The case of immigration and citizenship policy'. *European Journal of Social Theory* 8(1): 43–61.

Kok, L., Guillet, M. and Rosman, C. 2016. 'Kliklijn van consulaat splijt Turken', *Het Parool*, 22 April.

Kooper, A. 2011. 'Woede, maar wel in stilte', *Dagblad De Limburger*, 31 January.

Levitsky, S. and Way, L. A. 2010. *Competitive Authoritarianism: Hybrid Regimes after the Cold War*. Cambridge: Cambridge University Press.

Lewis, D. 2015. '"Illiberal spaces:" Uzbekistan›s extraterritorial security practices and the spatial politics of contemporary authoritarianism'. *Nationalities Papers* 43(1): 140–59.

Markus, N. 2017a. 'Gülen-aanhangers geïntimideerd na aantijgingen Turkse pers', *Trouw*, 15 March.

McMann, K. M. 2006. *Economic Autonomy and Democracy: Hybrid Regimes in Russia and Kyrgyzstan*. Cambridge: Cambridge University Press.

Michaelsen, M. 2018. 'Exit and voice in a digital age: Iran's exiled activists and the authoritarian state'. *Globalizations* 15(2): 248–64.

Miller, M. 1981. *Foreign Workers in Western Europe: An Emerging Political Force*. New York: Praeger.

Ministerie van Buitenlandse Zaken. 2019. 'Kamerbrief Sancties tegen Iran wegens ongewenste inmenging' [Foreign Ministry letter to Parliament on sanctions against Iran because of undesirable interference], 8 January.

Mouissie, S. 2015. 'Asielverzoek brengt Oeigoeren al in gevaar', *Nederlands Dagblad*, 15 June.

Moss, D. M. 2016. 'The ties that bind: Internet communication technologies, networked authoritarianism, and 'voice' in the Syrian diaspora'. *Globalizations*.

Mountz, A. 2011. 'The enforcement archipelago: Detention, haunting, and asylum on islands'. *Political Geography* 30: 118–28.

Pinedo, D. and Schravesande, F. 2017. 'Er hoeft weinig te gebeuren of mensen denken: wéér die lange arm van Ankara', *NRC Handelsblad*, 1 April.

Plaut, M. 2016. 'How Eritrea is turning to Dutch courts to silence its critics', *The Guardian*, 1 March.

Polman, J. 2016. 'Ambassade onder vuur', *De Telegraaf*, 14 December.

'Protest and lose your passport'. 2016. *The Economist*, 26 November.

Quintaneiro, T. 2006. 'The concept of figuration or configuration in Norbert Elias' sociological theory", translated by Maya Mitre from *Teoria & Sociedade* 2(2): 54–69.

Schedler, A. 2013. *The Politics of Uncertainty: Sustaining and Subverting Electoral Authoritarianism*. Oxford: Oxford University Press.

Shain, Y. 2005. [First published 1989]. *The Frontier of Loyalty: Political Exiles in the Age of the Nation-state*. Ann Arbor: University of Michigan Press.

Sterkenburg, N. 2016. 'Erdogans macht: daar en hier', *Elsevier Weekblad*, 23 July.

Sunier, T., Van der Linden,, H. and Van de Bovenkamp, E. 2016. 'The long arm of the state? Transnationalism, Islam, and nation-building: the case of Turkey and Morocco'. *Contemporary Islam* 10(3): 401–20.

Tansey, O. 2016. *The International politics of Authoritarian Rule*. Oxford: Oxford University Press.

To, J. J. H. 2014. *Qiaowu: Extra-territorial Policies for the Overseas Chinese*. Leiden: Brill.

Torpey, J. 1999. *The Invention of the Passport: Surveillance, Citizenship and the State*. Cambridge: Cambridge University Press.

Tsourapas, G. 2018. *The Politics of Migration in Modern Egypt: Strategies for Regime Survival in Autocracies*. Cambridge University Press: Cambridge.

Van der Kooy, C. 2016. 'Oproep consulaat te gek voor woorden'. *Algemeen Nederlands Persbureau ANP*, 21 April.

VluchtelingenWerk and Amnesty International. 2013. *Geen weg terug, risico's bij gedwongen terugkeer van Oeigoeren*, 10 April.

VPRO Argos. 2021.

Vugts, P. 2019. '"Noffel" krijgt levenslang voor aansturen liquidatie Ali Motamed', *Het Parool*, 18 July.

Wedeen, L. (2015 [1999]). *Ambiguities of Domination: Politics, Rhetoric, and Symbols in Contemporary Syria*. Chicago: University of Chicago Press.

Wimmer, A. and Glick Schiller, N. 2002. 'Methodological nationalism and beyond: Nation-state building, migration and the social sciences'. *Global Networks* 2(4): 301–34.

Yanasmayan, Z. and Kaşlı, Z. 2019. 'Reading diasporic engagements through the lens of citizenship: Turkey as a testcase'. *Political Geography* 70: 24–33.

2

GLOBAL AUTOCRACIES: STRATEGIES OF TRANSNATIONAL REPRESSION IN WORLD POLITICS

Gerasimos Tsourapas

When you tie a hen with a long rope, she may think she is free.
– Amharic proverb repeated by Ethiopian Prime Minister Meles Zenawi[1]

Introduction

The aim of this chapter[2] is to contribute to a broader understanding of the transnational illiberal practices of authoritarian states. As Moss and Furstenberg note in the Introduction to this volume, transnational repression practices within non-democratic contexts are attracting increasing attention from policymakers and in academic circles. Indeed, the scholarly literature observes that there has been a global shift towards illiberalism, with autocracies frequently emboldened to project their power abroad with the aims of challenging liberal norms, sabotaging accountability and thereby threatening democratic processes. As authoritarianism continues to gain power across the global arena, there is a growing need to understand *how*, *when* and *why*

---

[1] Quoted in Aalen (2011: 53).

[2] This chapter is a modified and abridged version of Gerasimos Tsourapas (2021), 'Global autocracies: Strategies of transnational repression, legitimation, and co-optation in world politics'. *International Studies Review* 23(3): 616–44. It has been adapted to this volume with the publisher's permission.

non-democracies take repressive action against their citizens beyond their own national borders.

In the first part of this chapter, I adopt an interdisciplinary perspective that places the works of Albert O. Hirschman (1970, 1978) and James F. Hollifield (2004) in conversation with each other and with research on the international politics of autocratic rule. This maps the historical evolution of transnational authoritarianism. I argue that transnational authoritarianism emerged out of autocracies' contradictory needs as they sought to resolve, to paraphrase Hollifield, an *illiberal paradox* – namely, the contrast between the desire to allow mass emigration and the urge to maintain control over political dissent. In the second part of this chapter, I draw on insights from political sociology and international relations to identify four types of state-led transnational authoritarianism strategies: transnational repression, legitimation, co-optation, and co-operation with non-state actors. I conclude by discussing how this analysis paves the way for a novel area of research in international studies.

Transnational Authoritarianism and the Illiberal Paradox

Political scientists researching authoritarianism have traditionally adopted an intrastate focus. More recently, scholars have examined the drivers that motivate international actors to promote or hinder democratisation abroad (Whitehead 1996; Levitsky and Way 2006), while others investigate the effects of such actions on authoritarian regime durability (Yom 2016). Another strand of the literature has focused on the politics of cross-border mobility in terms of Western destination countries' relations with authoritarian countries of origin and/or transit, either in the context of Cold War bipolarity (Zolberg 1995) or in the management of forced migration (Betts and Loescher 2011). An emerging line of research examines how authoritarian regimes themselves behave in the international arena (Tansey 2016) by focusing on processes of diffusion (Darwich 2017), learning (Heydemann and Leenders 2011) or interstate co-operation (Weyland 2017). Yet, while this work identifies key sociopolitical and security dynamics in transnational authoritarian contexts, it does not theorise on specific policies towards citizens beyond the territorial boundaries of the authoritarian nation-state. This absence is particularly noticeable given the importance of citizens abroad for the survival of an autocratic regime: research has identified that they may challenge non-democracies via diasporic activism (Betts and Jones 2016), or they may reinforce the position of a hegemonic party via out-of-country voting (Brand 2010). Migrant remittances might strengthen authoritarianism in certain sending states (Ahmed 2012) or destabilise it in others (Escribà-Folch, Meseguer and Wright 2018). Expatriates may affect processes of conflict at home (Miller and Ritter 2014) and transmit information back about social and political norms, including democratic values (Pérez-Armendáriz 2014).

A similar gap exists in migration studies due to the historical tendency to view approaches to the management of cross-border mobility through a Western lens focusing on immigration (Adamson and Tsourapas 2020a). This perspective has identified the considerable material gains that countries of origin – authoritarian or otherwise – stand to benefit from through mass emigration, primarily in the form of remittances (De Haas 2010). Yet, contrary to the expectations of this line of thinking, not all autocracies allow mass emigration (Miller and Peters 2020). Even those that do may continue to target specific citizens living abroad. A subfield of diaspora studies has shed some light on such practices, but the sizeable literature on democracies' diaspora policies is not mirrored in work on authoritarian states' extraterritorial practices, which remains limited to single- or small-N research (Østergaard-Nielsen 2003; Brand 2006; Glasius 2017; Baser and Öztürk 2020). It is debatable whether autocracies' specific strategies towards political exiles, émigrés or other individuals abroad who are perceived as threats to a regime constitute part of a state's broader 'diaspora' policy. In fact, in the context of Global South politics, these would tend to fall under the jurisdiction of ministries of interior, security or defence rather than of foreign affairs, migration or diaspora.

Smaller literature streams on security studies, propaganda and intelligence shed more light on the rationales behind autocracies' strategies towards political dissidents abroad (for a recent example, see Furstenberg, Lemon and Heathershaw 2021). Scholars of Cold War politics identify how political calculations influenced autocracies' management of their citizens' cross-border mobility, as communist countries feared an exodus of dissatisfied citizens – in this context, material considerations appear to matter less than security exigencies: the German Democratic Republic's decision to construct the Berlin Wall was a clear demonstration of political calculations (Dowty 1989).

If dissidents did escape abroad, certain autocracies would seek to punish them from afar, as in the case of the Soviet Union (Krasnov 1985). Other regimes appear to downplay security concerns in favour of the economic gains of liberalising their border controls – for instance, Mexico and Egypt in the 1970s (Fitzgerald 2006; Tsourapas 2015) – or, at least, allowing groups of people to emigrate at specific points in time as a 'safety valve' strategy that would help to stabilise the regime, as in the case of Cuba (Hoffmann 2005; cf. Barry et al. 2014). These states often devised strategies of monitoring citizens' behaviour abroad and, when necessary, taking action against émigrés' political activism. For much of the second half of the twentieth century, Algeria, Morocco and Tunisia maintained large networks of surveillance, control and punishment of members of their communities across Western Europe (Brand 2006; Collyer 2006). Overall, there appears to be a cost–benefit analysis of mass emigration from the perspective of authoritarian regimes, as they seek to maximise the material benefits of liberalising emigration and border controls while minimising the political and security risks associated with it. As mass migration tends to become the norm rather than the exception in world politics, how can this tension (or, more broadly, autocracies' policymaking vis-à-vis their citizens abroad) be theoretically and historically understood?

James F. Hollifield (2004) established that contemporary states are 'migration states', for which the control of cross-border mobility is central to state logic. By examining immigration policymaking in Western Europe and North America, Hollifield identified the existence of a 'liberal paradox'. Although states wish to encourage the free flow of immigrant labour for economic purposes, they also seek to maintain immigration restrictions for political and security reasons. Put differently, contemporary migration states remain trapped in their need to balance economic and political exigencies: '[I]n order to maintain a competitive advantage, governments must keep their economies and societies open to trade, investment and migration. But unlike goods, capital and services, the movement of people involves greater political risks' (Hollifield 2004: 886–7). Notwithstanding its contribution to the literature on the politics of migration, the liberal paradox thesis focuses exclusively on policymaking across liberal democratic destination countries of the Global North (Adamson and Tsourapas 2019b). Do countries of origin across the Global South – frequently authoritarian – face a similar dilemma between maximising economic gains and minimising political and security risks from mass emigration? I argue for the existence of an *illiberal paradox* across authoritarian migration states: on the one hand, autocracies seek to control their borders and restrict emigration because of domestic political and security reasons – citizens' right to travel abroad comes into conflict with autocracies' wish to maintain order and eliminate dissent; on the other hand, autocracies wish to encourage emigration under an economic rationale that relies on free cross-border mobility to increase migrant remittances, lower unemployment and address the pressures of overpopulation.

How do autocracies attempt to escape the illiberal paradox? For much of their history, authoritarian regimes have tended to prioritise politics over economics by securitising emigration at the border: the freedom to travel abroad was a privilege rather than a right for citizens of mercantilist regimes or, more recently, communist regimes. This securitisation assumed various forms, from the creation of 'blacklists' of political dissenters banned from travelling abroad to the denaturalisation of nationals who emigrated without authorisation – measures prevalent in much of the 'Second' and 'Third' Worlds (Messina 1994). Although autocracies continue to prioritise border controls today, mass migration has become more prevalent due to the rise of economic interdependence, technological advances and, more broadly, processes of globalisation. Numerous autocracies, such as Turkey and Mexico, already had bilateral migration agreements with Global North states for much of the twentieth century. Since the 1970s, a number of authoritarian regimes, including China and Egypt, have espoused mass emigration, while another such wave of liberalisation occurred in the aftermath of the collapse of the Soviet Union. Arguably, the Democratic People's Republic of Korea is the only remaining authoritarian regime today that adheres to an isolationist policy that forbids emigration.

Although the shift towards mass emigration offers autocracies considerable material benefits, it does not automatically resolve the illiberal paradox. In fact, Albert Hirschman (1970, 1978) has identified the mutually exclusive processes of *exit* versus *voice*. In the context of migration politics, citizens who are dissatisfied in an existing polity can either protest against it – that is, exercise voice – or emigrate – that is, engage in exit (cf. Dowding et al. 2000). In recent years, work on transnationalism and diaspora mobilisation has demonstrated that Hirschman's binary is not clear-cut. Migrants are able to exercise their voice against authoritarian rule back home, as research on transnational advocacy networks and human rights issues also demonstrates (cf. Keck and Sikkink 2014).[3] How do autocracies respond to the political and security risks generated by the émigré voice? One possibility would be for them to return to the mercantilist and communist tradition of restricting mass emigration, but that would have severe economic and political implications in an era of global interconnectedness. In fact, recent trends suggest that autocracies are attempting to bypass the illiberal paradox altogether: they seek to reap the material benefits of free movement while ensuring that migrant and diaspora groups pose little political or security threat to their survival via the emergence of *transnational authoritarianism*.

I conceptualise transnational authoritarianism as any effort to prevent acts of political dissent against an authoritarian state by targeting one or more existing or potential members of its emigrant or diaspora communities (Tsourapas 2019b). While autocracies' attempts to silence dissent abroad may go as far back as the emergence of the nation-state, transnational authoritarianism emerges in the context of specific bilateral and regional migration agreements, as well as on a global scale, when state borders soften in the second half of the twentieth century. The growth of extraterritorial repressive action in recent years is further buttressed by a variety of factors – for one, technological advances have facilitated individuals' physical mobility across state borders as well as their ability to mobilise across them. As discussed by Michaelsen (Chapter 3) in this volume, information and communications technologies (ICTs) have also minimised the cost of disseminating information on a global scale. At the same time, autocracies are increasingly able to monitor, discipline and punish dissenters abroad, with surveillance technology becoming widely available. Importantly, in the aftermath of the War on Terror, a wider global shift towards illiberalism in recent years has provided the normative underpinnings for autocracies to extend their repressive strategies beyond state borders. The next section discusses how specific strategies of transnational repression – surveillance, threats, coerced return, enforced disappearances, coercion-by-proxy and lethal retribution – contribute to the growing repertoire of transnational authoritarianism.

---

[3] Hirschman also introduced the concept of 'loyalty', which he downplayed in later work and which is not discussed here.

Strategies of Authoritarian Transnational Repression

Surveillance

Domestic surveillance may serve as an instrument in controlling 'voice' abroad in multiple ways: mirroring extensive repression within Uzbekistan itself, the Uzbek government has 'designed a system where surveillance and the expectation of surveillance [abroad] is not the exception, but the norm', according to Amnesty International (2020b). As one refugee activist in Sweden argued, 'if we call our relatives, friends and families [in Uzbekistan], everything will be heard, we know that' (ibid.). Some authoritarian regimes have attempted to control émigrés abroad indiscriminately, as in the case of some countries in North Africa (Collyer 2006; Brand 2006). The Syrian authorities systematically note the activities of expatriates abroad, including recording street demonstrations and other protests, and monitoring mobile phones and Internet usage across Canada, Chile, France, Germany, Spain, Sweden, the United Kingdom and the United States (Amnesty International 2011).

Other regimes appear more focused: Turkey engages in 'long-distance policing' of specific opposition groups abroad, predominantly Kurdish organisations such as the Kurdistan Workers' Party (Østergaard-Nielsen 2003: 118–19). Turkmenistan pays particular attention to monitoring the activities of its students abroad (Human Rights Watch 2018b), as does China: a Chinese student in Vancouver argued that '[w]e self-police ourselves . . . Everybody is scared. Just this fear, I think creating the fear, it actually works' (Human Rights Watch 2020). Autocracies also adopt specific methods of transnational surveillance – Cuba, Sudan and the Persian Gulf countries depend on ICTs, as discussed below (Lamoureaux and Sureau 2019; Suárez 2019). Ethiopia has been accused of using FinSpy, a software programme that pulls users' passwords, records calls made on computer microphones, turns on webcams, logs keystrokes and reads text messages (Timberg 2014). Other regimes rely on their embassy and consular networks: in Egypt, where exiles have fled in a number of waves over the last seventy years (Dunne and Hamzawy 2019), the military regime tasks staff abroad with spying on the activities of its diaspora communities (cf. Aswany 2008). Beyond allegations of specific embassies reporting back to Cairo on citizens (Ahram Online 2016), embassy delegates and diplomats frequently attend lectures, events and exhibitions on Egypt – even academic conferences – to gather intelligence on speakers and attendees (Ramadan 2016).

Threats

The Chechen community in Germany, some 50,000 people, has been the target of threats by Ramzan Kadyrov's regime, the Kremlin-backed leader of the autonomous Russian republic of Chechnya. Movsar Eskarkhanov, the first openly gay Chechen refugee to publicly denounce Kadyrov in an interview with *Time*, renounced his claims during a second interview with a German-based correspondent for ChGTRK, the Chechen state broadcaster, stating that 'the Western journalists gave me drugs [and] forced me to disgrace the Chechen leader'. He apologised for 'disgracing' Chechnya, claiming to regret that his 'mental illness' had spurred him to say 'even one bad word' about Kadyrov. Eskarkhanov later admitted that his second interview was coerced: 'they made it clear that if I continued to talk, there would be problems' (*The Moscow Times* 2017). Elsewhere, autocracies may threaten host states: when the Dutch authorities placed restrictions on Turkish officials seeking to promote the campaign for a 'yes' vote in the 2017 constitutional referendum across Turkish citizens living in the Netherlands, President Recep Tayyip Erdoğan did not mince his words: he called the Dutch 'Nazi remnants' and threatened to retaliate in the 'harshest ways', including sanctions (Koinova 2017). In 2019 China asserted that Sweden would 'suffer the consequences' for awarding a freedom of speech prize to the detained Chinese-born Swedish publisher Gui Minhai (Flood 2019). While evaluating the success of intimidation is beyond the scope of this piece, such tactics appear to have an effect on migrant communities. Chechens in Germany, for instance, have often voiced their disappointment with their lack of protection from the local authorities. According to one Chechen in Berlin, 'the Russians and Kadyrovtsy have their own headquarters here, right here in Germany . . . dogs here have more rights than us. You kill a dog, you face punishment. You kill a Chechen? Go on, no problem' (Hauer 2019). Exiles are aware of the long reach of autocratic regimes: back in 1991, Saad al-Jabr, an outspoken Iraqi critic of the Saddam Hussein regime living in Britain, recalled how:

> The Iraqi cultural attaché in London came to visit me [with] a message for me from Saddam. He said there were just a few words . . . The message was, 'If Saad hides in a matchbox, I will find him.' It always stayed with me, that message . . . In other words, there was no escaping Saddam if he wanted to get me. (Sciolino 1991: 92)

An Arab leader who relied on intimidation in managing political opposition abroad was Muammar Gaddafi, who seized power in Libya in 1969. As the regime liberalised emigration for economic purposes, it addressed the illiberal paradox via transnational repression: Gaddafi would publicly describe many of those who had fled abroad as traitors to the Libyan state or, more frequently, *kullāb ḍāla* ('stray dogs'), and he would threaten to enact vengeance (Pargeter 2012). The regime would often conflate threats against émigrés who sought refuge in Europe or North America with anti-Westernism: in his 1982 'Day of Vengeance' speech, Gaddafi claimed that 'these stray dogs composed of ex-premiers who are traitors and hirelings . . . They demean the Libyan people because they sold out Libya . . . There shall be no mercy for the agents of America. The escaped hirelings, enemies of the Libyan people, shall not escape from this people' (quoted in Ross 1982). Libya also carried such threats through, and violence against émigrés was commonplace. An assassination programme in the United Kingdom was reportedly spearheaded by Moussa Koussa, nicknamed *mab'ūth al-mawt* ('envoy of death'). In 1980 Koussa was formally removed from his position as public envoy in London after publicly admitting these practices to *The Times* (11 June 1980): 'We killed two in London, and there were another two to be killed . . . I approve of this.' One of the most chilling instances involved Al-Sadek Hamed al-Shuwehdy, a Libyan student in the United States. He was forcibly returned to Libya in 1984 and placed in the middle of a packed stadium. After he tearfully confessed that he had been one of the 'stray dogs', a gallows was brought into the arena and al-Shuwedhy was hanged on live state television (Black 2011). Not surprisingly, Libyans abroad would rarely discuss homeland politics:

> When we met Libyans, a lot of them were scared. If I say hey, 'Gaddafi-this', everybody was like, 'shut the hell up . . . I can't even hang around with you!' They're here [in the United States] and they didn't even have free speech. (Moss 2016: 487)

Coerced Return

Authoritarian regimes also develop a range of strategies aiming at coercing citizens to return to the homeland. One form is renditions, particularly when linked to interstate migration diplomacy strategies (cf. Adamson and

Tsourapas 2019a): Öztürk and Taş describe how Turkey requested the extradition of 504 people suspected of being part of the Gülen movement from ninety-one countries – 107 'fugitives' had been brought back by March 2019 (2020: 63). Similar reports exist on the Rwandan community in Uganda (Betts and Jones 2016: 148). The Tanzanian authorities unlawfully coerced more than 200 unregistered asylum seekers into returning to Burundi on 15 October 2019 by threatening to withhold their legal status in Tanzania (Amnesty International 2019c). Georgian authorities have been suspected of aiding in the May 2017 disappearance of Azeri opposition journalist Afgan Mukhtarli in Tbilisi, where he had been living in self-imposed exile since 2015. At the time of his disappearance, Mukhtarli had been investigating the business holdings of the family of Azeri President Ilham Aliyev in Georgia for the Organised Crime and Corruption Reporting Project (BBC 2017). Two months later, Mukhtarli resurfaced in Azerbaijan and was sentenced to a six-year prison term. In 2017 the Egyptian government arrested hundreds of Uyghurs living in Egypt and handed them to the Chinese government; many were never seen again (Amnesty International 2019a). Beyond renditions, another extralegal strategy is that of forcing individuals either to appear at consulates or embassies abroad, where they are apprehended, or to fly back to their country of origin themselves: in 2017 Uighurs studying abroad were ordered to return home, with family members being held hostage by Chinese authorities until they did (Radio Free Asia 2017).

Co-operation on matters of coerced return is frequent in the case of Thailand, which has yet to respect the principle of *non-refoulement* that prohibits states from returning an individual to a country where they may face torture or other human rights violations. In fact, Thailand has invariably co-operated with authoritarian regimes' requests for extradition of refugees, asylum seekers and other individuals in its territory. In 2017, despite United Nations warnings, Thai authorities transferred Muhammet Furkan Sökmen, a Turkish national accused of ties to the Gülen movement, to Turkey (Human Rights Watch 2017b). In 2015 Thailand also reportedly returned to China approximately 100 alleged Uyghurs (Human Rights Watch 2017c). The country has also been known to subject prominent Chinese critics to illicit renditions: journalist and activist Li Xin disappeared while seeking refuge in Thailand in January 2016, only to reportedly reappear in China a few days later (Buckley

2016). Jiang Yefei and Dong Guanping, two Chinese citizens who had been designated as refugees by the United Nations High Commissioner for Refugees and relocated to Thailand, were deported to China in November 2015 in what Amnesty International called 'a worrying new pattern of China putting pressure on third-party countries to repatriate dissidents and others who have left China for economic and social reasons', including a rising number of ethnic Uyghurs (Buckley 2015). Thailand has also been identified as endangering the lives of refugees and asylum seekers via unofficial deportations – namely, towing boats of people out to sea, particularly Rohingas, a Muslim minority group in Burma (Bhaumik 2011).

Enforced Disappearances

The use of enforced disappearances frequently targets high-profile dissidents: in Rwanda, the Rwandan Patriotic Front does not tolerate political opponents or outspoken critics abroad, who frequently vanish (Human Rights Watch 2014). The disappearance of five people associated with the Causeway Bay Books independent bookstore in Hong Kong (specialising in books on Chinese politics that are not available in the People's Republic) sparked concerns about state-led renditions and contributed to the rise of Hong Kong's Anti-Extradition Law Amendment Bill Movement (Palmer 2018). Under Gaddafi, many Libyan dissidents also mysteriously disappeared, such as former Minister of Foreign Affairs (1972–3) Mansour Rashid El-Kikhia, who was granted American citizenship and helped found the Arab Organisation of Human Rights. He disappeared in Cairo in 1993, and his remains were only discovered in Libya in 2012 (Tsourapas 2020). Declassified documents reveal the extent of Operation Condor, under which the United States worked with South American military regimes to 'disappear' hundreds of political émigrés from Argentina, Bolivia, Brazil, Chile, Paraguay and Uruguay in the 1970s, and later from Ecuador and Peru (McSherry 2002; Lessa 2022). Beyond the involvement of liberal democracies, such as the United States, in such strategies, a pattern of interstate autocratic co-operation appears to emerge: for instance, numerous Thai political dissidents have disappeared since going into exile following the 2014 military coup d'état (Chachavalpongpun 2019), particularly in Laos (Human Rights Watch 2019a).

Among the authoritarian regimes that have relied on enforced disappearances to target dissent abroad is Saudi Arabia, which encourages its citizens' mobility for educational and developmental purposes but seeks to control 'voice' abroad. Beyond the Khashoggi assassination (Hearst 2018), Saudi Arabia frequently attempts to abduct émigrés who it considers enemies of the state. In 2018 the Saudi embassy in Cairo contacted Prince Khaled bin Farhan al-Saud, a critic of the regime's human rights record, to 'mend relations' by offering him $5.5 million. Bin Farhan realised there was 'a dangerous catch' when he was told that 'he could collect his payment only if he personally came to a Saudi embassy or consulate'. The regime extended similar overtures to Saudi dissident Omar Abdulaziz in Canada: 'they encouraged him to stop his activism and return home, urging him to visit the Saudi embassy to renew his passport' (Mohyeldin 2019). Loujain al Hathloul, a Saudi women's rights activist, was kidnapped while studying in the United Arab Emirates in 2018 and rendered to Saudi Arabia. Back in 2003, regime critic Sultan bin Turki bin Abdulaziz, a member of the royal family, was allegedly drugged in Geneva and taken to Riyadh. He escaped to Europe but was reportedly lured into boarding a Saudi plane once more in 2016 and has since disappeared. In fact, such Saudi practices date back to the 1979 abduction of opposition leader Nasser al-Saeed in Beirut. His whereabouts remain unknown (Allinson 2019).

Coercion-by-proxy

Rather than target a particular dissenter abroad, autocracies may choose to threaten or punish their family members or close associates back home. Coercion-by-proxy constitutes the actual or threatened use of physical or other sanctions against an individual within the territorial jurisdiction of a state for the purpose of repressing a target individual residing outside its territorial jurisdiction (Adamson and Tsourapas 2020b). In Iran, the regime interrogated the family of Vahid Pourostad, a digital activist working abroad, in an effort to dissuade him from publishing. They also targeted the father of journalist Masih Alinejad, who campaigns for women's rights online: 'nine times they took him and told him that his daughter is morally corrupt, that she is against Islam, she works with Israel against our country. My father doesn't talk to me anymore' (Michaelsen 2018: 258). Similar reports appear in the cases of Djibouti (MENA Rights Group 2019), Bahrain (Human Rights Watch 2019b) and Turkey (Öztürk and Taş 2020). Uzbek refugees in Europe are 'too afraid to contact their loved ones at home due to the terrible risk it can expose them to' (Amnesty International 2020b). Numerous reports point to

Venezuelans abroad fearing for the safety of their family members back home (Garsd 2018), but coercion-by-proxy extends beyond threats to exiles' networks back home. Chinese dissident student leaders testified before the United States Congress about family members being threatened with the loss of their jobs and instructed to ask students to cease any political activism (Eftimiades 2017). Similarly, the United Arab Emirates employs harassment techniques against not only family members but also friends and mere acquaintances of dissidents abroad: 'Our cousins and friends all cut us off, because anyone who would frequent our home would be summoned and asked detailed questions about us and our lives', argued one dissident's relative abroad. 'You become a pariah in society', said another (Human Rights Watch 2019d).

Lethal Retribution

Lethal retribution involves the actual or attempted assassination of dissidents residing abroad. In some instances, authoritarian regimes are unwilling to accept responsibility: in 2019 the European Union imposed sanctions against Iran in response to allegations that it was involved in plots to assassinate Iranian émigrés across Europe, including the death of two Dutch nationals of Iranian origin. The Iranian Foreign Minister responded that 'accusing Iran won't absolve Europe of responsibility for harbouring terrorists' (Schwirtz and Bergman 2019). In July 2019, an improvised explosive device was discovered at the television station of Nicaraguan investigative journalist Carlos Fernando Chamorro Barrios in Costa Rica, where he had been living and working in exile for less than half a year (Thaler and Mosinger 2019). The Karimov regime in Uzbekistan has been known to conduct assassinations in Turkey and elsewhere (Farooq 2015). In other instances, autocracies may be more likely to identify themselves as culprits, as in the case of Gaddafi's Libya or Rwanda: in January 2014, the body of former intelligence chief Patrick Karegeya was found, apparently murdered, in South Africa. When asked about this, Rwandan President Paul Kagame warned that 'whoever betrays the country will pay the price'. Regime insider James Kabarebe remarked that 'when you choose to be a dog, you die like a dog . . . There is nothing we can do about it, and we should not be interrogated over it' (quoted in Thomson 2018: 234). Saddam Hussein arguably 'made assassination part of Iraq's official foreign policy' from 1980 onwards, as Iraqi exiles were publicly targeted in London, California and across the Middle East. Mahdi al-Hakim, a political dissident and member of the Shiite al-Hakim family, was lured out of Britain for an Islamic conference in Sudan, where he was gunned down in the lobby of the Khartoum Hilton hotel in January 1988. It emerged that the Iraqi intelligence service had organised the conference with the aim of luring al-Hakim out of Britain, as they 'did not want to assassinate al-Hakim on British soil and thus risk damaging their good relations with the government of Prime Minister Margaret Thatcher' (Sciolino 1991: 92).

One state with a long tradition in engaging in lethal retribution in terms of transnational authoritarianism is Russia (Krasnov 1985). A history of violence against its citizens abroad dates back to the early Soviet years, as Moscow targeted those who opposed the Bolsheviks and had migrated abroad (the so-called 'white émigrés'). The Soviet secret police, the OGPU, was believed to be implicated in the political assassinations of both Pyotr Wrangel and Alexander Kutepov in Paris, among others. From 1934 onwards, the People's Commissariat for Internal Affairs (NKVD) became responsible for such efforts, including the 1940 assassination of high-profile political dissident Leon Trotsky in Mexico City. Since the collapse of the Soviet Union, Russia has been implicated in violence against citizens who have received political asylum in Western countries – most notably, the poisoning of Alexander Litvinenko in London in 2006, and Sergei and Yulia Skripal in Salisbury in 2018. Many of these cases remain unresolved – for instance, Mikhail Lesin, the former media director of Gazprom who had relocated to the United States in 2011, was found dead in a Washington, DC hotel room as a result of blunt-force trauma to his head; and former business tycoon Boris Berezovsky, who had been granted asylum in the United Kingdom in 2003, was found dead in 2013 under mysterious circumstances, following two alleged unsuccessful assassination attempts in 2003 and 2007 (Erickson 2018).

Conclusion

'Anyone who says anything [bad] about our country, what happens to them?' Nabila Makram, Egypt's Minister for Immigration, asked during a private party for Toronto expatriates in July 2019. 'We cut', she said as she made a throat-slitting gesture with her hand while audience members laughed and burst into applause (BBC 2019). Despite the rising frequency of autocracies' extrastate repressive actions, the field of international studies lacks a coherent framework that explains how, when and why governments engage in repressive action against their citizens beyond their national borders. In this chapter, I have drawn on a range of sources to examine the historical evolution of the phenomenon of *transnational authoritarianism*, which involves strategies of repression, legitimation, co-optation and co-operation with non-state actors. While such strategies are not novel in the context of international relations, I have demonstrated how transnational authoritarianism emerged in the twentieth century as states attempted to tackle an *illiberal paradox* – namely, the need to maintain open borders for economic purposes while wishing to continue to control citizens' political activity once abroad. Such extrastate practices are bound to increase in intensity, fostered by technological change, rising global levels of cross-border mobility and a growing climate of illiberalism.

While I have inductively demonstrated how each type of transnational authoritarianism operates to crush dissent abroad via a range of cases from Africa, Asia, the Middle East and South America, autocracies are not expected to limit their strategies to one type. In fact, authoritarian regimes are keen on combining these strategies, rather than using them in isolation, to maximise their effectiveness. Victims' reports demonstrate this all too clearly: Negar Mortazavi, an Iranian-American digital activist, has argued that strangers would approach her on Facebook by using 'fake accounts that have a generic name with a generic photo or without a photo . . . They tried to add us as friends with these new weird accounts and to get into our circles and monitor us' (quoted in Michaelsen 2018). In fact, the combination of various strategies produces an environment of fear that prevents exiles from escaping the long arm of their state – whether this is real or imagined. As Syrian refugees abroad would report, the Syrian regime's totalitarian-style state repression has produced 'a disposition of silence . . . carried beyond the homeland' (Pearlman 2017).

I pave the way in this chapter for new research on an unexplored dimension of authoritarian politics: for one, the illiberal paradox thesis suggests conflicting interests between regimes' desires for material benefits from emigration and the security needs for repression. Future researchers could attempt to focus on exploring potentially causal relationships between these conflicting interests – for example, primary material (such as intelligence reports or historical accounts from regime dissenters) would be helpful in demonstrating whether and when internal deliberations focused on the trade-offs between economic openness and risk to the regime. Beyond this, should we expect certain types of autocracies to develop distinct transnational authoritarian practices? Would monarchical regimes engage with political dissent abroad in different ways from personalist regimes or military juntas? How may state strength affect variation, and does this explain why some states may not engage in transnational authoritarianism? What is the importance of the country of destination's regime type in the development of autocracies' strategies? Moving beyond autocratic politics, a key question also concerns the effects of transnational authoritarianism on liberal democracies. The American government's recent emphasis on diverting flows of highly qualified Chinese research talent to other countries to combat espionage has created fears of undue suspicion of immigrants with a Chinese connection (Yang 2020). In the United Kingdom, a Foreign Affairs Committee (2019) identified that the drive to recruit more international students led universities to be 'undermined by overseas autocracies' via 'financial, political and diplomatic pressure'. A sustained discussion on the nature of transnational authoritarianism has the potential for revealing the wide repertoire of illiberal practices at the disposal of the modern state.

References

Aalen, L. 2011. *The Politics of Ethnicity in Ethiopia: Actors, Power and Mobilisation Under Ethnic Federalism*. Leiden: Brill.

Adamson, F. B. and Tsourapas, G. 2020a. 'The migration state in the Global South: Nationalizing, developmental, and neoliberal models of migration management'. *International Migration Review* 54(3): 853–82.

——. 2020b. 'At home and abroad: Coercion-by-proxy as a tool of transnational repression'. *Freedom House*.

Ahmed, F. Z. 2012. 'The perils of unearned foreign income: Aid, remittances, and government survival'. *American Political Science Review* 106(1): 146–65.

Ahram Online. 2016. 'Egypt embassy in Berlin denies sending reports on activists to Cairo'. http://english.ahram.org.eg/NewsContent/1/64/186501/Egypt/Politics-/Egypt-embassy-in-Berlin-denies-sending-reports-on-.aspx.

Allinson, T. 2019. 'How Saudi Arabia monitors and intimidates its critics abroad'. https://www.dw.com/en/how-saudi-arabia-monitors-and-intimidates-its-critics-abroad/a-51159148

Amnesty International. 2011. 'Syria: The long reach of the Mukhabaraat: Violence and harassment against Syrians abroad and their relatives back home'. https://www.amnesty.org/en/documents/MDE24/057/2011/en/

——. 2019a. 'Help us find Yiliyasijiang Reheman'. https://www.amnesty.org/en/get-involved/take-action/w4r-2019-china-yiliyasijiang-reheman/

——. 2019b. 'Eritrea: Government officials and supporters target critics abroad as repression stretches beyond borders'. https://www.amnesty.org/en/latest/news/2019/06/eritrea-government-officials-and-supporters-target-critics-abroad-as-repression-stretches-beyond-borders/

——. 2019c. 'Tanzania: Confidential document shows forced repatriation of Burundi refugees imminent'. https://www.amnesty.org/en/latest/news/2019/09/tanzania-confidential-document-shows-forced-repatriation-of-burundi-refugees-imminent/

——. 2020a. 'Nowhere feels safe'. https://www.amnesty.org/en/latest/research/2020/02/china-uyghurs-abroad-living-in-fear/

——. 2020b. 'Uzbekistan: Tentacles of mass surveillance spread across borders'. https://www.amnesty.org/en/latest/news/2017/03/uzbekistan-tentacles-of-mass-surveillance-spread-across-borders/

Aswany, A. al. 2008. *Chicago*. London: Fourth Estate.

Barry, C. M., Clay, K. C., Flynn, M. E. and Robinson, G. 2014. 'Freedom of foreign movement, economic opportunities abroad, and protest in non-democratic regimes'. *Journal of Peace Research* 51(5): 574–88.

Baser, B. and Öztürk, A. E. 2020. 'Positive and negative diaspora governance in context: From public diplomacy to transnational authoritarianism'. *Middle East Critique* 29(3): 319–34.

BBC. 2017. 'Afgan Mukhtarli: Did Georgia help abduct an Azeri journalist?' https://www.bbc.com/news/world-europe-40606599

——. 2019. 'Egypt minister downplays threat to "cut" critics abroad'. https://www.bbc.com/news/world-middle-east-49101954

Betts, A. and Jones, W. 2016. *Mobilising the Diaspora: How Refugees Challenge Authoritarianism*. Cambridge: Cambridge University Press.

Betts, A. and Loescher, G. (eds). 2011. *Refugees in International Relations*. Oxford: Oxford University Press.

Bhaumik, S. 2011. 'Thailand "sent back" Rohingyas'. https://www.bbc.com/news/world-south-asia-12445480

Black, I. 2011. 'Gaddafi's Libyan rule exposed in lost picture archive'. http://www.theguardian.com/world/2011/jul/18/gaddafi-brutal-regime-exposed-lost-archive

Bozzini, D. M. (ed.). 2015. 'The fines and the spies: Fears of state surveillance in Eritrea and in the diaspora'. *Social Analysis* 59(4): 32–49.

Brand, L. A. 2002. 'States and their expatriates: Explaining the development of Tunisian and Moroccan emigration-related institutions'. La Jolla: University of California, San Diego.

——. 2006. *Citizens Abroad: Emigration and the State in the Middle East and North Africa*. Cambridge: Cambridge University Press.

——. 2010. 'Authoritarian states and voting from abroad: North African experiences'. *Comparative Politics* 43(1): 81–99.

Buckley, C. 2015. 'Thailand deports 2 dissidents to China, rights groups say'. https://www.nytimes.com/2015/11/19/world/asia/thailand-deports-2-dissidents-to-china-rights-groups-say.html?module=inline

——. 2016. 'Journalist who sought refuge in Thailand is said to return to China'. https://www.nytimes.com/2016/02/04/world/asia/china-thailand-li-xin.html

Chachavalpongpun, P. 2019. 'The case of Thailand's disappearing dissidents'. https://www.nytimes.com/2019/10/14/opinion/thailand-dissidents-disappearance-murder.html

Collyer, M. 2006. 'Transnational political participation of Algerians in France. Extra-territorial civil society versus transnational governmentality'. *Political Geography* 25(7): 836–49.

Darwich, M. 2017. 'Creating the enemy, constructing the threat: The diffusion of repression against the Muslim Brotherhood in the Middle East'. *Democratization* 24(7): 1289–1306.

De Haas, H. 2010. 'Migration and development: A theoretical perspective'. *International Migration Review* 44(1): 227–64.

Dowding, K., John, P., Mergoupis, T. and Vugt, M. 2000. 'Exit, voice and loyalty: Analytic and empirical developments'. *European Journal of Political Research* 37(4): 469–95.

Dowty, A. 1989. *Closed Borders: The Contemporary Assault on Freedom of Movement*. New Haven, CT: Yale University Press.

Dunne, M. and Hamzawy, A. 2019. 'Egypt's political exiles going anywhere but home'. https://carnegieendowment.org/2019/03/29/egypt-s-political-exiles-going-anywhere-but-home-pub-78728

Eftimiades, N. 2017. *Chinese Intelligence Operations: Espionage Damage Assessment Branch, US Defence Intelligence Agency*. London: Routledge.

Escribà-Folch, A., Meseguer, C. and Wright, J. 2018. 'Remittances and protest in dictatorships'. *American Journal of Political Science* 62(4): 889–904.

Farooq, U. 2015. 'The hunted'. https://foreignpolicy.com/2015/04/02/the-hunted-islam-karimov-assassination-istanbul-russia-putin-islamic-state-human-rights/

Fitzgerald, D. 2006. 'Inside the sending state: The politics of Mexican emigration control'. *International Migration Review* 40(2): 259–93.

Flood, A. 2019. 'China threatens Sweden after Gui Minhai wins free speech award'. https://www.theguardian.com/books/2019/nov/18/china-threatens-sweden-after-gui-minhai-wins-free-speech-award

Freedom House. 2019. 'Freedom in the World 2019: Democracy in retreat'. https://freedomhouse.org/report/freedom-world/freedom-world-2019/democracy-in-retreat

Furstenberg, S., Lemon, E. and Heathershaw, J. 2021. 'Spatialising state practices through transnational repression'. *European Journal of International Security* 6(3): 358–78.

Garsd, J. 2018. 'For many in Venezuela, social media is a matter of life and death'. https://www.npr.org/2018/09/11/643722787/for-many-in-venezuela-social-media-is-a-matter-of-life-and-death

Ghebreselasse, D. 2010. *The Escape*. New York: Unpublished.

Glasius, M. 2017. 'Extraterritorial authoritarian practices: A framework'. *Globalizations* 15(2): 179–97.

Glasius, M. and Michaelsen, M. (2018). 'Authoritarian practices in the Digital Age: Illiberal and authoritarian practices in the digital sphere – Prologue. *International Journal Of Communication* 12: 19. Retrieved from https://ijoc.org/index.php/ijoc/article/view/8899/2459

Hauer, N. 2019. 'If someone speaks the truth, he will be killed'. https://www.theatlantic.com/international/archive/2019/12/chechnya-ramzan-kadyrov-vladimir-putin/603691/

Hearst, D. 2018. 'Saudi journalist Jamal Khashoggi criticised the regime – and paid with his life'. https://www.theguardian.com/commentisfree/2018/oct/08/saudi-journalist-jamal-khashoggi-istanbul.

Hepner, T. M. R. 2009. *Soldiers, Martyrs, Traitors, and Exiles: Political Conflict in Eritrea and the Diaspora*. Philadelphia: University of Pennsylvania Press.

Heydemann, S. and Leenders, R. 2011. 'Authoritarian learning and authoritarian resilience: Regime responses to the "Arab Awakening"'. *Globalizations* 8(5): 647–53.

Hirschman, A. O. 1970. *Exit, Voice, and Loyalty: Responses to Decline in Firms, Organizations, and States*. Cambridge, MA: Harvard University Press.

——. 1978. 'Exit, voice, and the state'. *World Politics* 31(1): 90–107.

Hirt, N. and Mohammad, A. S. 2017. 'By way of patriotism, coercion, or instrumentalization: How the Eritrean regime makes use of the diaspora to stabilize its rule'. *Globalizations* 15(2): 232–47.

Hoffmann, B. 2005. 'Emigration and regime stability: The persistence of Cuban socialism'. *Journal of Communist Studies and Transition Politics* 21(4): 436–61.

Hollifield, J. F. 2004. 'The emerging migration state'. *International Migration Review* 38(3): 885–912.

Human Rights Watch. 2014. 'Rwanda: Repression across borders'. https://www.hrw.org/news/2014/01/28/rwanda-repression-across-borders

——. 2017a. 'Oman: Activist's family barred from traveling abroad'. https://www.hrw.org/news/2017/02/14/oman-activists-family-barred-traveling-abroad

——. 2017b. 'Burma/Thailand: Deported Turkish man at risk'. https://www.hrw.org/news/2017/06/01/burma/thailand-deported-turkish-man-risk

——. 2017c. 'Thailand: Implement commitments to protect refugee rights'. https://www.hrw.org/news/2017/07/06/thailand-implement-commitments-protect-refugee-rights

——. 2018a. 'Human rights abuses of Eritreans, at home and abroad'. https://www.hrw.org/news/2018/04/18/human-rights-abuses-eritreans-home-and-abroad

——. 2018b. 'World Report 2019: Rights trends in Turkmenistan'. https://www.hrw.org/world-report/2019/country-chapters/turkmenistan

——. 2019a. 'Laos: Investigate disappearance of 3 Thai dissidents'. https://www.hrw.org/news/2019/01/22/laos-investigate-disappearance-3-thai-dissidents

——. 2019b. 'Bahrain: Drop charges against activist's family'. https://www.hrw.org/news/2019/02/24/bahrain-drop-charges-against-activists-family

——. 2019c. 'Egypt: Families of dissidents targeted'. https://www.hrw.org/news/2019/11/19/egypt-families-dissidents-targeted

——. 2019d. 'UAE: Unrelenting harassment of dissidents' families'. https://www.hrw.org/news/2019/12/22/uae-unrelenting-harassment-dissidents-families

——. 2020. 'China's global threat to human rights'. https://www.hrw.org/world-report/2020/china-global-threat-to-human-rights

Jones, S. 2015. 'Diaspora tax for Eritreans living in UK investigated by Metropolitan Police'. https://www.theguardian.com/global-development/2015/jun/09/eritrea-diaspora-tax-uk-investigated-metropolitan-police

Jörum, E. L. 2015. 'Repression across borders: Homeland response to anti-regime mobilization among Syrians in Sweden'. *Diaspora Studies* 8(2): 104–19.

Keck, M. E. and Sikkink, K. 1998. *Activists Beyond Borders: Advocacy Networks in International Politics*. Ithaca, NY: Cornell University Press.

Krasnov, V. 1985. *Soviet Defectors: The KGB Wanted List*. Washington, DC: Hoover Press.

Lamb, K. 2019. 'Thai government pressed over missing Lao activist Od Sayavong'. https://www.theguardian.com/world/2019/sep/07/thai-government-pressed-over-missing-lao-activist-od-sayavong

Lamoureaux, S. and Sureau, T. 2019. 'Knowledge and legitimacy: The fragility of digital mobilisation in Sudan'. *Journal of Eastern African Studies* 13(1): 35–53.

Lessa, F. 2022. *The Condor Trials: Transnational Repression and Human Rights in South America*. New Haven, CT: Yale University Press.

Levitsky, S. and Way, L. A. 2006. 'Linkage versus leverage: Rethinking the international dimension of regime change'. *Comparative Politics* 38(4): 379–400.

McSherry, J. P. 2002. 'Tracking the origins of a state terror network: Operation Condor'. *Latin American Perspectives* 29(1): 38–60.

MENA Rights Group. 2019. 'Member of Djibouti's opposition party subjected to reprisals for her husband's cyber-activism'. https://www.menarights.org/en/caseprofile/member-djiboutis-opposition-party-subjected-reprisals-her-husbands-cyber-activism

Messina, C. 1994. 'From migrants to refugees: Russian, Soviet and post-Soviet migration'. *International Journal of Refugee Law* 6(4): 620–35.

Michaelsen, M. 2018. 'Exit and voice in a digital age: Iran's exiled activists and the authoritarian state'. *Globalizations* 15(2): 248–64.

Miller, G. L. and Ritter, E. H. 2014. 'Emigrants and the onset of civil war'. *Journal of Peace Research* 51(1): 51–64.

Miller, M. K. and Peters, M. E. 2020. 'Restraining the huddled masses: Migration policy and autocratic survival'. *British Journal of Political Science* 50(2): 403–33.

Mohyeldin, A. M. 2019. 'No one is safe: How Saudi Arabia makes dissidents disappear'. https://www.vanityfair.com/news/2019/07/how-saudi-arabia-makes-dissidents-disappear

Mosadiq, H. 2015. 'My journey to defend human rights in Afghanistan'. https://www.amnesty.org/en/latest/news/2015/12/my-journey-to-defend-human-rights-in-afghanistan/

Moss, D. M. 2016. 'Transnational repression, diaspora mobilization, and the case of the Arab Spring'. *Social Problems* 63(4): 480–98.

Østergaard-Nielsen, E. 2003. *Transnational Politics: Turks and Kurds in Germany*. London and New York: Routledge.

Öztürk, A. E. and Taş, H. 2020. 'The repertoire of extraterritorial repression: Diasporas and home states'. *Migration Letters* 17(1): 59–69.

Palmer, A. W. 2018. 'The case of Hong Kong's missing booksellers'. https://www.nytimes.com/2018/04/03/magazine/the-case-of-hong-kongs-missing-booksellers.html

Pargeter, A. 2012. *Libya: The Rise and Fall of Qaddafi*. New Haven, CT: Yale University Press.

Pearlman, W. R. 2017. *We Crossed a Bridge and It Trembled: Voices from Syria*. New York: Custom House.

Pérez-Armendáriz, C. 2014. 'Cross-border discussions and political behavior in migrant-sending countries'. *Studies in Comparative International Development* 49(1): 67–88.

Radio Free Asia. 2017. 'Uyghurs studying abroad ordered back to Xinjiang under threat to families'. https://www.rfa.org/english/news/uyghur/ordered-05092017155554.html

Ramadan, N. 2016. 'Egypt's embassy in Berlin: Part of Sisi's oppressive apparatus?' https://www.alaraby.co.uk/english/indepth/2016/2/2/egypts-embassy-in-berlin-part-of-sisis-oppressive-apparatus

Ross, J. 1982. 'Qaddafi threatens dissidents overseas'. https://www.washington-post.com/archive/politics/1982/12/06/qaddafi-threatens-dissidents-overseas/d7bfa1d3-22b5-419a-a8df-a39805e9ed26/

Schenkkan, N. 2018. 'Turkey just snatched six of its citizens from another country'. https://www.washingtonpost.com/news/democracy-post/wp/2018/04/01/turkey-just-snatched-six-of-its-citizens-from-another-country/

Schwirtz, M. and Bergman, R. 2019. 'E.U. imposes sanctions on Iran over assassination plots'. https://www.nytimes.com/2019/01/08/world/europe/iran-eu-sanctions.html

Sciolino, E. 1991. *The Outlaw State: Saddam Hussein's Quest for Power and the Gulf Crisis*. Hoboken, NJ: Wiley.

Suárez, Y. 2019. 'Under a watchful eye: Cyber surveillance in Cuba'. https://iwpr.net/global-voices/under-watchful-eye-cyber-surveillance-cuba

Tansey, O. 2016. *International Politics of Authoritarian Rule*. Oxford: Oxford University Press.

Thaler, K. M. and Mosinger, E. S. 2019. 'Repression and resilience in Nicaragua'. https://revista.drclas.harvard.edu/book/repression-and-resilience-nicaragua

The Moscow Times. 2017. 'First Chechen to come out as gay says public apology was forced'. https://www.themoscowtimes.com/2017/12/27/first-chechen-gay-to-come-out-as-gay-says-public-apology-was-forced-a60059

The White House. 2018. 'Statement from President Donald J. Trump on standing with Saudi Arabia'. https://www.whitehouse.gov/briefings-statements/statement-president-donald-j-trump-standing-saudi-arabia/

Thomson, S. 2018. *Rwanda: From Genocide to Precarious Peace*. New Haven, CT: Yale University Press.

Timberg, C. 2014. 'U.S. citizen sues Ethiopia for allegedly using computer spyware against him'. https://www.washingtonpost.com/business/technology/us-citizen-sues-ethiopia-for-allegedly-using-computer-spyware-against-him/2014/02/18/b17409c6-98aa-11e3-80ac-63a8ba7f7942_story.html

Tsourapas, G. 2015. 'Why do states develop multi-tier emigrant policies? Evidence from Egypt'. *Journal of Ethnic and Migration Studies* 41(13): 2192–2214.

———. 2019a. *The Politics of Migration in Modern Egypt: Strategies for Regime Survival in Autocracies*. Cambridge: Cambridge University Press.

———. 2019b. *A Tightening Grip Abroad: Authoritarian Regimes Target Their Emigrant and Diaspora Communities*. https://www.migrationpolicy.org/article/authoritarian-regimes-target-their-emigrant-and-diaspora-communities

———. 2020. 'The long arm of the Arab state'. *Ethnic and Racial Studies* 43(2): 351–70.

———. 2021. 'Global autocracies: Strategies of transnational repression, legitimation, and co-optation in world politics'. *International Studies Review* 23(3): 616–44.

Weyland, K. 2017. 'Autocratic diffusion and cooperation: The impact of interests vs. ideology'. *Democratization* 24(7): 1235–52.

Whitehead, L. (ed.). 1996. *The International Dimensions of Democratization: Europe and the Americas*. Oxford: Oxford University Press.

Wintour, P. 2019. 'Mohamed Ali: Egyptian exile who sparked protests in shock at mass arrests'. https://www.theguardian.com/world/2019/oct/23/mohamed-ali-egyptian-exile-in-shock-over-street-protest-arrests

Yang, Y. 2020. 'US–China tech dispute: Suspicion in Silicon Valley'. https://www.ft.com/content/e5a92892-1b77-11ea-9186-7348c2f183af

Yom, S. L. 2016. *From Resilience to Revolution: How Foreign Interventions Destabilize the Middle East*. New York: Columbia University Press.

Zolberg, A. R. 1995. 'From invitation to interdiction: U.S. Foreign policy and immigration since 1945'. In: Teitelbaum, M. S. and Weiner, M. (eds), *Threatened Peoples, Threatened Borders: World Migration and US Policy*. New York: W. W. Norton & Company.

3

NOWHERE TO HIDE: DIGITAL TRANSNATIONAL REPRESSION AGAINST EXILED ACTIVISTS FROM THE MIDDLE EAST

Marcus Michaelsen

In October 2019, Omar Abdulaziz, a Saudi dissident living in Canada, filed a lawsuit against two major US American companies, Twitter and the McKinsey consulting firm. The complaint faulted McKinsey for writing a report to the Saudi government that singled out Abdulaziz as one of three influential voices on social media who criticised the economic reforms in the kingdom. Abdulaziz sued Twitter for failing to protect his private information because Saudi intelligence operatives had managed to recruit two co-nationals employed at the company to gather data on account activity of Saudi Twitter users, including Omar Abdulaziz (Benner et al. 2018). With their actions, stated the complaint, both companies had exposed the plaintiff, 'his family members, friends and political associates to imprisonment, torture, and even death' (*Abdulaziz v. Twitter*; McKinsey 2019).

Abdulaziz had become the target of threats and harassment from the Saudi regime when he amassed a large online following after moving to Canada, in 2009. In order to blackmail him into ceasing his social media activism, two government agents even brought one of his younger brothers from Saudi Arabia to a meeting in Montréal, in May 2018. Two of his brothers, along with seven of his friends, were arrested in Saudi Arabia (Shalaby 2018). Around the time, Abdulaziz's smartphone was infected with a powerful spyware which the Saudi government had purchased from an Israeli company called the NSO Group. The Pegasus surveillance tool gave the operatives access to his personal files, emails and chats; regime agents were able to monitor his communications and movements. They likely also eavesdropped on Abdelaziz's conversations with his close associate Jamal Khashoggi, the exiled journalist who was eventually murdered in the Saudi consulate in Istanbul, in October 2018. Shortly after, Abdulaziz filed a first lawsuit against the NSO Group highlighting a direct relationship between the hacking of his phone and the decision of Saudi state officials to go ahead with the murder plot against Khashoggi (Kirkpatrick 2018). He continued his activism unabated, but appeared weighed down by the role he had involuntarily played in the killing of his friend. 'The guilt is killing me,' Abdulaziz told CNN in an interview (dos Santos and Kaplan 2018).

To silence outspoken critics abroad, authoritarian governments increasingly rely on what I call *digital transnational repression*: the use of digital technologies for the purpose of exerting political control and coercion over exiles and diasporas. The attempts of sending-state regimes to prevent, constrain and punish dissent across borders by digital means have grown in parallel to the widespread usage of the Internet for transnational activism. A Freedom House (Schenkkan and Linzer 2021) investigation into the global scale of physical acts of transnational repression shows that digital threats are by now a key element in the repertoire of repressive regimes. Of the thirty-one states documented to having engaged in acts like assault, renditions and assassinations between 2014 and 2020, twenty-one used some form of digital threat against exiles and at least seventeen relied on spyware to target individuals across borders. Governments practising digital transnational repression included global players such as Russia and China, regional powers like Saudi Arabia, and smaller states, such as Kazakhstan and Vietnam.

This chapter examines digital transnational repression and its constraining effects on activism in diaspora and exile communities. It centres on North Africa and the Middle East, a region where digital technologies have played an important role in both the contestation and consolidation of authoritarian power (Lynch 2011; Howard and Hussain 2013). The chapter shows that digital technologies have given repressive regimes new tools to monitor and respond to the activities of political exiles and diasporas with increasingly greater scope and speed (Michaelsen 2018, 2020; Moss 2018). The case of Omar Abdulaziz demonstrates that threats like surveillance, online harassment and disinformation campaigns are often intertwined with other methods of transnational repression, such as pressure on home-country families, kidnappings and even assassinations, as documented in this volume. Digital repression extends the reach of regime agents far into foreign countries, enabling them to invade the professional activities and personal lives of targeted exiles (Al-Jizawi et al. 2022). Emigrants who leave their home countries to escape similar infringements on their personal and political liberties thus find themselves once again exposed to the authoritarian exercise of power.

The phenomenon of digital transnational repression underscores that contemporary authoritarian rule is not simply a regime type bound to a specific territory, but 'a mode of governing people through a distinct set of practices' (Glasius in Dalmasso et al. 2017: 95; see also Glasius's contribution in this volume). Authoritarian practices 'sabotage accountability to people over whom a political actor exerts control, or their representatives, by means of secrecy, disinformation and disabling voice' (Glasius 2018: 517). Considering the boundary-blurring nature of the Internet and the multitude of actors involved in shaping digital infrastructures, applications and usages, a practice approach is particularly helpful. The example of Omar Abdulaziz's lawsuits against Twitter, McKinsey and the NSO Group illustrates that authoritarian regimes are not alone in their attempts to silence dissent abroad. On the contrary, the practices of digital transnational repression emerge and unfold in constellations of actors that stretch across democratic and autocratic, state and non-state divides (Glasius and Michaelsen 2018).

The chapter starts by tracing the emergence of digital transnational repression at the juncture of two broader developments of the last two decades: first, the rise of Internet-supported networked political mobilisation; and second, the securitisation of digital space and the global proliferation of surveillance techniques. It then presents the toolkit of digital repression and the ways in which these practices propagate self-censorship, isolation, stress and uncertainty among diaspora activists. Finally, I will outline some forms of resistance to this form of repression and the curtailment of digital space.

Between 9/11 and the Arab Uprisings: The Emergence of Digital Transnational Repression

Digital transnational repression can be considered as a response of authoritarian regimes to intensified cross-border flows of migration and information

(Tsourapas 2021). With the advent of new communication technologies, transnational migrants were able to make new kinds of 'cheap calls' for maintaining relations with contacts at home (Vertovec 2004). The Internet and social media not only connected migrants more closely to families and friends, but also multiplied their options to remain involved in political debates and developments at home. For diaspora activists working for home-country change, digital technologies became key to inform, collaborate and mobilise across borders (Bernal 2014; Brinkerhoff 2009).

From the early 2000s onwards, civil society and opposition movements in authoritarian contexts began to benefit from online media, such as blogs and news websites, which circumvented mass media censorship. Emergent online counter-publics benefited diaspora members, many of whom seized this opportunity to exchange news and political opinion (Michaelsen 2015a; Sreberny and Khiabani 2010). The arrival of social media further strengthened transnational networks by amplifying the voices of diaspora activists. Eventually, these networks formed an important nucleus of the protest movements that erupted across the Middle East and North Africa between 2009 and 2011. The Internet did not bring these movements about, but it clearly helped civil society to connect and mobilise. Diaspora actors were able to channel information from the ground into international news cycles, bringing worldwide media attention to the protests and international scrutiny on the regimes (Moss 2022; Tufekci 2017).

During the 2009 election protests in Iran, for example, a handful of young exiled activists with close ties to the political opposition avidly compiled information about the tumultuous events in Tehran and other Iranian cities for dissemination to the international media (Michaelsen 2015b). Similarly, in the case of Syria, diaspora activists worked to transmit the voices of protesters inside the country to the outside world, translating and preparing social media content for foreign journalists and mainstream media (Andén-Papadopoulous and Pantti 2013; Moss 2022). Such information brokerage effectively represents one of the core functions that diaspora activists fulfil in support of home-country movements (Adamson 2013; Moss 2020). With access to international organisations, media and policy circles, they can raise awareness, scale up the demands of peers in their country of origin, and leverage critical information against repressive regimes (Keck and Sikkink 1998; Tarrow 2005). Social media also enabled these activists to reach broader audiences in their home countries.

The YouTube channels of individual critics in exile, for instance, repeatedly provoked the anger of governments in places such as Egypt and Saudi Arabia (Segal 2020; Walsh 2020).

On the international level, the rise of social media-fuelled political protests seemed to confirm the narrative, predominant at the time, casting the Internet as a 'liberation technology' that opened up closed regimes, and fostered political participation and critical debate (Diamond 2010). In Western capitals, the uprisings in the Middle East produced not only enthusiastic headlines about the 'Facebook Revolutions', but also a drive to exploit the potential of digital technologies for promoting political change and democracy. Most famously, in two notable speeches in 2010 and 2011, then-US Secretary of State Hillary Clinton tied the defence of Internet freedom to a fundamental battle against dictatorship, pledging support for Internet activists worldwide (Clinton 2010). The sudden interest of Western governments in Internet-induced democratisation translated into a surge of funding to support the development of censorship circumvention technologies, digital security trainings and citizen journalism (Christensen 2011; Hussain 2014).

Given the growing influence of social media on society and its potential to empower activism and dissent, Middle Eastern regimes moved swiftly to curtail digital space. Measures evolved from the simple blocking of websites to more severe interventions such as network disruptions, hacking attacks and online harassment, all embedded in stricter legal frameworks. Regimes also learned to use digital technologies for the purposes of surveillance and information manipulation (Gunitsky 2015; Deibert et al. 2011). The Western support for Internet freedom pushed regimes to further tighten their grip and crack down on activists who might be connected to these programmes within and beyond their territory. In 2020, for instance, the Iranian Revolutionary Guard arrested the prominent software engineer Behdad Esfahbod, a dual-national from Canada on a family visit in Tehran, to pressure him into spying on Iranian tech activists abroad (Fassihi 2020).

The Proliferation of Surveillance and Security in the War on Terror Context

Digital transnational repression is not only an outcome of the authoritarian backlash against transnational human rights advocacy and diaspora mobilisation. It is also closely linked to, and stimulated by, global patterns and practices of state security. Worldwide, surveillance has become a key security approach as fields like counterterrorism, border control and crime policing increasingly foreground prediction and prevention. The attacks of 11 September 2001 and the turn to counterterrorism pushed particularly Western governments to rapidly expand their capabilities for monitoring and data collection. The War on Terror intensified a demand for security technologies and services, fuelling a trend towards privatisation and the emergence of a 'security-industrial complex' (Hayes 2012). Today, more than ever, the reach of law enforcement and security agencies stretches across national borders in complex collaborations of state and non-state actors (Mitsilegas 2016).

These developments 'have given rise to understandings and technologies of security with global impacts' (Abrahamsen and Williams 2011: 176). The 2013 revelations of Edward Snowden, former contractor of the US National Security Agency, exposed the extensive surveillance programmes of the United States and their allies, setting new standards which other governments tried to follow. Hacking and digital espionage became important instruments of statecraft (Buchanan 2017; Segal 2016). In the Middle East, Saudi Arabia and Iran, for instance, have repeatedly targeted each other with disinformation campaigns and operations against critical infrastructure (Kausch 2017). The threat actors versed in advanced hacking techniques who operate against foreign adversaries are often identical or overlapping with those targeting civil society at home and abroad (Anderson and Sadjadpour 2018). State security agencies also cultivate relationships with non-state proxies or 'cyber-militias', ranging from patriotic hackers to cybercriminals, who play an increasingly active role in cyberattacks (Maurer 2018). After 2011, the Assad regime, for instance, relied on the self-proclaimed Syrian Electronic Army for aggressive attacks and surveillance operations against foreign and opposition targets (Abas and Al-Masri 2018).

The increasing demand for surveillance technology in the Middle East was met by a burgeoning private industry. At the time of the Arab uprisings in 2011, the sales of spyware in the region surged, with businesses based in the UK, France, Germany and Israel being among the top exporters (Deibert 2020: 147). The powerful spyware of the Israeli NSO Group, which was found on the phones of Jamal Khashoggi's associates, was particularly sought after by Saudi Arabia and other wealthy Gulf monarchies for the purpose of targeting opponents inside and outside their territories (Bergman and Mazetti 2022). Countries with fewer resources gained access to the market, too. Egypt bought equipment from German, Italian, French and American manufacturers, and received technical support from China (Privacy International 2019; Weber 2019). Despite sanctions blocking their access to Western technology, Iran and Syria found ways to purchase tools for the mass monitoring of communications. In the years before the 2011 uprising, Syria established a nationwide surveillance system with German, Italian and US-American equipment (Privacy International 2016). In Iran, repression against the Green Movement in 2009 used monitoring technology produced by the Finnish-German Nokia Siemens company (Center for Human Rights in Iran 2010). Owing to a globalised commodification of surveillance, these examples show, authoritarian regimes had little difficulty in acquiring technologies for invasive surveillance and information controls, which they then readily deployed against civil society, both within and beyond their borders.

The Toolkit of Digital Transnational Repression

Without even relying on sophisticated spyware, regimes can use social media and the Internet to monitor dissidents abroad for free. Sharing information, engaging in public debates and building networks by using digital tools are essential tasks for diaspora activists advocating for political change at home. However, an active online presence reveals important information to regimes about their activities and social relations (Hankey and Ó Clunaigh 2013). Agents are able to exploit so-called 'open-source intelligence' – publicly accessible information – to launch threats. This includes refining the social engineering that accompanies a malware attack, launching a smear campaign against individuals in the diaspora, or uncovering their in-country collaborators (Marczak and Paxson 2017).

In addition to monitoring, regimes use targeted attacks to infiltrate activists' devices and accounts. Such targeted surveillance is a response to the increasing use of encrypted communications in emails and messengers by civil society. Because encrypted messages cannot be intercepted and read while transiting through the Internet, regime agents try to get into the computer or mobile phone of a target person as a work-around method (Guarnieri 2015). With the help of spyware, they can turn these devices into surveillance tools and siphon off confidential data, often without being noticed. Access to such information gives the regime a decisive advantage when it comes to curtailing activities in the diaspora and cracking down on opponents. In the case of Khashoggi, so the conclusion of an investigation by UN Special Rapporteur Agnes Callamard found, the Saudi regime decided to go ahead with the murder plot once it had penetrated the smartphone of Omar Abdulaziz and gathered information about the projects the two exiles were planning (United Nations Human Rights Council 2019a).

Although the use of advanced spyware for purposes of digital transnational repression is increasing, attacks against civil society can also be technically simple, relying on basic tools of cybercrime and targets' security failures. Perpetrators compensate for a lack of technical sophistication with thorough social engineering to spread their efforts for delivering simple malware in carefully crafted messages (Scott-Railton 2016). To lure targets into unwittingly downloading malware on their device, attackers send out messages impersonating the friends or colleagues of a target person or presenting information that is relevant to their work, such as recent news about human rights violations or fake interview requests and seminar invitations (Marczak and Paxson 2017).

Such phishing attempts rarely target one specific individual; rather, they build on ties among activists to unravel entire groups and networks. Access to the confidential information of one individual allows attackers to uncover new links and contacts. Iran's security agencies have used the accounts of individuals arrested inside the country to approach their contacts abroad (Alimardani 2015). Perpetrators also try to infiltrate the accounts of low-profile activists and inexperienced users – or family members – in order to reach more valuable targets. In one of my research interviews, for instance, an Iranian women's rights defender based in the US recalled that unknown agents used the Facebook profile of her niece, living in Tehran, to convince her into revealing the password for her own account.

The active presence of diaspora activists on social media not only facilitates monitoring and surveillance but also various forms of online harassment. Smear campaigns aim to silence outspoken exiles and taint their reputation. In interviews, diaspora activists agreed that such slander absorbed much of their focus and energy. An Iranian journalist explained: 'They attack and you have to defend yourself. You spend time for nothing, only responding to their lies. You spend time that you could have used for writing articles' (Personal interview). Others decide to entirely withdraw from social media as a consequence of these attacks. Furthermore, women journalists and activists are often targeted with degrading, misogynistic and sexually violent insults, which increases the risk of their withdrawal from public debate and of psychological harm.

Regime agents also deploy confidential information gathered through hacking operations for harassment and threats. After the phones of a number of high-profile women journalists and activists from the Gulf region got infected with the Pegasus spyware, their private photos were circulated on social media to intimidate them and smear their reputation (Solon 2021). An Iranian journalist explained that news agencies with ties to the security apparatus in Iran relied on similar methods to portray regime critics as 'immoral' and increase the pressure on their families. 'They will dig very deep in your personal life, to blackmail you, to threaten you, to stop you from what you are doing,' he told me in an interview, pointing out that in a rather conservative society like Iran's, women and LGBT activists were more sensitive to these forms of harassment.

An increasing number of countries also rely on social media manipulation brigades to influence online narratives, spread disinformation and silence critics. Similar to cyber militias, these so-called cyber troops or 'trolls' vary in their affiliation to the state, ranging from government-employed influencers to private contractors, paid citizens and volunteers. In contrast to the cyber militias mentioned above, however, they do not try to gain unauthorised access to accounts and networks. Instead, they actively shape and distort public opinion in the service of a political agenda by using real, fake or automated social media profiles to promote pro-government messages and threaten users with diverging positions (Maurer 2018; Monaco and Nyst 2018). Since the rise to power of Crown Prince Mohammed bin Salman after 2015, Saudi Arabia has massively invested in influence operations on Twitter. The regime groomed professional social media influencers to boost the image of the Crown Prince and lead attacks against critics such as Jamal Khashoggi, who was reportedly confronted with a large number of hateful social media comments every day (Benner et al. 2018).

Other countries are using Facebook for state-supported harassment campaigns against political opponents and independent news sources. The Azerbaijani regime, for instance, has relied on co-ordinated inauthentic accounts for trolling attacks against critical media, exploiting a loophole in the platform's functionality. Although a Facebook employee discovered the campaign, the company failed to take action, apparently because of a lack of interest in the relatively small market that the country represented for its operations (Wong and Harding 2021). This example highlights the central role that large, commercial platforms play in digital transnational repression, enabling authoritarian practices out of indifference, neglect or lack of proper contextual knowledge.

Finally, in their efforts to shut down online criticism and alternative information, regimes take aim at the websites of media and civil society organisations based abroad. Not only are these publications often blocked for audiences in the target country, but they are also taken offline by defacements and denial-of-service attacks which disrupt their availability to legitimate users with massive false requests. Other operations copy the design and layout of prominent news websites, such as BBC Persian, only to mock and falsify the content of the original sites (Personal interviews).

With these methods of digital transnational repression, authoritarian regimes are able to constrain a significant portion of diaspora activists' operations, outreach and influence. Moreover, regimes can escalate these digital threats by launching other forms of transnational repression to punish exiled dissidents for crossing a red line. Online monitoring gives state agents the opportunity to react swiftly to any activity taking place in the diaspora that they perceive as a threat. In fact, surveillance often lays the groundwork for operations of physical transnational repression, as the example of Omar Abdulaziz and Jamal Khashoggi shows.

Digital monitoring and surveillance are also closely intertwined with the more latent 'everyday' versions of transnational repression, such as the proxy punishment of home country families and smear campaigns in state media. Whenever regime agents become aware of a diaspora activist's critical writings or human rights advocacy, they can choose to threaten their parents at home (Moss, Michaelsen and Kennedy 2022). Often, digital tools grant traditional forms of collective punishment a greater reach and immediacy. In 2017, for example, the sister of a London-based BBC Persian journalist was held in solitary confinement for seventeen days by the Iranian authorities to force the journalist into a Skype-based interrogation, as well as to pressure her to spy on her colleagues in Britain (Saremi 2017).

The Silencing Effects of Digital Transnational Repression

With 'stories of security incidents spreading through peer groups, organizations and networks' (Kazansky 2016), digital threats do not just affect the targeted individual. Rather, they extend to their networks and contacts, perpetuating the silencing effects of surveillance and other attacks among diaspora communities. Building on these reinforcing dynamics, regimes often exaggerate their actual capacities and willingness to resort to repression to stoke fear, or they set examples through selected cases of drastic or widely publicised attacks against dissidents to keep the diaspora living in fear of reprisals (Moss 2016).

Surveillance, in particular, establishes an unequal power relation between the watcher and the watched, 'giving the watcher greater power to influence or direct the subject of surveillance' (Richards 2013: 1953). Activists are never certain if they are actually being monitored but, in interviews, often *imagine* regime surveillance to be comprehensive and permanent. An Iranian human rights defender based in the United States observed: 'I don't know how much they actually know about my work (. . .) but I always assume that they know the details of what I am doing' (Personal interview). Occasionally, regime agents signal to diaspora members that monitoring and surveillance are taking place, such as when they use information gathered through open-source intelligence and intercepted communications for direct threats, media propaganda or during interrogations of in-country collaborators. This way, regime surveillance becomes a means of control in and of itself. As underlined by the UN Special Rapporteur David Kaye, 'interference with privacy through targeted surveillance is designed to repress the exercise of the right to freedom of expression' (United Nations Human Rights Council 2019b: 7). The knowledge or suspicion of ongoing surveillance can have 'chilling effects' that not only deter people from speaking out but also bring them to behave 'in a way that conforms to, or is in compliance with, a perceived social norm' (Penney 2021: 1457).

The assumption of continuous online surveillance pushes activists towards various forms of self-restraint and undermines their ties to the home country, especially when they still have family living there. A Syrian activist pointed out during our interview in 2019 how he was effectively prevented from using all opportunities of activism from exile: 'I cannot be a kind of public activist. I cannot speak out in my real name. I cannot do something that puts international pressure on the regime. Even though I am heavily involved [in anti-regime activism], I have no full freedom of movement. I have to define limits.' The same activist explained that his family members in Syria were harassed by security agents after he had published photos of himself collecting donations for internally displaced persons on his Facebook profile. In response, he said, 'I just blocked all the family on Facebook' to protect them (Personal interview).

A Moroccan journalist and consultant in exile also emphasised the negative impact of surveillance on his professional and social relations. After it was discovered that his phone had been infected with the powerful Pegasus spyware, his clients withdrew and his relatives reduced their contact with him. Especially for his family members, the thought that their communications might still be monitored was 'emotionally distressing' (Access Now 2020). These examples show that the damage of intrusive surveillance goes far beyond the hacked accounts and devices. The entailed danger for in-country contacts places an enormous responsibility on the shoulders of activists in the diaspora and puts them under pressure.

The threat of digitised surveillance also curtails collaboration between activists inside and outside of the home country. An exiled Egyptian human rights defender involved in organising meetings between civil society members in Cairo and a delegation of parliamentarians from Europe concluded that his communications must have been monitored because all his in-country contacts received threats from security agencies not to proceed with the meetings. The risks entailed for people inside the country force many to reduce or end their collaboration with the diaspora. As a result, exiled journalists explained they were unable to quote sources by name, and even deliberately refrained from working with in-country contributors. An Iranian women's rights activist emphasised that exile gave her a lot of freedom and opportunities to engage in public activism, but pointed out the 'inverse relation between opportunity and threat' as her public activities risked endangering her contacts inside Iran 'day by day' (Michaelsen 2018: 258).

These effects of surveillance are further exacerbated by activists' difficulties in assessing the actual capabilities of regimes. The technical underpinnings of targeted and mass surveillance operations are understood by only a small cadre of forensic experts. Activist risk perceptions are therefore often shaped by reports on successful attacks and sophisticated, complex tools of surveillance. The complexity of digital technologies, the constant evolution of threats and the lack of precise information regarding the resources at the disposal of security agencies aggravate the feelings of uncertainty, stress and fear that activists experience. An Egyptian human rights defender co-ordinating with colleagues inside Egypt and across several other countries stressed the difficulty of everyday security choices: 'All the time when we talk in our online meetings we don't know if we can speak freely or not. We have no alternatives; we are between two options: to be practical or to be secure. Every discussion is a test for us, to mention a name, to say something or not, dates, passwords, etc.' (Personal interview).

Moreover, as a result of recurring reports on successful hacking operations or new security flaws in popular applications, activists feel easily overwhelmed by the idea that powerful state actors are capable of penetrating all layers of protection. This can lead to resignation and a sense of hopelessness. A Syrian security trainer described the mechanisms producing 'security paralysis' as follows: 'If you think about all the possibilities of getting hacked, then it can result in this attitude: OK, I will get hacked anyway. It is a kind of response mechanism to the level of stress' (Personal interview).

Finally, online harassment in the form of trolling, hate speech and smear campaigns can have detrimental effects on the wellbeing of activists and force them into self-censorship and silence. A Syrian journalist and trainer working to support female journalists explained that colleagues who had gone through a wave of trolling and threats felt physically affected and were 'thinking twice' before voicing their opinion again. As a result, according to this interviewee, the number of outspoken women in Syrian opposition media and civil society networks had decreased (Personal interview).

Resisting Digital Transnational Repression

Digital transnational repression does not unfold without resistance from the targeted communities and their allies in global civil society. During the last two decades, concerns about the proliferation of information controls and surveillance have led to the emergence of a 'digital security ecosystem' (Engine Room 2018): an internationally dispersed network of organisations, individuals and coalitions engaged in protecting civil society against the harms of mass surveillance, targeted intrusions and Internet censorship. The activities of this community encompass the development of privacy-enhancing technologies, trainings and capacity-building, as well as research and advocacy aiming to expose and constrain usages of digital technology that are harmful to human rights (see also Beraldo and Milan 2019).

For their online activities, civil society actors generally rely on commercial platforms and programmes that are not designed for confronting resourceful state actors seeking to compromise their communications and data. Therefore, different tools aim to support online anonymity and secure browsing, circumvent censorship, and encrypt and protect messages. Their usage is typically taught in trainings held by digital security experts and civil society organisations. In addition, a number of international organisations and their regional offshoots offer technical helplines and emergency support for activists who have been attacked.

Despite existing networks of support, activists often have to fend for themselves and find ad hoc solutions for threats occurring in their daily routines. Most of the time, they do not have the capacity to comprehend the exact technical set-up of surveillance campaigns and intrusions. In the attempt to 'tame the uncertainties of contemporary surveillance, turning political strife and unpredictable danger into a "manageable" problem', activists develop 'anticipatory data practices' that help them to assess risks and come up with practical responses (Kazansky 2021: 2). The solutions resulting from such threat perceptions often reflect the complex technopolitical environment in which they must navigate. A Syrian journalist based in Turkey, for instance, explained how, at the height of the Syrian conflict, he had developed different routines depending on the location of his contacts:

> When I call a journalist in the regime area, they use fake names and I also use a fake name. We connect by email, they use VPN, I don't. The danger is for them, not for me. I don't say anything about them, nobody knows their names. When a publication asks me about the name of my source, like who is this journalist, I don't answer. I'd rather cancel my article. The same thing for contacts in [ISIS-held] area[s] before. For areas under control of the SDF [Syrian Democratic Forces], I use a fake name to be safe, because I am in Turkey, and they use their real name, no problem for them.(Personal interview)

Challenging the Enablers of Digital Repression

In addition to technical and educational strategies, resistance to digital transnational repression also takes the form of countersurveillance and advocacy work. Technical investigations coupled with media campaigns work to expose and disrupt surveillance operations against civil society. Experts at organisations like the Citizen Lab at the University of Toronto and Amnesty International build on their relationships with targeted communities to collect and analyse suspicious messages that might serve as vectors for spyware infections (e.g. Amnesty International 2018; Marczak et al. 2018). Samples from targeted or compromised devices are used to scan the Internet for traces of surveillance programmes, which allow them to identify their operators and ultimately the governments behind these operations. Successful investigations can uncover and disable existing infections and warn potential targets of ongoing surveillance campaigns. They also help the companies behind the applications and programmes that are exploited for malware attacks to patch vulnerabilities.

The countersurveillance against state operations also draws attention to the detrimental effects that the unregulated sale of commercial spyware has on the human rights of targeted individuals and communities. The disclosure of vendor–client relationships can put governments under increased scrutiny and pressure. Investigations may also lead to legal action against the perpetrating governments as well as the involved companies. As highlighted in the Introduction to this chapter, digital platforms and spyware firms can be targeted by litigation from non-governmental organisations and affected activists. A number of lawsuits have been filed against the Israeli NSO group for the infection of devices with the Pegasus spyware to date. Other companies, such as FinFisher and Gamma Group, also became defendants in formal complaints and lawsuits for the use of their products by repressive regimes (Anstis 2018).

Investigative research, public advocacy and legal action from civil society actors clearly challenge the commercial interests of the private industry furnishing surveillance tools to rights-abusing governments. In response, however, companies strike back. Netsweeper, a Canadian firm selling Internet censorship and monitoring tools, sued the Citizen Lab for defamation after its researchers released a report revealing the proliferation of Netsweeper's products around the world (Deibert 2016). Moreover, the Citizen Lab became the target of a spying operation conducted by the private intelligence firm Black Cube, based in Israel. An agent met with two staff members and tried to record their conversations, apparently in an attempt to use these recordings as incriminating evidence for legal proceedings or even blackmail. The fact that the operation occurred as the NSO Group was facing several lawsuits *because* of the Citizen Lab's reporting suggests that the company was trying to pressure researchers into ceasing their investigations. As the director of the Lab, Ron Deibert, pointed out, 'it was as if we were becoming one of the very targets we had been studying' (2020: 255).

Adapting to the exposure of surveillance operations and increasing security precautions in civil society, the perpetrating governments and their commercial enablers constantly improve the obfuscation and effectiveness of spyware operations. The NSO Group, for instance, provided its customers with packages exploiting rare and expensive vulnerabilities in popular applications and devices, such as the WhatsApp messenger and Apple's iPhone (Perlroth 2021). Investigations of the WhatsApp abuse identified over a hundred cases of targeted human rights defenders and journalists in at least twenty countries across the globe, including in the Middle East, Africa and Asia (Citizen Lab 2019). The incidents revealed the substantial resources that private companies devote to identifying unknown software vulnerabilities (which are referred to as 'zero-days') in order to market their lucrative products to government clients.

Conclusion

Digital transnational repression enables authoritarian regimes to enforce self-censorship, undermine cross-border ties and raise the psychosocial costs of activism by spreading tension, stress and mistrust among diaspora communities. These practices build on the networked nature of diaspora activism, which generally involves dispersed communities across different countries and contexts. Activists' reliance on digital media creates vulnerabilities and exposes sensitive information that state agents use to threaten dissidents abroad and their home-country contacts. Digital threats aim to unravel their networks and diffuse a silencing fear that extends far beyond the immediate target. Moreover, these threats are often interwoven with other tactics of transnational repression, such as proxy punishment against home-country families and other, more blatant methods of kidnapping and assassination (Schenkkan and Linzer 2021).

Authoritarian regimes perceive diaspora activists as a threat when such activists are able to raise public attention, garner support for civil society and opposition in the country, and disseminate alternative news and opinions (both at home and abroad). With close ties to the home country as well as contacts to international organisations, media and policy circles, diaspora activists occupy a strategic position to leverage critical information against regimes. To a significant extent, therefore, practices of digital transnational repression are information controls used by regimes to disrupt information flows across borders. These practices are coercive strategies of 'authoritarian image management' that target opponents abroad whose claims risk gaining traction inside the country and may increase international pressure (Dukalskis 2021: 25).

As demonstrated in this chapter, digital threats against transnational activists build on constellations of actors, networks and infrastructures that involve democratic and authoritarian governments, private and other non-state actors (Glasius and Michaelsen 2018). The counterterrorism policies of Western democracies and the global securitisation of digital space have increasingly paved the way for a proliferation of offensive information controls and surveillance capabilities. The chilling effects of targeted surveillance and online harassment are exacerbated by the complexity of today's digital platforms and applications, which often leave potential targets in the dark as to the actual capabilities of regimes to infiltrate communications and devices.

In these dynamics, technology companies play a significant role in facilitating digital transnational repression. Whereas large digital platforms sometimes fail to recognise and remediate threats against civil society actors and organisations, the surveillance industry wittingly *promotes* the development and sale of tools that facilitate practices of extraterritorial authoritarian rule (see also Chapter 1 of this volume by Glasius). In defending their commercial interests and concealing their relationships with repressive governments, spyware companies themselves occasionally resort to authoritarian practices by systematically obscuring access to information and attempting to silence those who try to hold them accountable.

Echoing numerous other authors in this volume, I suggest that future research further disentangle these relations and the different actors involved in sustaining practices of digital transnational repression. As Picard and Moss argue in Chapter 13, scholars and practitioners must also focus more on the role and responsibilities of the host countries in curtailing these practices which, after all, threaten their very own security and sovereignty in addition to the fundamental rights of targeted individuals (see also Anstis and Barnett 2022). The investigations into abuses enabled by the Pegasus spyware have shown how swiftly invasive surveillance by authoritarian regimes against dissidents abroad has spread to a range of other, foreign targets, including journalists, lawyers and high-ranking political figures.[1] It is thus in the immediate interest of the host countries, chosen by many emigrants from authoritarian contexts precisely

---

[1] For an overview of the investigations: https://forbiddenstories.org/case/the-pegasus-project/

because of their openness and rule of law, to counter digitised authoritarian repression across borders.

References

All online resources retrieved 8 June 2022.

Abas, A. and Al-Masri, A. 2018. 'The new face of the Syrian Electronic Army'. *Open-Canada*, 17 May 17. https://www.opencanada.org/features/new-face-syrian-electronic-army

Abdulaziz vs. Twitter; McKinsey. 2019. *Complaint and Demand for Jury Trial*. United States District Court: Northern District of California. https://digitalcommons.law.scu.edu/cgi/viewcontent.cgi?article=3058&context=historical

Abrahamsen, R. and Williams, M. C. 2011. 'Security privatization and global security assemblages'. *The Brown Journal of World Affairs* 18(1): 171–80.

Access Now. 2020. 'From India to Rwanda, the victims of NSO Group's WhatsApp hacking speak out'. 17 December. https://www.accessnow.org/nso-whatsapp-hacking-victims-stories

Adamson, F. B. 2013. 'Mechanisms of diaspora mobilization and the transnationalization of civil war'. In: Checkel, J. (ed.), *Transnational Dynamics of Civil War*. Cambridge: Cambridge University Press, pp. 63–88.

Alimardani, M. 2015. 'The arrest of Arash Zad, Iran's start-up kid'. *Global Voices Advox*, 23 September. https://advox.globalvoices.org/2015/09/23/the-arrest-of-arash-zad-irans-start-up-kid

Aljizawi, N., Anstis, S., Barnett, S., Chan, S., Leonardt, N., Senft, A. and Deibert, R. 2022. 'Digital transnational repression in Canada'. The Citizen Lab. https://citizenlab.ca/wp-content/uploads/2022/03/Report151-dtr_022822.pdf

Amnesty International. 2018. 'When best practice isn't good enough: Large campaigns of phishing attacks in Middle East and North Africa target privacy-conscious users'. 19 December. https://www.amnesty.org/en/latest/research/2018/12/when-best-practice-is-not-good-enough

Andén-Papadopoulos, K. and Pantti, M. 2013. 'The media work of Syrian diaspora activists: Brokering between the protest and mainstream media'. *International Journal of Communication* 7: 2185–2206.

Anderson, C. and Sadjadpour, K. 2018. 'Iran's cyber threat: espionage, sabotage and revenge'. *Carnegie Endowment for International Peace*. http://carnegieendowment.org/files/Iran_Cyber_Final_Full_v2.pdf

Anstis, S. 2018. 'Litigation and other formal complaints concerning targeted digital surveillance and the digital surveillance industry'. The Citizen Lab. https://citizenlab.

ca/2018/12/litigation-and-other-formal-complaints-concerning-targeted-digital-surveillance-and-the-digital-surveillance-industry

Anstis S. and Barnett, S. 2022. 'Digital transnational repression and host states' obligation to protect against human rights abuses'. *Journal of Human Rights Practice*, online first.

Benner, K., Mazetti, M., Hubbard, B. and Isaac, M. 2018. 'Saudi's image makers: A troll army and a Twitter insider'. *New York Times*, 20 October. https://www.nytimes.com/2018/10/20/us/politics/saudi-image-campaign-twitter.html

Beraldo, D. and Milan, S. 2019. 'From data politics to the contentious politics of data'. *Big Data & Society*, 6(2): 1–11.

Bergman, R. and Mazetti, M. 2022. 'The Battle for the world's most powerful cyberweapon'. *New York Times Magazine*, 28 January. https://www.nytimes.com/2022/01/28/magazine/nso-group-israel-spyware.html

Bernal, V. 2014. *Nation as Network: Diaspora, Cyberspace, and Citizenship*. Chicago: University of Chicago Press.

Brinkerhoff, J. M. 2009. *Digital Diasporas: Identity and Transnational Engagement*. New York: Cambridge University Press.

Buchanan, B. 2017. *The Cybersecurity Dilemma: Hacking, Trust, and Fear between Nations*. Oxford: Oxford University Press.

Center for Human Rights in Iran. 2010. 'Shirin Ebadi: Nokia Siemens action a major accomplishment for Iranians and for the people of the world'. 6 October. https://www.iranhumanrights.org/2010/10/shirin-ebadi-nokia-siemens-action-a-major-accomplishment-for-iranians-and-for-the-people-of-the-world

Christensen, C. 2011. 'Discourses of technology and liberation: State aid to net activists in an era of "Twitter Revolutions"'. *The Communication Review* 14(3): 233–53.

Citizen Lab, The. 2019. 'NSO Group/Q Cyber Technologies. Over one hundred new abuses'. https://citizenlab.ca/2019/10/nso-q-cyber-technologies-100-new-abuse-cases

Clinton, H. R. 2010. 'Remarks on Internet freedom'. 21 January. https://2009-2017.state.gov/secretary/20092013clinton/rm/2010/01/135519.htm

Dalmasso, E., Del Sordi, A., Glasius, M., Hirt, N., Michaelsen, M., Mohammad, A. S. and Moss, D. 2018. 'Intervention: Extraterritorial authoritarian power'. *Political Geography* 64: 95–104.

Deibert, R. 2016. 'On research in the public interest: A statement from Professor Ron Deibert'. 26 July. https://citizenlab.ca/2016/07/research-interest

——. 2020. *Reset: Reclaiming the Internet for Civil Society*. Toronto: House of Anansi Press.

Deibert, R., Palfrey, J., Rohozinski, R. and Zittrain, J. 2011. *Access Contested: Security, Identity and Resistance in Asian Cyberspace*. Cambridge: MIT Press.

Diamond, L. 2010. 'Liberation technology'. *Journal of Democracy* 21(3): 69–83.

dos Santos, N. and Kaplan, M. 2018. 'Jamal Khashoggi's private WhatsApp messages may offer new clues to killing'. *CNN*, 4 December. https://edition.cnn.com/2018/12/02/middleeast/jamal-khashoggi-whatsapp-messages-intl/index.html

Dukalskis, A. 2021. *Making the World Safe for Dictatorship*. Oxford: Oxford University Press.

Engine Room. 2018. 'Ties that bind: Organisational security for civil society'. *Ford Foundation*. https://www.theengineroom.org/wp-content/uploads/2018/03/Ties-that-Bind-Full-Report.pdf

Fassihi, F. 2020. 'He was Iran's home-grown tech star. The Guards saw a blackmail opportunity'. *New York Times*, 21 August. https://www.nytimes.com/2020/08/21/world/middleeast/Iran-technology-arrest-spy.html

Glasius, M. 2018. 'What authoritarianism is . . . and is not: A practice perspective'. *International Affairs* 94(3): 515–33.

Glasius, M. and Michaelsen, M. 2018. 'Illiberal and authoritarian practices in the digital sphere'. *International Journal of Communication* 12: 3788–94.

Guarnieri, C. 2015. 'Helping the helpless: Targeted threats to civil society'. Talk at the Chaos Communication Camp, 16 August. https://media.ccc.de/v/camp2015-6848-helping_the_helpless

Gunitsky, S. 2015. 'Corrupting the cyber-commons: Social media as a tool of autocratic stability'. *Perspectives on Politics* 13: 42–54.

Hankey, S. and Ó Clunaigh, D. 2013. 'Rethinking risks and security of human rights defenders in the Digital Age'. *Journal of Human Rights Practice* 5(3): 535–47.

Hayes, B. 2012. 'The surveillance-industrial complex'. In: Ball, K., Haggerty, K. and Lyon, D. (eds), *Routledge Handbook of Surveillance Studies*. London: Routledge, pp. 167–75.

Howard, P. N. and Hussain, M. M. 2013. *Democracy's Fourth Wave? Digital Media and the Arab Spring*. Oxford: Oxford University Press.

Hussain, M. M. 2014. 'Digital infrastructure politics and Internet freedom stakeholders after the Arab Spring'. *Journal of International Affairs* 68(1): 37–56.

Kausch, K. 2017. 'Cheap havoc: How cyber-geopolitics will destabilize the Middle East'. *German Marshall Fund of the United States*, Policy Brief No. 35. http://www.gmfus.org/publications/cheap-havoc-how-cyber-geopolitics-will-destabilize-middle-east

Kazansky, B. 2016. 'Digital security in context: Learning how human rights defenders adopt digital security practices'. *Tactical Technology Collective*. https://secresearch.tacticaltech.org/media/pages/pdfs/original/DigitalSecurityInContext.pdf

——. 2021. '"It depends on your threat model": The anticipatory dimensions of resistance to data-driven surveillance'. *Big Data & Society* 8(1).

Keck, M. E. and Sikkink, K. 1998. *Activists Beyond Borders: Advocacy Networks in International Politics*. Ithaca, NY: Cornell University Press.

Kirkpatrick, D. 2018. 'Israeli software helped Saudis spy on Khashoggi, lawsuit says'. *New York Times*, 2 December. https://www.nytimes.com/2018/12/02/world/middleeast/saudi-khashoggi-spyware-israel.html

Lynch, M. 2011. 'After Egypt: The limits and promise of online challenges to the authoritarian Arab state'. *Perspectives on Politics* 9(2), 301–10.

Marczak, W. and Paxson, V. 2017. 'Social engineering attacks on government opponents: Target perspectives'. *Proceedings on Privacy Enhancing Technologies* 2: 172–85.

Marczak, B., Scott-Railton, J., McKune, S., Razzak, B. A. and Deibert, R. 2018. 'Hide and seek: Tracking NSO Group's Pegasus spyware to operations in 45 countries'. The Citizen Lab. https://citizenlab.ca/2018/09/hide-and-seek-tracking-nso-groups-pegasus-spyware-to-operations-in-45-countries

Maurer, T. 2018. *Cyber Mercenaries*. Cambridge: Cambridge University Press.

Michaelsen, M. 2015a. 'The politics of online journalism in Iran'. In: Rahimi, B. and Faris, D. (eds), *Iran and Social Media*. New York: SUNY Press, pp. 101–22.

——. 2015b. 'Beyond the "twitter-revolution": Internet and political change in Iran'. In: Weibel, P. (ed.), *Global Activism. Art and Conflict in the 21st Century*. Cambridge, MA: MIT Press, pp. 384–95.

——. 2018. 'Exit and voice in a digital age: Iran's exiled activists and the authoritarian state'. *Globalizations* 15(2): 248–64.

——. 2020. 'Silencing across borders: Transnational repression and digital threats against exiled activists from Egypt, Syria, and Iran'. *Hivos*. https://hivos.org/assets/2020/02/SILENCING-ACROSS-BORDERS-Marcus-Michaelsen-Hivos-Report.pdf

Mitsilegas, V. 2016. 'Surveillance and digital privacy in the transatlantic war on terror: The case for global privacy regime'. *Columbia Human Rights Law Review* 47(3): 1–77.

Monaco, N. and Nyst, C. 2018. 'State-sponsored trolling: How governments are deploying disinformation as part of broader digital harassment campaigns'. *Institute for the Future*. https://www.iftf.org/fileadmin/user_upload/images/DigIntel/IFTF_State_sponsored_trolling_report.pdf

Moss, D. M. 2016. 'Transnational repression, diaspora mobilization, and the case of the Arab Spring'. *Social Problems* 63(4): 480–98.

——. 2018. 'The ties that bind: Internet communication technologies, networked authoritarianism, and "voice" in the Syrian diaspora'. *Globalizations* 15(2): 265–82.

——. 2020. 'Voice after exit: Explaining diaspora mobilization for the Arab Spring'. *Social Forces* 98(4): 1669–94.

——. 2022. *The Arab Spring Abroad: Diaspora Activism against Authoritarian Regimes*. Cambridge: Cambridge University Press.

Moss, D. M., Michaelsen, M. and Kennedy, G. 2022. 'Going after the family: Transnational repression and the proxy punishment of Middle Eastern diasporas'. *Global Networks* 22(4), 735–51.

Penney, J. W. 2021. 'Understanding chilling effects'. *Minnesota Law Review* 106: 1451–1530.

Perlroth, N. 2021. 'Apple issues emergency updates to close a spyware flaw'. *The New York Times*, 13 September. https://www.nytimes.com/2021/09/13/technology/apple-software-update-spyware-nso-group.html

Privacy International. 2016. 'Open season: Building Syria's surveillance state'. https://privacyinternational.org/sites/default/files/2017-12/OpenSeason_0.pdf

——. 2019. 'State of privacy in Egypt'. https://privacyinternational.org/state-privacy/1001/state-privacy-egypt

Richards, N. M. 2013. 'The dangers of surveillance'. *Harvard Law Review* 126(7): 1934–65.

Saremi, N. 2017. 'Iran's persistent attacks on BBC Persian journalists'. *Iran Wire*, 28 October. https://iranwire.com/en/features/4934

Schenkkan, N. and Linzer, I. 2021. 'Out of sight, not out of reach. Understanding transnational repression'. https://freedomhouse.org/report/transnational-repression

Scott-Railton, J. 2016. 'Security for the high-risk user: Separate and unequal'. *IEEE Security & Privacy* 14(2): 79–87.

Segal, A. 2016. *The Hacked World Order: How Nations Fight, Trade, Manoeuvre, and Manipulate in the Digital Age*. London: Hachette UK.

Segal, D. 2020. 'He mocks Saudi Arabia on YouTube. Yes, he fears for his safety'. *The New York Times*, 3 January. https://www.nytimes.com/2020/01/03/business/media/saudi-arabia-dissident-al-masrir.html

Shalaby, S. 2018. '"I do not accept blackmail": Saudi activist in Canada defiant after brothers arrested'. *Middle East Eye*, 23 August. https://www.middleeasteye.net/news/i-do-not-accept-blackmail-saudi-activist-canada-defiant-after-brothers-arrested

Solon, O. 2021. '"I will not be silenced": Women targeted in hack-and-leak attacks speak out about spyware'. *NBC News*, 1 August. https://www.nbcnews.com/news/amp/ncna1275540

Sreberny, A. and Khiabany, G. 2010. *Blogistan: The Internet and Politics in Iran*. London: Bloomsbury Publishing.

Tarrow, S. 2005. *The New Transnational Activism*. Cambridge: Cambridge University Press.

Tsourapas, G. 2021. 'Global autocracies: Strategies of transnational repression, legitimation, and co-optation in world politics'. *International Studies Review* 23(3): 616–44.

Tufekci, Z. 2017. *Twitter and Tear Gas: The Power and Fragility of Networked Protest*. New Haven, CT: Yale University Press.

United Nations Human Rights Council. 2019a. 'Annex to the report of the special rapporteur on extrajudicial, summary or arbitrary executions: Investigation into the unlawful death of Mr. Jamal Khashoggi'. https://www.ohchr.org/EN/HRBodies/ HRC/RegularSessions/ Session41/Documents/A_HRC_41_CRP.1.pdf

——. 2019b. 'Surveillance and human rights: Report of the Special Rapporteur on the promotion and protection of the right to freedom of opinion and expression'. https://documents-dds-ny.un.org/doc/UNDOC/GEN/G19/148/76/PDF/ G1914876.pdf

Vertovec, S. 2004. 'Cheap calls: the social glue of migrant transnationalism'. *Global Networks* 4(2): 219–24.

Walsh, D. 2020. 'Outside Egypt, critics speak freely. Inside, families pay the price'. *The New York Times*, 14 May. https://www.nytimes.com/2020/05/14/world/middleeast/egypt-critics-arrests.html

Weber, V. 2019. 'The worldwide web of Chinese and Russian information controls. Centre for Technology and Global Affairs'. University of Oxford. https://ctga.web. ox.ac.uk/files/theworldwidewebofchineseandrussianinformationcontrolspdf

Wong, J. C. and Harding, L. 2021. 'Facebook isn't interested in countries like ours: Azerbaijan troll network returns months after ban'. *The Guardian*, 13 April. https://www.theguardian.com/technology/2021/apr/13/facebook-azerbaijan-ilham-aliyev

4

TRANSNATIONAL REPRESSION, NON-STATE AUTHORITARIANISM AND DIASPORA POLITICS

Fiona B. Adamson

Can diaspora politics be authoritarian? Some, like Betts and Jones (2016), see diaspora politics as a form of transnationalism that can potentially challenge authoritarian regimes. Especially in the wake of the Arab uprisings of 2011, increased attention has been paid to the roles that citizens abroad can play in fostering political change at home (e.g. Moss 2016; 2022). Since they are able to operate beyond the territorial limits of the state, diasporic opposition groups can arguably take advantage of their position as actors both 'outside the nation-state' and 'inside the people' (Shain and Barth 2003: 461). By using political resources and opportunities available in their host countries, diasporic opposition groups often show a potential to contribute to processes of democratisation in their homelands.

At first glance, then, diaspora politics appears to be anything but authoritarian. The 'diaspora' is regularly celebrated as a space of freedom from state control, in which grassroots organising and bottom-up social movements can emerge to challenge repressive regimes in the home state. However, this view downplays the extent to which diaspora politics can become oppressive and contain elements of transnational repression.[1] Indeed, non-state groups may

---

[1] Moss (2016) introduced the concept of 'transnational repression'. In this chapter, I build on her seminal work, as well as on that of Cooley and Heathershaw (2017), Glasius (2018a, 2018b) and Lewis (2015). See also Garvey (1980) and Shain (1989).

employ illiberal, anti-democratic or authoritarian practices as part of their overall political strategy. Sometimes this emerges from constraints imposed on the diasporic actors' structural positions. In other cases, it may be due to ideological reasons or to the preferences or leadership styles of diasporic and organisational elites. Just as different states have different regime types, so too does diaspora politics vary across the political spectrum. Diaspora politics is therefore not just a form of transnationalism that interacts with or contests state power; it also encompasses modalities of political control.

In this chapter I examine the use of authoritarian strategies and transnational repression[2] by non-state actors engaged in diaspora mobilisation and compare it with strategies employed by the state. I argue that non-state actors engaged in diaspora politics at times use the same authoritarian policies and transnational repressive measures as some states, including extreme ones such as assassinations, intimidation and threats. Through the cases of diasporic politics pertaining to Turkey and Sri Lanka, I demonstrate that state and non-state actors alike can use authoritarian strategies to mobilise and consolidate power in the diaspora, discourage internal opposition, and weaken or eliminate political rivals. The study expands our understanding of the repertoires and strategies that political entrepreneurs use to mobilise the diaspora, as well as shedding light on forms of authoritarianism beyond the territorial state. Ultimately, the analysis also points to some of the spatial complexities of the liberal international order, in which liberal and illiberal spaces overlap and become intertwined in ways that create policy conundrums that transcend state boundaries.

The rest of this chapter proceeds as follows. First, I provide a brief review of the literature on diaspora politics and how it intersects with debates on authoritarianism. Second, I discuss the concept of non-state authoritarianism as a form of transnational repression. In so doing, I point to a range of authoritarian practices used by states and look at the extent to which they have also

---

[2] Such strategies are not limited to authoritarian states. In 2011 the United States killed three of its citizens with an extraterritorial drone, including Anwar al-Awlaki, a Muslim cleric and senior operative in al-Qaeda in Yemen who had been born in New Mexico and retained his US citizenship (Mazetti et al. 2013). Moreover, as Moss (2018) reminds us, much of the surveillance equipment that authoritarian states use to spy on their citizens in the diaspora originates from Western governments.

been used by transnational and non-state actors. Third, I provide examples of non-state organisations and movements that have used these practices and suggest that competing forms of state- and non-state authoritarianism characterise some political behaviour in the diaspora. I conclude by discussing the implications for research and policy.

Diaspora Politics and Authoritarianism

Political science, sociology and migration studies all have growing literatures on diaspora politics (Adamson 2016; Adamson and Demetriou 2007; Brinkerhoff 2009; Cohen 2008; Koinova 2010, 2012; Østergaard-Nielsen 2001; Ragazzi 2009; Shain 2007; Shain and Barth 2003; Sheffer 2003, 2006). Until recently, however, this literature has had little to say about authoritarianism and transnational repression, aside from noting that diasporas often engage in political activities that can challenge certain aspects of authoritarian regimes. By drawing on existing national and transnational political opportunity structures, diasporic groups can use various forms of transnational mobilisation to transform and reshape the homeland (Adamson 2002; Wayland 2004). This can include activities such as sending remittances (Brinkerhoff 2008; Kapur 2010; Levitt 1998; Levitt and Lamba-Nieves 2011; Nyberg-Sørensen et al. 2003), protesting or engaging in symbolic politics, lobbying for changes in foreign policy towards the homeland (Hägel and Peretz 2005; Saideman 2001), agitating for political reform or, in extreme cases, pursuing change via armed conflict and violence (Adamson 2013; Kaldor 2013; Van Hear and Cohen 2017).

The interventions of external diasporic organisations have also been shown, in some cases, to improve the quality of governance in home states. Brinkerhoff (2005), for example, argued that, by using the Internet to foster greater transparency, Coptic organisations in the United States helped to support more democratic forms of governance in Egypt. Other studies suggest that diasporic remittances can place pressure on authoritarian regimes by making populations less dependent on the state (Escribà-Folch et al. 2015). More generally, diasporas have been viewed as actors that can, under certain conditions, promote democratisation through the diffusion of liberal and democratic norms (Koinova 2009; Shain 1999). Betts and Jones (2016), for instance, suggest that diasporas in general, and refugee diasporas in particular, should be understood as key players in targeting and challenging authoritarian regimes at home. Such arguments often hold to the view that diasporic groups can influence authoritarian states from the outside inwards. Yet, a growing literature (including chapters in this edited volume) is focusing more on the opposite dynamic – how homeland states influence and shape diaspora politics from the inside outwards. This literature challenges the notion that diasporas are autonomous actors operating in transnational spaces removed from the interests and policies of their states of origin. Rather, states are increasingly reaching out to and shaping politics in the diaspora through their so-called 'diaspora management policies' (Adamson 2019; Collyer 2013; Délano and Gamlen 2014; Fitzgerald 2006a; Gamlen 2008; Levitt and de la Dehesa 2003; Naujoks 2013; Varadarajan 2010). These include diaspora engagement, diaspora integration and diaspora-building policies which can vary depending on where the diasporas are located and the political interests of the sending state (Gamlen 2014; Mylonas 2013; Tsourapas 2015). These policies can range from giving members of the diaspora VIP status, encouraging remittances and investment, and promoting dual citizenship and overseas voting, to using diasporic groups as a tool of public diplomacy to promote state interests abroad (Adamson and Demetriou 2007; Bauböck 2005; Collyer 2014; Fitzgerald 2006b; Lafleur 2011).

Some scholars regard state programmes for the diaspora as a benign form of 'migration governance' in which states respond to norms promoted by international organisations and design diasporic engagement policies for the purposes of facilitating more efficient and stable migration management and economic development (Gamlen 2014). Yet others note that states engage with 'their' diasporas for different reasons, and thus produce different types of engagement policies, ranging from a focus on harnessing remittances, building 'global nations' and enhancing a state's soft power and ability to engage in public diplomacy, to a focus on surveillance (Ragazzi 2014; Tsourapas 2019). Transnational nation-building policies may rely on essentialised notions of who constitutes the nation, thus activating the dynamics of transnational 're-ethnicization' (Joppke 2003), in which states seek to enhance their power by extending their transnational constituencies through diaspora-building processes (Abramson 2017).

In this context, a state's regime type[3] is important for understanding variations in types of state–diaspora relations. Apart from structuring diaspora political engagement vis-à-vis the homeland (Østergaard-Nielsen 2003; Shain and Barth 2003), the regime type determines the nature of the diaspora's role in a state's bilateral relations. In fact, diasporas are likely to play a positive part in forging bilateral relations in democratic dyads – that is, when the country of origin and the country of residence are both democratic – but are sidelined in other dyadic formations, as in authoritarian–authoritarian or democratic–authoritarian dyads (Mirilovic 2016). Semi-authoritarian states may also use their emigrants to achieve foreign policy goals or national prestige, or as a way of projecting state power and gaining regional advantage (Tsourapas 2016). Moreover, different regime types may promote similar policies, albeit for different reasons. For example, whereas stable democracies may promote voting abroad as a way of expanding democratic participation, authoritarian states may promote it for reasons that have more to do with controlling emigrants, using the process to register and monitor their overseas citizens (Brand 2010).

Transnational Repression and Non-state Authoritarianism

As this volume demonstrates, the use of authoritarian strategies to target political exiles and activists in the diaspora can extend into the space of liberal democratic states.

Yet, such strategies are not necessarily limited to states. Non-state actors may also use them in some cases to intimidate members of the diaspora as part of their strategies of political mobilisation. Indeed, there is evidence to suggest that diaspora mobilisation by non-state actors can potentially contain a wide range of authoritarian elements. In addition to the strategies of transnational repression listed by Tsourapas in this volume, these include the use of personalistic forms of authority and personality cults; centralised power combined with political exclusion and internal repression; the use of propaganda and coercion to enforce loyalty and ideological hegemony; militarism;

---

[3] See, for example, the Polity IV Project: http://www.systemicpeace.org/polityproject.html as well as the extensive literature on authoritarianism in political science (Cheibub et al. 2010; Gasiorowski 1996; Geddes et al. 2014; Linz 2000).

mass mobilisation; forcible extraction of resources; hierarchical and secretive organisational networks; patronage and patrimonialism; and hegemonic single-party apparatuses that penetrate society and civic life. These strategies are not meant to constitute an exhaustive list, but they are indicative of aspects of authoritarianism that are found in a number of non-state organisations that have a strong diasporic presence.

In many respects, one would expect certain subsets of non-state actors to have authoritarian proclivities that extend into their relations with the diasporic populations they seek to mobilise. National liberation movements, separatist organisations, rebel groups or other bodies that have used violence in the homeland and have a political presence in the diaspora are prime candidates for the use of techniques of political mobilisation that, at least in part, rely on authoritarian ideologies, strategies and tactics. Some non-state organisations involved in diaspora mobilisation resemble de- territorialised quasi states as much as they do social movements; they seek to emulate states and ultimately achieve statehood, so have their own governments-in-exile, diplomatic strategies, welfare organisations and armed wings.[4] Furthermore, such organisations need constantly to mobilise a constituency because they face competition from other political actors; the loyalty of their constituency cannot necessarily be guaranteed via formal forms of membership, such as citizenship, and this may also provide incentives to turn to more authoritarian forms of securing and maintaining political support.

Just as different regime types approach diaspora politics in different ways, so too is there a variation in how different non-state actors approach diaspora mobilisation and engagement. Some forms of diaspora politics may simultaneously be about contesting an authoritarian regime abroad and exercising internal control and hegemony within the diaspora. Ordinary people living in the diaspora may therefore in some cases be subject to intimidation, threats and forms of transnational repression from both state and non-state actors – in addition to possibly being marginalised as migrants, minorities or refugees in their states of residence.

---

[4] See the literature on rebel governance (Arjona 2016; Arjona et al. 2015; Mampilly 2011; Staniland 2014), rebel diplomacy (Huang 2016) and governments-in-exile (Shain 1991, 2010).

State and Non-state Transnational Repression: The Turkish Case

The political mobilisation of Turks and Kurds living in Europe provides illustrative evidence of the various forms of transnational repression that both state and non-state actors use. In the case of Turkey, a variety of political actors, including the Turkish state, far-right nationalist organisations, Kurdish groups and religiously defined groups such as Alevi, Yazidi and dissident Islamist movements, all compete for support. Østergaard-Nielsen (2003: 107) noted that the political activities of emigrants 'may be perceived as a threat when dissidence unfolds on the political stage of their receiving countries, outside the reach of the homeland state. The relationship between the Turkish State (and government) and its citizens and former citizens amply illustrates this ambiguity.' As discussed by Böcü and colleagues in this volume, the Turkish state has a history of using various forms of state control to monitor, shape and deter the political activities of Turks and Kurds in Europe and has for many years engaged in the surveillance and 'long-distance policing' of political activists in Germany, France and elsewhere.

The Kurdistan Workers' Party (PKK), which has been involved in armed conflict with the Turkish state since 1984, has been the main target of Turkish state activities, though the state has also targeted other leftist organisations, dissident Islamist groups and, more recently, members of the broader Hizmet ('Service') movement linked to Fethullah Gülen. Germany banned the PKK in 1993 and, under pressure from the Turkish state, other PKK-related organisations and media groups operating abroad were also banned during the 1990s, including MED-TV, Firat News Agency in the Netherlands; ROJ-Groupa and Denge Mezopotamya Radio in Belgium; ROJ TV and MMC TV in Denmark; Newroz TV in Norway; the House of Kurdish People in Marseille, France; and the newspaper *Yeni Özgur Politika* in Germany (Baser 2015: 77; Eccarius-Kelly 2008; Hassanpour 1998; Karagoz 2017: 89; Romano 2006: 153–9).

There have also been several assassinations of PKK supporters in Europe, with the Turkish Intelligence Service (MİT) or organisations close to the state widely suspected of carrying them out. The most notable of these was in 2013, when Sakine Cansiz, one of the co-founders of the PKK, was executed in the Kurdistan Information Centre in Paris along with two other women, Fidan Doğan and Leyla Söylemez. In 2016 an assassination plot was uncovered that allegedly involved the Turkish Intelligence Service targeting the leaders of two

Kurdish organisations. German police detained a suspected MİT agent in Hamburg in connection with this in December 2016 (Yaş 2017).

However, the Turkish state has used less obvious sources of control, some of which emerged historically out of agreements between Turkey and Western European states over migration recruitment in the 1960s to 1980s. These included expanding the role of the Turkish Ministry of Religious Affairs (Diyanet) in the diaspora; sending Turkish schoolteachers and other officials to Germany and other European states; increasing the activities of embassies, consulates and the MİT; and using diplomatic pressure (Østergaard-Nielsen 2003: 107). In the 1990s, for example, there were at least 470 Turkish teachers in Germany sent by the Turkish Ministry of Education to teach the Turkish language and history, as well as Diyanet imams who serviced approximately 775 mosques throughout Germany. The situation has changed little since then, with accusations made in April 2017 that Turkey was using imams in the Diyanet-linked Türkisch-Islamischen Union (DİTİB) to spy on Turkish communities abroad.[5]

As Böcü et al. explain in this volume, since the attempted military coup of 15 July 2016, the Turkish government has accelerated its attempts to pursue activists in the diaspora. Kurdish individuals and organisations are still a main target, but a second one now includes individuals and organisations connected with the Hizmet movement associated with Fethullah Gülen, a cleric residing in Pennsylvania, USA, whom Turkish President Recep Tayyip Erdoğan has accused of being behind the coup attempt. In addition to asking the United States government to extradite Gülen, Turkey has tried to persuade numerous states to close Gülen schools and organisations, and its intelligence agencies have been involved in keeping track of activists abroad and putting pressure on governments to pursue members of Hizmet within their own borders (Schenkkan 2018).

The PKK: Both Target and Perpetuator of Transnational Repression

The Kurdistan Workers' Party (PKK) has undoubtedly been a target of transnational repression by the Turkish state, and the violent conflict between

---

[5] The figures come from the Turkish Ministry of Education and Turkish Parliament (TBMM) as cited in Østergaard-Nielson (2003: 108). A more recent count of mosques engaging Diyanet imams is 800 (Zeit Online 2017a).

the two entities has extended into the diaspora. The PKK has also at various points in its history resorted to authoritarian strategies and exercised transnational repression in the diaspora. This has changed over time, especially in relation to levels of repression in Turkey; for example, during the 2013–15 peace process, the PKK shifted its strategy in the diaspora in an attempt to 'normalise' and reach out to public officials. Furthermore, since 2011, the conflict in Syria, the fight between PKK-linked factions and ISIL, and the extension of the PKK into northern Syria, including the setting up of the quasi state of Rojava, have also changed the dynamics in the diaspora and given more legitimacy to Syrian-based organisations affiliated with the PKK. There has also been a shift in ideological orientation in the PKK towards principles of 'democratic consociationalism'.[6]

Nevertheless, at some points the PKK, like the Turkish state, has used violence and intimidation against rival organisations in the diaspora, including against the more moderate social democratic KOMKAR group, which it saw as a competitor. In fact, it assassinated Kurdish members of KOMKAR in Sweden in the 1980s and in Germany in the 1990s (Adamson 2013: 80; Baser 2015: 136). In the diaspora, the PKK sought to dominate large areas of civic life and to assert hegemony over local and cultural institutions. For example, in London it managed to dominate several local Kurdish institutions, which more apolitical Kurds had previously run. The PKK periodically used intimidation and threats to secure the support of the community. For example, Sözer and Yilmaz (2016: 8) recounted one restaurant owner saying that,

> They [the PKK] wanted to take my son to the Iraqi mountains. I strongly opposed the idea. As a result, one day the PKK raided my restaurants and beat both my employees and me . . . my sister was not as lucky as I was. The PKK took her son to the mountains, and he was killed in an armed conflict.

Many in the community were especially vulnerable because they had refugee or questionable status or were working illegally in the UK, and thus were hesitant to go to the authorities with their concerns. In Germany, it has been estimated

---

[6] See Biehl (2012) and Leezenberg (2016).

that almost 70 per cent of all incidents of extortion that took place in the 1990s were connected with the PKK. In the Netherlands, extortion was used regularly against Kurdish-owned pizza parlours (Adamson 2013). There are also reports of the PKK using the legal system in Britain to exercise control over the local community, by finding ways to sue local businesses for legal infractions if they failed to give enough money to the organisation (Sözer and Yilmaz 2016).

Another way of putting pressure on the local community was via trade in illicit substances. In London, the PKK managed to gain hegemony over the local drugs trade and a symbiotic relationship formed between it and local gangs (Sözer and Yilmaz 2016). These dynamics meant that the Kurdish community in London was at times caught between the PKK and the local police and British intelligence services, whose activities were shaped in part by Britain's relationship with Turkey or wider forces such as the Global War on Terror. Similar situations were experienced in other European states. Kurds were told that they could engage with the local Kurdish community, but not the PKK. In effect, however, the PKK had gained a strong degree of hegemony over the community and it became difficult for people to disentangle themselves from some of its activities (Sentas 2016).

More broadly, despite its ideology having changed over time, the level of centralisation in the PKK has at times resembled a form of transnational authoritarianism. It was at its most extreme in the 1980s and 1990s, but the PKK is still centrally organised and symbolically allied to its imprisoned leader, Abdullah Öcalan, who remains the primary figurehead for the PKK-centred Kurdish movement. While the PKK has changed its ideology over time – it has been Marxist-Leninist and separatist; it has focused on human rights and cultural autonomy; and it has espoused localism and democratic confederalism – the focus on Öcalan has remained constant.

State and Non-state Transnational Repression: The Sri Lankan Case

Sri Lanka offers another example of politics in the diaspora characterised by state and non-state transnational repression. Its government, like Turkey's, fought a civil war with an armed separatist organisation, the Liberation Tigers of Tamil Eelam (LTTE). Although the conflict ended with the LTTE's military defeat in 2009, the relationship between Sri Lanka and 'its' diaspora continues to be heavily securitised, even in the post-conflict period.[7] As Guyot (2017: 4) notes, 'after its victory, the Sri Lankan regime identified the diaspora as the new existential threat the country faced'. Indeed, the Sri Lankan Defence Minister vowed to seize international assets belonging to the Tamil Tigers and to 'eradicate the LTTE from the entire world' (Sentas 2012: 97).

According to reports, the Sri Lankan government has engaged in the direct surveillance of its diaspora abroad. Tamils in the United Kingdom and elsewhere have been subjected to the same kind of surveillance as those in the predominantly Tamil areas of Sri Lanka. People have been presented with photographs of themselves or of members of their family taken by the Sri Lankan security forces at Tamil protests or commemorative gatherings in the diaspora, and some UK Tamil organisations have reacted to this by banning cameras at events to ensure the safety of participants.[8] Others have noted that the Sri Lankan authorities 'take a strong interest in the activities of the Tamil diaspora in the UK and many returning to Sri Lanka . . . have been tortured and interrogated about their activities and contacts in the UK'.[9] Tamils abroad, even after 2009, faced problems when they sought to return to Sri Lanka, which suggests that surveillance, intelligence gathering and intelligence sharing occurs in the diaspora.[10] Additional reports claim that abductions in Sri Lanka target the families of diaspora activists, and that intermediaries based in the diaspora assist the Sri Lankan government in gathering relevant intelligence (TamilNet 2015).

An additional means of exerting control over the diaspora has been through the use of proscription. Throughout the duration of the conflict, Sri Lanka put pressure on Western governments to ban the LTTE. The UK designated it a terrorist organisation in 2001 and forced it to shut down its London office; the European Union and Canada did so in 2006 (Nadarajah and Sriskandarajah

---

[7] The notion of who constitutes a 'diaspora' is always political and contested. Sinhalese and Tamils often do not consider themselves to be part of the same diaspora, just as Turks and Kurds may identify as being part of different diasporas. For a discussion on diasporas as social constructions, see Adamson (2012). For the role of sending state policies in generating multiple diasporas and shaping intradiasporic politics, see Adamson (2019). I thank an anonymous reviewer for emphasising this point.

[8] Asylum Research Centre (2016: 5) citing ITJP Sri Lanka (2015: 13, 92).

[9] Asylum Research Centre (2016: 6) citing Freedom from Torture (2015: 9).

[10] Various corroborations of these allegations exist; see, for example, Miller (2013).

2005; Orjuela 2011). Even after the armed conflict ended, the Sri Lankan state continued to accuse diasporic organisations of being terrorist groups and used this to justify maintaining domestic anti-terror laws in Sri Lanka (Guyot 2017: 4). As Sentas (2012: 111) put it, the use of proscription 'facilitates a legal framework in which the counter-insurgency logic of the front is embedded in the criminal justice system transnationally'. Sri Lankan foreign service officers and anti-LTTE civil society organisations in the diaspora, such as Sinhala nationalist groups (Orjuela 2008: 443), were among those lobbying for proscription. Sri Lankan officials were outspoken in urging governments in Europe and elsewhere to ban the LTTE, noting that 'it is not something the Government of Sri Lanka can do on European soil, but must necessarily be initiated by the respective governments themselves' (Aryasinha 2008: 28). By lobbying to brand the LTTE a 'terrorist organisation', the Sri Lankan state triggered the apparatuses of the Global War on Terror, including national and international legislation, thus demonstrating the power that rests in the ability to deploy the language of terrorism (Nadarajah and Sriskandarajah 2005).

The LTTE: Both Target and Perpetrator of Transnational Repression

The Sri Lankan state targeted the LTTE globally but the organisation itself also at times wielded transnational repression within the diaspora. Like the PKK, the LTTE had a centralised structure and, by managing to capture and politicise civic life and institutions, it exerted a great deal of control in the diaspora (Fair 2005; Orjuela 2008: 441). It used authoritarian-like strategies to secure internal hegemony and to marginalise rival Tamil groups, such as the Tamil Eelam Liberation Organisation (TELO), the People's Liberation Organisation of Tamil Eelam (PLOTE) or the Eelam People's Democratic Party (EPDF) (Gazagne and Sanchez-Cacidedo 2015: 4; McDowell 2005). The LTTE's organisational structure placed the political wing of the organisation below its military wing and there was a significant personality cult around its leader Velupillai Prabhakaran, who was killed in 2009. While many Tamils hailed him as a hero, Prabhakaran's critics described him as 'a street thug with a background specializing in extortion and smuggling who developed political ambitions in the early 1970s' (Thompson 2008, cited in Orjuela 2011: 123).

At the height of the conflict in Sri Lanka, the LTTE kept a computer database and used information from its supporters to keep track of and closely follow the movements of individuals in the diaspora (Becker 2006: 12). At the time, Human Rights Watch recorded that: 'Tamils in the West have been subject to death threats, beatings, property damage, smear campaigns, fabricated criminal charges, and even murder as a consequence of dissent' (Becker 2006: 1). For example, in 2005 several German Tamils were threatened, attacked and severely beaten after organising an event in honour of a Tamil whom the LTTE had allegedly assassinated in Sri Lanka. In another prominent case, assailants beat a Tamil journalist with baseball bats in Toronto for having written articles that were critical of the LTTE. There has also been at least one assassination in the diaspora; Sabaratnam Sabalingam, who was on the verge of publishing an anti-LTTE book, was killed in Paris in 1994. In addition, prominent Tamils in Australia and London received death threats in 2005. Although the number of overtly violent incidents has been relatively low, they nonetheless create a climate of uncertainty, intimidation and fear in the diaspora (Becker 2006: 14–20, 33). Thus, Tamils in the diaspora suffered from transnational repression not only from a state but also from a non-state entity with a global reach. As one Tamil community activist in Toronto explained (Becker 2006: 1):

> Ninety per cent of people, even if they don't support the LTTE, they are scared. The killing doesn't just happen back home in Sri Lanka. It happens in Paris, in Canada. They burned the library, they broke the legs of DBS Jeyaraj. They tried to stop the CTBC radio from organizing. A journalist was killed in Paris. The threat is not only in Sri Lanka. It's everywhere, all over the world.

According to Human Rights Watch (Becker 2006), the LTTE sometimes used threats to family members and relatives as a means of controlling the diaspora. Numerous cases have been documented of individuals speaking out in the diaspora, only to have their family in Sri Lanka suffer harassment and intimidation (Becker 2006: 19–20). Like the PKK, the LTTE attempted to exercise hegemony in the diaspora by controlling a range of civic organisations, including NGOs and Hindu temples. Its attempts to control religious institutions abroad bear some resemblance to the Turkish state's use of the Diyanet to control mosques in its diaspora, although the LTTE's primary aim was to use temples as fundraising sites. As Orjuela (2011: 131) notes, 'it was an open secret that the LTTE was behind the greater part of Tamil organizations and activities in the diaspora, while political initiatives taken outside of the control of the LTTE were opposed or silenced'. In cities such as London, Toronto and Paris, 'the LTTE and its supporters [took over and monopolised] social structures, from refugee relief in the 1980s to newspapers, shops and temples' (Becker 2006: 14). In addition, the LTTE at times used extortionist tactics to force people in the diaspora to pay up to $2,000 and businesses between $10,000 and $100,000 (Becker 2006: 25ff). La (2004: 379) noted that it 'developed a system to extract remittances in Canada by exploiting transnational social ties. They threaten migrants about the security of relatives or property in Sri Lanka.' There are also accounts of the LTTE in Sri Lanka forcing returnees or visitors from the diaspora to pay according to how much time they had spent in the West (for example, a dollar or pound a day) and, in a non-state version of 'passport harassment', confiscating their passports and not allowing them to leave again until they had paid up (Becker 2006: 2).

Diasporic LTTE politics and Tamil gang violence were implicated in at least twelve deaths in London since 2000. A police operation in 2007 estimated that Tamil gangs engaging in extortionist practices against local businesses accounted for £70 million worth of credit card fraud. Similar patterns in Toronto, Paris and Oslo showed that there was an 'overlap between the techniques used by the Tigers in Sri Lanka and the gangs' (Orjuela 2011: 130). Because many people in the Tamil community are marginalised, or fear for their legal status, such activity often took place unnoticed and its effects were largely felt within the Tamil diaspora itself. Thus, the Tamil diaspora came under pressure from both the LTTE activities and the lobbying of the Sri Lankan state, which at times resulted in a criminalisation of the entire Tamil community (Brun and Van Hear 2012; Nadarajah and Sriskandarajah 2005; Orjuela 2011; Sentas 2012).

Conclusion

In this chapter, I have argued that diaspora engagement by both state and non-state actors can be characterised by long-distance authoritarianism and transnational repression. The brief case studies above suggest that non-state organisations are as capable as states of including transnational repression in their repertoires of diaspora engagement. This is especially likely among those involved in armed conflict in the homeland, which is hardly surprising given the propensity of such organisations to use violence and repression to achieve their aims. Nevertheless, it raises broader questions about the possibilities for other forms of 'diasporic authoritarianism' to emerge from non-state actors operating transnationally. While the authoritarian practices of non-state organisations resemble the transnational authoritarian practices of states in some ways, they also differ in other respects. For example, non-state actors are unlikely to have the same resources and infrastructure as a state with which to monitor and repress populations. At the same time, a number of non-state organisations with 'diaspora engagement' policies do mimic states in a number of respects. Armed groups that seek to establish a state of their own often have sophisticated structures of 'rebel governance' (Arjona 2016; Arjona et al. 2015; Mampilly 2011) that can be used to control populations at home and abroad. These include structures of diplomacy and welfare, as well as internal security apparatuses that can be utilised for the surveillance, repression and policing of 'their' diaspora populations.

At the very least, raising the issue of non-state authoritarianism opens up a space for examining the complexity of intradiasporic dynamics and the multiple ways in which diaspora politics can create a 'globalization of domestic politics', including a globalisation of authoritarianism (Cooley and Heathershaw 2017; Koslowski 2006; Lyons and Mandaville 2010). Such an approach also has important policy implications. It shows how global and local factors can become intertwined in particular contexts and the policy conundrums this creates at different levels – from the micro-level of local policing, to the national level of managing bilateral relations, where such processes connect with broader global narratives around terrorism, conflict and transitional justice. Finally, the analysis points to the multiple stresses to which many 'ordinary' members of diasporic populations may be subject, especially in cases where they are required to navigate their way through a complex combination of transnational repression from both state and non-state actors, as well as – in some cases – marginalisation and securitisation in their adopted home.

References

Abramson, Y. 2017. 'Making a homeland, constructing a diaspora: The case of Taglit-Birthright Israel'. *Political Geography* 58: 14–23, doi: 10.1016/j.polgeo.2017.01.002

Adamson, F. B. 2002. 'Mobilizing for the transformation of home: Politicized identities and transnational practices'. In: Al-Ali, N. and Koser, K. (eds), *New Approaches to Migration? Transnational Communities and the Transformation of Home*. London: Routledge, pp. 155–68.

Adamson, F. B. 2005a. 'Globalisation, transnational political mobilisation, and networks of violence'. *Cambridge Review of International Affairs* 18(1): 31–49, doi: 10.1080/ 09557570500059548

——. 2005b. 'Global liberalism versus political Islam: Competing ideological frameworks in international politics'. *International Studies Review* 7(4): 547–69, doi: 10.1111/j.1468-2486.2005.00532.x

——. 2012. 'Constructing the diaspora: Diaspora identity politics and transnational social movements'. In: Lyons, T. and Mandaville, P. (eds), *Politics from Afar: Transnational Diasporas and Networks*. New York: Columbia University Press, pp. 25–46.

——. 2013. 'Mechanisms of diaspora mobilization and the transnationalization of civil war'. In: Checkel, J. T. (ed.), *Transnational Dynamics of Civil War*. Cambridge: Cambridge University Press, pp. 63–88.

——. 2016. 'The growing importance of diaspora politics'. *Current History* 115(784): 291–7, available at: https://tinyurl.com/y8ewakng

——. 2019. 'Sending states and the making of intra-diasporic politics: Turkey and its diaspora(s)'. *International Migration Review* 53(1): 210–36, doi: 10.1177/0197918318 767665

Adamson, F. B. and Demetriou, M. 2007. 'Remapping the boundaries of "state" and "national identity": Incorporating diasporas into IR theorizing'. *European Journal of International Relations* 13(4): 489–526, doi: 10.1177/1354066107083145

Arjona, A. 2016. *Rebelocracy: Social Order in the Colombian Civil War*. New York: Cambridge University Press, doi: 10.1017/9781316421925

Arjona, A., Kasfir, N. and Mampilly, Z. (eds). 2015. *Rebel Governance in Civil War*. New York: Cambridge University Press.

Aryasinha, R. P. 2008. 'Time to act: The LTTE, its front organizations, and the challenge to Europe'. EU–US International Seminar on LTTE, 9–10 December, available at: www.srilankaembassy.be/old/PressRealease/PressReleaseFullText.pdf

Aylum Research Centre. 2016. 'Sri Lanka COI query response: update', available at: www.refworld.org/pdfid/56e2e1584.pdf

Baser, B. 2015. *Diasporas and Homeland Conflicts: A Comparative Perspective*. Abingdon: Routledge.

Bauböck, R. 2005. 'Expansive citizenship: Voting beyond territory and membership'. *PS: Political Science & Politics* 38(4): 683–7, doi: 10.1017/S1049096505050341

Becker, J. 2006. *Funding the 'Final War': LTTE Intimidation and Extortion in the Tamil Diaspora*. New York: Human Rights Watch, available at: www.hrw.org/report/2006/03/14/ funding-final-war/ltte-intimidation-and-extortion-tamil-diaspora

Betts, A. and Jones. W. 2016. *Mobilising the Diaspora: How Refugees Challenge Authoritarianism*. Cambridge: Cambridge University Press.

Biehl, J. 2012. 'Bookchin, Öcalan and the dialectics of democracy'. New Compass, speech at conference entitled 'Challenging capitalist modernity: alternative concepts and the Kurdish question', Hamburg, Germany, 3–5 February, available at: http://new-compass.net/articles/ bookchin-öcalan-and-dialectics-democracy

Bob, C. 2005. *The Marketing of Rebellion: Insurgents, Media, and International Activism*. Cambridge: Cambridge University Press.

——. 2012. *The Global Right Wing and the Clash of World Politics*. Cambridge: Cambridge University Press.

Brand, L. A. 2006. *Citizens Abroad: Emigration and the State in the Middle East and North Africa*. Cambridge: Cambridge University Press.

——. 2010. 'Authoritarian states and voting from abroad: North African experiences'. *Comparative Politics* 43(1): 81–99, doi: 10.2307/25741388

Brinkerhoff, J. M. 2005. 'Digital diasporas and governance in semi-authoritarian states: The case of the Egyptian Copts'. *Public Administration and Development* 25(3): 193–204, doi: 10.1002/pad.364

—— (ed.). 2008. *Diasporas and Development: Exploring the Potential*. Boulder, CO: Lynn Rienner.

——. 2009. *Digital Diasporas: Identity and Transnational Engagement*. Cambridge: Cambridge University Press.

Brun, C. and Van Hear, N. 2012. 'Between the local and the diasporic: The shifting centre of gravity in war-torn Sri Lanka's transnational politics'. *Contemporary Southeast Asia* 20(1): 61–75, doi: 10.1080/09584935.2011.646070

Cheibub, J. A., Gandhi, J. and Vreeland, J. R. 2010. 'Democracy and dictatorship revisited'. *Public Choice* 143(1/2): 67–101, doi: 10.1007/s11127-009-9491-2

Cohen, R. 2008. *Global Diasporas: An Introduction*, second edition. London: Routledge.

Collyer, M. 2013. *Emigration Nations: Migration, Diasporas and Citizenship*. New York: Palgrave Macmillan.

Collyer, M. 2014. 'A geography of extra-territorial citizenship: Explanations of external voting'. *Migration Studies* 2(1): 55–72, doi: 10.1093/migration/mns008

Cooley, A. A. and Heathershaw, J. 2017. *Dictators Without Borders: Power and Money in Central Asia*. New Haven, CT: Yale University Press.

Dalmasso, E., Del Sordi, A., Glasius, M., Hirt, N., Michaelsen, M., Mohammad, A. S. and Moss, D. 2018. 'Intervention: Extraterritorial authoritarian power'. *Political Geography* 64: 95–104, doi: 10.1016/j.polgeo.2017.07.003

Délano, A. and Gamlen, A. 2014. 'Comparing and theorizing state–diaspora relations'. *Political Geography* 41: 43–53, doi: 10.1016/j.polgeo.2014.05.005

Eccarius-Kelly, V. 2008. 'Interpreting the PKK's signals in Europe'. *Perspectives on Terrorism* 2(11): 10–14, available at: www.terrorismanalysts.com/pt/index.php/pot/article/view/56/116

Escribà-Folch, A., Meseguer, C. and Wright, J. 2015. 'Remittances and democratization'. *International Studies Quarterly* 59(3): 571–86, doi: 10.1111/isqu.12180

Fair, C. C. 2005. 'Diaspora involvement in insurgencies: Insights from the Khalistan and Tamil Eelam movements'. *Nationalism and Ethnic Politics* 11(1): 125–56, doi: 10.1080/ 13537110590927845

Fitzgerald, D. 2006a. 'Inside the sending state: The politics of Mexican emigration control'. *International Migration Review* 40(2): 259–93, doi: 10.1111/j.1747-7379.2006.00017.x

——. 2006b. 'Rethinking emigrant citizenship'. *New York University Law Review* 81(1): 90–116, available at: https://bit.ly/2GCSkjI

Freedom from Torture. 2015. 'Tainted peace: Torture in Sri Lanka since May 2009', report, available at: https://tinyurl.com/ycu8c6k3

Gamlen, A. 2008. 'The emigration state and the modern geopolitical imagination'. *Political Geography* 27(8): 840–56, doi: 10.1016/j.polgeo.2008.10.004

Gamlen, A. 2014. 'Diaspora institutions and diaspora governance'. *International Migration Review* 48(S1): S180–217, doi: 10.1111/imre.12136

Garvey, J. I. 1980. 'Repression of the political émigré: The underground of international law: A proposal for remedy'. *Yale Law Journal* 90(1), 78–120, available at: https://digital commons.law.yale.edu/ylj/vol90/iss1/2

Gasiorowski, M. J. 1996. 'An overview of the political regime change dataset'. *Comparative Political Studies* 29(4): 469–83, doi: 10.1177/0010414096029004004

Gazagne, P. and Sánchez-Cacidedo, A. 2015. 'Understanding the politics of the Sri Lankan diaspora in Switzerland'. Global Migration research paper 14, Global Migration Centre (GMC), The Graduate Institute Geneva, available at: https://bit.ly/2IDxtPy

Geddes, B., Wright, J. and Frantz, E. 2014. 'Autocratic breakdown and regime transitions'. *Perspectives on Politics* 12(2): 313–31, doi: 10.1017/S1537592714000851

Glaser, B. G. and Strauss, A. L. 2017. *Strategies for Grounded Theory: Strategies for Qualitative Research* (first copyrighted in 1967). New York: Routledge.

Glasius, M. 2018a. 'Extraterritorial authoritarian practices: A framework'. *Globalizations* 15(2): 179–97, doi: 10.1080/14747731.2017.1403781

——. 2018b. 'What authoritarianism is . . . and is not: a practice perspective'. *International Affairs* 94(3): 515–33, doi: 10.1093/ia/iiy060

Glasius, M., de Lange, M., Bartman, J., Dalmasso, E., Lv, A., Del Sordi, A., Michaelsen, M. and Ruijgrok, K. 2018. *Research Ethics and Risk in the Authoritarian Field*. Basingstoke: Palgrave Macmillan, doi: 10.1007/978-3-319-68966-1

Guyot, L. (2017) 'From arms to politics: The new struggle of the Tamil diaspora', Network of researchers in international affairs (Noria) website, available at: https://tinyurl.com/ybz69f7p

Hägel, P. and Peretz, P. 2005. 'States and transnational actors: Who's influencing whom? A case study in Jewish diaspora politics during the cold war'. *European Journal of International Relations* 11(4): 467–93, doi: 10.1177/1354066105057893

Hassanpour, A. 1998. 'Satellite footprints as national borders: MED-TV and the extra-territoriality of state sovereignty'. *Journal of Muslim Minority Affairs* 18(1): 53–72, doi: 10.1080/13602009808716393

Huang, R. 2016. 'Rebel diplomacy in civil war'. *International Security* 40(4): 89–126, doi: 10.1162/ISEC_a_00237

ITJP Sri Lanka. 2015. 'A still unfinished war: Sri Lanka's survivors of torture and sexual violence 2009–2015', International Truth and Justice Project report, available at: www.itjpsl.com/assets/stoptorture_report_v4_online.pdf

Joppke, C. 2003. 'Citizenship between de- and re-ethnicization'. *European Journal of Sociology* 44(3): 429–58, doi: 10.1017/S0003975603001346

Kaldor, M. 2013. *New and Old Wars: Organised Violence in a Global Era*, third edition. Cambridge: Polity Press.

Kapur, D. 2010. *Diaspora, Development, and Democracy: The Domestic Impact of International Migration from India*. Princeton, NJ: Princeton University Press.

Karagoz, Z. 2017. 'The Kurdish diasporic mobilization in France: From a restricted political national frame to a translocal sphere of contention? The case of Kurds in Marseille'. *Journal of Mediterranean Knowledge* 2(1): 79–100, doi: 10.26409/2017JMK2.1.05

Koinova, M. 2009. 'Diasporas and democratization in the post-communist world'. *Communist and Post-Communist Studies* 42(1): 41–64, doi: 10.1016/j.postcomstud.2009.02.001

——. 2010. 'Diasporas and international politics: Utilising the universalistic creed of liberalism for particularistic and nationalist purposes'. In: Bauböck, R. and Faist, T. (eds), *Diaspora and Transnationalism: Concepts, Theories and Methods*. Amsterdam: Amsterdam University Press, pp. 149–66.

——. 2012. 'Autonomy and positionality in diaspora politics'. *International Political Sociology* 6(1): 99–103, doi: 10.1111/j.1749-5687.2011.00152_3.x

——. 2013. 'Four types of diaspora mobilization: Albanian diaspora activism for Kosovo independence in the US and the UK'. *Foreign Policy Analysis* 9(4): 433–53, doi: 10.1111/j.1743-8594.2012.00194.x

Koslowski, R. 2006. *International Migration and the Globalization of Domestic Politics*. London: Psychology Press.

La, J. 2004. 'Forced remittances in Canada's Tamil enclaves'. *Peace Review* 16(3): 379–85, doi: 10.1080/1040265042000278630

Lafleur, J.-M. 2011. 'Why do states enfranchise citizens abroad? Comparative insights from Mexico, Italy and Belgium'. *Global Networks* 11(4): 481–501, doi: 10.1111/j.1471-0374.2011.00332.x

Leezenberg, M. 2016. 'The ambiguities of democratic autonomy: The Kurdish movement in Turkey and Rojava'. *Southeast European and Black Sea Studies* 16(4): 671–90, doi: 10.1080/14683857.2016.1246529

Levitsky, S. and Way, L. 2010. *Competitive Authoritarianism: Hybrid Regimes after the Cold War*. Cambridge: Cambridge University Press.

Levitt, P. 1998. 'Social remittances: Migration driven local-level forms of cultural diffusion'. *International Migration Review* 32(4) 926–48, doi: 10.2307/2547666

Levitt, P. and de la Dehesa, R. 2003. 'Transnational migration and the redefinition of the state: Variations and explanations'. *Ethnic and Racial Studies* 26(4): 587–611, doi: 10.1080/0141987032000087325

Levitt, P. and Lamba-Nieves, D. 2011. 'Social remittances revisited'. *Journal of Ethnic and Migration Studies* 37(1): 1–22, doi: 10.1080/1369183X.2011.521361

Lewis, D. 2015. '"Illiberal spaces:" Uzbekistan's extraterritorial security practices and the spatial politics of contemporary authoritarianism'. *Nationalities Papers* 43(1): 140–59, doi: 10.1080/00905992.2014.980796

Linz, J. J. 2000. *Totalitarian and Authoritarian Regimes*. Boulder, CO: Lynne Rienner.

Lyons, T. and Mandaville, P. 2010. 'Think locally, act globally: Toward a transnational comparative politics'. *International Political Sociology* 4(2): 124–41, doi: 10.1111/j.1749-5687.2010.00096.x

McDowell, C. 2005. 'Asylum diaspora: Tamils in Switzerland'. In: Ember, M., Ember, C. R. and Skoggard, I. (eds), *Encyclopedia of Diasporas: Immigrant and Refugee Cultures Around the World*, volume I. Yale: Springer, 534–43.

Mampilly, Z. C. 2011. *Rebel Rulers: Insurgent Governance and Civilian Life during War*. Ithaca, NY: Cornell University Press.

Mazetti, M., Savage, C. and Shane, S. 2013. 'How a US citizen came to be in America's cross hairs'. *The New York Times*, 9 March, available at: https://tinyurl.com/apum8x8

Miller, M. J. 1981. *Foreign Workers in Western Europe: An Emerging Political Force*. New York: Praeger.

Miller, P. 2013. 'Deportation of Tamils helped the Sri Lankan state'. *New Internationalist* blog, 18 July, available at: https://newint.org/blog/2013/07/18/tamil-deportation-britainsri-lanka

Mirilovic, N. 2016. 'Regime type and diaspora politics: A dyadic approach'. *Foreign Policy Analysis* 14(3): 346–66, doi: 10.1093/fpa/orw038

Moss, D. M. 2016. 'Transnational repression, diaspora mobilization, and the case of the Arab Spring'. *Social Problems* 63(4): 480–98, doi: 10.1093/socpro/spw019

Moss, D. M. 2018. 'The ties that bind: Internet communication technologies, networked authoritarianism, and "voice" in the Syrian diaspora'. *Globalizations* 15(2): 265–82, doi: 10.1080/14747731.2016.1263079

Mügge, L. 2012. 'Ideologies of nationhood in sending-state transnationalism: Comparing Surinam and Turkey', *Ethnicities* 13(3): 338–58, doi: 10.1177/1468796812451096

Mylonas, H. 2013. 'The politics of diaspora management in the Republic of Korea'. Asian Institute for Policy Studies, issue brief 20 November, available at: https://bit.ly/2Wc0uos

Nadarajah, S. and Sriskandarajah, D. 2005. 'Liberation struggle or terrorism? The politics of naming the LTTE'. *Third World Quarterly* 26(1): 87–100, doi: 10.1080/014365904200 0322928

Naujoks, D. 2013. *Migration, Citizenship, and Development: Diasporic Membership Policies and Overseas Indians in the United States*. Oxford: Oxford University Press.

Nyberg-Sørensen, N., Van Hear, N. and Engberg-Pedersen, P. 2003. 'The migration–development nexus: evidence and policy options'. *International Migration* 40(5): 3–47, doi: 10.1111/1468-2435.00210

Orjuela, C. 2008. 'Distant warriors, distant peace workers? Multiple diaspora roles in Sri Lanka's violent conflict'. *Global Networks* 8(4): 436–52, doi: 10.1111/j.1471-0374.20 08.00233.x

——. 2011. 'Violence at the margins: Street gangs, globalized conflict and Sri Lankan Tamil battlefields in London, Toronto and Paris'. *International Studies* 48(2): 113–37, doi: 10.1177/0020881712469457

Østergaard-Nielsen, E. 2001. 'Diasporas in world politics'. In: Josselin, D. and Wallace, W. (eds), *Non-state Actors in World Politics*. London: Palgrave Macmillan, pp. 218–34, doi: 10.1057/9781403900906

——. 2003. *Transnational Politics: The Case of Turks and Kurds in Germany*. Abingdon: Routledge.

Ragazzi, F. 2009. 'Governing diasporas'. *International Political Sociology* 3(4): 378–97, doi: 10.1111/j.1749-5687.2009.00082.x

——. 2014. 'A comparative analysis of diaspora policies'. *Political Geography* 41: 74–89, doi: 10.1016/j.polgeo.2013.12.004

Romano, D. 2006. *The Kurdish Nationalist Movement: Opportunity, Mobilization and Identity*. New York: Cambridge University Press.

Saideman, S. M. 2001. *Ties That Divide: Ethnic Politics, Foreign Policy and International Conflict*. New York: Columbia University Press.

Schenkkan, N. 2018. 'The remarkable scale of Turkey's "global purge": How it became a threat to the rule of law everywhere'. *Foreign Affairs*, online article, 29 January, available at: https://tinyurl.com/ycfljg26

Sentas, V. 2012. 'One more successful war? Tamil diaspora and counter-terrorism after the LTTE'. In: Poynting, S. and Whyte, D. (eds), *Counter-terrorism and State Political Violence*. London: Routledge, pp. 97–115.

Sentas, V. 2016. 'Policing the diaspora: Kurdish Londoners, MI5 and the proscription of terrorist organizations in the United Kingdom'. *British Journal of Criminology* 56(5): 898–918, doi: 10.1093/bjc/azv094

Shain, Y. 1989. 'The war of governments against their opposition in exile'. *Government and Opposition* 24(3): 341–56, doi: 10.1111/j.1477-7053.1989.tb00727.x

——. 1991. *Governments-in-exile in Contemporary World Politics*. London: Routledge.

——. 1999. *Marketing the American Creed Abroad: Diasporas in the US and their Homelands*. New York: Cambridge University Press.

——. 2007. *Kinship and Diasporas in International Affairs*. Ann Arbor: University of Michigan Press.

——. 2010. *The Frontier of Loyalty: Political Exiles in the Age of the Nation-state*. New York: Cambridge University Press.

Shain, Y. and Barth, A. 2003. 'Diasporas and international relations theory', *International Organization* 57(3): 449–79, doi: 10.1017/S0020818303573015

Sheffer, G. 2003. *Diaspora Politics: At Home Abroad*. New York: Cambridge University Press.

——. 2006. 'Transnationalism and ethnonational diasporism'. *Diaspora: A Journal of Transnational Studies* 15(1): 121–45, doi: 10.1353/dsp.0.0029

Smith, H. A. and Stares, P. 2007. *Diasporas in Conflict: Peace-makers or Peace-wreckers?* Tokyo: United Nations University Press.

Sözer, M. A. and Yilmaz, K. 2016. 'The PKK and its evolution in Britain (1984–present)'. *Terrorism and Political Violence*, online early, 1–19, doi: 10.1080/09546553.2016.1194269

Staniland, P. 2014. *Networks of Rebellion: Explaining Insurgent Cohesion and Collapse*. Ithaca, NY: Cornell University Press.

TamilNet. 2015. 'White-van abductions continue in North with "UNP sophistication"', online article, 30 December, available at: www.tamilnet.com/art.html?catid=13&artid=38067

Thompson, J. C. 2008. 'The tigers die hard', *The Island*, 18 November, available at: www.island.lk/2008/11/18/features5.html

Tsourapas, G. 2015. 'Why do states develop multi-tier emigrant policies? Evidence from Egypt'. *Journal of Ethnic and Migration Studies* 41(13): 2192–214, doi: 10.1080/ 1369183X.2015.1049940

——. 2016. 'Nasser's educators and agitators across al-Watan al-'Arabi: Tracing the foreign policy importance of Egyptian regional migration, 1952–1967'. *British Journal of Middle Eastern Studies* 43(3): 324–41, doi: 10.1080/13530194.2015.1102708

Van Hear, N. and Cohen, R. 2017. 'Diasporas and conflict: Distance, contiguity and spheres of engagement'. *Oxford Development Studies* 45(2): 171–84, doi: 10.1080/13600818.2016.1160043

Varadarajan, L. 2010. *The Domestic Abroad: Diasporas in International Relations*. New York: Oxford University Press.

Wayland, S. 2004. 'Ethnonationalist networks and transnational opportunities: the Sri Lankan Tamil diaspora'. *Review of International Studies* 30(3): 405–26, doi: 10.1017/ S0260210504006138

White, P. 2000. *Primitive Rebels or Revolutionary Modernizers? The Kurdish National Movement in Turkey*. London: Zed Books.

——. 2015. *The PKK: Coming Down from the Mountains*. London: Zed Books.

Yaş, P. 2017. 'Germany hides Turkish intelligence MİT's assassination list', *ANF News*, 12 May, available at: https://bit.ly/2Vl9Xgm

Zeit Online. 2017a. 'Ermittlung gegen 20 mutmassliche türkische Spion', *Die Zeit*, 6 April, available at: https://tinyurl.com/yacno9jq

——. 2017b. 'Türkischer geheimdienst: stümperhafte spione', *Die Zeit*, 5 April, available at: www.zeit.de/2017/15/tuerkischer-geheimdienst-spionage-mit-resul-oezcelik

——. 2017c. 'Türkischer geheimdienst: hunderte türken in Deutschland ausspioniert', 27 March, available at: https://tinyurl.com/ybkxvguf

PART II

CONDITIONS AND CAUSAL
MECHANISMS FACILITATING
TRANSNATIONAL REPRESSION
OVER TIME

5

AUTOCRATISATION AS A FACILITATOR OF TRANSNATIONAL REPRESSION IN EAST AND SOUTHEAST ASIA

Alexander Dukalskis and Redmond Scales

Introduction

Authoritarianism has never stayed neatly contained within the borders of authoritarian states. Some autocracies evangelise their political models, others receive support from powerful patrons in the name of stability, and still others benefit indirectly from authoritarian norms in their region.[1] There is almost inevitably external spillover generated by authoritarian rule. Even tightly insulated authoritarian states like North Korea or Eritrea generate refugees and exiles due to military conflict with neighbours and/or the consequences of their domestic governance.

As the contributions to this volume illuminate, one common externality of authoritarian rule is transnational repression. Exiled critics or opponents of a dictatorship present a threat to the ruling regime, whether real or perceived, and thus become targets for repression, because they can generate negative publicity for the government, build links with internal activists and lobby foreign states to pressure the government for change (notable contributions to this literature include Lewis 2015; Moss 2016; Cooley and Heathershaw 2017; Dalmasso et al. 2018; Glasius 2018; Michaelsen 2018; Adamson 2019; Lemon 2019;

---

[1] Unless referring to a specific subtype of regime, this chapter uses the terms authoritarianism, dictatorship and autocracy interchangeably to refer to non-democratic governments.

Tsourapas 2020; Furstenberg et al. 2021; Dukalskis 2021; Moss 2021). While democracies may repress their citizens abroad, there are solid theoretical reasons to suggest that autocracies will do so more extensively. Because of free-speech guarantees and institutional avenues to pursue change domestically, democracies generate fewer exiles in the first place. Those interested in creating political change – even radical political change, assuming it is non-violent – can usually attempt to do so from within the structures of a liberal democratic society. Furthermore, democracies may be less willing to repress whatever exiles they have abroad because of legal limits on what they can or will do and oversight mechanisms that may expose wrongdoing, leading to political consequences for principals. The transnational repression of a sending state's citizens abroad who are engaged in lawful forms of dissent and activism in their host states is thus primarily, although not exclusively, an authoritarian phenomenon.

This chapter explores patterns of transnational repression in East and Southeast Asia between 1991 and 2019. The chapter draws its analysis from the Authoritarian Actions Abroad Database (AAAD) and describes patterns in East and Southeast Asia, which reveal that China and North Korea are among the most frequent transnational repressors in the region, and indeed the world. After providing an overview of the data, the chapter illustrates how the region's autocratisation enabled states to co-operate in their transnational repression. Specifically, it highlights how the autocratisation of Thai and Cambodian politics in recent years has led to an increase in transnational repression in the region, as Cambodia has become a more active source state and Thailand a more frequent source *and* host state.

Our overarching argument is that deepening authoritarianism in a region facilitates more authoritarian co-operation, which in turn increases transnational repression. Authoritarian states certainly threaten and repress their exiles in democratic states. Indeed, it is surprisingly common, but an authoritarian partner is advantageous for several reasons. First, the repression can take place in a more controlled media environment and is thus more difficult to discover. Intimidation, threats and attacks can be perpetrated with more impunity. Second, the repression can obtain the veneer of legality. A 'terrorist' may be handed over by an autocracy to be extradited back to their autocratic home state, which appears as routine co-operation between states. Of course, if the 'terrorist' is a pro-democracy activist or a critical journalist, then the transaction is an act of transnational repression masquerading as international legal co-operation.

An increasingly authoritarian neighbourhood creates a friendlier context for transnational repression (on authoritarian regional contexts, see Obydenkova and Libman 2019; Lemon, this volume). This chapter begins by presenting AAAD and its methodology. It then presents patterns of transnational repression in the context of East and Southeast Asia and describes the case studies of Thailand and Cambodia. The chapter concludes by summarising the findings from the case studies and their broader implications for the studies of transnational repression and authoritarianism.

The Authoritarian Actions Abroad Database (AAAD)

The Authoritarian Actions Abroad Database (AAAD) attempts to record the efforts by authoritarian states globally to repress their exiles abroad between 1991 and 2019 (for further details, see Dukalskis 2021).[2] The coding and data were inspired by and are similar in some respects to the Central Asian Political Exiles (CAPE) but differ in some key ways (see Heathershaw and Furstenberg 2020; Dukalskis et al. 2022). The AAAD contains information about cases in which autocracies threaten, threaten the family of, arrest or detain, attack, extradite, abduct or assassinate their exiled critics. Attempts that are ultimately unsuccessful are included for extraditions, abductions and assassinations. Targets include journalists, activists, opposition members, former government officials, and a residual category of 'citizens' that captures people who may not be especially politically active abroad but are targeted because some aspect of their identity renders them politically threatening to the government. By far the most common instances of the citizen category in the AAAD involve Uyghurs caught up in China's post-2014 crackdown and North Koreans who have defected. Cases are recorded at the incident level, so the AAAD is an events database with the individual incident as the unit of analysis.

The information underlying the AAAD is all publicly available and was gathered using four steps. First, existing databases such as CAPE, the Xinjiang Victims Database and Front Line Defenders were used. Second, a research team used Google News and search terms to cast a wide net of articles and reports that bear on the subject. A complete list can be found in Dukalskis (2021), but combinations of terms like COUNTRY, THREATENED, EXILES were used. Third, Google-based searches were supplemented by

---

[2] The full database can be seen here: https://alexdukalskis.wordpress.com/data/

Lexis Advance UK, particularly to gather information on earlier years in the dataset. Fourth, follow-up searches were completed in six languages beyond English: Arabic, Chinese, French, Korean, Turkish and Russian. Information from credible NGOs, international watchdog groups and journalistic sources were used and included if deemed reliable by the team. The coding team cross-checked questionable cases to determine if they should be included and conducted several spot tests throughout the process. Transnational repression is often designed to be secretive and responsibility for it is usually deliberately obscured, so there is little doubt that the information compiled and analysed is incomplete. It likely also includes a disproportionate number of cases in which the 'host' country was democratic, given that it is easier to report on transnational repression in the freer context of a democracy. Nonetheless, while the true extent of authoritarian transnational repression is likely unknowable, the data gives us a glimpse of global patterns of transnational repression.[3]

Details are reported more thoroughly in Dukalskis (2021), but in summary, the AAAD captured 1,177 total incidents of transnational repression between 1991 and 2019. Some of the incidents involved multiple people, so the minimum number of individuals involved is about 2,585, not including the family members of critical exiles who must deal with domestic difficulties due to their relative's actions or status. The top five most frequently offending countries are Uzbekistan (195 events), China (167), North Korea (156), Turkey (111) and Russia (74). By target, citizens comprised just over 37% of cases, activists just over 33%, journalists nearly 14%, former government officials almost 10% and political opposition members just over 6%. Actions were spread relatively evenly, with threats (18.9%), arrest or detention (18.3%), extradition attempts (17.3%), extradition (14.8%) and threatening the family of the exiled person (14.7%) the most common. Of special note because of their consequences are assassinations (4.4% of cases, or 52 incidents) and assassination attempts (2.6% of cases, or 30 incidents). It should be underscored that these are aggregate numbers over the entire time period; transnational repression varied by political context and time over this period.

The data confirm that transnational repression is a global phenomenon, with thirty-five offending states recorded just from publicly available sources. As also shown by Freedom House (Schenkkan and Linzer 2021), authoritarian states

---

[3] On data difficulties in transnational repression research, see Dukalskis et al. 2022.

around the world appear willing and able to target their exiled citizens. Targeting critics abroad helps regimes to control criticisms and mitigate perceived threats to their internal and external security. While transnational repression is a demonstrably global issue, it is also likely to display regional variation. The following section investigates patterns of transnational repression found in the AAAD in the context of East and Southeast Asia.

Patterns of Transnational Repression in East and Southeast Asia

Before interrogating the data from Asia in the AAAD, it is worth first considering patterns of democracy and authoritarianism in East and Southeast Asia since 1991. Figure 5.1 captures annual average scores for the region on the Varieties of Democracy (V-Dem) Liberal Democracy Index. The measure captures several dimensions of democracy, including electoral quality, suffrage, protection for expression and co-ordination rights, and institutional checks (V-Dem 2018). The scale ranges between 1 and 0, with scores closer to 1 indicating a higher degree of liberal democracy and scores closer to 0 indicating a lower degree of liberal democracy. Figure 5.1 shows a general upward trajectory on average

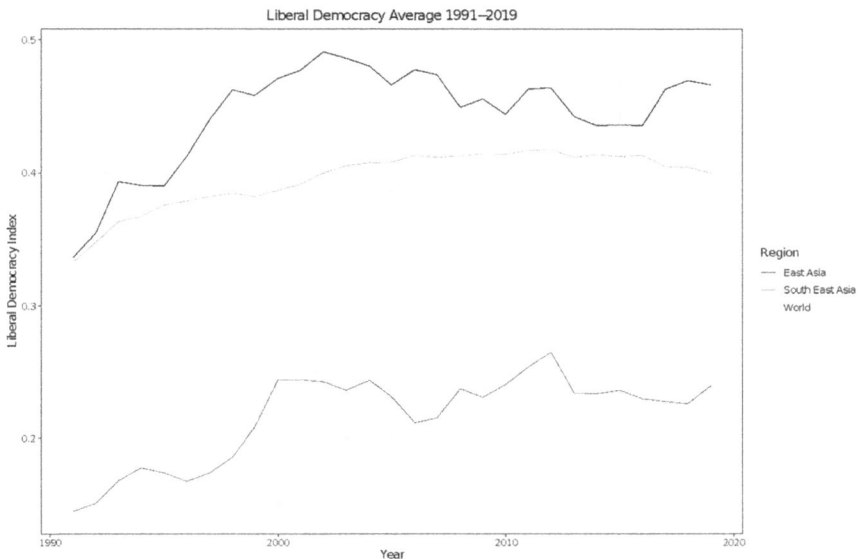

Figure 5.1 Average liberal democracy scores of East and Southeast Asian states as measured by V-Dem

for both East and Southeast Asian states since 1991. However, despite overall improvement within Southeast Asia in terms of the average liberal democracy score, Southeast Asia lags behind East Asia on average.

Figure 5.2 shows the trajectory for each of the region's countries that features at any point in the AAAD as a source state of transnational repression. These include: China, North Korea, Thailand, Cambodia, Laos and Vietnam. As the data show, the four single-party communist states in the region display little variation, but there is a notable decline in Thailand and a less dramatic but still noticeable decline in Cambodia. Aside from Thailand, all the countries in Asia found to have been transnational repressors in the dataset are well below the liberal democracy index average for Asia for the entire three decades captured in the data.

Figure 5.3 compares the average non-democratic state in the region (as defined by Morgenbesser 2020) that does not feature as a source state in the AAAD, namely Brunei, Singapore, Myanmar and Malaysia. Figure 5.3 shows that the source states within the AAAD dataset (China, North Korea, Thailand, Laos, Cambodia and Vietnam) are among the most autocratic states in Asia. Authoritarian states that do not engage in apparent transnational repression

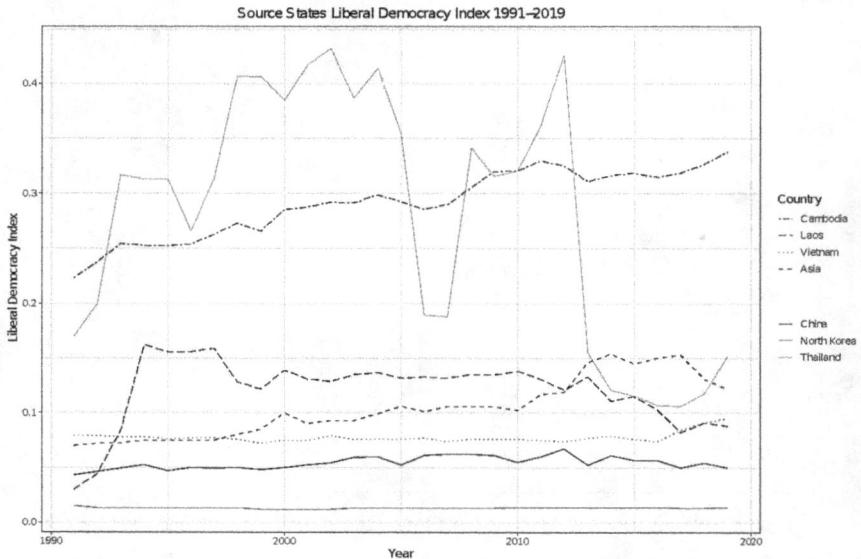

Figure 5.2 V-Dem liberal democracy scores of source states in AAAD compared to Asian average

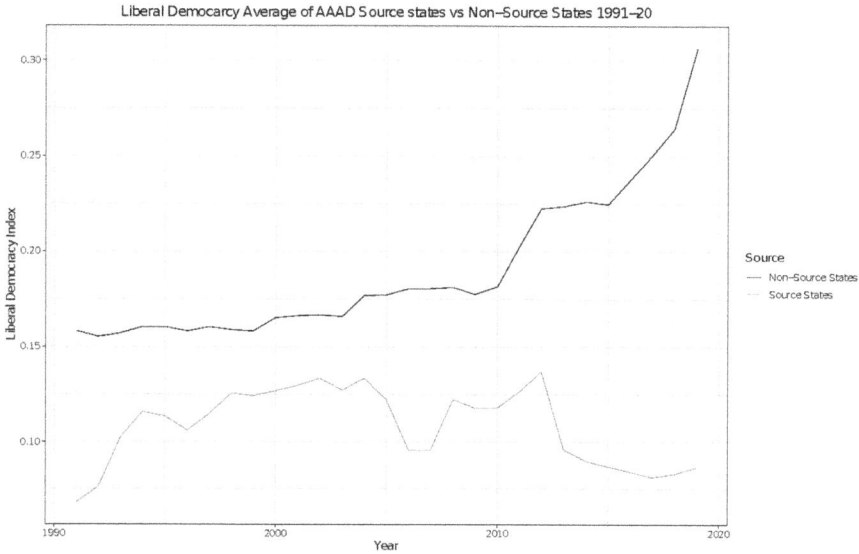

Figure 5.3 V-Dem liberal democracy scores of Asian source states in AAAD versus Asian non-source states

appear more respectful of liberal democratic norms than authoritarian states that do repress abroad, although both sets of states still have low overall scores. Put differently, this suggests that the more autocratic a state is, the more likely it is to take part in transnational repression.

Taken together, these data show that the region is characterised by some extremely stable authoritarian regimes (most importantly China) and a few that have notably autocratised when the latter is understood as becoming more authoritarian (Lührmann and Lindberg 2019). This gives us an opportunity to explore whether autocratisation in some regional states facilitates transnational repression (see also Lemon, this volume). The remainder of this section provides descriptive statistics about transnational repression in the region, while subsequent sections focus on Thailand as an increasingly active source country and a more pliant host country for transnational repression, and on Cambodia as a more frequent source country targeting its opposition abroad.

Table 5.1 shows details of the actions of source states from Asia in the AAAD broken down by number of cases and transnational repression practices. Extraditions and extradition attempts are the most used practices of authoritarian source states, with North Korea displaying the highest number

Table 5.1 Source states and repressive methods, 1991–2019

				Source States and Repressive Methods				
	Abducted	Arrested/Detained	Assassinated	Assassination Attempt	Attacked	Extradited	Extradition Attempt	Family Threatened	Threatened
Cambodia	0	3	0	0	1	0	0	0	5
China	16	16	1	0	0	15	16	74	29
North Korea	10	9	3	9	0	100	0	5	20
Thailand	4	0	2	0	0	3	7	2	19
Vietnam	1	0	0	0	0	0	0	0	0

*Source: AAAD

of extraditions from 1991 to 2019. Threats to individuals and their families overseas and at home have also proven to be one of the most common tactics used by source states, with China being the most prevalent user of both methods. It must be noted that some arrests and detentions were later dropped by host states due to the lack of evidence of the charges that targets were accused of in their home country. False accusations varied from embezzlement and corruption to murder.

Table 5.2 shows details of the actions of source states from Asia in the AAAD broken down by the number of cases and target. Table 5.2 shows that ordinary citizens abroad are the most common target for authoritarian states in Asia, driven almost entirely by China and North Korea. In the Chinese case, the vast majority of the citizens in question are Uyghurs who have been targeted by Chinese authorities abroad even if they are not especially politically active (for more details, see Jardine et al. 2021). Simply by virtue of being abroad, they are deemed politically threatening to General Secretary Xi Jinping's China. In the North Korean case, most of the citizens have left the country due to economic reasons, primarily from the extremely poor northeastern provinces that border China. These defections are usually not due to political protest but rather in search of better economic opportunities and/or to be reunited with family members who have previously escaped. Nevertheless, they are deemed politically threatening by North Korean authorities because 'the act of defection or border crossing announces the limitations and failures of the state. Without

Table 5.2 Source states and targets of repression, 1991–2019

	Source States and Targets of Repression				
	Activist	**Citizen**	**Former Government Official**	**Journalist**	**Opposition**
Cambodia	1	0	0	0	8
China	50	97	3	17	0
North Korea	11	116	25	4	0
Thailand	27	3	2	0	5
Vietnam	1	0	0	0	0

*Source: AAAD

saying a word, border crossers articulate the varied failures of North Korea' (Fahy 2019: 131). In both cases – for Uyghurs and North Koreans abroad – exiles are in a position to speak about domestic repression by their home states, which makes them a potential threat. Activists were the next most targeted category and were particularly targeted by Thailand, which will be covered in more detail below.

Table 5.3 shows the most frequent host states for transnational repression in Asia, including those states that are not authoritarian and/or do not appear as source states, broken down by the number of cases and the individuals most targeted. The most targeted democratic host states include Australia, Germany and Spain. Appearing on this list are some states that are also source states of transnational authoritarian repression, such as Egypt, Russia, Thailand and Turkey. States can be both sources and hosts of transnational authoritarian repression, sometimes willingly and sometimes reluctantly in the latter case.

Table 5.3 Host states for transnational repression emanating from East/Southeast Asia

	Host States and Targets of Repression				
	Activist	**Citizen**	**Former Government Official**	**Journalist**	**Opposition**
Australia	3	15	3	2	0
China	0	79	6	1	0
France	7	7	1	0	3
Laos	5	13	0	0	1
Russia	0	12	1	0	0
South Korea	11	1	15	3	0
Thailand	10	6	0	4	1
Turkey	0	24	0	0	0
United Kingdom	4	1	0	0	1
United States	14	12	0	10	0

Source: AAAD
[†]The ten most frequently targeted host states

Taken together, this overview shows a region with several stable authoritarian states (including the world's largest), along with a few displaying notable autocratisation. Furthermore, it establishes the basic context of transnational repression in the region. The following sections delve into two sides of the transnational repression relationship. The next section analyses the forces that have driven Thailand to become a much more active source country and a cooperative host country in facilitating the repression of nationals in neighbouring states. The subsequent section focuses on Cambodia as an increasingly active source country for transnational repression, targeting its now transnationally dispersed opposition.

Case Study 1: Thailand's Autocratic Turn and Transnational Repression

The last several years of Thai politics have seen a dramatic increase in transnational repression. The AAAD records 37 instances in which Thailand repressed its critics abroad, with 34 of them coming after 2014. It has also been the site of transnational repression by other states 23 times in the database, with 22 of them occurring from 2014 onwards. Of those 23 instances, 18 involved repression of Chinese nationals, including an infamous case in which Thai authorities extradited more than 100 Uyghurs to China.

These patterns can be explained by Thailand's 2014 military coup and subsequent autocratisation of Thai politics. The Thai political system is notoriously coup-prone, although not all coups or their outcomes in Thailand are the same. The roots of the relationship between the country's military, electoral system, monarchy and political economic structure are complex (McCargo 2005; Baker 2016; Chambers and Waitoolkiat 2016). A coup in 2006 was aimed at removing Thaksin Shinawatra from the position of prime minister and neutralising his support base (Kanchoochat and Hewison 2016). A new constitution drafted on the military's watch and promulgated in 2007 saw some changes, but an election in 2007 saw Thaksin's party, the People's Power Party (PPP), win again. This was followed by renewed efforts to sideline the PPP, culminating in the prime ministership of Abhisit Vejjajiva until 2011 (Kanchoochat and Hewison 2016). But elections in 2011 revealed the resilience of support for Thaksin, as his sister Yingluck Shinawatra headed a party that easily defeated Abhisit's. However, after months of protests and political instability in 2013 and 2014, Shinawatra was removed from power, and the military ultimately took power in May 2014 (Prasirtsuk 2015).

The 2014 coup was more severe than many of its predecessors insofar as the military did not step back quickly, but rather spent the next five years trying to reshape Thai politics. In so doing, 'the junta used repressive regulations and techniques of intimidation to silence opposition in a more aggressive way than any coup since 1976' (Baker 2016: 390). The military imposed martial law for over ten months and, even after lifting it, granted junta leader Prayuth Chan-ocha enormous powers to repress dissent (Baker 2016: 390). Political discourse and collective action were likewise severely restricted. Elections were held in 2019 under the new 2017 constitution, with Prayuth emerging as the prime minister despite a lack of widespread popular support. In 2020 a large protest movement challenged the government after a popular opposition party was forced to disband, with protests expanding to advocate for curtailing the authority of the royal family.

However, the junta repressed domestic opposition and activism (see Phasuk 2019). Activists were arrested on dubious grounds, and censorship limited what could be discussed and debated publicly. Furthermore, the death in 2016 of the previous monarch meant that Prince Vajiralongkorn was crowned in December of that year. The new king has proven to be much more assertive than his father in terms of controlling resources, involving himself in politics and taking control of a military guard unit of several thousand soldiers (McCargo 2019: 124). During the junta, enforcement of the country's draconian laws against criticising the monarchy were more strictly enforced than they were previously, with nearly a hundred cases in the first three years of military rule (Reuters 2020).

Domestic repression pushed some activism beyond Thailand's borders. With domestic space for political society restricted, some activists and critics fled abroad to escape repression. Thai authorities attempted to extend their repression beyond borders to neutralise them. As mentioned earlier, the AAAD records thirty-seven instances of transnational repression with Thailand as the source state, with almost all of them occurring after the 2014 coup. By far the most common category of targets for the Thai junta were activists.

A group of cases involving Laos as the host state illustrates well the dispersion pressure that the junta put on activism and the government's determination to rein it back in. Prominent political activist Surachai Danwattananusorn fled to Laos in 2014, fearing prosecution under the lese-majesty law. Suracahai, in his seventies at the time, is a well-known and long-time critic of the monarchy. While in Laos, he operated online radio and YouTube programmes critical of the monarchy and junta. In December 2018, he and two of his associates, Kraidet Leulerd (or Kasalong) and Chatchan Bupphawan (or Phuchana), disappeared. Later that month the bodies of Kasalong and Phuchana were caught in the nets of a fisherman on the Mekong River. Their faces had been mutilated and their bodies disembowelled and filled with concrete blocks. Surachai remains missing as of this writing (for further information about the cases, see BBC 2019; Human Rights Watch 2019; Cochrane 2019; Ellis-Petersen 2019; Prachatai 2020).

This case also highlights the facilitating role that an authoritarian partner, also focused on regime security, can have on transnational repression. Laos has been a single-party authoritarian state since 1975 and is therefore immune from scrutiny by a free press, opposition parties or the rule of law. This makes it a convenient partner for transnational repression. One year prior to the disappearances, in December 2017, Thailand's Deputy Prime Minister and Defence Minister Prawit Wonsuwon and his counterpart, Lao Defence Minister Chansamone Chanyalath, agreed that the two countries should co-operate to ameliorate threats to each other's security emanating from the other (Wassana 2017). This included criminal gangs and drug smugglers, but also the general category of 'groups of people who threaten the security' of countries across the border from the other. Indeed, months before this meeting, Thailand sought assistance from Laos to locate and extradite Wuthipong Kochathamakun, a political opponent of the junta and monarchy (Wassana 2017). In December 2018, just a few days before the disappearance of the three activists mentioned above, the two defence ministers met again and the discussion reportedly explicitly included the issue of Thai political dissidents operating in Laos, with Chansamone promising to deal with the issue (Prachatai 2019). Five days after the meeting between the defence ministers in December 2018, Thai junta leader Prayuth visited Laos for a bilateral meeting and reportedly also requested Laos's help in extraditing Thai dissident exiles in Laos (Ellis-Petersen 2019).

The authoritarian environment of Laos also helped reduce scrutiny in the aftermath of the disappearance and murders. The government has not investigated the episodes, nor has it looked into previous disappearances of Wuthipong Kochathamakun in 2017 or Itthipol Sukpaen in 2016 (Human

Rights Watch 2019). The lack of an independent judiciary or press surely reduces pressure on the Lao government to do so, which the government undoubtedly prefers. Indeed, the authoritarian co-operation between Laos and Thailand is a two-way street. Lao pro-democracy activist Od Sayavong has been missing from his Bangkok home since August 2019, with the Thai government apparently showing little enthusiasm to investigate the case (Lamb 2019; Radio Free Asia 2020).

In fact, Thailand is an increasingly friendly host state for transnational authoritarian repression. Several instances involving China illustrate this. Thai–Chinese relations warmed significantly in the aftermath of the 2014 coup (Hewison 2018). The coup made Bangkok's relationship with the United States more difficult, as Washington condemned the move. China framed the coup as an internal matter and co-operation between the two countries was boosted in several areas, including on matters of defence (Hewison 2018).

This co-operation apparently extends to the realm of transnational repression. (This and the following three paragraphs draw on the first author's previous work published in Dukalskis (2021: 136–7)). As mentioned previously, the AAAD documents eighteen cases in which Chinese citizens were targeted in Thailand, all of which occurred after the coup. Thailand had long been thought of among the Chinese dissident community as a relatively safe space, but warming relations between Beijing and Bangkok have since changed that perception (Marshall 2016; Leong et al. 2016).

The most famous incident involves Gui Minhai, a Chinese-born naturalised Swedish citizen. He was abducted from Thailand in October 2015 and resurfaced in China early in 2016 via a forced confession on China Central Television. Gui had been one of a group of five booksellers in Hong Kong who were abducted and/or detained in various locations and renditioned to the mainland. The bookstore was known for selling sometimes sensationalistic books critical of Chinese leaders, and Gui himself authored several books in the genre. Gui remains in prison in China; to date there have been no discernible public findings of investigations in Thailand, nor any public concerns articulated by Thai leaders, about the apparent state-backed kidnapping of Gui on Thai soil.

Gui is not the only case of a Chinese Communist Party (CCP) critic abducted from Thailand. In 2016 Li Xin, a journalist and activist, was abducted from a train in Thailand, only to reappear the next month in China (Phillips and Holmes 2016). Li had been a pro-democracy activist and apparently had been pressured by Chinese authorities to spy on other dissidents. One of his friends in Thailand, himself an activist who had fled China, warned Li 'to be very careful in Thailand. It is very dangerous here. The CCP is very strong here' (Phillips and Holmes 2016). It appears that he is still detained, but little information is available about his case.

Sometimes covert abduction is not necessary. In October 2015, Thai immigration authorities willingly co-operated with China's transnational repression by detaining two pro-democracy activists, Dong Guangping and Jiang Yefei (Front Line Defenders 2020). Even though both had been granted refugee status by the UN High Commissioner for Refugees, Thai authorities nonetheless deported them to China in November 2015. After being held in detention for two years in China, both were tried and found guilty. Jiang was convicted of 'subverting state power' and Dong of 'inciting subversion of state power' (ibid.). They were given prison sentences of six and a half years and three and a half years, respectively.

Overtly political activists are not the only group in China vulnerable to transnational repression. Thailand has become a common transit point for Uyghurs escaping the harsh repression that the Chinese government visits on the ethnic group domestically (see Jardine et al. 2021: 38–9; Roberts, this volume). Some attempt to enter Thailand and apply for refugee status there, or use Thailand as a transit point to make it to Turkey, where there is also a significant Uyghur population. Since the coup, however, Thai authorities have been detaining escaped Uyghurs and, in some cases, repatriating them back to China. The most infamous case occurred in July 2015, when Thai authorities sent back 109 Uyghurs to China to face detention in Xinjiang's now well-known network of re-education camps, or perhaps worse. Reflecting willing authoritarian co-operation, Thai leaders at the time justified their decision publicly. Referring to a previous decision to send a group of Uyghurs from Thailand to Turkey, a spokesperson for the military government said 'Thailand has worked with China and Turkey to solve the Uighur Muslim problem. We have sent them back to China after verifying their nationality' (Campbell 2015). Prayuth went further, arguing that Thailand could not take sides in Chinese domestic issues, and reportedly said that 'China has guaranteed their safety. If we send them back and there is a problem, that is not our fault' (Wong and Amatatham 2015). The larger issue of Uyghur escapees in Thailand continues. Uyghurs are held in detention centres in Thailand and some chance to escape rather than be sent back to China (Bangkok Post 2020).

Clearly, Thailand's autocratic turn after the 2014 military coup opened the valves of transnational repression in both directions – with Thailand as a source and a willing host. The coup pushed some Thai activists abroad, which prompted the Thai military government to extend its repressive reach beyond its borders. Domestically, Thai authorities seemed willing to return the favour if troublesome critics from neighbouring states had sought refuge in Thai territory. The logic of co-operation in these examples involving Laos, China and Thailand appears to be mainly driven by regime security concerns. Activists and opposition members represent perceived threats to authoritarian regimes, with regional autocratic co-operation used to break their associated networks and capture their leaders as a way to help secure authoritarian rule.

Case Study 2: Cambodia as a Source State of Transnational Repression

As seen in Figure 5.2, Cambodia has not reached high levels of liberal democracy since 1990. This is understandable given that the country suffered in the 1970s and 1980s from extensive bombing by the United States, the genocidal Khmer Rouge regime of 1975 to 1979 that by some estimates killed over a quarter of the population (approximately 3 million people), and invasion by Vietnam in the closing days of 1978. These were not fortuitous conditions for liberal democracy, to say the least, and despite United Nations-administered elections in 1993, the current leader Hun Sen has ruled the country since 1985. Even so, democracy in Cambodia deteriorated from an already low mark in the 2010s as Hun Sen and his Cambodia People's Party (CPP) entrenched their power and repressed opponents. As of this writing, the CPP holds 125 out of 125 seats in the National Assembly and all 58 elected seats in the Senate.

Throughout its time in power, the CPP had often been able to preserve dominance in part because of a divided opposition (Un and Lou 2020: 120). However, national elections in 2013 saw the opposition unite under the banner of the new Cambodia National Rescue Party (CNRP) and perform surprisingly well, trailing the CPP by only 44 per cent to the incumbent's

49 per cent. This seems to have put Hun Sen and the CPP on high alert, as the state intensified its repression of the opposition, civil society, media and foreign-linked organisations in the following years (Croissant 2018; Morgenbesser 2019: 165–6). Nevertheless, the CNRP again performed well in local elections in 2017, despite the campaign of repression against it. While the CPP ultimately won those elections, the CNRP 'made remarkable gains over its previous commune elections performance, with a twelvefold increase in the overall number of communes won and shifts in some provinces that would have seemed unthinkable in 2012' (Croissant 2018: 195).

Again, Hun Sen's government responded with repression. Sam Rainsy, co-founder of the CNRP, had already fled Cambodia in 2015, fearing arrest stemming from a defamation case against him by Hun Sen in 2011 (Moregenbesser 2019: 165). His CNRP co-founder Kem Sokha took over as party leader a few months before the 2017 local elections. After the CNRP's strong performance, however, Kem Sokha was arrested in September of that year on the grounds that he was colluding with the United States to overthrow the Cambodian government (Croissant 2018: 196). He was released to house arrest the next year and banned from politics for five years. The CNRP itself was formally dissolved in November 2017 by the CPP-led government under new legislation allowing it to ban political parties for a variety of vague and expansively worded offences. Thus, the 2018 'election' resulted in the CPP holding unchecked power over the Cambodian political system.

The scope and severity of the crackdown against the opposition drove many government critics abroad. Dispersal prompted Hun Sen to extend his repressive horizons beyond Cambodia's borders. This was dramatically showcased in November 2019. Sam Rainsy announced he would return to Cambodia from his self-exile in France on 9 November, Cambodia's independence day. Several other CNRP leaders, including deputy leader Mu Sochua, indicated they would also return to Cambodia on that day (Al Jazeera 2019).

Hun Sen, with the collaboration of neighbouring states, thwarted their plans. Rainsy had posted details of his plane ticket on Twitter, which indicated that he would transit via Bangkok. Thailand's junta leader Prayuth commented that 'according to our commitment to ASEAN, we will not interfere in each other's internal affairs, and we will not allow an anti-government person to use Thailand for activism. I have ordered this, so he probably won't get in' (Al Jazeera 2019). Rainsy was ultimately prevented from boarding his flight from Paris to Bangkok. Mu Sochua, a dual Cambodian and American citizen, was detained in Kuala Lumpur by Malaysian authorities and later released. Two others, Ngoeum Keatha and Heng Seang Leang, were also detained and released by Malaysian authorities (Amnesty International 2019a).

The CPP claims publicly that the CNRP leadership are criminals who wish to perpetrate a treasonous coup (see also Chapter 1 of this volume by Marlies Glasius on the treatment of exiles as traitors by sending states). The government has therefore indicated on multiple occasions that they would be arrested and face legal consequences should they return (Al Jazeera 2019; VOD 2020). However, as the November 2019 events demonstrate, it simultaneously prevented them from entering the country. Cambodian authorities revoked the passports of twelve CNRP leaders, thus making their entry more complex (Amnesty International 2019a). In 2020 there was a mass trial of more than 120 CNRP-linked activists who had been charged with treason for their political opposition (Cheang 2020). Only thirty-three showed up to the first day of the trial, in part because so many are abroad. Mu Sochua, who is one of the CNRP leaders with a revoked Cambodian passport, has indicated that she wishes to return to defend herself in court, but is being barred from entering by the Hun Sen government (Vantha and Flynn 2020a). She and colleagues are in a position of being summoned by the court but simultaneously banned from appearing. The CPP appears to prefer keeping these high-profile CNRP leaders outside the country so they cannot organise domestically or become symbols of resistance through their trials. Keeping them abroad minimises their voice domestically. It also can still harass them while they are abroad, as demonstrated by Hun Sen trying to pursue a defamation case against Sam Rainsy in French courts (Vantha and Flynn 2020b). More directly, CNRP member Chamroeun Suon was beaten and nearly abducted in Bangkok by two men speaking Khmer in late 2019 (Ruffles 2020).

The autocratic deepening in Cambodia over the last several years has pushed significant actors of the political opposition abroad. Cambodian electoral politics now transcends continents in ways that have prompted the Hun Sen government to extend its repressive reach beyond its borders. It has actively prevented opposition leaders from entering Cambodia and has persuaded other Southeast Asian states to frustrate the movements of CNRP members.

It has also complicated the movements of opposition leaders by revoking their passports and begun to extend its transnational reach further with attacks and legal cases against its exiled opponents.

Concluding Remarks: Exploring the Autocratisation–Transnational Repression Nexus

Transnational repression is meant to enhance the internal and external regime security of authoritarian states (Dukalskis 2021). In most cases, authoritarian states would prefer to avoid exercising transnational repression because the 'necessity' of repression indicates the reality of dissent, which undermines their claim to support by the people to rule. However, 'as politics moves beyond borders, so too does repression' (Cooley and Heathershaw 2017: 190). In order to advance our understanding of this phenomenon, this chapter has focused on mapping patterns of transnational repression in East and Southeast Asia. It provided an overview of descriptive statistics based on a unique dataset followed by in-depth examination of the cases of post-2014 Thailand and the tightening grip on power of Cambodia's Hun Sen. In so doing, we argued that as authoritarianism deepens, so does transnational repression. This is true at the country level insofar as repressed politics domestically pushes opposition actors and critics abroad. It is also true at the regional level, as deepening authoritarianism facilitates authoritarian co-operation between states that facilitates transnational repression.

This autocratisation–transnational repression nexus could be explored further in several ways (Moss 2022). Specifically, it would benefit from cross-national analysis to specify the relationship, timing and sequencing of the nexus. This would help us to understand broad relationships and the conditions under which particular actions are likely. The subject could also be better understood by comparing regions with different levels of transnational repression co-operation to capture the drivers and barriers at play. Disaggregating by behaviour, target and method can also help to understand the relationship between different repressive actors within the source state and their counterparts in the host state. Archival and/or elite interview methods applied to historical cases (e.g. Lessa 2022) could illuminate more details about how autocratisation helps spread and sustain authoritarian co-operation (and vice versa), and by extension facilitates transnational repression.

For now, an important task in this area is to pay attention to processes of data collection, comparison and replicability (see Dukalskis et al. 2022). This is a challenging task because transnational repression events are varied by nature, ranging from assassination to Internet threats, which necessitates different types of sources and levels of verification. States often work to hide their transnational repression, which makes the researcher's job more difficult, and journalists pay attention to some cases disproportionately over others. Some victims may not wish to publicise their ordeals, which means that some cases may never be reported and therefore not analysed. These problems may be impossible to overcome entirely, but many can be mitigated, with the ultimate result being better data that can facilitate new understandings of transnational repression patterns and processes.

References

Adamson, F. 2019. 'No Escape: Long-Distance Repression, Extraterritorial States and the Underworld of IR'. Paper presented at the 2019 European Consortium of Political Research Joint Sessions of Workshops, April 2019.

Al Jazeera. 2019. 'Cambodian opposition leader Sam Rainsy announces Saturday return'. *Al Jazeera*, 6 November. Available at: https://www.aljazeera.com/news/2019/11/6/cambodian-opposition-leader-sam-rainsy-announces-saturday-return (accessed 1 December 2020).

Amnesty International. 2019. 'Cambodia: Stop pressuring regional neighbours to harass opposition figures'. *Amnesty International*, 7 November. Available at: https://www.amnesty.org/en/latest/news/2019/11/cambodia-stop-pressuring-regional-neighbours-harass-opposition-figures/ (accessed 7 January 2020).

Baker, C. 2016. 'The 2014 Thai coup and some roots of authoritarianism'. *Journal of Contemporary Asia* 46(3): 388–404.

Bangkok Post. 2020. 'Last Uighur escapee recaptured'. *Bangkok Post*, 14 January 14. Available at: https://www.bangkokpost.com/thailand/general/1835469/last-uighur-escapee-recaptured (accessed 1 December 2020).

BBC. 2019. 'Mutilated Thai bodies on Mekong shore are activist's aides'. *BBC News*, 22 January. Available at: https://www.bbc.com/news/world-asia-46965839 (accessed 30 November 2020).

Campbell, C. 2015. 'Thailand defends its decision to forcibly return Uighur migrants to China'. *Time*, 10 July. Available at: https://time.com/3952498/china-uighur-xinjiang-deportations-turkey-thailand-human-rights/ (accessed 1 December 2020).

Chambers, P. and Waitoolkiat, N. 2016. 'The resilience of monarchised military in Thailand'. *Journal of Contemporary Asia* 46(3): 425–44.

Cheang, S. 2020. 'Cambodia begins mass trial of opposition activists'. *Associated Press*, 26 November. Available at: https://apnews.com/article/election-2020-trials-general-elections-elections-cambodia-fa4654b4c8eda338a92da7e73f44 7f03 (accessed 1 December 2020).

Cochraine, L. 2019. 'Thai dissidents living in exile fear for their lives after a string of disappearances and murders'. *ABC News*, 22 May. Available at: https://www.abc. net.au/news/2019-05-23/fears-for-thai-band-and-missing-activists-after-bodies-found/11137196 (accessed 30 November 2020).

Cooley, A. and Heathershaw, J. 2017. *Dictators Without Borders: Power and Money in Central Asia*. New Haven, CT: Yale University Press.

Croissant, A. 2018. 'Cambodia in 2017: Descending into dictatorship?' *Asian Survey* 58(1): 194–200.

Dalmasso, E., Del Sordi, A., Glasius, M., Hirt, N., Michaelsen, M., Mohammad, A. S. and Moss, D. 2018. 'Intervention: Extraterritorial authoritarian power'. *Political Geography* 64: 95–104.

Dukalskis, A. 2021. *Making the World Safe for Dictatorship*. New York: Oxford University Press.

Dukalskis, A., Furstenberg, S., Gorokhovskaia, Y., Heathershaw, J., Lemon, E. and Schenkkan, N. 2022. 'Transnational repression: Data advances, challenges, and possibilities'. *Political Research Exchange* 4(1): 2104651.

Ellis-Petersen, H. 2019. 'Murder on the Mekong: Why exiled Thai dissidents are abducted and killed'. *The Guardian*, 17 March. Available at: https://www.theguardian.com/world/2019/mar/17/thailand-dissidents-murder-mekong-election (accessed 30 November 2020).

Fahy, S. 2019. *Dying for Rights: Putting North Korea's Human Rights Abuses on the Record*. New York: Columbia University Press.

Furstenburg, S., Lemon, E. and Heathershaw, J. 2021. 'Spatialising state practices through transnational repression'. *European Journal of International Security* 6(3): 358–78.

Glasius, M. 2018. 'Extraterritorial authoritarian practices: A framework'. *Globalizations* 15(2): 179–97.

Heathershaw, J. and Furstenberg, S. 2020. 'Central Asian Political Exiles Database (CAPE), Parameters and Definitions'. Available at: https://excas.net/projects/political-exiles/ (accessed 3 January 2020).

Hewison, K. 2018. 'Thailand: An old relationship renewed'. *Pacific Review* 31(1): 116–30.

Human Rights Watch. 2019. 'Laos: Investigate disappearance of 3 Thai dissidents." *Human Rights Watch*, 22 January. Available at: https://www.hrw.org/news/2019/01/22/laos-investigate-disappearance-3-thai-dissidents (accessed 30 November 2020).

Jardine, B., Lemon, E. and Hall, N. 2021. *No Space Left to Run: China's Transnational Repression of Uyghurs*. Washington, DC: Uyghur Human Rights Project and Oxus Society for Central Asian Affairs.

Kanchoochat, V. and Hewison, K. 2016. 'Introduction: Understanding Thailand's politics'. *Journal of Contemporary Asia* 46(3): 371–87.

Lamb, K. 2019. 'Thai government pressed over missing Lao activist Od Sayavong'. *The Guardian*, 7 September. Available at: https://www.theguardian.com/world/2019/sep/07/thai-government-pressed-over-missing-lao-activist-od-sayavong (accessed 30 November 2020).

Lemon, E. 2019. 'Weaponizing Interpol'. *Journal of Democracy* 30(2): 15–29.

Leong, J., Gooch, L. and Lee, L. 2016. 'Why Thailand is no longer safe for Chinese dissidents'. *Al Jazeera*, 26 July. Available at: https://www.aljazeera.com/features/2016/07/26/why-thailand-is-no-longer-safe-for-chinese-dissidents/ (accessed 30 November 2020).

Lessa, F. 2022. *The Condor Trials: Transnational Repression and Human Rights in South America*. New Haven, CT: Yale University Press.

Lewis, D. 2015. '"Illiberal spaces": Uzbekistan's extraterritorial security practices and the spatial politics of contemporary authoritarianism'. *Nationalities Papers* 43(1): 140–59.

Lührmann, A. and Lindberg, S. I. 2019. 'A third wave of autocratization is here: What is new about it?' *Democratization* 26(7): 1095–113.

Marshall, A. R. C. 2016. 'Dissidents fearful as Thailand, once a haven, favors China'. *Reuters*, 17 February. Available at: https://www.reuters.com/article/us-thailand-china-dissidents-idUSKCN0VQ2ZU (accessed 30 November 2020).

McCargo, D. 2005. 'Network monarchy and legitimacy crises in Thailand'. *Pacific Review* 18(4): 499–519.

——. 2019. 'Democratic demolition in Thailand'. *Journal of Democracy* 30(4): 119–33.

Michaelsen, M. 2018. 'Exit and voice in a digital age: Iran's exiled activists and the authoritarian state'. *Globalizations* 15(2): 248–64.

Morgenbesser, L. 2019. 'Cambodia's transition to hegemonic authoritarianism'. *Journal of Democracy* 30(1): 158–71.

——. 2020. *The Rise of Sophisticated Authoritarianism in Southeast Asia*. Cambridge: Cambridge University Press.

Moss, D. M. 2016. 'Transnational repression, diaspora mobilization, and the case of the Arab Spring'. *Social Problems* 63(4): 480–98.

——. 2021. *The Arab Spring Abroad: Diaspora Activism against Authoritarian Regimes*. New York: Cambridge University Press.

Obydenkova, A. V. and Libman, A. 2019. *Authoritarian Regionalism in the World of International Organizations: Global Perspectives and the Eurasian Enigma*. New York: Oxford University Press.

Phasuk, S. 2019. 'Unending repression under Thailand's military junta'. *Human Rights Watch*. Available at: https://www.hrw.org/news/2019/05/22/unending-repression-under-thailands-military-junta (accessed 30 November 2020).

Phillips, T. and Holmes, O. 2016. 'Activist who vanished in Thailand is being held in China, says wife'. *The Guardian*, 3 February 3. Available at: https://www.the-guardian.com/world/2016/feb/03/activist-li-xin-vanished-in-thailand--held-in-china-says-wife (accessed 9 April 2020).

Prachatai. 2020. '1 year on, disappeared activist Siam Theerawut's whereabouts remain unclear'. *Prachatai English*, 16 May. Available at: https://prachatai.com/english/node/8524 (accessed 30 November 2020).

Prasirtsuk, K. 2015. 'Thailand in 2014: Another coup, a different coup?' *Asian Survey* 55(1): 200–6.

Radio Free Asia. 2020. 'Lao democracy activist still missing after a year, as Thai police investigation "stalls"'. *Radio Free Asia*, 25 August. Available at: https://www.rfa.org/english/news/laos/missing-08252020101554.html (accessed 30 November 2020).

Reuters. 2020. 'Explainer: Thailand's Lese Majeste Law'. *Reuters*, 4 August. Available at: https://www.reuters.com/article/us-thailand-protests-monarchy-explainer-idUSKCN2501Q1 (accessed 30 November 2020).

Ruffles, M. 2020. 'Hun Sen branded him a traitor. He fled the country but thugs found him'. *Sydney Morning Herald*, 2 January. Available at: https://www.smh.com.au/world/asia/hun-sen-branded-him-a-traitor-he-fled-the-country-but-thugs-found-him-20191229-p53ndd.html (accessed 1 December 2020).

Tsourapas, G. 2020. 'Global autocracies: Strategies of transnational repression, legitimation, and co-optation in world politics'. *International Studies Review* early view doi: https://doi.org/10.1093/isr/viaa061

Un, K. and Lou, J. J. 2020. 'Cambodia in 2019: Entrenching one-party rule and asserting national sovereignty in the era of shifting global geopolitics'. *Southeast Asian Affairs* 2020: 117–34.

Vantha, P. and Flynn, G. 2020a. 'CNRP leaders plan to return to Cambodia on Jan. 4, 2021'. *Cambodianess*, 1 December. Available at: https://cambodianess.com/article/cnrp-leaders-plan-to-return-to-cambodia-on-jan-4-2021 (accessed 1 December 2020).

——. 2020b. 'PM Hun Sen annoyed by delays to Rainsy defamation case in French courts'. *Cambodianess*, 25 November. Available at: https://cambodianess.com/article/pm-hun-sen-annoyed-by-delays-to-rainsy-defamation-case-in-french-courts (accessed 1 December 2020).

V-Dem. 2018. *Democracy for All? V-Dem Annual Democracy Report 2018*. Gothenburg, Sweden: Varieties of Democracy. Available at: https://www.v-dem.net/media/filer_public/3f/19/3f19efc9-e25f-4356-b159-b5c0ec894115/v-dem_democracy_report_2018.pdf (accessed 30 November 2020).

VOD. 2020. 'Hun Sen vows to arrest economic subversives, three From CNRP jailed'. *VOD*, 3 June. Available at: https://vodenglish.news/hun-sen-vows-to-arrest-economic-subversives-three-from-cnrp-jailed/ (accessed 1 December 2020).

Wassana, N. 2017. 'Laos agrees to tackle threats to Thai govt'. *Bangkok Post*, 21 December. Available at: https://www.bangkokpost.com/thailand/general/1383234/laos-agrees-to-tackle-threats-to-thai-govt (accessed 30 November 2020).

Wong, E. and Amatatham, P. 2015. 'Ignoring protests, Thailand deports About 100 Uighurs back to China'. *The New York Times*, 9 July. Available at: https://www.nytimes.com/2015/07/10/world/asia/thailand-deports-uighur-migrants-to-china.html (accessed 1 December 2020).

6

BIOPOLITICS WITHOUT BORDERS: CHINA'S RACIALLY PROFILED TRANSNATIONAL REPRESSION OF THE UYGHUR PEOPLE

Sean R. Roberts

Introduction

In 2018, while I was in Oslo, Norway doing interviews for my book *The War on the Uyghurs: China's Internal Campaign against a Muslim Minority* (Roberts 2020), numerous Uyghur refugees, most of whom were completely uninvolved in diaspora political activities, told me that the authorities from China frequently called them to ask for detailed information about their lives. They posed queries such as: Where do you work? What is your address? How many children do you have? Are you married, and, if so, to whom? Do you participate in any Uyghur groups in Norway or elsewhere? I heard similar stories from Uyghur exiles in Turkey, Australia and the United States. Those who contacted local law enforcement to complain about these extraterritorial phone interrogations found that there was no way to trace the calls, which were presumably routed via Voice-Over-Internet-Protocol.[1] These unsolicited phone calls and related intimidation tactics represent a form of transnational repression that is explicitly racially profiled and all-encompassing in its application. The People's Republic of China (PRC) does not determine those to be

---

[1] Voice-Over-Internet Protocol (VOIP) is a means of calling a telephone number via the Internet. This can mask the number that is calling and make it difficult to trace.

targeted by the extent of one's political activity, but by virtue of one's identity. In this sense, it mirrors the PRC's domestic policies towards Uyghurs, Kazakhs, Kyrgyz, Uzbeks, Tatars and other Turkic Muslims since 2017, which have also involved racially targeted repression that ultimately seeks to erase the identities of Turkic Muslims who view the Xinjiang Uyghur Autonomous Region (XUAR) of China as their homeland.[2]

Probes by Chinese officials into the lives of Uyghur refugees were unfolding at the same time that the world was learning about the Chinese state's notorious Integrated Joint Operations Platform (IJOP) database. The IJOP is a racially profiled database that contains extensive information on Uyghurs and other indigenous peoples of the XUAR, gathered from mass surveillance (HRW 2019). This database has played a central role in facilitating the massive campaign of repression targeting Uyghurs and related peoples in the region, which several countries, including the US, Canada, the Netherlands, the UK and Lithuania have deemed to constitute genocide (Basu 2021). The information collected in the IJOP is used to evaluate individual Uyghurs' loyalty to the state in determining who should be either imprisoned or interned in 're-education' camps (see: Leibold 2020). Given the aforementioned information being collected from Uyghur exiles, it appears that the IJOP may also profile Uyghurs beyond the borders of the PRC as a means of determining future efforts at transnational repression.

By recounting the historical roots of this transnational repression and its evolution since 1990, this chapter seeks to understand how its racialisation and global reach has so rapidly accelerated over the last thirty years. The racialised nature of the PRC's transnational repression vis-à-vis Uyghurs is part and parcel of the historical nature of structural racism against Uyghurs and other Turkic Muslims in the PRC, but this racialisation has also been solidified by the US-led Global War on Terror (GWOT). The GWOT allowed the PRC to dehumanise the Uyghurs as a people by branding them as inherently prone to 'terrorism' by virtue of their cultural and religious identity. This also provided the Chinese state with a convenient justification for its actions against

---

[2] The PRC's crackdown on Uyghurs since 2017 has also targeted related Central Asian ethnic groups in the Uyghurs' homeland, including Kazakhs, Kyrgyz, Uzbeks and Tatars. Throughout this chapter, I often refer to 'Uyghurs and related peoples' to reflect this fact.

Uyghurs abroad as 'counterterrorism' measures that were posited as being in concert with the goals of the US-led GWOT and, thus, were tolerated by the international community. At the same time, China's growing global influence allowed the PRC to secure the co-operation of an increasing number of states in the implementation of repressive measures against Uyghur exiles. As a result, the geographic reach of the PRC's transnational repression of Uyghurs has expanded exponentially over the last three decades, at the same time that it has shifted from targeting politically active exiles to targeting all Uyghurs by virtue of their identity.

In what follows, these points are elucidated using Michel Foucault's concept of 'biopolitics'. The chapter first explores the historical roots of the PRC's structural racism towards Uyghurs and its identification of this people as a biopolitical threat to Chinese society. This is followed by an historical examination of PRC transnational repression of Uyghurs since 1990, culminating in the racially imbued and expansive nature of the repression of Uyghur exiles since 2017. The chapter concludes with a discussion of the implications of China's present racially profiled transnational repression of Uyghurs for the future of transnational repression and for the possibilities of transnational genocidal actions.

Understanding China's Biopolitics vis-à-vis Uyghurs at Home and Abroad

As I have argued elsewhere, the PRC's actions against Uyghurs and related peoples in the Uyghur region since 2017 represent an extreme manifestation of what Michel Foucault has called 'biopolitics' (cf. Roberts 2018, 2020). Foucault has used the term biopolitics to describe a certain style of governance ubiquitous among modern states, which focuses on the productive force of individual bodies, or citizens, as either productive or unproductive to the polity and society. The productive bodies within society (those whom the state views as furthering state objectives) are viewed as both the object of governance and as a critical tool in the hands of government, while unproductive bodies (those perceived by the state as hindering state objectives) are viewed as dangerous to the polity, almost like a biological threat such as a virus, which can infect the productive portion of the population. As such, the unproductive, or counterproductive, population must be 'banished, excluded, and repressed' by the state, a process in which the productive are asked to assist in realising (Foucault 1997: 32).

The Chinese state's actions towards Uyghurs since 2017 represent a particular form of biopolitics that is racially determined. While Foucault intended biological infection to serve as a metaphor in his description of modern states' targeting of people as a threat to society, the PRC's actions against Uyghurs and related peoples represent a truly biological form of biopolitics that frames an entire racial or ethnic group as a threat to society. The state is not attacking a subset of Uyghurs who are deemed unproductive or counterproductive; rather it has deemed the Uyghur identity itself to be unproductive and a threat to Chinese society deserving of banishment, exclusion, repression, and ultimately erasure. Such a racially imbued biopolitics is not uncommon in history, serving as the embodiment of racist politics, but when it has been fully implemented in state policy, its logical conclusion is genocide – the destruction of the racial or ethnic group that has been framed as the threat to society.

It is important to understand that the Uyghur people have always been subject to structural racism based on a particular biopolitics by the PRC inside and outside China's borders. Since its inception in 1949, the state has identified a substantial part of its Uyghur population as an existential threat to society, leading the state to treat Uyghurs as an 'exception' within Chinese society and holding them to different standards than other citizens. At the same time, it has always identified this perceived domestic threat from Uyghurs to be involved with external actors, usually associated with Uyghurs' cultural links to peoples outside China, but also often ambiguously framed to evoke China's geopolitical foes, making Uyghurs simultaneously an outside threat. I would argue that the reason the state has continually framed Uyghurs as both an inside and outside threat is due to the ambiguous position this population and its historical homeland holds in Chinese society. As David Tobin has recently argued, the Chinese state perceives Uyghurs simultaneously both as outsiders and as a constituent part of China (Tobin 2020). On the one hand, the Chinese state goes to great lengths to claim that the Uyghur people and their homeland have always been a part of an ahistorical vision of Chinese civilisation (see SCOIPRC 2009). On the other hand, within Chinese society Uyghurs and their homeland are clearly perceived as foreign and exotic because they have stronger cultural and historical connections to Central Asia and the Turkic world than to China (see Tobin 2020). These connections are apparent because the Uyghurs and their homeland were incorporated into modern China through imperial conquest and colonial subjugation, an uncomfortable history that Chinese official sources seek to ignore.

Modern China's conquest and subjugation of the Uyghur region began in the mid-eighteenth century, when the Qing Empire first took control of the region, but it was arguably not consolidated until the establishment of the PRC in 1949. From the PRC's perspective, China's control of the region was hindered by the involvement of foreign imperialists from Europe and Japan, who exploited China beginning with the Opium Wars of the mid-nineteenth century and lasting until the establishment of the PRC, a period which Chinese historians often call the 'century of humiliation'. Viewing all of China's history from the mid-nineteenth century to the founding of the PRC through the lens of the 'century of humiliation', the PRC has sought to ignore China's own imperial projects and the local resistance to them during this time, including that in the Uyghur region.

In particular, the PRC has erased the history of twentieth-century anti-colonial struggles in the Uyghur homeland by dismissing them as being provoked by Western and Japanese imperialists. This is especially germane to its historical narrative about the two independent proto-states established by local Muslims in the Uyghur region, both known as the Eastern Turkistan Republic (ETR). If the PRC characterises the first ETR (1933–4 in the south of the Uyghur region) as provoked by Western and Japanese imperialists, it has traditionally explained the second ETR (1945–9 in the north of the region and supported by the USSR) as merely a part of the Chinese revolution.

If the memory of these states as Turkic anti-colonial resistance to Chinese rule has been erased by the PRC, it has been preserved by Uyghurs, especially in exile. When the Communist Party of China (CPC) invaded and established complete control of the Uyghur region in 1949, many of those involved in or inspired by the first ETR fled the country, most ultimately settling in Turkey with pockets finding refuge elsewhere in South Asia and the Middle East. Many of those involved in and inspired by the second ETR, after a brief period of being accepted into the CPC, fled to the USSR, especially to Kazakhstan and Kyrgyzstan (Roberts 1998). As a result, during the early years of Communist rule in China, two large Uyghur diaspora communities formed in Turkey and the Soviet Union respectively that maintained the memory of Uyghurs' struggle for independent statehood. In this context, the PRC since its inception has viewed Uyghur exiles, especially in Turkey and Central Asia, as agents of external powers and an existential threat bent on dividing China, particularly if they are able to 'infect' the Uyghur population inside China.

However, China's perceptions of Uyghur exiles as a threat have also changed over time. From the late 1950s to the late 1980s, the PRC was mostly concerned with Uyghurs in the Soviet Union influencing those still in China via a propaganda war that was waged in the context of the Sino-Soviet split (Karklins 1975). During the 1990s, as China opened to the world, the PRC worried that "good" Uyghurs who were loyal to the state would be 'infected' by 'bad' Uyghurs and other negative influences from abroad, a concern that expanded during the 2000s to encompass the less territorially bound external influences of 'religious extremism' and 'terrorism'. However, since 2017 the state's concerns have extended to virtually all Uyghurs at home and abroad, perceiving them all as an 'inside/outside' threat by virtue of their cultural identity and historical connection to the outside world that could 'infect' the larger Chinese society.

This evolution of the PRC's perception of Uyghurs as an 'inside/outside' threat to Chinese society has amounted to a history of incrementally increasing transnational repression of Uyghur exiles since the 1990s that is well documented in a recent report published by the Uyghur Human Rights Project (UHRP) and authors Bradley Jardine, Edward Lemon and Nathalie Hall (UHRP 2021a). The report chronicles 1,546 cases where Uyghurs or related Turkic Muslims from the XUAR were either detained in a third country at Beijing's request and/or extradited to China since 1997 (UHRP 2021a). The report shows that the PRC's deployment of such tactics has increased incrementally and has expanded in their geographical reach during that time, attaining staggering numbers and broad geographic application in the last seven years. From 1997 to 2007, the study documented eighty-nine cases of detention or extradition primarily in South and Central Asia. Between 2008 and 2013, that number had increased to 130 in half the time and had expanded geographically to Southeast Asia as well, and over the last seven years this number has skyrocketed to 1,327, expanding to also include the Middle East, North Africa and even Eastern Europe (UHRP 2021a: 1). Furthermore, this data does not account for the more mundane surveillance and intimidation since 2017 of virtually all Uyghurs who have left China in the last decade, irrespective of their place of residence, tactics that are freely employed by the PRC even in the liberal democracies of North America, Western Europe and Australia. In the following sections, I describe this evolution of transnational repression practices against Uyghur exile populations since the 1990s. I do so by highlighting how they began with China's opening up to the world, became more racialised by the GWOT and expanded geographically as China's global influence increased.

The Evolution of Transnational Repression and the Targeting of Uyghurs since the 1990s

China's Transnational Repression of Uyghurs during the 1990s

The PRC had little need to employ direct methods of transnational repression against Uyghurs until the 1990s, when China's opening to the world allowed the people of the region to more freely travel abroad and to host exile relatives who had previously left China. This reunification of Uyghurs across borders was most pronounced between those in China and Central Asia respectively. By the mid-1990s, there was substantial cross-border travel among Uyghurs between China and the former Soviet states of Kazakhstan, Kyrgyzstan and Uzbekistan to visit relatives and conduct trade. For a brief period in the 1990s, while I was doing fieldwork in Kazakhstan, the country, and especially the city of Almaty, provided a free space for Uyghurs from both sides of the border to communicate about the nature of their nation and its political ambitions, and Uyghur exiles from Turkey even came on occasion to partake in this process (see Roberts 2007). In the context of the dissolution of the Soviet Union in 1991, this situation created an internal contradiction in China's engagement with the newly independent states of Central Asia. On the one hand, the PRC encouraged Uyghurs with linguistic, cultural and familial connections in the region to jump-start cross-border trade and cultural engagement in former Soviet markets that held great promise for China's rapidly growing export-oriented economy (Roberts 2004). On the other hand, the security apparatus of the state was concerned about China's Uyghurs being influenced by Uyghur exiles known to harbour a desire for independent statehood (Roberts 2004).

The PRC dealt with this contradiction through the 'Shanghai Five', a series of diplomatic meetings during the 1990s between the PRC and the former Soviet states bordering on China (Russia, Kazakhstan, Kyrgyzstan and Tajikistan). In these meetings, the Chinese government placed increased pressure on the Central Asian states, and especially Kazakhstan, to dismantle any political space for Uyghurs that had been established in their countries (see Iwashita 2004). While Kazakhstan initially appeared to allow Uyghur political activism to be practised freely in the country, apparently as a means of establishing leverage with the PRC on border demarcation negotiations, once those negotiations had been mostly resolved, it followed through on virtually all of Beijing's requests to close off this space (Roberts 2004). Kyrgyzstan, the home of the region's second-largest Uyghur diaspora, would subsequently follow suit and take similar actions.

In the data collected for the UHRP report on transnational repression targeting Uyghurs, China's security co-ordination with Kazakhstan and Kyrgyzstan at this time is visible. For 1998–2000, the report documents two extraditions from Kazakhstan to China that include a total of ten Uyghurs, one forced return from Kyrgyzstan to China including two Uyghurs, and the mysterious death of one Kazakhstani Uyghur activist who had left China in the 1960s (see Oxus 2021).[3] However, having conducted fieldwork among Uyghurs of Central Asia at this time, I can attest that the actions of the Kazakhstan and Kyrgyzstan states against Uyghurs at the end of the 1990s were much more expansive than these extraditions indicate. Between 1998 and 2000, both Kazakhstan and Kyrgyzstan began limiting the ability of local Uyghur activists to publicly carry out advocacy and arrested numerous Uyghurs under murky circumstances (see Millward 2004). Others who had come from China to Kazakhstan and Kyrgyzstan used their networks among local Uyghurs at this time to find ways to leave the region and seek refuge in the European Union, the US or Turkey. The result of these actions was the dismantling of what had become a relatively free transnational space for Uyghurs to organise around the aspirations of their nation. By the end of the 1990s, the former Soviet states of Central Asia were no longer safe refuges for Uyghurs fleeing China. The PRC had established strong security co-operation with all these states for this express purpose, a relationship which was formalised in 2001 with the founding of the Shanghai Cooperation Organization (SCO).

At the same time, the PRC also established security co-operation with Afghanistan and Pakistan to neutralise any Uyghur political activity in those countries. Fewer Uyghurs travelled to these countries than to Central Asia, but there was a steady flow of Uyghurs to Pakistan either to conduct trade or

---

[3] In the data set, one of the extraditions is wrongly identified as having been from Kazakhstan, but the source cited clearly discusses Kyrgyzstan.

to study in the country's religious schools throughout the 1990s. While the PRC initially encouraged Uyghurs to study in other Muslim countries in the early 1990s (see Gladney 1992), by the later 1990s the state began suspecting Uyghurs exposed to religious ideas outside China of disloyalty to the state. It was in this context that the PRC would request Pakistan extradite fourteen Uyghur religious students in 1997 to China, where they were subsequently executed on charges of separatism (UHRP 2021b: 40–1). In the years that followed, Pakistan would continue to monitor and limit the activities of Uyghurs in the country, closing down guesthouses frequented by Uyghur traders and students and evicting hundreds from their shelter (UHRP 2021b: 41). Far fewer Uyghurs travelled to Afghanistan in the 1990s than to Pakistan, but some did come to the country via Pakistan. The PRC engaged the Taliban in 1998–9 to ensure that no Uyghurs could organise militant groups in Afghanistan from which to attack China, an agreement that the Taliban appears to have honoured in exchange for economic assistance (Roberts 2020: 108–9). Yitzhak Shichor suggests that, as part of those agreements, the Taliban handed over thirteen Uyghurs who had been in Afghanistan to Chinese authorities (Shichor 2004: 158). Additionally, the Taliban immobilised a small group of Uyghur would-be militants in the country to ensure they could pose no threat to the PRC (see Roberts 2020: 108–10).

If the PRC's transnational repression of Uyghurs in the 1990s focused on those Uyghurs it viewed as a political threat to the status quo inside China, it also employed a liberal definition of what constituted a 'threat'. Some who were sought for extradition had been identified as subversive already while in China where they had previously served prison time, but others, like the Uyghur students studying religion in Pakistan, were extradited because Chinese authorities viewed them as potentially subversive due to their religiosity. Even if the PRC cast a wide net in pursuing Uyghurs abroad in the 1990s, it was limited in its geographic reach to those countries where it had substantial influence and stifled international criticism. However, the Chinese state soon found ways to address both of these obstacles to their transnational repression of Uyghurs.

The Global War on Terror, China's Growing Global Influence and Uyghur Transnational Repression during the 2000s

There were two factors that led to an increase in the transnational repression of Uyghurs in the early 2000s – the US-led Global War on Terror (GWOT) and China's growing influence around the world through its outsized role in the global economy. As pointed out by Marcus Michaelsen in this volume, the US declaration of the GWOT provided, in the form of 'counterterrorism cooperation', a justification for states around the world to employ transnational repression against its citizens abroad. The PRC quickly used this justification to target Uyghurs outside China. At the same time, China's critical role in the global economy gave the PRC increased leverage with states to facilitate its repression of Uyghurs abroad, especially if the states had close economic ties to China.

The PRC quickly exploited the GWOT after its declaration in late 2001, and it immediately sought to characterise its concerns with Uyghurs abroad as a matter of 'counterterrorism' (see Roberts 2020: 69–75). Within months of the 9/11 attacks on the US, the PRC's Mission to the United Nations (UN) issued a paper suggesting that some forty Uyghur diaspora organisations around the world were part of a terrorist network funded by Osama bin Laden and al-Qaeda (PMUNPRC 2001). While the international community did not find China's claims about a substantial Uyghur 'terrorist threat' to be credible, this sentiment dramatically changed in August 2002, when the US government suddenly recognised one previously unknown Uyghur militant group, allegedly known as the Eastern Turkistan Islamic Movement (ETIM), as a 'terrorist' organisation linked to al-Qaeda and the Taliban (see Federal Register 2002) and a month later joined the PRC and Kyrgyzstan to convince the UN Security Council to recognise ETIM on the UN 'Consolidated list of Terrorist Groups' (Reeker 2002). Recently, then-US Deputy Assistant Secretary of State for South and Central Asian Affairs, Richard Boucher, stated that the US initially resisted PRC requests to recognise Uyghurs as a 'terrorist threat', given the paucity of evidence of such a threat, but the US finally recognised ETIM, in Boucher's words, 'to help gain China's support for invading Iraq' (Magnier 2021). While the US apparently believed there was no harm in recognising a marginal Uyghur group in Afghanistan as a 'terrorist organisation', the decision to do so would have grave consequences for the transnational repression of Uyghurs during the twenty-first century.

At the same time, given its experience with the Central Asian states, Pakistan and Afghanistan during the 1990s, China was becoming more comfortable in translating its global economic power into influence over other countries to assist in repressing Uyghur exiles. While China had yet to announce the Belt and Road Initiative (BRI) in the early 2000s, its investments throughout countries in Asia and in the Middle East already allowed the PRC to put more pressure on states to extradite Uyghurs, particularly when framed as 'counter-terrorism cooperation'. Between 2001 and 2004, the PRC continued its extra-ditions from Kazakhstan, Kyrgyzstan and Pakistan, from which there were at least twenty-one known cases of Uyghurs being sent back to China (Oxus Society 2021). Additionally, the PRC appears to have pressured the Nepal govern-ment to extradite at least three Uyghurs in 2002, two of which had already been awarded refugee status by the UNHCR and were awaiting settlement in a third country (Amnesty 2004: 19–23). In doing so, Nepal became the first country outside Central Asia, Pakistan or Afghanistan to extradite Uyghurs to China, but more would follow in the coming years as the PRC used the GWOT to pursue politically active Uyghurs in other countries where it had leverage.

To do so, the PRC, like many other countries at the time, began issuing lists of 'terrorists' to justify its pursuit of specific Uyghurs abroad. While China's first list of 'terrorists' released in December 2003 named a handful of people allegedly associated with the shadowy group in Afghanistan that had become known internationally as ETIM, it also included others who were active in peaceful and secular advocacy groups in Turkey and Europe, claiming that these people were also associated with ETIM (Xinhua 2003). This list was especially debilitating for the present President of the World Uyghur Con-gress, Dolqun Isa, who at the time led the World Uyghur Youth Congress. Although he was already flagged with an Interpol 'Red Notice' in 1999, the PRC's new accusations that he was associated with the internationally listed ETIM 'terrorist' organisation caused increased international travel problems for Isa, who was subsequently denied entry to the US until getting his 'Red Notice' removed only in 2018 (Reuters 2018).

In addition to its internationally publicised 'terrorist lists', the PRC appar-ently provided discrete lists of alleged 'terrorists' to different countries at this time to request the deportation of Uyghur exiles. In 2004, for example, Syria deported a Uyghur poet who had lived in the country for fifteen years and was married to a Syrian woman because he was allegedly associated with 'terrorist' groups (RFA 2004). The poet, Ahmadjan Osman, was able to leave for Turkey rather than be extradited to China, and he eventually received refugee status in Canada, but his deportation represented the first time that a country outside South and Central Asia had acted against a Uyghur at Beijing's request. If these machinations by the Chinese state to repress Uyghurs abroad were expanding in geographic reach with the assistance of the GWOT, the actions taken on Beijing's behalf were also becoming more brazen.

Kazakhstan and Kyrgyzstan remained discreet in their extradition of Uyghurs to China at this time, but Uzbekistan more openly did so. Most notably, Uzbekistan abducted a Uyghur who was a Canadian citizen at Beijing's request in 2006 and extradited him to China, where he was given a life prison term (Desai 2021). Additionally, Uzbekistan would extradite a prominent Uyghur businessman the following year to China, and it began jailing many of its local Uyghur activists (Isa 2007). At the same time, the PRC was applying pressure on Uyghur exile activists around the world by threatening to punish relatives remaining in China. In 2006, for example, the Chinese government arrested three of the children of Rabiya Kadeer, then President of the World Uyghur Congress, in order to silence her advocacy in the US (UCA 2006).

Most of these actions continued to elicit criticism from the international community, but the GWOT softened the impact of such criticism as the PRC framed its requests for extraditions or detention as 'counterterrorism' efforts. However, it is notable that between 2001 and 2008, there was little evidence that there were any active Uyghur-led 'terrorist organisations' or militant groups of any kind that were threatening China. There had been very little violence in the Uyghur region of China during this time, and there was no credible evidence of Uyghurs being involved in international 'terrorist networks'. The alleged leader of ETIM had been killed by the Pakistani military in December 2003, after which nothing had been heard of the organisation (BBC 2003). Furthermore, while the US was holding twenty-two Uyghurs, who had been apprehended in Afghanistan and Pakistan, in Guantanamo Bay Detention Center at this time, US military officials were already questioning whether these people had anything to do with international terrorism, having released six of them to Albania in 2006 and considering ways to release others without sending them back to the PRC (BBC 2006). Given these events, many doubted the veracity of the PRC's claims about the alleged Uyghur 'terrorist threat', which had been used to justify China's transnational repression of Uyghurs.

However, a cascade of events in 2008–9 would alter this situation substantially. The first event was the March 2008 Internet broadcast of a video threatening to attack the Beijing Olympics made by a previously unknown Uyghur militant group calling itself the 'Turkistan Islamic Party' (TIP) (see TIP 2008a). If there were no disruptions of the Games as threatened in TIP's videos, the videos made life much more difficult for Uyghurs in the Olympics's aftermath, while also lending more credibility internationally to PRC claims of a Uyghur 'terrorist threat'. Subsequently, 'counterterrorism' sweeps throughout the Uyghur region added to the tensions already being cultivated by top-down state-led development efforts that were bringing more Han settlers to the area. These tensions would bubble over during the summer after the Olympics when mass ethnic riots broke out in the capital city of the Uyghur region, Urumqi, in July 2009.

The details about these riots, which started when security forces clashed with peaceful protesters, have been analysed elsewhere in great depth (Ryono and Galway 2015). While the violence that broke out was obviously spontaneous and involved both Uyghur-on-Han violence and vigilante Han-on-Uyghur attacks, the state suggested that it had been a premeditated act of Uyghur-led 'terrorism' planned by Uyghur exiles in the US (Xinhua 2009). This incident, especially in the context of the TIP video threatening the Olympics a year earlier, was a turning point in the PRC's treatment of Uyghurs. As scholar Thomas Cliff, who was conducting fieldwork in the Uyghur region at the time, has suggested, the riots took on a significance for many Chinese not unlike 9/11 did for the US, leading to an ethnically profiled demonisation of all Uyghurs (Cliff 2012). I have argued that it was at this time that the PRC's biopolitics vis-à-vis the Uyghurs first became racialised to identify the Uyghur people and their cultural attributes as an existential threat to China's stability, but it remained primarily focused on rural religious Uyghurs in the Uyghur-majority southern areas of the XUAR (see Roberts 2018, 2020).

Following the July 2009 riots, the government shut down communications with the outside world in the region for a year while it established security sweeps, especially in the Uyghur-majority south, for Uyghurs accused of being involved in the violence (Ryono and Galway 2015). In the face of this repression, thousands of rural Uyghurs fled the country via human-trafficking networks through Southeast Asia between 2009 and 2014, with the intention of reaching Turkey (see WUC 2016). Under the pretence that these Uyghurs were fleeing China to join 'terrorist' groups, the PRC would successfully get various Southeast Asian countries to extradite Uyghurs from their countries over the next several years, leading to sixty-five extraditions from Cambodia, Laos, Myanmar, Thailand, Malaysia and Vietnam combined between 2009 and 2012 (Oxus Society 2021). In combination with these extraditions, the PRC also stepped up its pressure on Uyghur activists in exile, particularly those associated with the WUC and Rabiya Kadeer, whom the PRC blamed for the Urumqi riots. Uyghurs from China were sent into exile communities to infiltrate and collect intelligence on these communities' activists for the PRC, leading to at least two arrests of Uyghurs on espionage charges in Sweden and Germany respectively (cf. RFA 2010; DW 2021).

In addition to motivating this mass exodus of Uyghurs from China via Southeast Asia, the heavy-handed security tactics employed in the Uyghur-majority southern part of the XUAR only cultivated more violent resistance from Uyghurs, resulting in what I have called a cycle of 'violent repression–resistance–repression' that would steadily escalate during the five years following the Urumqi riots (Roberts 2020: 165–70). By late 2013 and early 2014, these tensions had escalated enough to facilitate a self-fulfilling prophecy where Uyghurs allegedly carried out acts of violence that looked much more like 'terrorism' than anything else perpetrated by Uyghurs inside China before (see Roberts 2020: 161–98).

Although there is no evidence that this violence was attributable to an organised 'terrorist' group, the PRC continued to suggest it was provoked by Uyghurs' links with 'terrorist groups' abroad. As a result, the PRC started a massive campaign in 2014 to prevent such influences and to 're-educate' those who may have already been influenced. This campaign, called 'The People's War on Terror', again particularly targeted religious Uyghurs, leaving most of the more secular Uyghurs unscathed. However, it would lay the groundwork for a more expansive campaign that started in 2017 and targeted all Uyghurs. During 'The People's War on Terror', the PRC would beta-test methods of 're-education' that were subsequently unleashed on large swaths of the Uyghur population in mass internment camps, it laid the groundwork for the legal justification to target virtually all religious beliefs as signs of 'extremism', and it started constructing the IJOP database and omnipresent surveillance that has been used since 2017 as a means of mass control and repression in the region (see Roberts 2020: 201–4).

Cultural Genocide and Total Control, 2017–Present

In 2017 the PRC's repression of Uyghurs both at home and abroad underwent another transformation that solidified a purely racialised biopolitics vis-à-vis Uyghurs. Suddenly, Xi Jinping's government placed all Uyghurs and related Turkic Muslims under suspicion, starting in 2017 with the arrest of Uyghur government functionaries who were accused of being 'two-faced' and deliberately supporting the three evils of 'separatism, terrorism, and extremism' inside China (Wen 2018). This campaign quickly extended to virtually all levels of society, with an emphasis on those with contacts abroad, employing a network of newly established mass internment camps to 're-educate' those thought to be prone to dissent and imprisoning those it accused of actual dissent. The state would use its existing ubiquitous surveillance system and the related IJOP database, that had been in development since 2014, to determine who should be 're-educated' in internment camps, who should be sent to prison and who should be allowed to continue their lives outside penal institutions (Leibold 2020). These actions laid the basis for an unprecedented police state inside the Uyghur region that sought to establish complete control over the population based on an idea of 'preventative repression' that targeted not only those who were viewed as subversive, but also those who might become so (see Greitens, Lee and Yazici 2020). This campaign of 'preventative repression' would inevitably also extend abroad, given the PRC's persistent perception of Uyghurs as an 'inside/outside' threat.

The Chinese state presumed any Uyghur with contacts or family members abroad to be a potential source of subversion, and my Uyghur exile acquaintances began telling me that they had been told by family inside China to cease communications with them. The state also actively began asking Uyghurs abroad, including students and especially those in Muslim countries, to return to China (Feng 2017). Some of these students came home on their own accord and were promptly either imprisoned or sent to 're-education' camps (see Special Correspondent 2018), but others defied state orders. As a result, the PRC began requesting their extradition, convincing Egypt, Saudi Arabia and Kyrgyzstan to extradite a total of over a hundred Uyghurs and related peoples, primarily students, between 2016 and 2018 (see Oxus Society 2021).

In this context, the PRC's pressure on Uyghur exiles around the world has increased substantially. In Kazakhstan, those ethnic Uyghurs and Kazakhs who somehow managed to escape China after having spent time in 're-education' camps either have faced extradition or have been forced to leave the country once their stories appeared in international media. In Turkey, the Uyghur exile population, which includes an estimated 30,000 Uyghurs who fled China since 2009, has been constantly worried about its fate since 2017. While the Turkish government has been one of the few Muslim governments globally to speak out against the PRC's treatment of Uyghurs, it has not offered most of these recently arrived Uyghurs either citizenship or refugee status, forcing them to annually apply for residency permits using their Chinese passports. Furthermore, the PRC has negotiated an extradition treaty with Turkey and has tried to persuade the Turkish public that Uyghurs are dangerous 'terrorists' (Butler 2021; Klimes 2020). Although Turkey has yet to fully ratify the extradition treaty as of the writing of this chapter (Al Jazeera 2021), since 2017 there have been some quiet extraditions of Uyghurs from Turkey via Tajikistan, and the state has detained some Uyghurs in the country (Ullah 2020; Kakissis 2020).

As a result, over the past several years there have been numerous cases of Uyghurs leaving Turkey to escape this uncertainty. While most were able to eventually find safe refuge in a European country, several found themselves stuck in third countries where they had been detained at Beijing's behest, whether via formal mechanisms like Interpol 'red notices' or through diplomatic requests to the country in question. This includes Uyghurs who, after leaving Turkey, were detained for an extended period in Serbia (Kashgary 2021), Morocco (AP 2021) and Montenegro (Uighurian 2021). A similar situation was recently experienced by an ethnic Kazakh from China fleeing Kazakhstan to Ukraine. After receiving threats from Chinese authorities in Ukraine, he tried to cross into Slovakia, where he was deported back to Ukraine and detained (Lakhanuly 2021). While he was finally released under pressure from local and international activists, it is likely that Ukraine faced substantial pressure from China not to do so.

In the Americas, Australia and most of Europe, exiles from the Uyghur region of the PRC have not feared extradition to China since 2017, but they are continually monitored and harassed by Chinese security organs using a variety of methods (UHRP 2021c: 18–20). This includes the phone calls discussed at this chapter's outset, but it has also included calls or electronic messages from relatives in China to their exiled family members urging them not to speak out about what is happening in the Uyghur region of the PRC. A recent report from UHRP suggests that the Chinese state also appears to be targeting Uyghurs and related peoples abroad through cyber surveillance using a variety of malware that allows state agents access to the victims' digital communications (UHRP 2021c: 10–16). While these tactics have not necessarily succeeded in silencing Uyghurs abroad and may even encourage more activism among those Uyghurs living in liberal democracies (see UHRP 2021c: 10–14), they have inflicted severe psychological harm and have created an environment of intense fear and guilt about the fate of relatives (see Qin and Wee 2021).

In this context, it is useful to ask a fundamental question: why is the PRC collecting substantial personal information on Uyghur exiles around the world, particularly about those who are not political? If the PRC is indeed building a database of Uyghur exiles akin to the IJOP that tracks Uyghurs inside China, it may be a mechanism of 'preventative repression', which can allow the state to mobilise tactics of transnational repression against them as soon as they are perceived as a direct threat to China. Such 'preventative repression' of exiles mirrors the tactics of the PRC vis-à-vis Uyghurs within its own borders. It is a decisively racialised form of biopolitics that identifies all Uyghurs and related peoples, both inside and outside the PRC, as an existential threat to Chinese society, which, in Foucault's words, must be 'banished, excluded, and repressed' by the state. The UHRP has succinctly summed this up by noting that 'mass targeting based on ethnicity and culture has become the norm for Chinese security services' in its transnational repression of Uyghurs (UHRP 2021c: 5). For Uyghur exiles, it feels as if the PRC is hunting them down at a time when their friends and family inside China are being erased.

Conclusion

The PRC's transnational repression of Uyghurs and related peoples shares many similarities with other states' efforts to control the activism of exiles from their country living abroad. Like other examples of state-led transnational repression documented in this volume, the Chinese regime uses international mechanisms to facilitate extraditions that are followed by political show trials at home, surveillance technology to track exiles' activities, and intimidation tactics to silence these exiles' criticism and activism regarding political issues in their countries of origin. However, there are two particularly unique aspects to the PRC's transnational repression of Uyghurs and other Turkic Muslims that appear unprecedented. One aspect is the expansive geographic reach of the PRC's transnational repression, which is a product of China's growing global influence as the second-largest economy in the world at a time when globalisation has fostered an unprecedented economic interdependence between countries. This aspect of the PRC's transnational repression is likely to remain unique to China, given that it cannot easily be replicated by other authoritarian states that wield far less global influence. The second notable aspect of the PRC's transnational repression of Uyghurs, while grounded in the PRC's history of structural racism, is one that could serve as a dangerous precedent to be replicated by other states, especially given the growth of populist nationalism globally. This is its racialisation, its targeting of an entire ethnic group by virtue of their identity and culture.

Such a form of transnational repression is primarily limited to states involved in genocidal actions at home, but it also brings these genocidal actions into the transnational realm, which makes them more difficult for other states to ignore without being themselves complicit. Arguably, the PRC is engaging in such an expansive campaign of transnational repression targeting Uyghurs and related peoples because it is concerned that these exiles may speak out about what is happening to relatives and friends inside China. However, the state's systematic erasure of Uyghur identity inside China means that all exiles who have fled their home country in the last decade are impacted by this campaign and could potentially bring international attention to it. This causes the PRC to cast an incredibly wide net in its transnational repression of Uyghurs that eventually could lead to a campaign to erase the culture and identity of Uyghurs both at home and abroad, raising the possibility of a transnational genocide as the logical conclusion of racialised transnational repression.

References

Al Jazeera. 2021. 'Turkey raises Uyghur issue with China as hundreds protest'. *Al Jazeera*, 25 March.

Amnesty International. 2021. *Amnesty International Report 2020/21: The State of The World's Human Rights Situation*. London, UK.

——. 2004. *Uighurs Fleeing Persecution as China Wages its 'War on Terror'*. London, UK.

——. 2002. *China's Anti-terrorism Legislation and Repression in the Xinjiang Uyghur Autonomous Region*. London, UK.

——. 1999. *People's Republic of China: Gross Human Rights Violations in the Xinjiang Uighur Autonomous Region*. New York, NY.

Associated Press (AP). 2021. 'Morocco authorities arrest Uyghur activist at China's request'. *The Guardian*, 27 July.

——. 2008. 'China releases blacklist in Olympics terror plot'. *Associated Press*, 22 October.

Basu, Z. 2021. 'Lithuanian parliament becomes latest to recognize Uyghur genocide'. *Axios*, 20 May.

British Broadcasting Corporation (BBC). 2006. 'Albania takes Guantanamo Uighurs'. BBC, 6 May.

——. 2003. 'Chinese militant "shot dead"'. BBC, 23 December.

Butler, D. 2021. 'Looming China extradition deal worries Uyghurs in Turkey'. Reuters, 8 March.

Cliff, T. 2012. 'The partnership of stability in Xinjiang: State-society interactions following the July 2009 unrest'. *The China Journal* 68: 79–105.

Desai, D. 2021. 'Five things to know about the forgotten Canadian still behind bars in China'. *National Post*, 27 September.

Deutsche Well (DW). 2021. 'Germany charges man with spying for China'. *Deutsche Welle*, 7 June.

Federal Register. 2002. 'Determination Pursuant to Section 1(b) of Executive Order 13224 Relating to the Eastern Turkistan Islamic Movement (ETIM)' [FR Doc. 02–22737], *Federal Register*, 63:173 (19 August), p. 57054.

Feng, E. 2017. 'China targets Muslim Uyghurs studying abroad'. *Financial Times*, 1 August.

Foucault, M. 1997. *'Society Must Be Defended': Lectures at the College De France, 1975–76*. New York: Picador Press.

Grietens, S. C., Lee, M. and Yazici, E. 2020. *Understanding China's 'Preventative Repression' in Xinjiang*. Brookings Institution, Washington, DC, 4 March.

Human Rights Watch (HRW). 2019. *China's Algorithms of Repression: Reverse Engineering a Xinjiang Police Mass Surveillance App*. New York, NY/Washington, DC.

Isa, D. 2007. 'Uyghur situation in Central Asian States (in Kazakhstan, Kyrgyzstan, and Uzbekistan): Statement by Dolqun Isa, World Uyghur Congress'. OSCE Human Dimension Implementation Meeting, 25 September.

Iwashita, A. 2004. 'The Shanghai Cooperation Organization and its implications for Eurasian Security: A new dimension of "partnership" after the post-Cold War period'. In: Iwashita, A. and Tabata, S. (eds), *Slavic Eurasia's Integration into the World Economy and Community.* Sapporo, Japan: Slavic Research Center, Hokkaido University.

Kakissis, J. 2020. '"I thought it would be safe": Uighurs in Turkey now fear China's long arm'. *National Public Radio*, 13 March.

Karklins, R.1975. 'The Uighurs between China and the USSR'. *Canadian Slavonic Papers* 17(2–3): 354–5.

Kashgary, J. 2021. '"Nobody can say it is not a great tragedy": Sinologist on Uyghur poet fleeing Xinjiang for France'. *Radio Free Asia*, 15 March.

Kaufman, A. A. 2010. 'The "Century of Humiliation," then and now: Chinese perceptions of the international order'. *Pacific Focus: Inha Journal of International Studies* 25(1), April. Klimes, O. 2020. 'China's propaganda and united front work in Turkey: Actors and content'. *Monde Chinois* 62: 44–71.

Leibold, J. 2020. 'Surveillance in China's Xinjiang region: Ethnic sorting, coercion, and inducement'. *Journal of Contemporary China* 29 (121).

Magnier, M. 2021. '9/11, 20 years later: How China used the attacks to its strategic advantage'. *South China Morning Post*, 2 September.

Millward, J. 2004. *Violent Separatism in Xinjiang: A Critical Assessment.* East-West Center. *Policy Studies*, No. 6. Washington, DC.

Oxus Society for Central Asian Affairs. 2021. *Dataset of Transnational Repression Against Uyghurs.* Washington, DC. https://oxussociety.org/viz/transnational-repression/ (accessed 28 October 2021).

Permanent Mission of the People's Republic of China to the United Nations (PMPR-CUN). 2001. *Terrorist Activities Perpetrated by 'Eastern Turkistan' Organizations and Their Links with Osama bin Laden and the Taliban.* New York, NY, 29 November.

Putz, C. 2020. '2020 Edition: Which countries are for or against China's Xinjiang policies'. *The Diplomat*, 9 October.

Qin, A. and Wee, S.-L. 2021. '"A daily cloud of suffering": A crackdown in China is felt abroad'. *The New York Times*, 6 November.

Radio Free Asia. 2010. 'Sweden: Uyghur sentenced for spying'. *Radio Free Asia*, 11 February.

——. 2004. 'Uyghur poet expelled by Syria seeks refugee status'. *Radio Free Asia*, 9 March.

Reeker, P. T. 2002. 'Designation of the Eastern Turkistan Islamic Movement under UNSC Resolutions 1267 and 1390'. *Homeland Security Digital Library*, 11 September.

Reuters (2018). 'Interpol lifts wanted alert for exiled Uygur leader, angering China'. Reuters, 24 February.

Roberts, S. R. 2020. *The War on the Uyghurs: China's Internal Campaign Against a Muslim Minority*. Princeton, NJ: Princeton University Press.

——. 2018. 'The biopolitics of China's "war on terror" and the exclusion of the Uyghurs'. *Critical Asian Studies* 50(2): 232–58.

——. 2007. "Daily negotiations of Islam in Central Asia: Practicing religion in the Uyghur Neighborhood of *Zarya Vostoka* in Almaty, Kazakhstan'. In: Zanca, R. and Sahadeo, J. (eds), *Everyday Life in Central Asia, Past and Present*. Bloomington: University of Indiana Press.

——. 2004. 'A land of borderlands: Implications of Xinjiang's trans-border interactions'. In: Starr, S. F. (ed.), *Xinjiang: China's Muslim Borderlands*. New York: M. E. Sharpe.

——. 1998. 'The Uyghurs of the Kazakstan borderlands: Migration and the nation'. *Nationalities Papers* 26(3): 511–30.

Ryono, A. and Galway. M. 2015. 'Xinjiang under China: Reflections on the multiple dimensions of the 2009 Urumqi uprising'. *Asian Ethnicity* 16(2): 235–55.

Shichor, Y. 2004. 'The great wall of steel: Military and strategy in Xinjiang'. In: Starr, S. F. (ed.), *Xinjiang: China's Muslim Borderlands*. New York: M. E. Sharpe.

Special Correspondent. 2018. 'A summer vacation in China's Muslim gulags'. *Foreign Policy*, 28 February.

State Council Office of Information of the People's Republic of China (SCOIPRC). 2009. *Development and Progress in Xinjiang*. Beijing, PRC, October.

——. 2002.'*East Turkistan' Terrorist Forces Cannot Get Away with Impunity*. Beijing, PRC, January.

Turkistan Islamic Party (TIP). 2008. [Untitled] (initial video threatening the Olympics).

Uighurian. 2021. 'Montenegro, European country, holds Uyghur refugee for year, now hands him to Interpol interrogation'. *Uyghur Times*, 5 November.

Ullah, A. 2020. 'Turkey accused of deporting Uighurs back to China via third countries'. *Middle East Eye*, 27 July.

Uyghur Canadian Association (UCA). 2006. *UCA Press Release on Recent Arrest of Ms. Rabiya Kadeer Children*. Toronto, 17 June.

Uyghur Human Rights Project (UHRP) 2021a. *No Place Left to Run: China's Transnational Repression of Uyghurs*. Washington, DC.

——. 2021b. *Nets Cast from the Earth to the Sky: China's Hunt for Pakistan's Uyghurs*. Washington, DC.

——. 2021c. '*Your Family Will Suffer': How China is Hacking, Surveilling, and Intimidating Uyghurs in Liberal Democracies*. Washington, DC.

Wen, P. 2017. 'Fellow Uighurs should beware of "two-faced" people in separatism fight, official says'. Reuters, 10 April.

World Uyghur Congress (WUC). 2016. *Seeking A Place to Breathe Freely.* Washington, DC, 2 June.

Xinhua. 2009. 'Evidence shows Rebiya Kadeer behind Urumqi riot: Chinese gov't'. *Xinhua*, 9 July.

——. 2003. 'China seeks cooperation worldwide to fight "East Turkistan" terrorists'. *Xinhua*, 15 December.

7

HOW DIASPORAS CONTRIBUTE TO AUTHORITARIAN GOVERNANCE: THE CASE OF ERITREA

Nicole Hirt and Abdulkader Saleh Mohammad

Introduction

Eritrea is an autocratic state located in the Horn of Africa and has been governed by its unelected president, Isaias Afewerki, since 1991. He came to power as the leader of the Eritrean People's Liberation Front (EPLF), which renamed itself the People's Front for Democracy and Justice (PFDJ) in 1994. At the time of this writing, the PFDJ is the country's only legal party. Often referred to as the North Korea of eastern Africa, Eritrea has no implemented constitution, no parliament, no independent media and the rule of law is absent. Two decades ago, the government introduced an open-ended national service that amounts to forced labour; in addition to war and poverty, these conditions have driven hundreds of thousands of Eritreans out of the country (Hirt and Mohammad 2013; Kibreab 2018).

Despite harsh restrictions on leaving the country legally, the people of Eritrea are not simply caged within the country's borders; rather, they also constitute a transnational community (Bernal 2014). Diasporas are often forged through crises that include violence, political persecution and poverty, and the Eritrean case has been no exception. During the armed nationalist struggle from 1961 to 1991, roughly one million Eritreans fled the atrocities of war with Ethiopia, and the majority of them have remained in exile since that time. The government does not publish statistical data about population numbers, but today an estimated four million people live inside the country. Together with their offspring, Eritreans abroad make up approximately one-third to one-half of the Eritrean nation, although it is impossible to give exact numbers (Hirt and Mohammad 2018: 234). However, we know that their impact on developments inside their home country is significant (Hirt and Mohammad 2021). Informal remittance flows are mainly handled through clandestine, informal money transfers (known as the *hawala* system), and financial donations by diaspora Eritreans to the EPLF contributed to the military victory against Ethiopia in 1991. After de facto independence in 1991, the government formalised a 2 per cent tax, payable on all kinds of incomes to the diaspora.

At the same time, the Eritrean government uses transnational repression, including methods of legitimisation, coercion and oppression (Gerschewski 2013), to control its populations and their descendants abroad (Hirt and Mohammad 2018a; Hirt 2021). On the one hand, many diaspora members believe in the regime's legitimacy and trust the narrative that their homeland is a nation threatened by various conspiracies, including by traitors and outlaws within exile communities (see the classification of Glasius in Chapter 1 of this volume). However, diaspora members are also coerced into supporting the home-country regime through transnational repression. They are coerced into paying the 2 per cent tax owing to their dependence on consular services, such as passport extensions and the issuance of birth and marriage certificates. Many Eritreans abroad also fear that their relatives at home will be targeted by the regime if they do not show their support from abroad. This threat of proxy punishment (see also Chapter 2 by Tsourapas, this volume, and Moss 2016) against their families keeps many of them silent and avoidant of criticising the regime. Additionally, the government of Eritrea has established strong transnational institutions to procure remittances, control diaspora mobilisation and curtail diaspora 'voice' after 'exit' (Moss 2022). These include a network of diplomatic missions across the globe, the Young PFDJ, which serves as a youth organisation for the second-generation diaspora, and community organisations – the so-called *mahbere.koms* that exist in cities across the globe with sizeable diaspora communities.

In this chapter, we draw from prior studies (e.g. Hirt and Mohammad 2021) to explore the transnational character of the Eritrean state and the effects of transnational repression on the diaspora and the regime itself. We begin by reviewing Eritrea's short history as an independent nation, the dispersion of its national community and the state's coercive policies towards its citizens abroad. We then show that the Eritrean state perpetuates authoritarian rule across borders by both exploiting diaspora patriotism – also referred to as 'long-distance nationalism' (Anderson 1998; Glick Schiller and Fouron 2001) – and by coercing its diaspora into performing loyalty through transnational institutional engagement. These tactics keep the political opposition weak and exacerbate political rifts that keep the diaspora divided according to their subnational ethnic, regional and religious identities. Transnational repression also helps to explain why so many Eritreans abroad, and especially the refugees who fled forced conscription, resort to subnational forms of social organisation to contest the government's nationalist propaganda (Mohammad 2021). Despite growing political diversity in diaspora communities, remittances continue to facilitate the regime's survival, and the opposition abroad has yet to find a way to seriously challenge the leadership in Asmara. Accordingly, Eritrea serves as a contemporary case of state-perpetuated transnational repression that is highly effective in coercing a diaspora into stabilising and supporting a totalitarian-like regime in the homeland.

The Armed Struggle for Independence and the Seeds of Transnationalism

Eritrea was created as a transnational entity by the Eritrean liberation fronts even before its independence from Ethiopia. Once an Italian colony from 1889 to 1941, the territory was briefly administered by Great Britain and in 1952 it was federated with imperial Ethiopia. The Federation was controversial among the population, and especially among Muslims, who made up about half of all Eritreans supportive of national independence. The Muslim-dominated Eritrean Liberation Front (ELF) initiated an armed insurrection against Ethiopia in 1961, and when Haile Selassie annexed Eritrea in a breach of international law in 1962, the independence struggle gained momentum. This effort was also transnational; the ELF organised migrant workers in the Middle East in mass organisations to collect funds for the struggle (Thiollet 2011).

The overthrow of the Ethiopian emperor by a military council in 1974 led to the 'Red Terror' campaign, with the aim of eliminating political dissent against the new Marxist leadership. This meant that many Eritrea Christians lost privileges they had enjoyed during the Haile Selassie regime, and they increasingly joined the armed struggle. This led to political conflicts inside the ELF due to ideological differences, and in the mid-1970s the Eritrean People's Liberation Front (EPLF) emerged as a rival movement. The civil war between the ELF and the EPLF caused a mass flight from Eritrea. Refugees first settled primarily in Sudan, where almost 600,000 Eritreans were officially registered in 1994 (Kibreab 1996: 57). This excludes similar numbers of individuals and families who had managed to make an independent living in urban areas outside the refugee camps. According to World Bank estimates, at least one million Eritreans had fled their country at the time of independence in 1991 (World Bank 1994: ii), turning the Eritrean nation into a diasporic society even before the foundation of the independent state. While the majority of the refugees stayed in the region, Eritrean expatriate communities also emerged in Europe, the United States, Canada, Australia and on the Arabian Peninsula, and grew rapidly from the late 1970s onwards. Most of them received a secure residence status and eventually acquired the nationality of their host state, except for those living in the Middle East. Many of them dreamed to return to their home once independence was achieved.

The rival front of the EPLF was led by Isaias Afewerki, who evolved as the strongman of the struggle. After successfully ousting the ELF from the field in the early 1980s, he retained control of all major developments in Eritrea and retains control over independent Eritrea. The EPLF leadership deeply mistrusted the international community, albeit while also accepting aid from Western donors, especially since the devastating famine of the early 1980s (Duffield and Pendergast 1994). Yet, the EPLF only allowed sporadic visits of leftist Western supporters to liberated areas under its control and proclaimed a strict policy of self-reliance (Cliffe and Davidson 1988; Connell 1993; Pateman 1990). These visitors were a part of the Front's transnational strategy and worked to spread the EPLF's narrative of their struggle on a global scale.

One major pillar of the EPLF's tactic was organising the diaspora communities to support the struggle. EPLF followers abroad were organised in mass organisations for workers, and women and students, who were supposed to donate parts of their monthly income (Kibreab 2007; Radtke 2009: 124; Redeker Hepner 2008: 477). The EPLF regularly organised seminars and festivals for the purpose of political indoctrination and fundraising, the most prominent being the annual summer festival in Bologna, Italy. The front also ran restaurants, bars and cafés as an additional source of income. Since many Eritreans abroad suffered from survivor's guilt, many of them volunteered to support the EPLF financially. Oftentimes, they formed closed communities, regularly watching videos from the field that showed Ethiopian atrocities, and also romanticised life in the EPLF-controlled areas using other propaganda material (Conrad 2006: 257; Hirt 2021; Von Nolting 2002: 56). Through films, slogans and banners, the EPLF created its own national narrative and a strong martyr's cult. Thus, the political leadership managed to politicise Eritreans abroad, create strong support for its aims in the diaspora, and shape the transnational community's image of an emergent Eritrean nation (Conrad 2006: 257).

In addition to this 'soft' power, the regime also used close surveillance by government supporters who volunteered as spies and informants for the consulates and embassies to curb political dissent abroad. Methods such as 'character assassination' and social exclusion from the closed diaspora communities proved highly efficient in intimidating Eritreans in an emerging transnational field (Redeker Hepner 2005). Although there is no hard evidence of assassination, there were several cases of mysterious fatalities of former EPLF members who had criticised the leadership's policies in the late 1970s in West Germany (personal observation by the second author, who lived in Germany as a student at that time).

Accordingly, the roots of Eritrean-style authoritarian transnationalism date back to the early stages of the EPLF's armed struggle. The refugees of Eritrea's civil war, who would eventually form established diaspora communities, were a crucial component of the political leadership's economic, political and social survival strategy. Notably, the precondition for controlling the diaspora on a permanent basis was made possible by a strong transnational political surveillance network in all countries with significant diaspora communities.

Eritrea as a Transnational Society after Independence

In this volume, Glasius introduces a typology of the methods exercised by authoritarian governments to control their citizens by treating them either as patriots, clients, outlaws or traitors. What these labels have in common is that nationals are not regarded as citizens who are entitled to rights, but rather as subjects who are at the disposal of the government. The Eritrean regime's actions correspond to this scheme, with the exception that it has had little to offer its subjects in regard to clientelism. Instead, it built strong institution-alised transnational control mechanisms to exercise coercion and to spread legitimising narratives across borders. To this end, Afewerki – who renamed the triumphant EPLF party as the People's Front for Democracy and Justice (PFDJ) after independence – continued to use the diaspora as a tool for finan-cial support. It introduced a diaspora tax of 2 per cent, payable on all kinds of income, including social welfare benefits, and invested in a close network of diplomatic missions, including embassies and consulates, in places where Eritrean communities had been established during the time of the struggle. This included the United States, Canada, Australia, European countries and various states in the Middle East. Their tasks were to collect the 2 per cent tax; to issue a so-called 'clearance' after the annual payment had been received; to surveil diaspora communities; and to enforce top-down patriotism through political indoctrination.

While the transnational community was subjected to a common repertoire of transnational repression, the situation was much worse for those Eritrean migrants living and working in Middle Eastern countries due to their depen-dence on consular services and the lack of freedoms and civil liberties for residents more generally (Hirt and Mohammad 2018b, 2022). Most embas-sies maintained an unofficial network of spies that reported dissenting views, and their officials held regular seminars where Eritrean citizens abroad were informed about 'the objective situation in the country' as seen by the govern-ment. The regime also often collected additional funds to meet the so-called 'challenges' the young country faced (Hirt 2015a).

Initially, the EPLF enjoyed support due to its military victory over the Ethi-opian Derg Army and the liberation from Ethiopian suppression. However, most diaspora Eritreans in the Global North were reluctant to return to their home country, contrary to their earlier aspirations. Most of them had acquired a secure residence status abroad, employment, and education for their children in Western nations. Eritreans who were residing in Middle Eastern countries did not enjoy such privileges, but their economic situation was still better than the situation of Eritreans in their war-torn home country. The nascent state of Eritrea had no social services to offer, wages were extremely low, and the quality of education was poor. Therefore, even strong government supporters preferred to remain abroad and visit Eritrea during holidays only. Yet, most of them volunteered to pay the rehabilitation tax to foster development in the home country (Koser 2003: 114; Tecle and Goldring 2013: 8). Others were less eager to pay the tax because they lived in straitened financial conditions or because they opposed the government. This included a large group of ELF supporters who were often coerced to pay for services such as the renewal of passports, the issuance of birth or marriage certificates, and the right to own property; all of these needs were dependent on payment of a levy to the Eritrean government (Redeker Hepner 2008: 487; 2015: 196).

Four years after independence in 1991, a renewed war broke out between Eritrea and Ethiopia. Initially, the PFDJ had closely co-operated with the new ruling coalition in Ethiopia under the leadership of the Tigray People's Liberation Front (TPLF). The Tigrayans had been the EPLF's brothers in arms during the struggle, but even then, there had been confrontations between the movements (Young 1996). During the 1990s, there were economic rifts between both parties, especially since Eritrea had introduced its own currency, the Eritrean Nakfa, in 1997, and there were issues around the un-demarcated border. There were also personal rivalries between President Isaias and Ethiopia's Prime Minister Meles Zenawi. From 1998 to 2000, a devastating border war between Eritrea and Ethiopia evolved, with immense human and economic costs (Negash and Tronvoll 2001).

As observed by the authors, diaspora Eritreans were shocked about these unexpected developments and many feared for the survival of their nascent home state. Accordingly, even those who had been less engaged in transnational politics volunteered to make financial contributions. According to sources of the late Eritrean scholar Tekie Fessehatzion, the diaspora contributed $142.9 million to the war effort in the 1990s. The state remobilised partially dormant community organisations (*mahbere.koms*), and embassies and consulates actively mobilised and indoctrinated Eritreans abroad to promote long-distance nationalism and patriotic loyalty (Redeker Hepner 2008: 486, personal observation by authors). Eritrea also issued bonds purchased by the diaspora, which helped to raise an additional US$70 million (Tecle 2012: 32).

The war did not go well for Afewerki. When a ceasefire ended the military confrontation in summer 2000, large chunks of Eritrean territory had been temporarily occupied by Ethiopian forces, and the image of the invincible EPLF fighters had been eroded (Reid 2020). The political leadership's failure to avoid needless bloodshed had grave implications not only inside Eritrea, but also among the diaspora. Eritrean long-distance nationalism, which had been at its peak during the first two years of the war, gave way to profound confusion, and many disappointed Eritreans residing abroad retreated from homeland politics.

Open-ended National Service, Mass Exodus and Diasporisation

Back home, Afewerki moved to capture power for himself and his supporters. He crushed dissent in 2001 by arresting his challengers, a group of reformers known as the 'G-15', without due process. Protesting students and independent journalists met the same fate. Through repression and coercion, the president rendered the judiciary and the legislature as dysfunctional. By the early 2000s, Afewerki had successfully established himself as an unchallenged incumbent president-for-life, governing as an autocrat without a constitution or the rule of law (Ogbazghi 2011).

The Algiers Peace Agreement of December 2000 ended the military conflict between Ethiopia and Eritrea, but it did not resolve underlying problems between ruling elites or resentments over the war's outcomes. Border disputes related to the symbolic place of Badme, which had been awarded to Eritrea by the Ethiopia-Eritrea Boundary Commission, continued to fuel enmity between the two countries. Meanwhile, Afewerki moved to militarise Eritrea's society and economy. The establishment of mandatory, open-ended national service – a form of forced labour – produced a state of social anomie (Hirt and Mohammad 2013), plunging the country into economic decline and marking the beginning of a new countrywide crisis (Kibreab 2018; UNHRC 2015). In combination with the absence of the rule of law and the prevailing dire human rights situation, Eritrea is today perceived as an 'open-air prison', which hundreds of thousands of young Eritreans have fled from over the past two decades. Approximately 100,000 of them made it to Europe between 2012 and 2018. Others reside in the oil-producing countries of the Arabian Peninsula as migrants labouring under precarious conditions. Yet, the majority of the refugees remain stranded in camps in Sudan and Ethiopia, where they live under perilous conditions with little hope of a dignified future. Even after the peace agreement with Ethiopia was reached in 2018, Eritreans were still obliged to go through military training. No trade agreements were put in place, and the borders were closed after only a few months of opening in autumn 2019.

Since November 2020, the Eritrean army has been involved in the military conflict in Ethiopia's northern province of Tigray against the TPLF (Tronvoll 2022). As a consequence of the war in Tigray, some of the 170,000 Eritrean refugees who lived in camps in the region were either displaced, deported back to Eritrea, killed or disappeared (UNHCR 2021). Despite the ongoing mass exodus, the government considers emigration from Eritrea as illegal. Citizens are not permitted to leave the country without an exit visa, which is almost impossible for persons between the ages of 10 and 50 to obtain. Only some government officials are granted visas to travel abroad to attend meetings or for medical treatment, and many of them have used this opportunity to defect and apply for asylum.

In his first decade Afewerki's authoritarian government attempted to prevent people from fleeing the country by enforcing shoot-to-kill orders at the border. It also punished the relatives of those who had fled by fining them ERN 50,000 (approximately $3,330). Those who were unable to pay ended up in prison. However, these measures did little to stem the tide of exit out of Eritrea. High-ranking military officers and other individuals began to profit from the exodus through human trafficking, and army commanders smuggled Eritrean conscripts across borders for a fee (Hirt and Mohammad 2013). Nevertheless, those who cross the borders to neighbouring countries illegally continue to be branded as traitors and are subjected to persecution upon return. Eritrean refugees who need consular services from their home government are made to sign a so-called letter of regret, a document provided by Eritrean consular missions abroad. To obtain consular services, they are required to confess to having committed an offence by failing to fulfil their national obligation (i.e. military service), and they must declare their readiness to accept any appropriate punishment upon their potential return to Eritrea.

The government never admitted that the open-ended national service made Eritreans risk their lives to escape and find a better life elsewhere. It has claimed that foreign conspiracies and the asylum policies of European governments are the cause of exit. At the same time, the government seems to have come to the conclusion that the exodus of young potential government critics has provided a benefit by providing a pressure-release valve for political change at home. Furthermore, Eritreans abroad feel a moral obligation to support their kin at home through remittances. Remittances benefit the regime by providing social welfare to people at home, most of whom remain in poverty, thereby supplementing the state's lack of clientelism for its subjects (Hirt and Mohammad 2021).

Political Rifts in the Diaspora

During the years following the border war, the political clampdown on reformers and the establishment of indefinite national service at home, the ruling party also lost support in the diaspora. Disgruntled PFJD supporters in exile formed the Eritrean Democratic Party, and in 2005, exiles established the Eritrean Democratic Alliance as a coalition of different opposition parties, including various ELF splinter groups, PFDJ dissidents, and religious and ethnic minority-based parties. While Alliance members tried to find a common ground in their struggle against the dictatorship in Eritrea, they were not very successful in taking concrete steps for action. The last notable attempt to bring regime opponents together, under the name Eritrean Congress for Democratic Change, took place during a congress in Awassa, Ethiopia in 2011 (Mohammad and Tronvoll 2015: 3–4), and since then the opposition has remained fragmented.

Inside Eritrea today, all political debate has been strictly prohibited, leaving the diaspora as the only field for a political discourse. However, the political programmes of the existing parties and groups have remained vague and diffuse over the decades, and there has been very little work on a sustainable political and institutional framework for a post-Afewerki Eritrea. The transmission of divisive internal conflicts – what Moss (2022) calls 'conflict transmission' – from Eritrea to the diaspora dates back to the 1950s, when Eritreans enjoyed relative political freedom under the British administration (Trevaskis 1960). Some contested issues at home and abroad include, for example, the role of Arabic as the lingua franca of the nation, and the appropriate degree of decentralisation in governance, which is linked to the dominance of ethnic Tigrinya over ethnic minorities.

However, one of the main weaknesses of the fragmented Eritrean opposition in exile has been the absence of a culture of compromise and tolerance for diverging opinions. Currently, both the established diaspora communities and the refugee communities are characterised by deep splits and fragmentation, and there is mutual mistrust between them. As Mohammad reports in earlier work, 'Many refugees and even diaspora members feel lost in the existing patchwork of groups, networks, and organisations claiming to represent the interests and needs of Eritrean minorities abroad and serving as a tool to resist the Eritrean government from afar' (Mohammad 2020: 16).

Countless calls for unity have failed because the Eritrean diaspora is a mirror of the home society (Hoehne et al. 2011), with its frictions along ethnic, religious and regional lines. Attempts to find a minimal consensus beyond getting rid of President Isaias Afewerki have so far failed. Opposition leaders seem to carry out their activities as an end in themselves, rather than seriously attempting to form a powerful parallel government in exile with a political programme and the capacity to convince actors such as the European Union, the United States or the African Union that they could be a viable alternative to the current government.

Notably, there is also a large group of staunch government supporters in the diaspora. Long-distance nationalism is a typical trait of many diaspora communities, and this often includes anti-democratic attitudes (Lyons and Mandaville 2012) or double standards in relation to the country of origin and the new home country. Many of those who supported the EPLF during the armed struggle are still organised in diaspora communities. They participate in the community organisations *(mahbere.koms)* run by the government via diplomatic missions abroad. Loyalists also attend seminars and follow pro-government websites, such as the Ministry of Information's shabait.com, tesfanews.com or madote. com. Government proponents are active on social media channels and act to keep their followers in line.

To keep control over the second diaspora-born generation, the government founded the Young PFDJ in 2004 to spread the EPLF ideology through festivals and other meetings. These events also serve as fundraisers for the government. Many second-generation diasporans still have a strong Eritrean identity, although most of them acquired their host country's nationality. To sustain its legitimacy among these younger generations, the Eritrean government strives to keep the memory of the armed struggle alive. The armed struggle is presented as a heroic struggle, during which Eritrean fighters were victorious against all odds and performed miracles in their fight against the Ethiopian army with no international support in order to liberate their country from suppression. This image is attractive for young Eritreans in the diaspora, who feel like underprivileged second-class citizens in their homeland. The government's narrative is built around a strong martyr's cult, all while completely ignoring today's harsh reality inside the country (Hirt 2021). Many Eritreans abroad admire President Afewerki despite his gross human rights violations, because he symbolises the state, the nation and the victorious struggle. Criticising the president and his style of government would mean the betrayal not only of the fragile Eritrean nation, but also a betrayal of the martyrs who gave their lives for independent Eritrea (Conrad 2006; Hirt 2021).

The government has proved that it is able to mobilise thousands of its supporters abroad. This support base is ready to condemn any accusations against the Eritrean leadership in regard to human rights violations. For example, several thousand Eritreans demonstrated against the imposition of sanctions against Eritrea in 2010 in cities like Washington, DC, Geneva and Canberra (Hirt 2015a). Even bigger demonstrations took place in 2015, after the UN Human Rights Council's Special Rapporteur on Eritrea, Sheila Keetharuth, concluded that the government of Eritrea had possibly committed crimes against humanity, including the systematic use of forced labour (UNHRC 2015). The organised opposition and other activists expressed their support for the work of the commission, but government supporters called it an 'unwarranted attack of Eritrea' (Eritrean-Smart.org 2015), following the government's narrative that any criticism against its policies means a betrayal of the Eritrean nation.

Many younger Eritreans growing up in the diaspora feel alienated from the older and more established opposition parties, including former ELF splinters and dissident EPLF veterans. As a result, they have founded various civil society movements with the aim of reaching out to oppressed Eritreans at home and to help refugees on the road, in addition to challenging the government and demanding reforms. Among the first of these organisations were Human Rights Concern Eritrea and *Arbi Harnet* ('Freedom Friday'), a group of diaspora members who mobilised to motivate their compatriots at home to engage in acts of civil disobedience, albeit without much success due to harsh surveillance and repression inside the country. The Eritrean Youth Solidarity for Change emerged in 2013, with the aim of discussing Eritrean solutions for Eritrean problems (Hirt 2015b). When Eritrean President Afewerki and Ethiopian Prime Minister Abiy Ahmed signed a peace agreement in 2018, many diaspora Eritreans believed that the time for political reforms had come, including a complete overhaul of open-ended national service. They started a social media campaign under the motto #Yiakl/#Kiffaya (#Enough!), in which Eritreans posted self-made video statements on Facebook and other platforms, demanding reforms and nominating fellow Eritreans to do the same. However, this campaign – like the earlier ones – also petered out, and generally both the old and the new diaspora generations have proved to be toothless against the regime in Asmara. At the same time, these political and social initiatives have been important tools in creating social belonging and in providing a counternarrative against the government's propagandistic picture of Eritrea.

There is also a growing number of Eritreans, especially among the refugees who fled Eritrea during the past two decades, who refrain from joining the conventional pro-government or anti-government communities. Instead, they have channelled their efforts into organising along regional, ethnic-based or religious lines. According to our field research in Germany, Norway, Sweden and the UK during 2018 and 2019, which involved interviews with a hundred Eritreans (about half of whom were first-generation emigrants or refugees), we found that this type of refugees avoids the established transnational institutions of the government, such as the *mahbere.koms* and the Young PFDJ. The majority of them had never visited any government-sponsored event. Instead, many of them were in search of alternative identities and had become members of ethnic-based, region-based or religious groups. Among the prominent ethnic-based associations are the Lowlanders League, which represents the Tigre-speaking communities of the western lowlands, and the Saho Cultural Association, which are active globally among the scattered diaspora communities from Sweden to Australia (Mohammad 2021).

It is important to mention that in spite of having suffered under the regime's policy of militarisation and political suppression, the majority of the refugees do not get involved in political anti-PFDJ activities. Many of them internalised the government's ideology, to which they have been exposed all their lives. However, they still disapproved of the dire consequences of PFDJ militarism for their personal lives and thus decided to flee the country. Many of them refrain from speaking up against the regime openly because they still have family in Eritrea and fear oppressive measures against their kin back home. Another reason mentioned by our informants for this avoidance was their disappointment with the existing opposition parties, which, in their perception, lacked clear agendas. They also realise that personal rivalries among 'hobby politicians' in the diaspora are often prioritised over bringing real change to the people in the homeland. They mistrust the leadership of these groups that have spent more than three decades in the diaspora and are unfamiliar with life in Eritrea (Mohammad 2021: 7). Belloni (2019: 9) found similar patterns of ambivalence among Eritrean refugees in her research.

Religious identities also contribute to subnational group formation in the diaspora. Muslims have been subjected to discrimination inside Eritrea due to their perceived critical stance against the government over the past thirty years, which detained hundreds of Muslim teachers, *sheikhs* and other religious leaders in the years following independence (Redeker Hepner 2014; Kibreab 2008; Mohammad 2017b). According to Redeker Hepner (2003), practising Eritrean identity through the medium of religion is seen as a challenge to the ideological hegemony of the Eritrean state in the transnational sphere. However, religious identity plays a decisive role as a politically unifying factor for most of the Muslims at home, in the diaspora and particularly among the refugee communities (Mohammad 2021: 12–13).

There are also differences between Tigrinya diaspora Eritreans and Christian refugees of recent years. While religion does not play an important role for the old diaspora, which has been influenced by the secular attitude of the EPLF, its nationalist narrative and the secular nature of most host states, many of the refugees seem to be deeply religious and adherent to Orthodox communities. According to our informants, the government has taken advantage of this situation by infiltrating church communities and extracting funds from the refugees in the form of baptism or marriage fees.

Despite these splits and diversification of identities among Eritreans abroad, one thing they have in common is a feeling of social obligation towards their fellow compatriots at home. The vast majority of our interviewees claimed that they send financial support to their relatives in Eritrea, irrespective of their political stance, their ethnic or religious background, and the time period they had spent abroad. The government relies on them as a social safety net that secures the subsistence of Eritreans inside the country in the absence of economic opportunities and grinding poverty (Hirt and Mohammad 2021). Thus, the government has more recently lost the strong control it has exercised over the diaspora during the struggle and during the earlier years of independence, but it still makes use of the diaspora as a tool of regime survival that helps to prevent the further breakdown of the fragile structures inside the country.

Conclusion: The Vicious Circle of Outmigration and Regime Stabilisation

Eritrea today is governed by a ruling elite and the cult of personality surrounding President Isaias Afewerki. There are no state institutions, the rule of law is absent, and the economy has been shattered through forced conscription and the suppression of private enterprise. The only functioning organisations in the nation are the omnipresent secret services and the military. The most relevant economic actor is the military, which employs national service recruits as forced labourers for the profit of high-ranking generals.[1] After decades of war and autocracy, the Eritrean diaspora has been forged through conflict, forced exile, poverty and ongoing political repression. During the past two decades of open-ended national service in Eritrea, hundreds of thousands of Eritreans have left their homeland as refugees who now reside across Ethiopia, Sudan and other surrounding countries. Thousands more live as labour migrants in Arab-majority states such as Saudi Arabia, Qatar and Egypt, and another hundred thousand Eritreans have been registered as asylum seekers in Europe during the influx of refugees beginning in 2015.[2]

There are good reasons why the government has put more effort into keeping transnational control over its diaspora communities than in developing the country's economy or institutions. The regime has invested heavily in the build-up and maintenance of strong transnational institutions that rely on mechanisms of legitimisation, coercion and oppression. As we discuss above, diaspora members are coerced into funding the government through taxes and fees, and retain a moral obligation to support their kin and relatives at home through private remittances. As a result, Eritreans abroad have contributed to

---

[1] In a 2021 TV interview, the president claimed that the Eritrean economy is merely an irrelevant subsistence economy with no productive added value (English translation by Asena TV 2021).

[2] Numbers according to UNHCR and Eurostat. Exact numbers of Eritreans in the Arab world are not known due to a lack of statistics.

the stabilisation of the faltering system at home, and in many ways have served as a regime saviour (see also Tsourapas 2020). Meanwhile, the opposition in exile and youth groups have remained fragmented and weak. Lacking unity and geopolitical support, they do not pose a challenge to the Eritrean regime. Our research has shown that diaspora communities are characterised by deep splits and fragmentations, and mutual mistrust prevails. This plays into the hands of the government, which can infiltrate both established and emerging associations to manipulate their behaviour in its favour. As a result, the government remains largely unchallenged from within the country and faces a weak opposition from abroad (Hirt and Mohammad 2021).

We conclude by noting that the diaspora has been further disempowered by weak international pressure on the Eritrean government. The large numbers of Eritreans arriving in the European Union starting in 2014 have not prompted the EU Commission to demand structural change in Eritrea. Instead, the EU granted the regime 200 million euros in development aid under the European Emergency Trust Fund for Africa, which is designed to curb migration towards Europe and is subject to few conditions for improvement in human rights, development or governance. It is doubtful that such measures will prevent young Eritreans from fleeing the decade-long national service or the lack of economic and social opportunities that plague their young nation. These funds, in conjunction with financial flows from the diaspora, have stabilised one of the most repressive and militarised polities on Earth, with bleak prospects for the future. Of course, the role of the diaspora in future political developments may change. For the time being, however, transnational repression coupled with a splintered opposition, political avoidance and weak international support has rendered the diaspora an important player in regime survival, rather than change.

References

Anderson, B. 1992. *Long-distance Nationalism: World Capitalism and the Rise of Identity Politics*. Amsterdam: Center for Asian Studies (CASA).

Asena TV. 2021. President Isaias TV interview, 17 February. https://asenatv.com/a-complete-english-translation-of-isaias-afwerkis-eritrean-tv-interview-17-february-2021/

BBC. 2020. 'Tigray crisis: Eritrea's role in Ethiopian conflict'. 28 December. https://www.bbc.com/news/world-africa-55295650 (accessed 30 July 2021).

Belloni, M. 2019. 'Refugees and citizens: Understanding Eritrean refugees' ambivalence towards homeland politics'. *International Journal of Comparative Sociology* 60(1–2): 55–73.

Bernal, V. 2006, 'Diaspora, cyberspace and political imagination: The Eritrean diaspora online'. *Global Networks* 6(2): 161–79.

Bernal, V. 2014. *Nation as Network. Diaspora, Cyber-Space and Citizenship.* University of Chicago Press.

Campbell, J. R. and Afework, S. 2015. 'Ethiopian and Eritrean immigrants in Britain, refugee organizing, transnational connections and identity, 1950–2009'. *African Diaspora* 8: 98–119.

Cliffe, L. and Davidson, B. 1988). *The Long Struggle of Eritrea for Independence and Constructive Peace.* Nottingham: Spokesman.

Connell, D. 1997. *Against All odds: A Chronicle of the Eritrean Revolution.* Lawrenceville, PA: Red Sea Press.

Conrad, B. 2006. 'Out of the "Memory Hole": alternative narratives of the Eritrean revolution in the diaspora'. *Africa Spectrum* 41(2): 249–71.

Duffield, M. and Prendergast, J. P. 1994. *Without Troops and Tanks: Humanitarian Intervention in Ethiopia and Eritrea.* Trenton, NJ: Red Sea Press.

Eritrean.smart.org. 2015. 'Demonstration against all hostilities, 22 June Geneva", http://www.eritrean-smart.org/content/june-22-eritrean-global-action-day-defiance-geneva (accessed 27 September 2015).

Firebrace, J. and Holland, S. 1985. *Never Kneel Down: Drought, Development and Liberation in Eritrea.* Trenton: Red Sea Press.

Gerschewski, J. 2013. 'The three pillars of stability: Legitimation, repression, and cooptation in autocratic regimes'. *Democratization* 20(1): 13–38.

Hirt, N. 2014. 'The Eritrean diaspora and its impact on regime stability: Responses to UN sanctions'. *African Affairs* 114(454): 115–35.

——. 2015. 'One Eritrean generation, two worlds: The established diaspora, the new exiles and their relations to the homeland'. *Horn of Africa Bulletin* 3: 23–9.

——. 2021. 'Eritrea's chosen trauma and the legacy of the martyrs: The impact of post-memory on political identity formation of second-generation diaspora Eritreans'. *Africa Spectrum* 56(1): 19–38.

Hirt, N. and Mohammad, A. S. 2013. 'Dreams don't come true in Eritrea: Anomie and family disintegration due to the militarization of society'. *Journal of Modern African Studies* 5(1): 139–68.

——. 2018. 'By way of patriotism, coercion, or instrumentalization: How the Eritrean regime makes use of the diaspora to stabilize its rule'. *Globalizations* 15(2): 232–47.

——. 2018b. 'The lack of political space of the Eritrean diaspora in the Arab Gulf and Sudan: Torn between an autocratic home and authoritarian hosts'. *Mashriq & Mahjar: Journal of Middle East and North African Migration Studies* 5(1): 104–29.

——. 2021. 'Eritrea's self-reliance narrative and the remittance paradox: Reflections on thirty years of retrogression'. *Remittances Review* 6(1): 21–39.

——. 2022. 'The limits of diaspora: Double vulnerabilities among Eritreans in Saudi-Arabia'. In: *Routledge Handbook of Middle Eastern Diasporas*, pp. 78–88.

Hoehne, M. V., Feyissa, D. and Abdille, M. 2011. 'Somali and Ethiopian diasporic engagement for peace in the Horn of Africa'. *African Conflict & Peacebuilding Review* 1(1): 71–99.

Kibreab, G. 1996. *Ready and Willing . . . But Still Waiting: Eritrean Refugees in Sudan and the Dilemma of Return*. Uppsala: Life and Peace Institute.

——. 2007. 'The Eritrean diaspora, the War of independence, post-conflict (re)-construction and democratisation'. In: Johansson, U. D. (ed.), *The Role of Diaspora in Peace, Democracy and Development in the Horn of Africa*. Research Report in Social Anthropology 1: 97–115. Lund: Lund University.

——. 2009. 'Forced labour in Eritrea'. *Journal of Modern African Studies* 47(1): 41–72.

——. 2018. *The Eritrean National Service: Servitude 'for the Common Good' and the Youth Exodus*. Woodbridge: Boydell & Brewer.

Koser, K. 2003. 'Mobilizing new African diasporas: An Eritrean case study'. In Koser, K. (ed.), *New African Diasporas*. London: Routledge, pp. 111–23.

Lyons, T. and Mandaville, P. 2012. 'Introduction: Politics from afar: Transnational diasporas and networks'. In: Lyons, T. & Mandaville, P. (eds), *Politics from Afar: Transnational Diasporas and Networks*. London: Hurst, pp. 1–23.

Mekonnen, D. R. and Van Reisen, M. 2014. 'Religious persecution in Eritrea and the role of the European Union on tackling the challenge'. In: Reilly, N. and Scriver, S. (eds), *Religion, Gender and the Public Sphere*. London and New York: Routledge, pp. 232–41.

Mohammad, A. S. and Tronvoll, K. 2015. 'Eritrean opposition parties and civic organisations'. Oslo: NOREF Expert Report.

Mohammad, A. S. 2013. 'Eritrea – National service, forced labour and mass exodus: Is there a way out?'. In: Bertelsmann Stiftung (ed.), *Escaping the Escape: Toward Solutions for the Humanitarian Migration Crisis*, pp. 231–44.

——. 2017. 'Faith, politics and the lack of religious freedom'. In: Ev. Missionwerk in Deutschland (ed.), *Eritrea: From Liberation to Oppression*, pp. 65–73.

——. 2021. 'The resurgence of religious and ethnic identities among Eritrean refugees: A response to the government's nationalist ideology'. *Africa Spectrum* 56(1): 39–58.

Moss, D. 2021. *The Arab spring abroad: Diaspora activism against authoritarian regimes*. Cambridge: Cambridge University Press.

Negash, T. and Tronvoll, K. 2000. *Brothers at War: Making Sense of the Eritrean–Ethiopian War*. Oxford: James Currey.

Ogbazghi, P. B. 2011. 'Personal rule in Africa: The case of Eritrea'. *African Studies Quarterly* 12(2): 1–25.

Pateman, R. 1990. *Eritrea: Even the Stones are Burning*. Trenton, NJ: Red Sea Press.

Pool, D. 2001. *From Guerillas to Government: The Eritrean People's Liberation Front*. Oxford: James Currey.

Radtke, K. 2009. *Mobilisierung der Diaspora: Die moralische Ökonomie der Bürgerkriege in Sri Lanka und Eritrea*. Frankfurt/Main: Campus Verlag.

Reid, R. 2020. *Shallow Graves: A Memoir of the Ethiopia–Eritrea War*. London: Hurst.

Redeker Hepner, T. 2015. 'Generation nationalism and generation asylum: Eritrean migrants, the global diaspora, and the transnational nation-state'. *Diaspora: A Journal of Transnational Studies* 18(1/2): 184–207.

——. 2014. 'Religion, repression, and human rights in Eritrea and the Diaspora'. *Journal of Religion in Africa* 44: 151–88.

——. 2008. 'Transnational governance and the centralization of state power in Eritrea and exile'. *Ethnic and Racial Studies* 31(3): 476–502.

——. 2003. 'Religion, nationalism, and transnational civil society in the Eritrean diaspora'. *Identities: Global Studies in Culture and Power* 10(3): 269–93.

Reuters. 2021. 'Ethiopian PM confirms Eritrean troops entered Tigray during conflict', 23 March. https://www.reuters.com/article/us-ethiopia-conflict-idUSK-BN2BF1NT

Rich, D. S. 2005. 'Narratives of nationalism in Eritrea: Research and revisionism'. *Nation and Nationalism* 11(2): 203–22.

Tecle, S. 2012. 'The paradoxes of state-led transnationalism: Capturing continuity, change and rupture in the Eritrean transnational field'. York University, Toronto, MA thesis.

Tecle, S. and Goldring, L. 2013. 'From "remittance" to "tax": The shifting meanings and strategies of capture of the Eritrean transnational party-state'. *African and Black Diaspora: An International Journal*. Doi 10.1080/17528631.2013.793137.

Thiollet, H. 2011. 'Migration as diplomacy: Labor migrants, refugees, and Arab regional politics in the oil-rich countries'. *International Labor and Working Class History* 79 (Spring 2011): 103–21.

Tronvoll, K. 2022. 'The anatomy of Ethiopia's civil war'. *Current History* 121(835): 163–9.

Tsourapas, G. 2021. 'Global autocracies: Strategies of transnational repression, legitimation, and co-optation in world politics'. *International Studies Review* 23(3): 616–44.

UNHRC. 2015. 'Report of the commission of inquiry on human rights in Eritrea'. UN Document A/HRC/29/42.

——. 2021. 'Eritrean refugees in Tigray caught up in conflict'. 27 July, https://www.unhcr.org/news/briefing/2021/7/60ffc4d44/eritrean-refugees-tigray-caught-conflict.html (accessed 30 July 2021).

van Reisen, M., Estefanos, M. and Rijken, C. 2014. *The Human Trafficking Cycle: Sinai and Beyond*. Oisterwijk: Wolf.

SAHAN/IGAD. 2016. 'Human trafficking and smuggling on the Horn of Africa-central Mediterranean Route', http://igad.int/attachments/1284_ISSP%20Sahan%20HST%20Report%20%2018ii2016%20FINAL%20FINAL.pdf. 3 June.

Von Nolting, N. 2002. *Gemeinschaft im Exil: Eritreische Flüchtlinge in Frankfurt am Main* [*Society in Exile: Eritrean Refugees in Frankfurt am Main*]. Arbeitspapier/Working Paper No. 11. Mainz: Gutenberg Universität Mainz, Institut für Ethnologie und Afrikastudien.

World Bank. 1994. 'Eritrea: Options and strategies for growth'. World Bank Report No. 12930-ER, Washington, DC.

Young, J. 1996. 'The Tigray and Eritrean People's Liberation Fronts: A history of tensions and pragmatism'. *The Journal of Modern African Studies* 34: 79–104.

PART III

TRANSNATIONAL REPRESSION
AND THE ROLE OF
HOST COUNTRIES

8

US–PHILIPPINE RELATIONS AND THE TRANSNATIONAL REPRESSION OF FILIPINO AMERICAN ACTIVISTS DURING THE MARCOS DICTATORSHIP

Sharon M. Quinsaat

Migrants and diaspora communities often act collectively to influence politics in their homelands, mobilising to undermine home-state regimes and marshalling support from their host-state governments for change. Because outspoken, well-resourced and mobilised diaspora members pose a threat to regimes from abroad, home-state regimes often enact transnational repression against them. As the chapters of this volume demonstrate, they do so in a number of ways, including by using direct and indirect forms of surveillance and violence. To date, the literature has made important advances by unpacking the ever-evolving toolkit of transnational repression used by authoritarian regimes to police and punish activists abroad. Yet, we know far less about the structural factors that enable authoritarian regimes to go after activists, and especially those who reside in liberal democracies. Accordingly, this chapter addresses the following question: how does the relationship between an authoritarian homeland and a democratic host state impact, and even enable, the transnational repression of diasporas and dissidents-in-exile?

I argue that the answer to this question resides in the character of the linkages between the home and host states. While diplomatic, economic and sociocultural connections between the home and host countries give diaspora activists political opportunities to lobby their host-country governments for regime change (Quinsaat 2013, 2019), these ties can also provide home-country regimes with opportunities and tools for repression. This is because robust linkages provide an infrastructure – including laws, policies and institutions – that facilitates the transnational repression. In other words, the relationship between the states in migrants' countries of origin and destination – particularly their bilateral relations, foreign policy and economic interests – poses a paradox for diaspora activism. Linkages provide political opportunities for diasporas to wield 'voice' after 'exit' against authoritarian regimes (Moss 2022), but they also provide home-country regimes with the means to surveil, target and repress their diasporas.

In this chapter, I use the case of Filipino American activism to show how the relationship between the US and Philippine governments enabled the Marcos regime to pursue transnational repression. Specifically, the character and strength of this linkage enabled the home-country regime to deploy surveillance and infiltration, legal statutes and treaties, assassination, proxy punishment and resource deprivation against diaspora activists. I show that the robustness of interstate ties paved the way for transnational repression, because the actors, laws, policies and institutions that characterise strong bilateral linkages can easily be exploited by homeland regimes as instruments of repression.

More specifically, in the context of the Cold War, the US needed the Subic Naval Base and Clark Air Base in the Philippines to pursue its invasion and war in Vietnam. This strategic interest gave Marcos the power to pursue his opponents in the US under the guise of protecting American national interests *through* the maintenance of his dictatorship. In short, Marcos was able to pursue transnational repression due to the strong relations between the US and the Philippines, epitomised by the US–Philippines Military Bases Agreement. In essence, Marcos suppressed Filipino American activists, many of whom were permanent residents and US citizens, with the consent of and in co-operation with US state agencies, because during the Cold War, national interests largely outweighed human rights concerns and civil liberties.

The chapter proceeds by first introducing the analytical concept of *issue linkages* and its role in the US–Philippines relations during the Marcos dictatorship. I then discuss the case of US-facilitated transnational repression within the anti-Marcos Filipino diaspora. I conclude with implications of the findings on the study of transnational repression for Filipino diaspora activists in particular in the post-Marcos political environment.

Issue Linkages and Interstate Co-operation

To better understand the ways homeland regimes are able to pursue their populations abroad with the help of host-state governments, I draw on work of scholars examining the concept of 'issue linkages' in international relations. Existing work on issue linkages defines them as a collaborative process involving interdependence and negotiations between state governments over two or more issues, with the aim of a joint settlement that is mutually agreeable (Haas 2011; Poast 2013). The prospect and the degree of co-operation is largely dependent on the relative power and the scope of existing interdependencies between the states involved (Betts 2008). As further argued by Poast (2013: 287), an issue linkage is a 'bargaining tactic' which '(1) increases the probability of states reaching a negotiated agreement and (2) motivates states to remain committed to an agreement'. Within the international co-operation literature, McGinnis (1986: 142) argues that issue linkages strategies are characterised by two different types: 'one that is a simple extension of 'tit for tat' or the other one that entails quid pro quo arrangements in which each actor sacrifices on some issues in order to gain in others'.

In the case of the Philippines and the US, multiple linkages in key strategic areas developed owing to forty-eight years of US colonisation of the Philippines. As a result, the two countries were inextricably linked in the six dimensions identified by Levitsky and Way (2010): economic, intergovernmental, technocratic, social, informational, and civil society. As McCann and Lovell (2020: 201) observe, 'in the post-World War II era, the Philippines emerged economically devastated, politically divided, and dependent on the US'. At the same time, the Cold War increased the strategic significance of the Philippines as a US client state, and particularly as a military and commercial outpost (Abinales and Amoroso 2017). After the war and following the Military Bases Agreement in 1947, the Philippines became a fundamental site for building US security and militarisation in the western Pacific (McCann and Lovell 2020: 202). As I describe in the following sections, the intensification of such ties further contributed to the consolidation of centralised autocratic power by President Ferdinand Marcos.

Marcos's Sultanistic Regime and US Support

Successive US administrations bestowed material and symbolic support to the presidency of Marcos – from President Lyndon B. Johnson lauding Marcos as 'my right arm in Asia' (Lee 2015), to Jimmy Carter agreeing to provide $450 million in military aid for five years (Bonner 1988), to Ronald Reagan inviting the dictator for an official state visit. A staunch anti-communist, Marcos capitalised on the US's military intervention in Vietnam to ensure US support of his candidacy in 1965. When he was elected as president eight months after the first US combat units arrived in Da Nang, Vietnam, the US wanted his commitment to send Filipino troops to fight in Vietnam. Marcos was aware of the US's need for his assistance, and he exploited this to its fullest potential.

Despite allegations of massive electoral fraud, Marcos was proclaimed Philippine president for a second term on 11 November 1969. US Vice President Agnew attended Marcos's inauguration in Manila, signalling Washington's full support for his administration. Public displays of militant opposition to the government persisted and intensified in the first two years of Marcos's second term, during which protesters targeted both the Philippine president and the US. Like the Pahlavi and Somoza dynasties in Iran and Nicaragua, respectively, Marcos's rule was sultanistic. This is a type of authoritarian regime based on personal ideology and personal favour to the autocrat in power; there is little ideological basis for the rule, except for the maintenance and exercise of personal power (Chebabi and Linz 1998). At the height of the dictatorship, the major opposition not only consisted of communist and Muslim separatist movements, but also encompassed an alienated oligarchy excluded from Marcos's inner circle.

When Marcos officially imposed martial law on 21 September 1972, the White House, the State Department and the American Chamber of Commerce publicly and unequivocally supported him (Bonner 1988). Marcos knew that the promotion and protection of US interests remained paramount in their granting of foreign aid. The essence of US–Philippines bilateral relations was forged through the US's maintenance of bases on Filipino soil, particularly the Clark Air Base and Subic Naval Base. In the context of the Cold War, Subic and Clark became the most strategic among all of the US's overseas facilities, allowing it to project its forces into both the Pacific and Indian Ocean regions and thus maintain dominance over the Asian continent (Steinmetz 1994).[1] Marcos used the bases agreement to its full advantage as leverage for aid negotiations and as a defence against US human rights policy.

Marcos's repression of his challengers in the Philippines prompted them to escape and seek asylum in liberal democratic countries in Western Europe and North America. Most of them went to the US, where migrants and second-generation Filipinos were forming groups against Marcos as early as 1970. As observed by Shain (1994/1995: 812), 'the openness of the American political system to ethnic politics has allowed many newly organized diasporas to acquire a meaningful voice in US foreign policy, especially on issues concerning countries of origin or symbolic homelands'. In this regard, many among the Filipino diaspora discovered that they were in a better position to mobilise their political efforts from inside the United States than in the Philippines. When Marcos declared martial law in 1972, political mobilisation among the diaspora grew and spread throughout major cities in the US and Canada. Because of the Marcos regime's reliance on US economic and military aid, activists pursued foreign policy lobbying as their primary strategy (Quinsaat 2019). Shain (1994/95: 830) considers the anti-Marcos campaign of Filipinos in the US as 'one of the most successful and multifaceted diasporic efforts to unseat a nondemocratic regime'. Reflecting on his downfall in 1986, Marcos stated that his negative reputation in the US was due to the activities of 'the articulate and well-financed representatives of anti-Marcos expatriates residing in North America', whose attendance at 'the hearings in the US Congress were given the widest circulation by the American press' (Marcos 1989: 94). Furthermore, Anderson (1998: 74) cites the involvement of substantial numbers of Filipinos 'not from political exile' in the struggle against Marcos as an example of effective long-distance nationalist mobilisation.

However, due to dense institutional ties and the common interest between the two governments in keeping Marcos in power, the dictator was able to exercise coercive power and inflict punishments over dissident citizens through

---

[1] During the Korean and Vietnam wars, these bases served as strategic camps for the deployment of US forces. American troops were also marshalled from Subic during the Iranian revolution, the North Yemen–South Yemen war and the Soviet intervention in Afghanistan. The US also used Clark as a staging point for the 1980 Iranian hostage rescue mission (Steinmetz 1994).

Philippine consulates and embassies, as well as the US State Department. He also attempted to suppress activists through the negotiation of an extradition treaty in 1981, although this failed to gain support in the Senate. Although Marcos mostly deployed these forms of repression to eliminate movement leaders, he also employed the soft tactics of ridicule and stigma to dissuade ordinary Filipinos from joining a movement that, in his words, was not representative of the Filipino people. For instance, Marcos's media propagandists portrayed activists from the Movement for a Free Philippines (MFP) and the Katipunan ng Demokratikong Pilipino (Union of Democratic Filipinos [KDP]) as disloyal to the nation and as 'steak commandos' (Vergara 2009: 113), an attack on their identity as Filipinos and their privileged class position. Because they had the resources to emigrate and remain in a foreign country, as well as because of their physical absence from the territory of the Philippine nation-state, they did not suffer like their compatriots. They were depicted, therefore, as lacking the lived experience to speak for all Filipinos. At the same time, the support of the US also enabled Marcos to pursue his opponents abroad through hard tactics of transnational repression, including violence. I explain these strategies below.

Strategies of Transnational Repression

Surveillance and Infiltration of Movement Organisations

The Marcos regime kept track of social movement organisations in the diaspora using the consulates and embassies as de facto intelligence agencies. Marcos also sent his own private security officers from the Philippines to spy on and harass well-known activists. Perhaps most disturbingly, according to a report on classified foreign intelligence operations in the US prepared for the Senate Foreign Relations Subcommittee on International Operations, the Philippine government had a liaison agreement with the Central Intelligence Agency to monitor opponents of Marcos in the US. The subcommittee report examined cases of harassment and surveillance, as well as suspected assassination plots, against US residents by intelligence agents of Chile, Iran, the Philippines, the Republic of China (Taiwan), the Soviet Union and Yugoslavia. US intelligence and law enforcement officials disclosed to Senate investigators that intelligence agencies of the five foreign governments conducted systematic campaigns inside the United States to spy on, harass, and in some cases plan assassinations of their opponents and 'operated with a relatively free hand' (*The Washington Post* 1979).

The report written by legal counsel for Senate Foreign Relations Committee member Michael Glennon stated: 'The CIA became aware in October 1973 that the Philippine government had become increasingly concerned that President Marcos's enemies in the US might be developing, or had already, an influence that would adversely affect the Philippine government ... in the 1970s the CIA successfully stopped Federal probes into the activities of those agents, fearing there would be retaliation against its own men in Manila' (Poole and Vanzi 1984). Beginning in May 1973, the Intelligence Service of the Armed Forces of the Philippines began infiltrating the US with secret agents assigned to neutralise political opponents of Marcos. The bodyguards of Marcos's daughter, who was studying at Princeton University, were disguised secret agents ordered to surveil anti-Marcos groups in the New York area. One of Marcos's spies reached out to the Federal Bureau of Investigation (FBI) office in San Francisco and offered to establish an information exchange on Filipino immigrants in the US. The FBI and the San Francisco Police Department, however, turned down the proposal. Marcos denied the existence of such operations (Anderson 1979).

The testimony of Los Angeles Consul General Armando Fernandez at a 1980 hearing at the Rizal Court of First Instance in the Philippines, which was convened to investigate the activities of the Marcos opposition in the US, confirmed Glennon's accounts. He admitted that one of his tasks was to monitor organisations in the US composed of Filipinos who sought to overthrow the Philippine government. Along with his statement, Fernandez submitted documents he gathered in fulfilment of his foreign post as evidence. These included an internal paper that laid out the Union of Democratic Filipinos's one-year plan, which had been restricted only to the group's members of this organisation within the United States (Villapando 1982).

Surveillance and infiltration initially threatened the movement, as they created fear and distrust in the Filipino community. Eventually, however, they emboldened activists to promote their agenda, especially since these acts of suppression created cleavages within Marcos's diplomatic corps. Activists exploited these divisions, which transformed into political opportunities for the expansion of their network of elite allies and sympathisers. On 18 May 1973, Philippine Consul General of Los Angeles Ruperto Baliao resigned from his post and turned over confidential documents to the *Los Angeles Times*, including a blacklist of 150 supposedly anti-Marcos Filipinos in the US.[2] Marcos had instructed the consulates not to renew their passports (Kalayaan 1973). The list consisted mostly of Filipinos who were American citizens by birth or naturalisation, or Philippine nationals with permanent residency in the US. Most were writers and editors of Filipino-American newspapers critical of the dictatorship, such as *Kalayaan International* and *Ningas Cogon*, and activists affiliated with KDP and National Committee on the Restoration of Civil Liberties in the Philippines (NCRCLP). However, the document also included leaders in the Filipino community, who were not members of anti-Marcos groups but were involved in activism on domestic issues confronting Filipinos in the US, such as employment, housing discrimination and access to social services. The exposure of the blacklist and the defection of Baliao was the first of a series of high-profile mutinies among Marcos's ambassadors and consuls. Philippine Ambassador to Australia, Joselito Azurin, and Assistant to the Foreign Information Representative in the Philippine Consulate in Chicago, Prospero Gotladera, left their posts in 1978 and 1980 respectively and joined the MFP.

In response to the blacklist, the NCRCLP formed the Blacklist Defense Committee to co-ordinate 'counter-offensive' work that comprised of framing Marcos's threats as an opportunity for mobilisation. After its formation, the committee released a statement that combined injustice and agency frames (Gamson 1992), foreshadowing a more pernicious act by the Philippine and US governments and exhorting the need to organise and resist:

> The only security we have is to organize and to launch an ever-mounting offensive against the Marcos dictatorship within the proper limits of our rights as citizens and permanent residents, and to let the new Hitler know unequivocably [*sic.*] that we do not want him or any part of his dictatorship around . . .
>
> . . . the immediate intent of the blacklisting is to intimidate and silence those who have actively opposed the Marcos dictatorship in the Philippines. Its

---

[2] *Philippine News* published the names of 150 Filipinos in the US accused of being against the government of Marcos.

ultimate intent is to have a ready list of Filipino community and student leaders who have been targetted [*sic.*] for extradition in the event that the US-RP extradition treaty becomes a reality. (Sarmiento 1973: 13)

With the help of the National Lawyers Guild, the committee decided to file a class-action suit against the Consuls General, spies and agents of the Philippine government, as well as the co-operating agencies and officials of the US government. The lawsuit would cover a range of grievances that ranged from a foreign government's attempt to curtail the freedom of speech and assembly of US citizens, to the personal and professional impact of being in the blacklist, such as loss of job and damage to one's reputation (Sarmiento 1973). The committee, however, was unable to move forward with this legal counteroffensive.[3]

Marcos's tactics of surveillance and infiltration persisted for eleven years. Days before his official trip to the US from 15 to 20 September 1982 (his first state visit in the country in sixteen years), members of the Coalition against the Marcos Dictatorship in the US and the Canada chapter of the International Association of Filipino Patriots were visited and harassed by presumed agents of Marcos. They also received death threats over the telephone. One of these regime agents attempted to volunteer for the coalition; when he was turned away, he and other agents showed up at several anti-Marcos protests thereafter. On the eve of the state visit, the car of a coalition member was broken into, and the activists' headquarters received a call warning of physical harm if their activities continued (De Guzman 2016).

Legal Statutes and Treaties

Marcos's surveillance and infiltration of movement organisations through the executive branches of the US and Philippine governments were critical in laying the basis for his pursuit of transnational repression using the legislative front. The two countries signed an extradition treaty on 27 November 1981, which was framed as part of an overall plan and partnership to deter crime and international terrorism. Marcos had first proposed an extradition treaty following a failed 'assassination' attempt against him in December 1972 by an American in collaboration with 'prominent Filipinos' (Sepulveda 1973). The

---

[3] No historical data including activists' recollections exist on the events that occurred after and the outcome of the committee's actions.

treaty stated that 'extradition shall not be granted if the offense for which it is requested is a political offense or is connected with a political offense'; however, it also specified the executive agencies, not the courts, as having the authority to determine the political nature of transgressions (Sepulveda 1982). But while the treaty was awaiting ratification in the US Senate, Marcos had already named his targets for extradition in the Manila newspaper, *Bulletin Today*. The list included fifteen Filipino nationals who were permanent residents of the US (PSN/CAMD 1982). The Philippine Court of First Instance also ordered the arrest of forty Filipinos residing in the US for violating the expanded Anti-Subversion Act of 1957 or Republic Act 1700, which made it a crime to be a member of any communist organisation in the Philippines.[4] The government issued arrest warrants against former senators and opposition leaders-in-exile, such as Benigno Aquino, Jr and Raul Manglapus, as well as the KDP leader and US permanent resident Rene Ciria Cruz (Sepulveda 1982).

Within two weeks of the State Department's release of copies of the agreement, the anti-Marcos group formed the National Commission Opposed to the US–RP Extradition Treaty, which included both movement adherents and allies. In its statement, it attacked President Reagan's support for undemocratic regimes: 'We must denounce the treaty as an abrasive infringement on the constitutionally-guaranteed rights of minorities, perpetuated by the Reagan administration in its effort to create domestic legitimacy for a reactionary foreign policy . . . we must expose it as one prong of a generalized assault on civil liberties that is now being mounted by the administration in the name of national security' (Ang Katipunan 1982: 1). The committee undertook a campaign to write letters to the Senate Foreign Relations Committee and organised protests and teach-ins across the country. In the end, the treaty was not forwarded to the Senate for advice and consent to ratification.

Assassination of Activists

As the anti-Marcos movement grew in the US with a network of support that had broadened to include American academics and public intellectuals, church organisations, labour unions and federations, and civil rights groups, the Philippine dictator escalated transnational repression. Unable to silence

---

[4] This Act was almost repealed in 1992 through Republic Act 7636.

Filipinos in the US through legal means, Marcos went after movement leaders through state-sponsored assassinations. Bob and Nepstad (2007: 1374) argue that while 'strategic use of deadly force to eliminate troublesome leaders' is usually undertaken by 'either state actors or nominally independent individuals who receive resources, support, or encouragement from the state', killings may have the opposite impact that the state has intended. Rather than demobilise the movement, it may increase support due to public attention and moral outrage, especially if those who are murdered are prophetic, rather than administrative, leaders. This was the outcome of the assassinations of Filipino-American labour leaders Silme Domingo and Gene Viernes, and Benigno Aquino, Jr.

Investigations implicated Marcos in the murders of Domingo and Viernes on 1 June 1981, inside the office of Local 37 of the International Longshoremen's and Warehousemen's Union (ILWU) in Seattle. The sons of Filipino Alaska cannery workers, Domingo and Viernes were well known in the movement community in Seattle. They were instrumental in passing an ILWU resolution to send an international team to the Philippines to investigate worker conditions and union repression under Marcos. Both were also at the forefront of reforming Local 37. Prior to his murder, Viernes had just returned from the Philippines, where he met with organisers of the Kilusang Mayo Uno (May First Movement), a militant labour federation with ties to the Communist Party of the Philippines-National Democratic Front. From Manila, he attended the ILWU biennial international conference in Honolulu, where he called on the ILWU to join the fight against the Marcos dictatorship. Because the ILWU possessed authority over the West Coast ports, which constituted a hub for trade relations between the Philippines and the US, Viernes's appeal would have a significant repercussion to the regime. According to political scientist Michael Mann (2020: 272), the ILWU 'had a history of building international solidarity with other trade union movements and could credibly threaten to impede access to US ports for countries that violated human rights and instrumental rights'. Domingo and Viernes drafted a resolution to send an ILWU team to investigate working conditions under the Marcos regime, and Kilusang Mayo Uno chair Felixberto Olalia and president of Local 42 in Hawaii supported the motion (De Guzman 2016), signalling a strong transnational union co-operation against the regime.

To anti-Marcos activists, the politically motivated killings proved the deception of Marcos's so-called repeal of martial law. KDP and community leaders in Seattle immediately formed the Committee for Justice for Domingo and Viernes to pursue legal remuneration. In September 1982, the same month of Marcos's state visit to the US, activists filed a $30 million civil suit in US District Court, charging that '1) the Marcos government had ordered the murders; 2) the murders stemmed from an illegal operation of Philippine agents in the US to monitor, harass, and silence the anti-dictatorship movement; and 3) US intelligence agencies cooperated with the Marcos regime to implement this plan and cover up the assassinations' (De Guzman 2016: 130). Tony Baruso, president of the ILWU at the time of the murders and owner of the gun used in the crimes, was convicted of murder in Viernes's death and acquitted in Domingo's. Baruso was a staunch Marcos supporter who had ties with regime officials and was also involved in corruption in the union. After gathering evidence in Manila and Seattle, the Committee for Justice for Domingo and Viernes also sued Ferdinand and Imelda Marcos in federal court. On 15 December 1989, a six-person federal jury found Marcos guilty of the murders and awarded $15.1 million in damages to the families of Domingo and Viernes (Mann 2020).

Another assassination occurred two years later. On 21 August 1983, after a three-year exile in the US, Aquino returned to the Philippines and was shot dead as he disembarked his plane at Manila International Airport. Aquino's murder drew an immediate condemnation from the State Department and precipitated hearings in the US Congress under the House Subcommittee on Asia (Bonner 1988). Diplomats in the US embassy in Manila, who knew of Marcos's involvement in the killing, began to reach out to the political opposition. Marcos's image underwent a negative transformation in the American press, resulting in a 'devastating restatement of past wrongs, which, combined with damaging new revelations associated specifically with his alleged involvement in the Aquino assassination, led to his virtual demonization in American reporting' (Soderlund 1994: 41).

With US mainstream media's regular reports of events in Manila, the Filipino diaspora – once divided on the Marcos dictatorship – gradually formed a consensus on the need for change in the Philippines. Demonstrations became a regular feature at Philippine consulates, and Marcos was a frequent topic at informal gatherings, social meetings and cultural events of Filipinos. Instead of sowing fear, Aquino's killing encouraged Filipinos in the US to come out publicly and express enmity towards Marcos. They also responded by making public claims and demands on behalf of their co-nationals in the Philippines. Aquino embodied the martyrdom of Filipinos, a narrative that resonated with a predominantly devout Catholic immigrant community.

Proxy Punishment in the Homeland

Adamson and Tsourapas (2020) argue that autocracies often use the strategy of coercion-by-proxy, because it's a '"low cost" form of transnational repression' that 'neither violates the sovereignty of other states nor is it likely to garner significant levels of diplomatic or media attention'. Along with assassination, Marcos utilised this violent form of repression as well. The convening of hearings on human rights in South Korea and the Philippines by the Subcommittee on International Organizations of the House of Representatives' Committee on International Relations in 1975 signalled to activists a transformed atmosphere for campaigns directed at US foreign policy. For the first time, Congress invited opponents of Marcos to testify on the political situation in the Philippines. A standard hearing turned into a media spectacle when news of the Philippine president offering $50,000 to one of the key witnesses, Primitivo Mijares, in exchange for his non-attendance and silence became public. Mijares was Marcos's former chief media propagandist. Philippine consul general Ambassador Trinidad Alconcel, who tried to persuade Mijares not to testify, was involved in the bribery[5] (Anderson and Whitten 1975).

After he exposed Marcos's attempt to buy him off, Mijares went on to corroborate claims of Marcos's corruption, electoral fraud and tyrannical rule to Congress. In retaliation for his testimony and publication of his book *The Conjugal Dictatorship of Ferdinand and Imelda Marcos* – a detailed first-hand account of the atrocities and excesses of the couple – Mijares disappeared under mysterious circumstances. He was last seen in Guam boarding a plane to the Philippines in January 1977. On 18 June 1977, the body of Mijares's sixteen-year-old son, Luis Manuel, who had been missing for two weeks, was

---

[5] The money was deposited in a San Francisco branch of Lloyds Bank of California under the names of Mijares and Alconcel; thus, Mijares could not withdraw the $50,000 on his own.

found with signs of physical abuse and torture. On the day he disappeared, the young Mijares was supposed to meet a pen pal. The supposed kidnappers, who called the family days later to demand a ransom, introduced themselves to the Mijares family as the Bangsa Moro Army. Based on later investigations, though, Luis Manuel was killed the day he vanished (Zamora 2017).

Although the older Mijares's whereabouts remained unknown, journalists and politicians speculated that his son was kidnapped to lure him to come home. Rumours circulated that the teenager was even tortured in front of his father. As Mijares's son-in-law, Joey Gurango, stated in an interview thirty years later: 'If they could do that to a 16-year-old boy, it shows what they were capable of doing. It had a chilling effect on people who were thinking of speaking out. We don't know for sure, but if that was the intent, it worked. People were very afraid' (Grande 2017).

Deprivation of Economic and Political Resources

Marcos's tactics also included denying the means for activists not only to engage in movement-related work but also to support themselves in the US. Philippine and US officials loyal to Marcos went after the staunchest and most prominent critics of the regime, who were living in expensive cities. Because they escaped without passports and access to funds in the Philippines, they depended on their social networks for short-term accommodations, housing and employment (Gaerlan 1999). The Carnegie Endowment for International Peace, based in Manhattan, eventually offered Raul Manglapus (a Marcos opponent-in-exile mentioned above) a position as a senior associate in its International Fact-Finding Center programme, which is partly financed through congressional appropriations (Fuentecilla 2013). When Manglapus applied to the Woodrow Wilson International Center for Scholars in Washington, DC, the State Department exerted its influence as member of the board and blocked Manglapus's nomination (Bonner 1988). The department's Office of Philippine Affairs stated: 'It was deemed inappropriate for the US Government to appear to be subsidizing a person who is actively engaged in activities directed against a government with which the US Government enjoys friendly relations' (Fuentecilla 2013: 12).

Marcos also inflicted transnational repression by cancelling the passports of dissidents living abroad. Walden Bello, who was teaching at University of

California Berkeley and City College of San Francisco while participating in the anti-Marcos law struggle, was rendered stateless after 1974 after the Philippine consulate in San Francisco confiscated his passport without explanation (Bello 2004). When Mila de Guzman tried to renew her passport so she could travel for work as an employee at the United Nations, a consular officer wrote on the first page of her old passport, 'Not to be renewed without the permission of the Department of Foreign Affairs, Manila' (De Guzman 2016). The Philippine government also used a network of agents to discourage subscribers and advertisers from supporting independent diaspora media outlets, such as the *Philippine News* and the Chicago-based newspaper *Philippine Times* (Lachica 1979). Marcos allegedly offered Alexander Esclamado, *Philippine News* editor, $100,000 in 1975 to temper the newspaper's criticism of the regime. When Esclamado rejected the bribe, Marcos pressured companies to stop advertising in the paper (Thompson 1995).

In sum, strong linkages between the US and the Philippines rooted in colonial ties and reinforced by the US–Philippines Military Bases Agreement facilitated Marcos's strategy of transnational repression. Because of US interests in maintaining the bases in the Philippines and its anti-communist strategies during the Cold War, Marcos was able to take advantage of executive support of his dictatorship. With the help of the US federal government through the Central Intelligence Agency and the Department of State, Marcos was able to surveil, intimidate and deprive activists of resources. Marcos also bolstered transnational repression through the negotiation of an extradition treaty with the US. (The treaty was not ratified in Congress, however, since foreign policy consensus in the legislature is less formidable in comparison to the executive.) Lastly, civil society linkages between the two countries offered Marcos a route to carry out assassination of activists.

The Evolution of Transnational Repression in the Post-Marcos Era

Despite many successful instances of transnational repression, the Marcos regime was unable to thwart the growth of anti-authoritarian resistance in the US through repression, whether at home or abroad. Instead of dissuading members of the Filipino community to support the movement, Marcos's attempt to isolate and suppress the activities of his critics offered evidence of his ability to extend his repressive reach. The resignation of a state official and the ensuing disclosure of the blacklist sent signals to activists of cleavages within Marcos's overseas emissaries and the presence of potential allies. The assassination of Domingo, Viernes and Aquino also galvanised the local communities due to their ties in the neighbourhood and city (as in the case of Domingo and Viernes) and to their prophetic leadership (Bob and Nepstad 2007). As Linden and Klandermans (2006: 226) describe, 'state repression is easier to overcome in a supportive social environment. In fact, in such a supportive social environment, a movement can get mileage out of backlash from state repression. But if the social environment is unsupportive or even hostile, it becomes much more difficult for activists to survive.'

Marcos's transnational repression, however, occurred within a unique conjuncture of the Cold War and the US's support for military dictators in Asia and elsewhere who served US economic and political interests. Other state leaders have included Lon Nol of Cambodia, Thanom Kittichakorn of Thailand and Park Chung Hee of South Korea. In this historical context, liberal democracies like the US can and have facilitated the transnational repression of diaspora activists in their own territories in order to placate authoritarian regimes that they consider allies. This persists today, as demonstrated by Furstenberg, Russo and Kennedy's chapter on Italian–Egyptian relations in this volume. But structural conditions can also change. Since the overthrow of Marcos in the People Power Revolution of 1986, Filipinos in the US have become partners in development and democratisation in the homeland, and each administration after Marcos has pursued the political project of diaspora formation, reincorporating overseas Filipinos through the Citizenship Retention and Reacquisition Act of 2003, which allows Filipinos to maintain dual nationality (Burgess 2020).

Unfortunately, democratisation in the Philippines took an illiberal turn with the election of populist Rodrigo Duterte in 2016. Under the Duterte presidency, various state-sponsored agents systematically killed thousands of civilians, including through extrajudicial killings, in the context of the 'war on drugs' campaign (Johnson and Fernquest 2018; Regilme 2021). Duterte's authoritarian practices also included jailing opposition leaders and harassing independent media outlets and journalists. During this time, activists from the anti-Marcos movement struggled to revive their networks and mobilise against Duterte's administration. In contrast to Marcos, however, Duterte did not directly repress his critics in the US. This has been owed in part to the fact that, although he erected an illiberal democracy in the Philippines, he also enjoyed popular support. As observed by Regilme (2021: 2), 'contestations and legitimation efforts of Duterte's illiberal and authoritarian regime emerged from various local, national, and transnational space[s]'. Specifically, the regime pulled its support from constituents with formal citizenship status abroad, as well as the transnational public sphere, including more powerful third-party states and groups (Regilme 2021: 4). In this regard, the Duterte regime systematically mobilised its political support from the Filipino diaspora to intimidate, slander and suppress political dissenters abroad. In this way, the regime has more effectively instrumentalised its diaspora for consolidating its illiberal practices while treating its diasporic individuals as outlaws or subjects to be repressed when rebellious (see Glasius, this volume).

On other occasions, however, Duterte asked for the deportation of critics of the regime, as for instance in the case of Elanel Ordidor, a Taiwan-based Filipino caregiver who was posting critical commentaries about the abuses and policy failures of the Duterte regime (Gotinga 2020, cited in Regilme 2021). His government also employed the softer tactic of transnational repression by deploying an army of cyber trolls to target individuals who have openly criticised his regime. Such tactics included social media influencers involved in ridicule, stigma and silencing in online spaces of movement actors. The impact is mostly individualised, with activists engaged in self-policing and censorship, especially in how diaspora members relate to their co-nationals.

Alongside these repressive actions, Duterte's regime introduced a transformative agenda in Philippine foreign policy which has, in turn, impacted issue linkages with the United States. He sought to separate from the country's long-standing treaty ally of the US in favour of building closer ties with China in pursuit of a more 'independent' foreign policy (Heydarian 2017; Castro 2019). According to Regilme (2021), close co-operation with the US became unfavourable to Duterte because this relationship threatened to challenge the legitimacy of Duterte's government over its human rights abuses. Additionally, the ideological alignment of Duterte's regime with countries like China and Russia further reinforced the regime's departure from liberal democratic principles. As Duterte told an audience in Beijing during his 2016 trip to China: 'I've realigned myself in your ideological flow and maybe I will also go to Russia to talk to [President Vladimir] Putin and tell him that there are three of us against the world – China, Philippines and Russia. It's the only way' (*Reuters*, 20 October 2016). Yet, the paradox discussed at the beginning of this chapter still holds. On the one hand, the Philippine government's shift away from the US and its diaspora may keep activists safer from 'hard' forms of transnational repression, which they experienced in the Marcos era. On the other hand, a reduction in issue linkages is also likely to undermine activists' leverage and their ability to gain external support when mobilising against human rights abuses in their homeland from the United States.

Conclusion

As this chapter has shown, homeland–hostland relations can facilitate the transnational repression of diaspora activists in liberal democracies. This case study demonstrates strong economic and military ties, security arrangements and strong diplomacy can fuel collaborative forms of transnational repression against citizens and lawful residents abroad. Transnational repression is also shaped by regime leaders' perceived threat of diaspora activism to the leader's legitimacy from a destination country's elites and public. For Marcos, US support was critical to sustaining his twenty-year rule. Accordingly, the existence of a movement against his regime in the US – which was composed of exiled political elites, members of the Philippine Left and second-generation Filipino Americans with deep roots to local diaspora and social movement communities skilled in foreign policy lobbying – posed a risk to the economic and military aid needed to maintain his regime. Marcos's policies on US investments and US military bases in the Philippines were also crucial to preserving US hegemony in the East Asian region.

Future studies would do well to investigate how issue linkages shape transnational repression in other liberal democracies, as well as how transnational repression will evolve in the wake of Marcos's son's election to the Philippine presidency in 2022. Whether transnational repression under Ferdinand 'Bongbong' Marcos, Jr will resemble that of his father, his predecessor Rodrigo Duterte or another form altogether, the protection of activists abroad is partly dependent on the response of the host country. As discussed in other chapters in this volume, transnational repression is not just a linear phenomenon directed by the homeland abroad, but co-constituted by sending and receiving states. For this reason, the effect of issue linkages on the mobilisation and suppression of diaspora activism warrants further investigation.

References

Organisational Documents

Ang Katipunan. 1982. 'Nat'l Group Formed to Fight Treaty'. *Ang Katipunan*, 16 January–6 February, pp. 1, 8.

Kalayaan International. 1973. 'Consul Baliao Denounces Marcos'. *Kalayaan International Special Issue*, 12 June, p. 1.

Philippine Solidarity Network/Coalition Against the Marcos Dictatorship (PSN/CAMD). 1982. 'Philippines Update: Extending Repression, Crackdown on the US Anti-Marcos Movement'. Brochure.

Sarmiento, N. 1973. 'Counter-Offensive: The Blacklist Defense Committee'. *Silangan* 1(1): 12–13.

Sepulveda, M. F. 1982. 'Senate Bills Tie Extradition to Foreign Policy'. *Ang Katipunan*, 16 January–6 February, pp. 1, 5.

Villapando, V. 1982. 'Target: KDP, Government Files Admit Extensive Spying'. *Ang Katipunan Special*.

Newspaper and Magazine Articles

Anderson, J. 1979. 'Filipino Agents Hunt Foes in The US'. *The Washington Post*, 11 August, p. B11.

Anderson, J. and Whitten, L. 1975. 'Marcos Bribe Offer Cited by Witness'. *The Washington Post*, 2 July, p. C7.

Grande, G. 2017. 'Who Was Primitivo Mijares? Gospel Truths and Urban Legends'. *ABS-CBN*, 20 February. Available from https://news.abs-cbn.com/focus/02/20/17/who-was-primitivo-mijares-gospel-truths-and-urban-legends

Lachica, E. 1979. 'Filipino Exiles Keep Opposition Movement Alive in US'. *The Asian Wall Street Journal*, 27 June, p. 1.

Poole, F. and Vanzi, M. 1984. 'Marcos's Secret War in America'. *The Nation*, 12 May, p. 577.

Reuters. 2016. 'Duterte aligns Philippines with China, says US has lost'. *Reuters*, 20 October. [Online]. Available at: https://www.reuters.com/article/us-china-philippines-idUSKCN12K0AS

Washington Post, The. 1979. 'Foreign Spy Activity Found Rampant in US'. *The Washington Post*, 9 August, p. A12.

Zamora, F. 2017. 'Family Secret: How Primitivo Mijares Disappeared'. *Philippine Daily Inquirer*, 19 February. Available from https://newsinfo.inquirer.net/872907/family-secret-how-primitivo-mijares-disappeared

Published books and journal articles

Abinales, P. N. and Amoroso, D. J. 2017. *State and Society in the Philippines*. Lanham, MD: Rowman & Littlefield Publishers.

Adamson, F. B. and Tsourapas, G. 2019. 'Migration diplomacy in world politics'. *International Studies Perspectives* 20: 113–28.

——. 2020. 'At home and abroad: Coercion-by-proxy as a tool of transnational repression'. Freedom House Special Report. Available from https://freedomhouse.org/report/special-report/2020/home-and-abroad-coercion-proxy-tool-transnational-repression

Amarasingam, A. 2015. *Pain, Pride, and Politics: Social Movement Activism and the Sri Lankan Tamil Diaspora in Canada*. Athens, GA: University of Georgia Press.

Anderson, B. 1998. *The Spectre of Comparisons: Nationalism, Southeast Asia and the World*. London: Verso.

Bello, W. 2004. 'The Global South'. In Mertes, T. (ed.), *A Movement of Movements: Is Another World Really Possible?* London and New York: Verso, pp. 49–69.

Betts, A. 2008. 'North–South cooperation in the refugee regime: The role of linkages'. *Global Governance* 14(2): 157–78.

Bob, C. and Nepstad, S. E. 2007. 'Kill a leader, murder a movement? Leadership and assassination in social movements'. *American Behavioral Scientist* 50(10): 1370–94.

Bonner, R. 1988. *Waltzing with a Dictator: The Marcoses and the Making of American Policy*. New York: Vintage.

Chebabi, H. E. and Linz, J. J. 1998. 'A theory of sultanism 1: A type of nondemocratic rule'. In Chebabi, H. E. and Linz, J. J. (eds), *Sultanistic Regimes*. Baltimore: Johns Hopkins University Press, pp. 3–25.

De Castro, R. C. 2018. 'Explaining the Duterte administration's appeasement policy on China: The power of fear'. *Asian Affairs: An American Review* 45(3–4): 165–9.

De Guzman, M. 2016. *Women Against Marcos: Stories of Filipino and Filipino Americans Who Fought A Dictator*. San Francisco: Carayan Press.

Fuentecilla, J. V. 2013. *Fighting from a Distance: How Filipino Exiles Toppled a Dictator*. Urbana, Chicago and Springfield: University of Illinois.

Gaerlan, B. S. 1999. 'The movement in the United States to oppose martial law in the Philippines, 1972–1991: An overview'. *Pilipinas* 33: 75–98.

Gamson, W. A. 1992. *Talking Politics*. New York: Cambridge University Press.

Gotinga, J. C. 2020. *DOLE asks Taiwan to deport OFW with Facebook posts criticizing Duterte*. *Rappler*. Retrieved from: https://www.rappler.com/nation/259053-dole-asks-taiw an-deport-ofw-facebook-posts-criticize-duterte?fbclid=IwAR0Dn8RHkQBTud jTMfEZALNO2Psoi1RNVXH8ro_Qvh7xXma_

Haas, E. B. 1980. 'Why collaborate? Issue-linkage and international regimes'. *World Politics* 32(3): 357–405.

Heydarian, R. J. 2017. 'Tragedy of small power politics: Duterte and the shifting sands of Philippine foreign policy'. *Asian Security* 13(3): 220–36.

Johnson, D. T. and Fernquest, J. 2018. 'Governing through killing: The war on drugs in the Philippines'. *Asian Journal of Law and Society* 5(2): 359–90.

Lee, T. 2015. *Defect or Defend: Military Responses to Popular Protests in Authoritarian Asia*. Baltimore: Johns Hopkins University Press.

Levitsky, S. and Way, L. 2010. *Competitive Authoritarianism: Hybrid Regimes After the Cold War*. New York: Cambridge University Press.

Linden, A. and Klandermans, B. 2006. 'Stigmatization and repression of extreme-right activism in the Netherlands'. *Mobilization* 11(2): 213–28.

Marcos, F. E. 1989. 'A defense of my tenure'. *Orbis* 33(1): 91–105.

McMann, M. W. and Lovell, G. I. 2020. *Union by Law: Filipino American Labor Activists, Rights Radicalism, and Racial Capitalism*. Chicago and London: University of Chicago Press.

McGinnis, M. D. 1986. 'Issue linkage and the evolution of international cooperation'. *Journal of Conflict Resolution* 30(1): 141–70.

Nepstad, S. E. 2004. *Convictions of the Soul: Religion, Culture, and Agency in the Central America Solidarity Movement*. New York: Oxford University Press.

Poast, P. 2013. 'Issue linkage and international cooperation: An empirical investigation'. *Conflict Management and Peace Science* 30(3): 286–303.

Quinsaat, S. M. 2019. 'Linkages and strategies in Filipino diaspora mobilization for regime change'. *Mobilization: The International Quarterly Review of Social Movement Research* 24(2): 221–39.

Regilme, S. S. F. Jr. 2021. 'Contested spaces of illiberal and authoritarian politics: Human rights and democracy in crisis'. *Political Geography* 89: 1–12. https://doi.org/doi:10.1016/j.polgeo.2021.102427

Shain, Y. 1994/5. 'Ethnic diasporas and US foreign policy'. *Political Science Quarterly* 109(5): 811–41.

Smith, C. 1996. *Resisting Reagan: US Central America Peace Movement*. Chicago and London: University of Chicago Press.

Soderlund, W. C. 1994. 'The impact of the Aquino assassination on the press image of Ferdinand Marcos: Transformation or amplification?' *Communication Reports* 7(1): 36–42.

Steinmetz, S. 1994. *Democratic Transition and Human Rights: Perspectives on US Foreign Policy*. Albany: State University of New York Press.

Thompson, M. R. 1995. *The Anti-Marcos Struggle: Personalistic Rule and Democratic Transition in the Philippines.* New Haven, CT: Yale University Press.

Vergara, B. M. Jr. 2009. *Pinoy Capital: The Filipino Nation in Daly City.* Philadelphia, PA: Temple University Press.

9

'BACKDOOR EXTRADITIONS': HOW AUTHORITARIAN REGIMES MANIPULATE INTERPOL AND THE US IMMIGRATION SYSTEM TO PERSECUTE DISSIDENTS

Sandra Grossman and Meg Hobbins

Introduction

The International Criminal Police Organization, commonly known as Interpol, is an intergovernmental organisation dedicated to facilitating police co-operation between member states.[1] Interpol co-ordinates global security by enabling member countries to share and access data on individuals who are accused of crimes or ordered to serve criminal sentences. In a globalised world, where crime often crosses borders, Interpol serves a critical law enforcement function. Interpol is not, however, without its faults. While Interpol's Constitution and accompanying neutrality mandate are intended to insulate the organisation from being complicit in human rights violations, Interpol has not done enough to protect its law enforcement functions from abuse.

Many authoritarian governments manipulate Interpol's data-sharing system, putting forth illegitimate criminal accusations against dissidents and

---

[1] Interpol. *What is Interpol?* Retrieved 10 April 2023 (https://www.interpol.int/Who-we-are/What-is-INTERPOL). 'Since INTERPOL is a global organization, it can provide [a] platform for cooperation; we enable police to work directly with their counterparts, even between countries which do not have diplomatic relations.'

regime opponents.[2] As shown by Lemon's contribution in this volume, authoritarian states often use international organisations for carrying out acts of transnational repression.[3] Interpol has not been an exception to such practices. It is now widely acknowledged that numerous countries routinely abuse the Interpol system to seek out dissidents abroad.[4] The following sixteen regimes have been censured for Interpol abuse in the State Department's Human Rights Reports: Azerbaijan (2020), Belarus (2021), Benin (2020), Côte d'Ivoire (2021), Ecuador (2021), Guinea Bissau (2021), Iran (2021) Kazakhstan (2020), Montenegro (2020 and 2021), Nicaragua (2020), People's Republic of China (2021), Russia (2020 and 2021), Saudi Arabia (2020 and 2021), Tajikistan (2020 and 2021), Turkey (2020 and 2021) and Venezuela (2021).[5] Many other countries, not listed in the State Department reports, such as Mexico, El Salvador, United Arab Emirates and Egypt, are also known to utilise Interpol's global police databases for purposes other than legitimate law enforcement.[6]

As argued by Lemon in his 2019 article, Weaponizing Interpol, 'the use of Interpol against political dissidents represents an important and understudied aspect of today's globalized autocracy' and poses a threat to individuals' civil liberties and freedoms.[7] In most cases, individuals targeted by Interpol notices face the risk of arrest and suffer from financial and reputational damage.

[2] Fair Trials. 2018. *Dismantling the Tools of Oppression: Ending the Misuse of INTERPOL.* Retrieved 21 July 2022 (https://www.fairtrials.org/app/uploads/2022/01/Dismantling-the-tools-of-oppression.pdf).

[3] *Infra* Part IV, Chapter 12.

[4] US Department of State. 2021. *2020 Country Reports on Human Rights Practices* (https://www.state.gov/reports/2020-country-reports-on-human-rights-practices/); see also Freedom House. 2021. *Out of Sight, Not Out of Reach* (https://freedomhouse.org/report/transnational-repression).

[5] *Id.*; see also US Department of State. 2022. *2021 Country Reports on Human Rights Practices* (https://www.state.gov/reports/2021-country-reports-on-human-rights-practices/).

[6] Article 77 of the Rules on the Processing of Data (RPD) establishes that the General Secretariat may not publish a Red Notice if the data provided do not meet the conditions of publishing a Notice and if publication of the Notice is not for the purposes of international police co-operation. See Interpol. 2019. *Rules of Processing Data*. Art. 77. Retrieved 25 July 2022 (https://www.interpol.int/en/Who-we-are/Legal-framework/Data-protection).

[7] Lemon, E. 2019. 'Weaponizing Interpol'. *Journal of Democracy* 30(2): 15–29.

Additionally, they are prevented from freely travelling across international borders (Lemon 2019), leading to separation from loved ones, as well as significant professional challenges. This is the intended outcome for targets of legitimate notices and diffusions, but not for unsuspecting victims of Interpol abuse.

Once Interpol publishes data about a particular person, law enforcement officials around the world are free to decide whether to arrest the target of the data if they are encountered within their borders.[8] As explained below, in the United States, Red Notices alone do not provide probable cause to effectuate a criminal arrest under the US Constitution. Nevertheless, immigration officials often utilise the data disseminated by Interpol to identify and target non-US citizens for 'civil' detention. These individuals often experience prolonged detention, visa cancellations, the denial of immigration benefits, and removal from the United States. Tragically, many US immigration officials, including judges working under the Department of Justice, justify this result by treating Red Notices and other types of Interpol communication as conclusive evidence of criminality, which they are not. US officials' inclination to view Interpol communications this way can be attributed to a variety of reasons, including lack of training on Interpol and how it functions, lack of communication between US law enforcement agencies, and perhaps, a desire to prevent even alleged criminals from obtaining protection in the United States. Further, as shown below, many US federal courts accord significant evidentiary weight to Red Notices when considering bars to asylum and other forms of protection in the United States.

An illegitimate Red Notice results in egregious human rights violations and what some advocates have termed 'backdoor extraditions'. In other words, authoritarian regimes accomplish through the US immigration system what they could not through an established extradition process: removal from the United States and forced repatriation. As the case examples in this chapter show, US immigration officials are denying foreign nationals a vast array

---

[8] See Interpol. *Red Notices* (https://www.interpol.int/en/How-we-work/Notices/Red-Notices):

'INTERPOL cannot compel the law enforcement authorities in any country to arrest someone who is the subject of a Red Notice. Each member country decides what legal value it gives to a Red Notice and the authority of their law enforcement officers to make arrests.'

of immigration benefits, including asylum and protection under the United Nations Convention Against Torture, solely on the basis of a Red Notice.[9]

Most individuals fleeing persecution are unaware that they are the target of a Red Notice. This is because most Red Notices are not made public on Interpol's website. At the time of writing this chapter, there are about 69,270 active Red Notices, of which some 7,192 are public.[10] Many individuals only learn about the Red Notice when they are arrested by the DHS or when they appear in immigration court. As a result, when repressive regimes utilise Interpol channels to persecute a dissident abroad, and US immigration officials act to arrest and detain individuals primarily because of a Red Notice or diffusion, Interpol's otherwise important data-sharing mechanisms become tools of transnational repression.

The political abuse of Interpol's notice system against critics and opponents of authoritarian regimes has drawn growing public attention in recent years. In the United States, for example, advocates for curbing Interpol abuse welcomed the passage of the Transnational Repression Accountability and Prevention (TRAP) provision as part of the National Defense Authorization Act (NDAA) for Fiscal Year 2022.[11] The provision provides important protections against abuse, such as a requirement that the Department of Justice and the Department of State produce a report on the political abuse of Interpol each year, specifically denouncing the most egregious violations.[12] As discussed below, the TRAP provisions are a significant recognition by the United States that Interpol needs to be monitored and its enforcement mechanisms improved. However, much more needs to be done to truly protect Interpol's data-sharing function from abuse.

Interpol has started to address some key issues on its own, and some would say the organisation has made significant improvements. For example, Interpol

---

[9] UN General Assembly. 1984. *Convention Against Torture and Other Cruel, Inhuman or Degrading Treatment or Punishment.* United Nations, Treaty Series, vol. 1465, p. 85. Retrieved 21 July 2022 (https://www.refworld.org/docid/3ae6b3a94.html).

[10] See Interpol. *Red Notices.* Retrieved 19 July 2022 (https://www.interpol.int/en/How-we-work/Notices/View-Red-Notices).

[11] National Defense Authorization Act for Fiscal Year 2022, Pub. L. No. 117-81, § 6503, 135 Stat. 1541 (2021).

[12] *Id.*

is now publishing more statistics about the number of Red Notices and other coloured Notices on its website.[13] Although this is a welcome change, issues of transparency remain. The review process for Red Notices remains largely confidential and the reforms in general have been slow and insufficient. Many in the international community question whether Interpol has the political will to meaningfully address its capacity to generate human rights violations. These concerns only grew during the 2021 Interpol 89th General Assembly meeting held in Istanbul, Turkey, where the organisation made significant decisions affecting its future. The General Assembly meeting failed to improve Interpol's image or to substantively address allegations of abuse. Holding the meeting in Turkey, one of the most notorious abusers of Interpol, sent the wrong message. The election of UAE Major General Ahmed Naser Al Raisi to the Presidency of the organisation was also extremely concerning. Numerous human rights groups have called out Al Raisi for his involvement in the torture of detainees.[14]

In this chapter, we will describe how US government agencies interact with Interpol in inconsistent and dangerous ways, ultimately unknowingly furthering the agenda of authoritarian regimes. We will also review how US courts are responding to asylum seekers, who challenge the legitimacy of persecutory Red Notices. Through select case studies we will illustrate how attempts to secure protection in the United States can be upended by persecutory Red Notices. Finally, we will provide our recommendations for safeguarding asylum seekers from the devastating effects of persecutory Red Notices.

The Administration and Effects of Interpol Red Notices in the US Immigration System

Thelma Aldana, former Attorney General and candidate for the Presidency of Guatemala, prosecuted over seven hundred government officials for corruption and investigated the very President who appointed her. In 2019 she became the leading presidential candidate in Guatemala, campaigning for an end to

---

[13] Interpol. *About Notices* (https://www.interpol.int/en/How-we-work/Notices/About-Notices).

[14] See, for example, Human Rights Watch. 2021. *Interpol: UAE Official's Candidacy Raises Human Rights Alarms*. Retrieved 21 July 2022 (https://www.hrw.org/news/2021/05/05/interpol-uae-officials-candidacy-raises-human-rights-alarms).

impunity and demanding accountability for government officials. Nevertheless, political enemies thwarted her candidacy and threatened her life. She fled to the United States for protection, where she had previously received the US State Department's Women of Courage award. However, Guatemalan authorities lodged false criminal charges against her and apparently attempted to obtain a Red Notice with Interpol to induce her arrest and extradition to Guatemala. As Ms Aldana's US immigration attorneys, given our previous experience in similar circumstances with the US Department of Homeland Security (DHS), we feared that immigration enforcement agents would arrest and detain Ms Aldana pursuant to the bogus criminal allegations and persecutory Red Notice. While Ms Aldana sought to rearrange her life in the US, seek asylum and protect her remaining family in Guatemala, she was also forced to try to delete a Red Notice that could derail all her efforts. She lived in fear of a DHS knock on her door and deportation to the very country she fled from. Ms Aldana's Interpol filing was successful, and she was ultimately issued a clearance showing she was not the subject of a Red Notice. She now has asylum protection.

'Juan', a Venezuelan citizen and well-known paediatric cardiologist/neonatologist, dedicated his life to treating acutely ill, vulnerable children. In 2008 he became the unfortunate victim of persecution instigated by the Venezuelan state. Through its court system, the media and the executive branch itself, the government of Venezuela set out to destroy Juan's reputation based on bogus criminal charges. The Venezuelan government's goal was clear: to divert attention from Venezuela's own failing public health system and to blame the nation's medical failings on a group of doctors labelled as 'elitist', 'westernized' and 'unpatriotic' because they were US-educated, employed in a private hospital and of the Jewish faith. The Venezuelan state further persecuted Juan through the machinery of Interpol, by issuing a request for a Red Notice. Because of this illegitimate and persecutory action, Juan, who was living in the US at the time, could not return to Venezuela, lest he be arrested and jailed unlawfully for a crime he did not commit. He could not travel abroad or even seek citizenship in the US because of the Interpol notice against him. In 2014 counsel for Juan filed a claim with Interpol arguing that the Red Notice violated Juan's fundamental human rights and dignity. Interpol deleted the Red Notice. Once the Red Notice was deleted, Juan was able to file for and obtain his US citizenship.

There are many myths surrounding Interpol and its most well-known communication: the Red Notice. Interpol's main function, however, is straightforward: it manages criminal databases and a network of communications transmitted among 195 member countries, including the United States.[15] Importantly, the co-operative base of Interpol's system is entirely voluntary. No state has the obligation to arrest an individual based on a Red Notice. As stated by Interpol: 'each member country decides for itself what legal value to give a Red Notice within their borders'.[16] Although Interpol is sometimes touted as an international police force, it is not. It has no authority to arrest individuals in its databases. The organisation is a conduit for communicating information between member states.

A Red Notice is often described as an 'international arrest warrant'. This is a common misconception and is incorrect, as Interpol itself confirms.[17] As defined by Interpol, a Red Notice is a 'request to law enforcement worldwide to locate and provisionally arrest a person pending extradition, surrender, or similar legal action'.[18] Red Notices apply to persons who are wanted either 'for prosecution or to serve a sentence', and are published at the request of a member country.[19] As indicated above, the organisation does not have the power to arrest or detain anybody. Rather, a Red Notice is a communication to all member countries that a person is wanted 'based on an arrest warrant or equivalent judicial decision issued by a country or an international tribunal'.[20] In this sense, the organisation facilitates co-ordination, as an international notice system that allows police in member states to share critical information. Red

---

[15] All below assertions, unless otherwise noted, are from Sandra Grossman and Meg Hobbins, Matter of W-E-R-B- and *The Reliability of Red Notices: How to Successfully Advocate for Victims of Persecution*, 25 Bender's Immigr. Bull. 875 (June 15, 2020) (citing Interpol. *What is INTERPOL?* Retrieved 20 April 2021 (https://www.Interpol.int/en/Who-we-are/What-is-INTERPOL)).

[16] Interpol. *Red Notices*. Retrieved 30 March 2022 (https://www.interpol.int/en/How-we-work/Notices/Red-Notices#:~:text=INTERPOL%20cannot%20compel%20the%20law,enforcement%20officers%20to%20make%20arrests).

[17] *Id.*

[18] *Id.*

[19] *Id.*

[20] *Id.*

Notices as such are a part of this system. Interpol has specific requirements to publish Red Notice requests, which are set out in Interpol's Rules for the Processing of Data (RPD).[21] They must concern serious ordinary-law crimes not related to behavioural or cultural norms, family or private matters, or private disputes that are not connected with organised crime. The underlying crime must also meet a penalty threshold.

Importantly, Red Notices must also comply with two broad protections set forth in Articles 2 and 3 of the Interpol Constitution.[22] Article 2 states that the organisation aims to promote international police co-operation within the 'spirit of the "Universal Declaration of Human Rights"'.[23] And Article 3, sometimes referred to as the neutrality clause, states that it is 'strictly forbidden for the Organization [Interpol] to undertake any intervention or activities of a political, military, religious, or racial character'.[24] Interpol notes that 'neutrality is, and has always been, paramount to INTERPOL', and the organisation's stated goal is to 'transcend domestic and international politics' in its noble quest to prevent and fight crime through international police co-operation.[25] Indeed, human rights protections are a critical and recurrent theme in Interpol's foundational documents.

Yet, despite these important safeguards against persecutory requests from member states, and despite some valuable efforts by Interpol to improve transparency and its review mechanisms, the organisation still fails to properly vet Red Notice requests for compliance. Too many bogus or persecutory communications slip through the review process, and while Interpol's Commission for the Control of Interpol's Files (CCF) does a commendable job at deleting most inappropriate data, the review process is lengthy and comes only after the target of the Red Notice or data has suffered some of its worst effects.

---

[21] Interpol. *Legal Documents*. Retrieved 20 April 2021 (https://www.Interpol.int/Who-we-are/Legal-framework/Legal-documents).

[22] Interpol. *Interpol Constitution* (https://www.Interpol.int/Who-we-are/Legal-framework/Legal-documents).

[23] *Id*. at art. 2.

[24] *Id*. at art. 3.

[25] Interpol. *Secretary General's Foreword to the Article 3 Repository of Practice*. Retrieved 4 October 2021 (https://www.interpol.int/en/content/download/12626/file/article-3-ENG-february-2013.pdf).

Interpol's internal safeguards against questionable Red Notices, many of which are contained in the RPD, have not led to consistent and meaningful review of arrest warrants and judicial notices. Additionally, Article 128 of the RPD provides a woefully inadequate framework for the treatment of requests by member states, establishing that '[d]ata are, *a priori*, considered to be accurate and relevant when entered by a National Central Bureau, a national entity or an international entity . . .'[26] This applies equally to all member states, whether shining examples of pluralistic democracies or notorious authoritarian regimes.

The presumption of legitimacy of the Red Notice request is only questioned 'if a doubt arises regarding compliance with the conditions for data processing'.[27] Nevertheless, Interpol is not an investigative body, and in most cases, a request for data sharing may appear facially legitimate. Even if somehow a doubt does arise, the same national entity that requested the Red Notice is consulted for clarification. While the organisation can take other, additional steps to ensure compliance with Interpol's rules, there is no mechanism by which the target of the Red Notice may be consulted. There is also no *a priori* determination, for example, that requests by states that are notorious abusers of Interpol receive greater scrutiny or require consultation with relevant human rights organisations.

The current process keeps the target of the Red Notice in the dark, and thus silenced, often only becoming aware of the Red Notice at the moment they are apprehended. As noted above, the reason being that most Red Notices are confidential and only known to law enforcement and related agencies. The burden of proof to delete an illegitimate Red Notice also falls on the targeted individual, who may already be detained. The deletion process is lengthy and demands technical legal knowledge, consisting of an application to the Commission for the Control of Interpol's Files (CCF).[28] The CCF, also located

---

[26] Interpol. *Rules on the Processing of Data*, art. 128(1). Retrieved 10 April 2023 (https://www.interpol.int/content/download/5694/file/24%20E%20RPD%20UPDATE%207%2011%2019_ok.pdf).

[27] *Id*. at art. 128(2).

[28] Interpol. *Commission for the Control of INTERPOL's Files*. Retrieved 10 April 2023 (https://www.interpol.int/About-INTERPOL/Commission-for-the-Control-of-Files-CCF).

in Lyon, France, independently reviews requests by targeted individuals to access data against them in the Interpol information-sharing system, as well as requests to delete that data. Their ability to process requests has improved in recent years, but they remain understaffed and underfunded.

In the United States, the bipartisan Commission on Security and Cooperation in Europe, better known as the US Helsinki Commission, 'has determined that there is widespread abuse of Interpol Red Notices for political ends'.[29] Given the defects in Interpol's review process, authoritarian nations harness the system to persecute individuals by accusing dissidents of crimes such as fraud or tax evasion, which on their face appear to be nonpolitical.[30] Authoritarian regimes in Russia, China, Turkey, Venezuela and a growing list of other countries are attempting to achieve through the backdoor of the US immigration system what they cannot accomplish through formal extradition proceedings: utilising the US justice system to apprehend and return political dissidents.

Examples of this manipulation abound. For example, a study published as early as 2011 by the International Consortium of Investigative Journalists reported that 'more than 2,200 of the 7,622 Red Notices that it examined were published as a result of requests from nations that did not respect human rights and that nearly half were from countries that Transparency International ranks as among the most corrupt in the world'.[31] Freedom House's 2022 report on transnational repression also tracks more recent examples of autocratic use of Interpol to detain political dissidents in countries around the world and highlights the use of 'digital tactics', including Interpol notices to find and detain dissidents (Gorokhovskaia and Linzer).[32]

---

[29] Morris, P. 2019. *Congress Seeks Reform of Red Notice Abuse*, Anticorruption blog (https://www.anticorruptionblog.com/u-s-congress/congress-seeks-reform-of-red-notice-abuse/).

[30] All below assertions, unless otherwise noted, are from Testimony: Sandra Grossman, *How Abusive Red Notices Affect People in the US Immigration System and Steps That Can Be Taken Within the US and at INTERPOL to Protect Victims* (US Helsinki Commission 2019).

[31] Bromund, T. and Kopel, D. 2013. *Necessary Reforms Can Keep Interpol Working in the US Interest*, Heritage Found (https://www.heritage.org/global-politics/report/necessary-reforms-can-keep-interpol-working-the-us-interest).

[32] Freedom House. 2022. *Defending Democracy in Exile, Policy Responses to Transnational Repression*. Retrieved 28 July 2022 (https://freedomhouse.org/sites/default/files/2022-05/Complete_TransnationalRepressionReport2022_NEW_0.pdf).

Often unchecked, abusive Red Notices begin to circulate in US law enforcement databases after they are communicated to the US National Central Bureau for Interpol, the entity handling direct communication between Interpol and the United States.[33] Law enforcement agencies – and in particular the Department of Homeland Security's enforcement branch, Immigration and Customs Enforcement (ICE) – utilise Red Notices to target foreign nationals for detention and deportation. If a person enters the United States on a valid visa that is then cancelled based on the publication of a Red Notice, the abusive foreign nation has essentially manufactured a false immigration violation in the US simply by lodging the Red Notice request.

Despite some increased interest in understanding persecutory notices, ICE has historically referred to those with Red Notices as 'violent criminals and other high priority fugitives who pose a danger to our communities'.[34] The agency targeted the subjects of Red Notices for arrest beginning in 2010, and under the name 'Project Red' beginning in 2015.[35] As recently as December 2018, ICE claimed to have arrested 105 people in Project Red.[36] While the public face of Project Red appears to have been limited to violent, dangerous fugitives, the net ICE continues to cast is much broader. While there are no official statistics, individuals with no criminal history, who are lawfully seeking asylum or other immigration benefits, are apprehended by ICE based on Red Notices and other INTERPOL data. Often these Red Notices allege vague, *non-violent* crimes. Unlike ICE, as a matter of policy, the US Department of Justice treats Red Notices simply as a request to look out for someone, rather than as a sufficient basis for arrest.[37]

---

[33] See Interpol. *National Central Bureaus (NCBs)*. Retrieved 10 April 2023 (https://www.interpol.int/en/Who-we-are/Member-countries/National-Central-Bureaus-NCBs).

[34] ICE. 2021. *Project Red*. Retrieved 28 July 2022 (https://www.ice.gov/features/project-red).

[35] Bromund, T. 2018. *ICE Wrongly Continues to Use Interpol Red Notices for Targeting*, Forbes (https://www.forbes.com/sites/tedbromund/2018/12/19/ice-wrongly-continues-to-use-interpol-red-notices-for-targeting/?sh=4435bc33175e#4bb6704c175e).

[36] *Id.*

[37] US Department of Justice. *Interpol Washington*. Retrieved 21 April 2021 (https://www.justice.gov/interpol-washington/frequently-asked-questions).

Challenging the Immigration Impact of a Red Notice Before US Immigration Agencies and US Federal Courts

Mr X, a citizen of China and successful entrepreneur in his 60s, fled his home country after he blew the whistle on rampant government corruption in his industry and was faced with death threats, physical assault and false criminal charges. After arriving in the United States on a valid visa, he was arrested at his home and placed in removal proceedings. Only then did he learn that he was the target of a Red Notice from China. The Immigration Judge denied him bond because he was allegedly a flight risk due to the Red Notice. Mr X's health deteriorated rapidly in detention, which was just as the Covid-19 pandemic began raging in jail facilities across the United States. After nine months of bond appeals, Mr X was released when a District Court granted his habeas corpus petition and the Immigration Court reversed its initial decision. Mr X was not able to challenge his Red Notice until his life was endangered from its consequences. Interpol ultimately deleted his Red Notice several months later, finding that it was not in compliance with the Universal Declaration of Human Rights and Interpol's Rules on the Processing of Data.

The negative impact of an abusive Red Notice on an individual's US immigration process cannot be overstated. While US constitutional protections apply to all persons in the United States, the rights of non-citizens are, in practice, extremely limited in the context of civil immigration law. US Immigration Courts have been described as conducting 'death penalty cases in a traffic court setting'.[38] In spite of the dire consequences to non-citizens, there is no guaranteed right to counsel. Once the target of a persecutory Red Notice has been apprehended and placed in removal proceedings, sometimes at their asylum interview, they face two formidable challenges: (1) seeking release from immigration detention to properly fight their case, and (2) proving they are not barred from seeking asylum.

How Red Notices Affect Eligibility for Release on Bond during Removal Proceedings

If the Department of Homeland Security seeks to remove a foreign national from the United States, then the agency will issue a document providing

---

[38] Marks, D. L. 2014. *Immigration judge: Death penalty cases in a traffic court setting.* CNN. (https://www.cnn.com/2014/06/26/opinion/immigration-judge-broken-system).

notice of the government's intent to remove them. This charging document, or Notice to Appear, signals to the foreign national that they must appear in Immigration Court and plead their case before an Immigration Judge. Some individuals may be subject to mandatory detention during the pendency of their removal proceedings due to certain criminal offences.[39] Others are detained at the discretion of ICE.[40] In order for someone detained in ICE custody to be granted bond by an Immigration Judge, he must show he is neither a danger to the community nor a flight risk.[41] This is a discretionary finding, meaning that the judge is largely unconstrained in their decision.[42] Case law establishes that a Red Notice is not a sufficient basis for denial of bond,[43] but immigration courts and US District Courts often inappropriately attribute dispositive, negative weight to a Red Notice without further analysis of its context and effect.

When evaluating 'danger to the community' and 'flight risk', multiple District Courts reviewing petitions for habeas corpus have determined that a Red Notice alone is not sufficient grounds for denial of bond.[44] This is particularly so when the petitioner can show evidence to rebut the Red Notice allegations, including that the country at issue is known for abusive Red Notices.[45] In *Kharis* v. *Sessions*, a habeas corpus decision from the Northern District of California, the court recognised that Red Notices may in fact *limit* a person's ability to travel, such that they cannot be the sole basis for establishing flight risk.[46] Subsequent cases, such as *Torres Murillo* v. *Barr*, echo that a Red Notice alone does not conclusively prove flight risk, but that it can be a contributing factor, especially when there is no indication of political persecution associated with the notice.[47]

[39] Immigr. & Nat'lity Act, 8 U.S.C. § 1226(c) (1996).

[40] 8 U.S.C. § 1226(a).

[41] *Matter of Guerra*, 24 I&N Dec. 37 (BIA 2006).

[42] *Id.*

[43] *Kharis* v. *Sessions*, Case No. 18-cv-04800-JST 2018 WL5809432 (N.D. Cal. Nov. 6, 2018).

[44] *Sato* v. *Sessions*, No. 18-CV-02891-EMC, 2018 WL 3619727, at *1 (N.D. Cal. July 30, 2018) (Red Notice issued as a result of interrogation).

[45] *Id.*

[46] *Kharis*, Case No. 18-cv-04800-JST 2018 WL5809432.

[47] *Torres-Murillo* v. *Barr*, Case No. 3:19-cv-05676 (N.D. Cal. Oct. 23, 2019).

In *Kharis* v. *Sessions*, a Russian citizen and asylum seeker in valid student visa status was the target of a Red Notice requested by Russia. The Red Notice was based on a Russian warrant for alleged embezzlement.[48] When Kharis attended his appointment to receive the decision on his asylum application, he was arrested by ICE and placed in removal proceedings. The Immigration Judge denied him bond for being a flight risk and the Board of Immigration Appeals (BIA or the Board)[49] affirmed. Kharis challenged these decisions and presented evidence undermining the reliability of the Red Notice, but was unable to win release during his proceedings. Having exhausted all options at the administrative level, Kharis petitioned for habeas corpus relief in District Court, challenging the government's authority to hold him in spite of strong evidence that he was entitled to bond.

The Northern District Court of California in *Kharis* concluded that a Red Notice is entitled to 'at least some weight' when considering whether a petitioner is a flight risk.[50] The court reasoned that it is common sense that the 'existence and seriousness of pending criminal charges' has an impact on assessing flight risk.[51] It emphasised that there is precedent that, though Red Notices do carry some weight, courts cannot look at criminal charges alone, especially when alleged only and that by 'a foreign nation [that] is allowed to initiate those charges without satisfying a probable cause standard'.[52] The court ultimately granted Kharis's habeas corpus petition, compelling the government to release him or conduct a bond hearing comporting with US Constitutional due process requirements.

Each favourable bond appeal or District Court decision nonetheless provides another example of an individual that has been detained unjustly and trapped in immigration detention for months, or even years. The individuals who overcome these unjust bond denials represent the extremely small minority that have

---

[48] No. 18-cv-04800-JST 2018 WL5809432 1 (N.D. Cal. 2018).

[49] The Board of Immigration Appeals (the Board or BIA) is an administrative appellate body that is part of the US Department of Justice (DOJ), with jurisdiction over appeals from Immigration Court decisions. Board decisions are binding on Immigration Courts nationwide unless they are modified or overruled by the Attorney General or a federal court.

[50] No. 18-cv-04800-JST 2018 WL5809432 1 (N.D. Cal. 2018) at 8.

[51] *Id.*

[52] *Id.*

the capacity and resources to challenge these decisions. Only 14 per cent of individuals in immigration detention have representation. [53]

This means that most who are wrongfully denied bond due to an abusive Red Notice will not have the resources to successfully challenge their detention. Equally troubling, immigration detention in the US, while formally considered civil detention, has many practical similarities to criminal detention.[54] Immigration detention restricts rights in a manner similar to criminal incarceration, resulting in diminished access to counsel and the creation of challenges to compiling the necessary evidence to prove eligibility. Further, unlike individuals with the benefits and protections of US citizenship, non-citizens seeking refuge are unlikely to overcome such hurdles. And as discussed below, asylum eligibility is significantly more challenging for those who are targets of abusive Red Notices.

How Red Notices Affect Eligibility for Asylum

The United States has long been a destination for individuals fleeing persecution around the world. The Refugee Act of 1980 incorporated into US law the definition of a refugee established by the United Nations 1951 Convention and 1967 Protocol: 'someone who is unable or unwilling to return to their country of origin owing to a well-founded fear of being persecuted for reasons of race, religion, nationality, membership of a particular social group, or political opinion'.[55] Through legislative changes, evolving case law, and agency

[53] Eagly, Ingrid, Esq. and Steven Shager, Esq. 2016. *Access to Counsel in Immigration Court*. American Immigration Counsel (https://www.americanimmigrationcouncil.org/sites/default/files/research/access_to_counsel_in_immigration_court.pdf).

[54] 'The entangled legislative history of incarceration as a method of sanctioning criminal conduct and immigration law violations would eventually lead to two detention regimes . . . Perhaps of greatest significance to the individuals whose liberty is at stake, however, and despite the civil labeling of immigration detention, both create an unmistakable penal reality for the people confined.' Garcia Hernandez, Cesar Cuauhtemoc. 2014. *Immigration Detention as Punishment*. 35 IMMIGR. & NAT'IITY L. REV 385.

[55] UN General Assembly. 1951. *Convention Relating to the Status of Refugees*. United Nations, Treaty Series, vol. 189, p. 137. Retrieved 21 July 2022 (https://www.refworld.org/docid/3be01b964.html); UN General Assembly. 1967. *Protocol Relating to the Status of Refugees*. United Nations, Treaty Series, vol. 606, p. 267. Retrieved 21 July 2022 (https://www.refworld.org/docid/3ae6b3ae4.html); Immigr. & Nat'lity Act, 8 U.S.C. § 1158 (1980).

action over the past four decades, the United States has created various barriers to asylum protection for individuals with criminal histories. The criminal allegations contained in a Red Notice can trigger these bars, even when the allegations themselves form part of the victim's persecution.

To be granted asylum protection, an applicant must show eligibility for asylum as a matter of law and a matter of discretion. As a matter of law, a foreign national cannot be subject to any statutory bars, including the conviction of an 'aggravated felony',[56] the persecution of others and commission of a *serious nonpolitical crime*.[57] As recent litigation demonstrates, the 'serious nonpolitical crime' bar, in particular, has resulted in the denial of asylum based only on criminal accusations that are contained in Red Notices. As explained below, this issue has been hotly litigated, yielding both administrative and appellate decisions that demonstrate the current understanding of Red Notices in US courts.

The Board of Immigration Appeals and Red Notices: Matter of W-E-R-B

The Board of Immigration Appeals is the highest administrative body for interpreting and applying immigration laws. In 2020 the Board issued the precedent decision, *Matter of W-E-R-B*,[58] holding that an Interpol Red Notice may constitute reliable evidence that an asylum applicant has committed a serious nonpolitical crime, rendering the applicant ineligible for asylum. A closer look at the decision reveals that the holding is narrow in scope, reflecting an imperfect but evolving understanding of abusive Red Notices.

The applicant in *Matter of W-E-R-B* is a citizen of El Salvador who conceded that he was deportable but applied for asylum. Based on Red Notice data stating that he was the subject of an arrest warrant in El Salvador for 'participation in an illicit organization',[59] an Immigration Judge found him ineligible for asylum and withholding of removal. The alleged crime was deemed sufficient to trigger the 'serious nonpolitical crime' bar to entry into the United States.[60]

---

[56] Immigr. & Nat'lity Act, 8 U.S.C. § 1158(b)(2)(B)i) (1994).

[57] 8 U.S.C. § 1158(b)(2)(A).

[58] *Matter of W-E-R-B*, 27 I&N Dec. 795 (BIA 2020).

[59] *Matter of W-E-R-B* at 795–6.

[60] See Section 208(b)(2)(A)(iii) of the Act (asylum); see also section 241(b)(3)(B)(iii) of the Act (withholding of removal); 8 C.F.R. § 1208.16(d)(2) (2019) (withholding of removal under the Convention Against Torture).

The applicant appealed, arguing that 'the Red Notice does not have any probative value because such a notice is insufficient to establish probable cause for an arrest in the United States under the Fourth Amendment'.[61]

The Board found that there were 'serious reasons for believing' that the applicant committed a serious nonpolitical crime, which triggers the bar to asylum. To establish that the serious nonpolitical crime bar did not apply, the Respondent provided a letter from an attorney in El Salvador attesting that the charges related to this offence were dismissed. No court documents were submitted.[62] Importantly, the Respondent conceded that the offence was nonpolitical. As a result, the Board only needed to assess whether the alleged offence was serious. With damning allegations of assault on a police officer and serving as a hitman for MS-13, it is no surprise that the alleged crime was found to be serious.

More concerning, there is *dicta* in *Matter of W-E-R-B* that betrays an exaggerated, misplaced faith in the legitimacy of Red Notices. While the Board confirms that a Red Notice is not 'a formal international arrest warrant', it quotes Department of Justice guidance stating that it 'is the closest instrument to an international arrest warrant in use today'.[63] Further, the decision indicates that because Interpol prohibits Red Notices regarding predominantly political offences, then all Red Notices are based on ordinary law crimes.[64] However, as previously discussed, just because a Red Notice is published by Interpol does not mean the underlying arrest warrant is valid, and it certainly does not mean the crime is 'not political' in nature.

---

[61] *Matter of W-E-R-B* at 798.

[62] It is relevant to note that often Interpol databases may be outdated and contain information that has otherwise been dismissed or cleared up in national databases. The authors are aware of several cases where an individual was issued a Red Notice due to underlying criminal proceedings that were later dismissed. Even though those proceedings were terminated in favour of the individuals, it can take years for Interpol to update its databases and then disseminate such information to its member states.

[63] See US Department of Justice Archives. Criminal Resource Manual, Section 611, Interpol *Red Notices*. Retrieved 7 April 2020 (https://www.justice.gov/archives/jm/criminal-resource-manual-611-interpol-red-notices).

[64] *Matter of W-E-R-B* at 798 ('The Immigration Judge further noted that a Red Notice may be published only if it fulfills all conditions for processing information, which include the criteria that the offense concerned is a serious ordinary law crime').

Fortunately, the Board includes *dicta* that serves as a guide to distinguishing the *W-E-R-B-* holding, particularly in cases where the Red Notice is illegitimate and persecutory in nature. The Board makes clear in a lengthy footnote that in cases where the individual provides evidence that the underlying criminal charges are politically motivated, the Immigration Judge 'should consider evidence in the record that the foreign country issuing the Red Notice abuses them for political reasons'.[65] While it is unfortunate that the most accurate acknowledgement of Red Notice vulnerabilities is placed in a Footnote, the message is clear: the Board acknowledges that some Red Notices are bogus, and it is up to the asylum applicant to prove it.

US Courts of Appeals and Red Notices

Although the holding of *Matter of W-E-R-B* had a significant foundation in prior Circuit Court precedent,[66] subsequent Circuit Court decisions provide essential language for mitigating it. In February 2021, the Eighth Circuit held in *Barahona* v. *Wilkinson* that a Red Notice, absent any other evidence, is insufficient to meet the probable cause standard.[67] Further supporting evidence is needed to trigger mandatory denial of asylum, based on committing a 'serious nonpolitical crime'.

In the *Barahona* case, DHS offered an Interpol Red Notice against Barahona, and the reviewing Immigration Judge denied his asylum request. The Judge concluded that 'serious reasons existed to believe that' Barahona committed serious nonpolitical crimes outside the United States.[68] The BIA affirmed that decision, finding that DHS met the probable cause standard for the 'serious nonpolitical crimes' bar, with 'some evidence' to support the bar's

---

[65] Matter of W-E-R-B- at n.5.

[66] See, for example, *Silva-Pereira* v. *Lynch*, 827 F.3d 1176 (9th Cir. 2016) (holding that an indictment alleging 'very specific facts', such as an eyewitness and an exact location, combined with a Red Notice, met the serious nonpolitical crime bar); *Khouzam* v. *Ashcroft*, 361 F.3d 161 (2d Cir. 2004) (holding that specific allegations, DNA evidence and eyewitness testimony sufficiently corroborated a Red Notice, triggering the serious nonpolitical crime bar).

[67] See *Barahona* v. *Wilkinson*, 986 F.3d 1090, 1095 (8th Cir. 2021) ('The parties did not cite, and we could not find, a case in which a court has found a Red Notice, alone, is sufficient to meet this standard').

[68] *Id.* at 1093.

application.[69] The Eighth Circuit Court of Appeals reversed and remanded the BIA's decision, holding that a showing of 'some evidence' does not establish 'probable cause'.[70] That is, a Red Notice alone did not suffice to support a finding of probable cause that a crime had been committed.

The Ninth Circuit Court of Appeals affirmed the same standard for the application of the serious nonpolitical crime bar to asylum in two cases. Most recently, in *Gonzalez-Castillo* v. *Garland*, the court held the government needed to provide more than just 'some evidence' to prove that the bar applied. Rather, a 'serious reason to believe standard' requires a fair probability that the non-citizen committed the crime.[71] The court thus held that the Red Notice cannot by itself establish probable cause.

The Ninth Circuit applied the same probable cause standard in *Villalobos Sura* v. *Garland*, holding that the existence on the record of a Red Notice *and* an arrest warrant established a fair probability that the non-citizen committed a serious nonpolitical crime, to wit, the murder of four men.[72] Nevertheless, although this holding follows the decisions cited above, it is problematic in the misplaced credence paid to the idea that Interpol Red Notices are inherently accurate and the best evidence of criminality.

Under the facts presented by the case, the non-citizen was the subject of an arrest warrant issued by the Special Examining Magistrate's Court in San Miguel, El Salvador. The warrant formed the basis of the Red Notice against the non-citizen (Villalobos Sura). Both the warrant and the Red Notice listed someone with Villalobos Sura's name, age, birthday and place of residence, and charged them with contempt of court in absentia for failure to appear to answer the charge of aggravated murder.[73] Villalobos Sura conceded in court that he matched the general description in the Notice, a concession that should have been paid little deference because an essential part of Villalobos Sura's claim was that he was framed for the alleged crime.[74]

---

[69] *Id.*

[70] *Id.* at 1095.

[71] See *Gonzalez-Castillo* v. *Garland*, 47 F.4th 971 (9th Cir. 2022).

[72] *Villalobos Sura* v. *Garland*, 8 F.4th 1161 (9th Cir. 2021).

[73] *Id.* at 1165.

[74] *Id.* at 1165, 1168.

Although the Ninth Circuit recognised that the arrest warrant for the aggravated murders was not part of the record, it found the warrant, when taken in conjunction with the Red Notice, to be sufficient evidence to establish probable cause that Villalobos Sura committed the alleged crime.[75] In other words, the Red Notice, a document with no independent probative value, containing the unsupported allegations of a notoriously weak judicial system, made all the difference in the application of the serious nonpolitical crime bar to asylum. The Ninth Circuit denied Villalobos Sura's applications for asylum and protection under the Convention Against Torture. The misplaced weight given to the Red Notice in this case is very troubling, and subsequent decisions arising on the basis of it should be carefully reviewed.

The above cases illustrate the evolving case law since *Matter of W-E-R-B*. The trend seems to be at least some understanding, at least among Circuit Courts, that the deference accorded to a Red Notice largely depends on the facts of the case, what the target of the Red Notice is willing to concede, and the other documents presented by the government in their attempt to apply the serious crime bar to asylum. Courts hearing protection claims from foreign nationals would be well served by understanding that Interpol communications are often nothing more than the unsupported allegations of a requesting government. The requirement for solid, independent, corroborative evidence is the best way to ensure the correct use of Red Notices.

Recommendations for Safeguards to Prevent Backdoor Extraditions

Interpol is required by its guiding principles and foundational documents to work '[t]o ensure and promote the widest possible mutual assistance between all criminal police authorities within the limits of the laws existing in the different countries and in the spirit of the "Universal Declaration of Human Rights"'.[76] Since Article 14 of the Universal Declaration of Human Rights expressly provides that '[e]veryone has the right to seek and to enjoy in other

---

[75] *Id.* at 1167–8.

[76] Interpol, Constitution, art. 2. Retrieved 10 April 2023 (https://www.interpol.int/content/download/590/file/01%20E%20CONSTITUTION%2011%202021.pdf); see also UN General Assembly. 1948. *Universal Declaration of Human Rights*, 217 A (III). Retrieved 21 July 2022 (https://www.refworld.org/docid/3ae6b3712c.html).

countries asylum from persecution', Interpol is accordingly obligated to ensure its practices do not infringe on the right to asylum. Given that the purpose of a Red Notice is to seek the location and arrest of wanted persons with a view to extradition, processing and maintaining such Notices, especially when the target of a Red Notice is an asylum seeker, is contrary to the rights of refugees under the Universal Declaration and as established by the 1951 Convention and the 1967 Protocol.[77]

With the recent increase in the number of Red Notices in circulation, and the prevalence of Interpol abuse by certain nations, more light is being shed on the potentially abusive aspects of the Interpol data-sharing system in the context of refugees and asylum seekers, highlighting the need for additional safeguards.

Strengthen Interpol's Refugee Policy

In 2017, after pressure from organisations like Fair Trials International, Freedom House and others, Interpol passed a resolution aiming to ensure that refugees and asylum seekers/asylees are afforded greater protections regarding Red Notices.[78] One of Interpol's stated goals was to bring Interpol procedures more in line with the safeguards contained in the 1951 Convention Relating to the Status of Refugees.[79] The resolution states that Red Notices could not be issued if: '1. The status of refugee or asylum seeker has been confirmed; 2. The notice/diffusion has been requested by the country where the individual fears persecution; 3. The granting of the refugee status is not based on political grounds vis-à-vis the requesting country.'[80] Practically speaking, however, asylum applicants in the United States continue to be the targets of bogus Red Notices and diffusions.

---

[77] UN General Assembly. 1951. *Convention Relating to the Status of Refugees*. United Nations, Treaty Series, vol. 189, p. 137. Retrieved 21 July 2022 (https://www.refworld.org/docid/3be01b964.html); UN General Assembly. 1967. *Protocol Relating to the Status of Refugees*. United Nations, Treaty Series, vol. 606, p. 267. Retrieved 21 July 2022 (https://www.refworld.org/docid/3ae6b3ae4.html).

[78] Fair Trials. 2018. *Dismantling the Tools of Oppression: Ending the Misuse of INTERPOL*. (https://www.fairtrials.org/sites/default/files/publication_pdf/Dismantling%20the%20tools%20of%20oppression.pdf) .

[79] *Id.*

[80] *Id.*

In many cases, it is not until after an individual informs the CCF that they have a pending asylum claim, or that they have been granted asylum, that the CCF will provisionally remove the Red Notice. The CCF deletion decision can be rescinded if asylum is denied. This continues to be problematic when judges apply the serious nonpolitical crime bar to asylum, in large part *because* of the Red Notice. As seen above, in these types of cases, despite the well-intentioned Refugee Policy, the Red Notice acts to thwart the asylum claim. The result is that the individual asylum seeker never gets a fair hearing on his request. The very reason the individual was fleeing persecution, pretextual criminal proceedings, becomes the basis for denying asylum. Interpol has a long way to go to improve and solidify its Refugee Policy.

Monitor Sources of Red Notice Requests and Prohibit US Immigration Authorities from Using Notices Issued by Repressive Governments

Interpol's intention to comply with the principles in the Universal Declaration of Human Rights (UDHR) certainly assists in curbing Interpol abuse, but immigration officials in the United States also have an important role to play. Under US immigration law and the 1967 Protocol, to which the United States is a signatory, the US is obligated to provide protection to individuals who qualify as refugees.[81] The Department of Homeland Security should thus refrain from targeting non-US citizens, especially asylum applicants, simply because of a Red Notice. Any person who has filed a bona-fide asylum application in the United States and is the target of a Red Notice from the country where they fear persecution, should be protected from arrest, detention and removal. The US National Central Bureau (NCB) can certainly work with the DHS to establish additional safeguards.

Notably, US immigration officials now have a mandate to take such corrective and ameliorative measures under the Transnational Repression and Accountability Prevention (TRAP) Provision (2021). The passage of the TRAP Provision was a key first step in recognising the potential for abuse of Interpol and initiating important policy reforms to help strengthen Interpol's

---

[81] UN General Assembly. 1967. *Protocol Relating to the Status of Refugees.* United Nations, Treaty Series, vol. 606, p. 267 (https://www.refworld.org/docid/3ae6b3ae4.html).

processes for reviewing Red Notices.[82] The provision introduces several monitoring mechanisms to help enhance transparency and accountability, all of which are valuable starting points.[83] Most importantly, the TRAP Provision requires the Secretary of State and the Secretary of Homeland Security to submit a report to Congress on Interpol abuse by member countries and how the US monitors and responds to these instances of abuse, particularly when they could affect the interests of US citizens, individuals lawfully admitted for permanent residence, and individuals that have pending asylum, withholding or removal, or Convention against Torture claims.[84] The Department of Justic is additionally required to regularly produce a report of any incidents in which US courts and executive departments or agencies have relied on Interpol communications in contravention of existing law or policy to seek the detention of individuals or render judgements concerning their immigration status.[85] As stated, these mechanisms are a great starting point, but much still needs to be done to enhance accountability and ensure the US is not complicit in abuse of Interpol's systems.

First and foremost, further protections need to be enacted for the most vulnerable targets of Interpol abuse – US asylum applicants. The TRAP Provision itself falls short in this regard. As noted by Interpol abuse experts Bromund and Reich, previous versions of the TRAP Provision contained a broad range of co-operative actions between US departments and agencies and had stronger language regarding the need for transparency reforms at the organisation itself.[86] This language is absent from the enacted legislation. In the

---

[82] Commission on Security and Cooperation in Europe. 2021. *Helsinki Commission Welcomes Passage of TRAP Provision in 2022 National Defense Authorization Act* (https://www.csce.gov/international-impact/press-and-media/press-releases/helsinki-commission-welcomes-passage-trap).

[83] National Defense Authorization Act for Fiscal Year 2022, Pub. L. No. 117-81, § 6503, 135 Stat. 1541 (2021).

[84] *Id.*

[85] *Id.*

[86] Bromund, T. and Reich, J. 2021. *Abuse of Interpol for Transnational Repression: Assessing the FY22 NDAA's Provisions for Prevention.* Retrieved 28 July 2022 (https://www.justsecurity.org/79161/abuse-of-interpol-for-transnational-repression-assessing-the-fy22-ndaas-provisions-for-prevention/).

current TRAP Provision, there is no mandate for ICE to review Red Notice requests more carefully for individuals with pending asylum claims. There is no requirement that US law enforcement refrain from processing requests from notoriously autocratic countries, even when the target of the Red Notice is an asylum applicant. Finally, the TRAP Provision calls for a prohibition against extradition based solely on an Interpol Notice or Diffusion. This does not address or ameliorate the more nuanced issue of 'backdoor extraditions' in which a Red Notice target may be placed in US removal proceedings because of a spurious request through Interpol.

Additionally, the TRAP Provision must be seriously administered by the various agencies that are subject to its reporting requirements. The true impact of TRAP is largely untested. However, the first joint US Department of State and Department of Justice Report, as mandated by the TRAP Provision for the purposes of reviewing instances of abuse and supporting CCF reforms, does not bode well. The report largely fails to recognise the extent to which US agencies continue to rely on potentially persecutory Red Notices and the broad impacts of those Notices, especially on individuals seeking immigration benefits.[87] The DOJ and DOS jointly published their report in accordance with NDAA FY 2022 on 14 September 2022, stating 'the US Government will continue to work at home and abroad to deter and thwart the misuse of Interpol systems and to support and strengthen Interpol reforms'.[88] The Report suggests, contrary to reports from Fair Trials International and other organisations, that transnational repression, at least through Interpol, 'seems to have receded' since Interpol's reforms in 2016 and 2017.[89] The report fails

---

[87] See generally US Department of State and US Department of Justice. 2022. *Assessment of INTERPOL Member Country Abuse of INTERPOL Red Notices, Diffusions and Other INTERPOL Communications for Political Motives and Other Unlawful Purposes*. Retrieved 10 April 2023 (www.justice.gov/d9/pages/attachments/2022/09/14/2022-transnational-repression-accountability-and-prevention-act-report_-_public.pdf).

[88] *Id*. at 6.

[89] *Id*. at 1. But see Fair Trials. 2022. *FAQs About INTERPOL* (https://www.fairtrials.org/articles/information-and-toolkits/faqs-about-interpol/) ('[Interpol] has introduced significant reforms to strengthen its internal vetting procedures for red notices and diffusions. These improvements have not halted the misuse of Red Notices and diffusions, and Fair Trials has continued to see cases of political activists and human rights campaigners being unjustly targeted'); Meacham, S.

to acknowledge the reality of how Red Notices jeopardise the rights of foreign nationals in the United States. Only one section discusses incidents in which US agencies have relied on Interpol communications in contravention to existing law.[90] The report also incorrectly states that the DOJ and DOS do not arrest or detain individuals based on Interpol notices or diffusions when, as discussed in previous sections, US agencies target the subjects of Red Notices with visa revocations and enforcement actions.[91]

Increase Interpol Transparency and Improve US Understanding of Interpol Operations

The US federal courts, with their distinct role in the immigration system, will also continue to play a significant role in establishing how Red Notices impact the removal proceedings of immigrants in the United States. As Red Notice abuse continues, hopefully courts and agencies alike will develop a more nuanced understanding of the meaning of Red Notices and Interpol's data-sharing system. The ability of individuals to apply for protection under US asylum laws and the Convention Against Torture must not be whittled away by misguided decisions. A great deal of important work needs to be done in the United States, and by Interpol itself, to stop authoritarian regimes from co-opting law enforcement mechanisms to engage in transnational repression.

2022. *Weaponizing the Police: Interpol as a Tool of Authoritarianism.* Harv. Int'l L. Rev. (https://hir.harvard.edu/weaponizing-the-police-authoritarian-abuse-of-interpol/#:~:text=Broadly%20speaking%2C%20the%20abuse%20of,weaponize%20them%20against%20global%20democracy); Jacobs, J. 2021. *Has Interpol Become the Long Arm of Oppressive Regimes? The Guardian* (https://www.theguardian.com/global-development/2021/oct/17/has-interpol-become-the-long-arm-of-oppressive-regimes).

[90] US Department of State and US Department of Justice. 2022. *Assessment of INTERPOL Member Country Abuse of INTERPOL Red Notices, Diffusions and Other INTERPOL Communications for Political Motives and Other Unlawful Purposes.* Retrieved 10 April 2023, pp. 5–6 (www.justice.gov/d9/pages/attachments/2022/09/14/2022-transnational-repression-accountability-and-prevention-act-report_-_public.pdf).

[91] *Id.* at 5; *see* Grossman, Young and Hammond. *INTERPOL Resources.* Retrieved 10 April 2023 (https://www.grossmanyoung.com/interpol-resources/) (listing cases in which DHS submitted an Interpol Red Notice to establish a respondent's ineligibility for immigration benefits, including asylum).

10

TURKEY'S DIASPORIC LANDSCAPES AMID AUTHORITARIANISM: TRANSNATIONAL REPRESSION, EVERYDAY DYNAMICS AND HOST-COUNTRY RESPONSES

Gözde Böcü, Bahar Baser and Ahmet Erdi Öztürk

Introduction

Over the last decade, Turkey has been going through a path-changing transformation towards authoritarianism under the rule of the Justice and Development Party (*Adalet ve Kalkinma Partisi*, hereafter AKP) and its leader President Recep Tayyip Erdoğan that has exacerbated the practice of transnational repression abroad. Although the AKP came to power with a promising agenda of democratisation reforms in the 2000s, events evolved differently as the ruling party gained more power over time. Today, Turkey is not only careening further away from the main pillars of democracy (Baser and Öztürk 2020; Topak 2017), but is in the process of consolidating a new authoritarian regime (Akçay 2021).

This process has been accelerated by the coup attempt in 2016 that has been followed by a massive crackdown on opposition groups at home and abroad (Esen and Gumuscu 2017). The night of 15 July 2016 represents one of the most important moments in Turkey's contemporary political history. A group of Turkish army flag officers attempted to mount a coup against the AKP government, but it was feeble compared to past attempts of military intervention in Turkey's history. The coup was repelled with the support of opposition parties and devoted civilians; 265 people died and 2,797 were wounded in the struggle. After the coup attempt was dismissed, more than 150,000 people were suspended and some 50,000 were jailed.[1] Some called this process a 'purge', where thousands of people who sympathised with the controversial Gülen Movement (GM) and others opposing the AKP in Turkey were sacked from their posts by emergency decrees, arrested and destined for civil death. As a result of these events and additional dismantling of democratic institutions and processes in Turkey, the country is increasingly classified as an electoral autocracy or competitive authoritarian regime (Esen and Gumuscu 2016).

The attempted coup in 2016 constitutes a turning point for the acceleration of emigration from Turkey to Europe, yet this process can be traced back to the aftermath of the Gezi protests in 2013. During this time, many people in Turkey lost hopes for further reforms and democratisation in the country. In these early days of democratic decline, many white-collar migrants, students and activists began leaving Turkey voluntarily to start a new life abroad. However, after the coup attempt, decisions to emigrate from Turkey were largely involuntary or taken out of severe necessity because of fear of persecution, arrest and torture (Öztürk and Baser 2021). High approval rates for asylum applications at the beginning of this process indicated immediate sympathy for vulnerable groups from Turkey. However, such processes have slowed down significantly and continue to be further affected by the Covid-19 pandemic – ultimately, impacting migration flows from Turkey to Europe. While migration waves triggered after 2013 are new, these newcomers tend to join older cohorts of emigrants abroad. Previous waves of mass migration from Turkey to Europe started in the 1960s in the form of labour migration and were followed by smaller waves of political emigration triggered by coups d'états and intensification of the low-scale civil war in the 1980s (Böcü 2022). During more recent decades, however, Turkey's diasporas have been changing dramatically through new waves of migration, which is increasingly transforming the composition of diasporic landscapes as well as the relations between the host countries and Turkey (Özturk and Baser 2021).

---

[1] DW. 2018. Germany: Turks still seeking asylum. 04.01.2018. [Online]. Available at: https://www.dw.com/en/turkish-diplomats-and-civil-servants-among-asylum-claimantssince-2016-failed-coup/a-43217296

Turkey, therefore, constitutes an important case study for those who want to understand how autocratisation in the homeland affects diaspora governance at large, as well as diasporic groups and their interactions with actors of the home and host countries. In recent decades, scholars have focused on how diasporas are formed (Butler 2001; Van Hear 2014), why they are mobilised (Adamson 2005; Sökefeld 2006; Moss 2022), how home and host countries respond to the ascending role they play (Bruneau 2010; Shain 1994), and their impact on political processes at home and abroad (Shain 2002; Shain and Barth 2003). Recent studies and contributions to this volume advance this literature by showing that authoritarian home states introduce, adapt and innovate their strategies to coerce dissident populations outside the borders of the home state when needed. This burgeoning literature demonstrates how authoritarian home states use an array of transnational strategies to suppress, coerce and control diaspora voices beyond the borders of the nation-state (Adamson 2018; Baser and Öztürk 2020; Cooley and Heathershaw 2017; Lemon 2019; Michaelsen 2017; Moss 2016; Tsourapas 2020) in places such as the Philippines (see Quinsaat in this volume), Eritrea (see Hirt and Mohammad in this volume), Egypt (see Furstenberg, Russo and Kennedy in this volume) and online spaces (see Michaelsen in this volume).

Although insights into transnational repression are evolving, we still need to better understand and conceptualise the complex dynamics which enable state-led repression in the diaspora and grant home states increasing authority over immigrant populations. First and foremost, there is a substantial gap in the literature regarding the responses of liberal host countries to such actions. Western states committed to democracy, human rights and freedom of speech find themselves in a challenging position when authoritarianism diffuses into their territories (Baser and Féron 2022). Host states usually treat these cases as an extension of homeland conflicts, and their existing foreign and domestic policies fall short in addressing the consequences of transnational repression within their borders.

Secondly, the existing literature mostly focuses on the visible and high-intensity forms of transnational repression that threaten dissident members of the diaspora through kidnapping, assassination, monitoring or proxy punishment. However, repression practices, as further discussed by Glasius in this volume, can take forms that are less visible and observable, and of lower intensity, which produce significant effects on members of the diaspora who may not define themselves as dissidents or exiles *per se* (Moss 2016, 2022).

Third, micro-level effects of transnational repression on group-level dynamics remain largely underexplored. Transnational repression mechanisms at times create a one-size-fits-all strategy to address the diaspora population as a whole and therefore engender mistrust and contention at the intra- and intergroup level in diverse diaspora groups which are divided along ethnic, religious and ideological cleavages, despite being originated from the same country. Moreover, host state–diaspora relations are also affected by the interferences from authoritarian home states, further impacting social and political dynamics within the diaspora.

The chapter addresses these gaps through an in-depth case study of Turkey's varying transnational repression efforts on European soil by specifically exploring its dynamics and host- country responses to these state-led processes. Turkey constitutes an important case for analysing issues pertaining to transnational repression policies and practices of authoritarian homelands as it has recently expanded the intensity, geographical scope and suddenness of its transnational repression efforts.[2] The chapter studies transnational repression by focusing on the triadic relationship between Turkey, its diasporas and various European host countries. It not only sheds light on elite-level political processes with regard to Turkey–European host state relations, but also brings to the fore everyday dynamics of transnational repression in Turkey's diaspora communities in Europe, revealing the visible and invisible effects of transnational authoritarianism on diaspora populations. The findings presented in this chapter are based on more than forty in-depth interviews with policy-makers, diaspora organisation representatives and members of the diaspora in Germany, France, Switzerland, Norway, the United Kingdom and Greece, conducted by the authors between 2017 and 2022. The chapter first attends to Turkey's authoritarian turn under the AKP regime, then describes the various transnational repression strategies and practices used in lieu of regime change. Finally, it examines everyday dynamics of transnational repression among different intradiasporic groups, as well as host states' responses to transnational repression. We close with a summary of our findings and concluding remarks.

---

[2] Freedom House. 2021. Out of sight, not out of reach. Case Study: Turkey. [Online]. Available at: https://freedomhouse.org/sites/default/files/2021-02/FH_TransnationalRepression Report2021_rev020221_CaseStudy_Turkey.pdf

Turkey's Authoritarian Turn under the AKP Regime

Founded in the early 2000s, and born of a branch of the religious-nationalist movement in Turkey, the AKP came to power in 2002 under the ostensible leadership of Abdullah Gül, and initially portrayed itself as a conservative party embracing democracy (Gumuscu and Sert 2009). In line with this image, the democratically elected AKP government subscribed to principles of democratisation and Europeanisation, and promised to create a freer society respecting freedom of religion and conscience, a stronger market economy, and to offer a resolution to the long-standing 'Kurdish question' (an armed conflict between the Turkish state and the Kurdistan Workers' Party (Partiya Karkerên Kurdistan, PKK)) (Dagi 2008).[3] Winning subsequent elections with sweepingly high vote shares allowed the AKP to advance domestic and foreign policy priorities by way of a series of legal and constitutional reforms.

Early in this process, the AKP also entered a coalition with various groups that supported its agenda, including the Gülen Movement – a multilayered religious organisation established in the mid-1960s by its leader Fethullah Gülen (Yavuz 2013). Although the AKP's founding cadre and the Gülen Movement had historically never seen eye to eye (Turam 2007), the coalition was initiated based on the common goal of weakening and eliminating the influence of Kemalist and secular elites over the state. As such, the Gülen Movement offered support for the AKP, granting access to media institutions, protecting the party and conducting joint operations with help from its members lodged within the state. This coalition soon started to settle accounts, and launch campaigns aimed at removing Kemalist, secular and Eurasian groups from pivotal positions within state structures through orchestrated plots. To legitimise these moves, the AKP thus launched various legal operations to jail more than five hundred Kurdish politicians between 2009 and 2013 under the guise of antiterrorism (Updegraff 2012).[4]

With the bureaucratic strengthening of Erdoğan's AKP after the 2010 constitutional referendum, the dominance of the Kemalist elites over the

---

[3] In this context, the AKP also distanced itself from a nationalistic discourse advanced by former ruling elites, and instead turned towards democratisation to further portray itself as a part of the Western bloc (Saatçioğlu 2010).

[4] The essential goal was to silence Kurdish groups that the ruling party and the Gülen Movement were unable to persuade to join their cause.

state was challenged, while the AKP grew increasingly authoritarian, both in terms of its political discourse and strategies –ultimately triggering processes of democratic decline. The growing discontent with the AKP's increasingly autocratic stance – in particular among young people and marginalised parts of society – resulted in the Gezi Park protests in May 2013. While the protests had initially started in opposition to an urban development project at the heart of Istanbul's Taksim Square, the government's incitement of violence against protests and dismissal of protesters as 'a few looters' triggered large-scale protests across seventy-nine provinces in Turkey (Arat 2013: 807–9). The Gezi protests, and the events that followed, marked the AKP's growing distance from the democratic principles that the party had subscribed to in the 2000s. In the aftermath of the Gezi protests, the Gülen–AKP coalition also started to deteriorate, and culminated in the failed coup attempt in July 2016. Backed by other politicians and media outlets, Erdoğan accused the Gülen Movement of attempting a coup, and introduced a permanent state of emergency. In order to legitimise this decision, Erdoğan declared repeatedly that 'the people' and 'the nation' faced an existential threat from the GM and that the AKP was essential to their survival. Under the conditions of the state of emergency, the AKP started ruling the country through statutory decrees, significantly limiting the powers of the parliament and judiciary and suspending democratic principles in practice.

A pivotal constitutional referendum held in 2017 under the conditions of a state of emergency transformed Turkey into a quasi-presidential autocracy, allowing for the ultimate dismantlement of democracy and transition to authoritarian rule under Erdoğan (Esen and Gumuscu 2017). To fill the gap left by the former alliance of the eradicated Gülen Movement, the regime ended resolution attempts with the Kurds and signalled a growing nationalistic stance, forming a new coalition with the nationalist branches of Turkish society, namely the Nationalist Movement Party (*Milliyetçi Hareket Partisi*). The coalition reflected the regime's growing attempts to legitimise and consolidate its rule by increasingly framing Kurds, Alevites, Leftists, Gülenists, Liberals and Kemalists as internal enemies that threaten Turkey's future, while blaming Western powers as external enemies for Turkey's ongoing economic and political problems. This ultimately constituted a new strategy of the AKP to unite its supporters, both at home and abroad (Böcü and Panwar 2022).

Turkey's Tightening Web of Transnational Repression across Europe

In line with these domestic trends, and Turkey's ongoing autocratisation, the AKP regime has extended and intensified its repressive policies and practices in the diaspora. While the intensive use of repressive practices by the AKP is new, transnational repression as a phenomenon shaping Turkey's diasporas is not. Since the early 1960s, Turkey's diasporas have been affected by political power struggles at home, including diaspora engagement and repression dynamics (Adamson 2018; Baser 2015). In the 1960s and 1970s, labour immigrants from Turkey emigrated to European countries such as Germany, France, the Netherlands and Austria under bilateral guest worker agreements that expected workers to return to Turkey upon completion of their contracts. However, as time passed and emigration continued, the permanency of migration became clear. Through family reunification schemes, workers brought their families abroad and the second-generation Turkish transnational community started emerging in the diaspora. In the meantime, political turmoil in Turkey pushed politically active groups such as leftists, Kurds, ultra-nationalists and religious groups opposing the secular state out of the country. Thousands of new migrants joined the labour migrants as asylum seekers, which resulted in the making of heterogeneous diasporas divided along ethnic, religious, class and political cleavages. At that time, much of Turkey's diasporic landscapes became a replica of political developments in Turkey, while political tensions and polarisation spilled over into these communities. As a result of the importation of homeland conflicts to transnational spaces (Baser 2015; Østergaard-Nielsen 2003) and competition for partisan influence in the diaspora (Senay 2012), Kemalist elites mobilised to curb the influence of 'undesirable' political movements abroad (ibid.). As such, between the late 1970s and 1980s, transnational repression of religious fundamentalist movements abroad became a major focus of Turkey's extraterritorial security practice. To this end, the Diyanet (the Presidency of Religious Affairs) was tasked with the goal to project a moderate Islam into the diaspora to prevent the spread of religious fundamentalism abroad (Mügge 2013; Öztürk and Sözeri 2018). As part of this process, the Diyanet established organisations across European host countries, provided financial assistance to their activities, and stocked the diaspora with homeland-educated imams (Maritato, Öktem and Zadrożna 2021). In the late 1980s and early 1990s, the intensification and escalation of armed conflict between the PKK and the state created a large-scale Kurdish emigration wave towards Europe, making Kurds one of the largest asylum-seeker communities in the world. Over time, different religious, ethnic and ideological diaspora groups established associations in European host countries, and diaspora mobilisation for homeland affairs became all the more visible (Baser 2015).

From the 1990s onwards, the state prioritised the repression of Kurdish diaspora activism as the low-scale civil war intensified in Turkey. In this context, Turkey used various *soft repression tactics*, including lobbying for the closure of Kurdish broadcasting and associations in Europe, extensive surveillance and monitoring of these communities, and using terrorism-based discourse to criminalise Kurdish nationalist activity in host-country contexts. While Turkey's transnational engagement with its European diasporas between the late 1970s and early 2000s was shaped by the preferences of secular and Kemalist elites and mainly characterised by soft and low-intensity repression, with the AKP's coming to power and the expansion of diaspora engagement characterised by the establishment of certain institutions, such as the Presidency for Turks Abroad and Related Communities (*Yurtdışı Türkler ve Akraba Topluluklar Başkanlığı*, hereafter YTB), dedicated to rejuvenating the diasporic ties between the Turkey-originated communities abroad and the Turkish state, a new era began for Turkey's engagement with its diaspora(s).

Turkey's turn towards *hard repression tactics* in the post-2016 period therefore should be understood in the context of state-led efforts to repress ideological, ethnic and religious minority groups in the diaspora with the aim of perpetuating authoritarian consolidation. Institutionalised forms of diaspora management strategies facilitated the outreach of such tactics, as they became more brazen and complex. Rather than using traditional diplomatic channels or covert and softer repression methods, Turkey has started using overt transnational repression tactics that (1) became more sophisticated and multilayered over time, and (2) sought to extend control over larger segments of the diaspora populations, rather than only smaller circles of political activists. Accordingly, although Turkey's repressive apparatus was already in place to some degree before the AKP came to power, the post-coup period was shaped by the expansion of transnational repression efforts towards all populations perceived as enemies of the state. While the specific targeting of the Gülen Movement, including those who fled after the coup attempt in 2016 and those who have been established abroad for a long time, constitutes an interesting target population of repression, other groups such as dissident academics, Kurdish and Alevite activists, leftists, seculars, dissident public intellectuals, journalists, athletes and students have also become the targets of transnational repression.

At the time of writing, the tactics employed by the regime include a variety of strategies such as proxy punishment of relatives at home through the seizure of their assets, intimidation, arrests, denial of services and preventing exit. Other tactics include threats of physical violence, verbal and online harassment, the refusal of consular services abroad and the confiscation of passports, monitoring and surveillance, slander of opponents as wanted terrorists, and the criminalisation of critical social media posts. To illustrate Turkey's use of new strategies, consider the digital transnational repression tactics used by the state such as the frequent arrest of regular diasporans who return to Turkey for holidays and their family members based on members' social media activities, thus preventing or deterring them from travelling back home or speaking up online.[5] In one case, a leader of the German Alevite Association was taken into custody at the airport in Istanbul as a strategy to intimidate dissidents more broadly.[6] Similarly, the arrest and detainment of German-Turkish journalist Deniz Yücel became equally prominent in the diaspora and succeeded in sending a message to opposition activists abroad.[7]

Besides targeted arrests upon return, the families of famous dissidents are often targets of repression. Many Turkish intellectuals who we interviewed expressed their concerns about the well-being of family members who they were forced to leave behind. For instance, Yavuz Baydar, the editor-in-chief of *Ahval* (an online news site published in English, Turkish and Arabic), remarked that the Turkish government took his wife's passport away for around nine months, putting them in a very difficult situation. In Europe, Turkish intellectuals and former politicians in exile regularly receive death threats and are being openly targeted by organised trolls on social media. At the same time, German authorities have warned several journalists (such as Celal Başlangıç) and former politicians (such as Ferhat Tunç) about potential attacks against

---

[5] For a definition of digital transnational repression, see Michaelsen in this volume.

[6] DW.2019. Alevi lidere havaalanında gözaltı. 11.10.2019. [Online]. Available at: https://www.dw.com/tr/alevi-lidere-havaalan%C4%B1nda-g%C3%B6zalt%C4%B1/a-50797081

[7] DW. 2019. Deniz Yücel: Erdogan let me be tortured. 05/10/2019May 10, 2019.[Online]. Available at: https://www.dw.com/en/deniz-y%C3%BCcel-Erdoğan-let-me-be-tortured-in-turkishprison/a-48686030

them, as several social media accounts shared an 'execution list' including their names. Another exiled journalist who works for a left-leaning newspaper, Erk Acarer, was further physically attacked in his home in Berlin by masked men wielding fists and knives.[8] Although physical intimidation is not a frequently employed strategy by the regime in Europe, our interviewees reveal that diaspora members live in fear over *potential future repression*.

Everyday dynamics of harassment – either online or offline – monitoring and surveillance are also commonly reported instances among members of the diaspora in Europe. The institutions that are allegedly accused of carrying out such everyday repression tactics are transnational state apparatuses such as diplomatic missions, intelligence services, branches of transnational religious institutions such as Diyanet, as well as members of the diaspora co-opted by the regime (Böcü and Baser 2022). For instance, several European states accused the Diyanet of extending its spying activities abroad and took measures to prevent Turkey's intelligence activities on their soil (Baser and Féron 2022). Diyanet's mosque networks were put under scrutiny in countries such as Germany and Austria as they were associated with extralegal activities, including illegal espionage.[9] At the same time, members of the diaspora and trolls-for-hire engage in online defamation against dissidents abroad.

According to several reports published by the Freedom House, Turkey has used transnational repression tactics in over thirty countries and, as of 2023, is ranked second among authoritarian regimes worldwide that employ repression transnationally.[10] As part of its global repression campaign, Turkey has also used renditions as a strategy to convince host states to extradite the 'wanted' individuals to Turkey.[11] In recent years, Turkey has therefore been increasingly

[8] DW. 2019. Exiled Turkish journalist attacked in Berlin. 07/08/2021July 8, 2021.[Online]. Available at: https://www.dw.com/en/erk-acarer-exiled-turkish-journalist-attacked-in-berlin/a-58198335

[9] Independent. 2017. Germany opens investigation into Turkish group accused of spying on Erdoğan opponents in 35 countries. 01.04.2017. [Online]. Available at: https://www.independent.co.uk/news/world/europe/turkey-spying-germany-europeaustria-35-countries-Erdoğan-coup-fethullah-gulen-diyanet-a7662096.html

[10] Freedom House. 2023. Still Not Safe: Transnational Repression in 2022. [Online]. Available at: https://freedomhouse.org/sites/default/files/2023-04/FH_TransnationalRepression2023_0.pdf

[11] Freedom House. 2021. Out of sight, not out of reach. Case Study: Turkey. [Online]. Available at: https://freedomhouse.org/sites/default/files/2021-02/FH_TransnationalRepressionReport2021_rev020221_CaseStudy_Turkey.pdf

exploiting international organisations such as Interpol[12] and its Red Notice system to capture political enemies abroad.[13] To this end, the regime has made a high number of extradition requests to Germany, the United States and other countries to return lawful Gülenist residents to Turkey.[14] Thus, a transition to authoritarianism in the post-coup period resulted in the extension of Turkey's long arm into diaspora communities and the increasing instrumentalisation of state apparatuses – what Svante Cornell coined 'weaponizing the diaspora' (Baser and Öztürk 2020).[15] Turkey's foreign missions, Diyanet's mosque networks and co-opted associations and organisations in the diaspora were then perceived as pawns in the implementation of the regime's hard transnational repression activities. This mistrust towards the Turkish state's outreach to its diaspora in both positive and negative ways (Baser and Öztürk 2020; Yanasmayan and Kaşlı 2019) paved the way for host-country responses to Turkey's overall diaspora governance policies, including its transnational repression aspects (Baser and Féron 2022). Several host countries, such as Germany and the Netherlands, banned Turkish political elites' visits to their countries before elections or became sceptical of Turkey-originated politicians, civil society organisations or diaspora entrepreneurs who had close relations with Turkey.

Host-country Responses: From Nonchalant Engagement to Reactive Restriction

Turkey's use of authoritarian politics and strategies of repression within its diaspora communities has not gone unnoticed by governments across Europe that host large numbers of Turkish immigrants and their descendants. In the early days of democratic decline in Turkey, the effects of regime change on the diaspora remained invisible and thus received little attention from European host-country governments. While solidarity protests supporting the call for democracy during

---

[12] See Edward Lemon's chapter in this volume to better understand how international organisations can be used as transnational tools of repression.

[13] VOA. 2019. How Authoritarian Governments Are Exploiting Interpol to Harass Political Enemies. 03.10.2019. [Online]. Available at: https://www.voanews.com/a/usa_how-authoritarian-governments-are-exploiting-interpol-harass-political-enemies/6176937.html

[14] BBC.2018. Turkey-Germany: Erdogan urges Merkel to extradite Gulen 'terrorists'. 28.09.2018.[Online]. Available at: https://www.bbc.com/news/world-europe-45684390

[15] Cornell, S. 2017. 'Weaponizing' the Diaspora: Erdoğan and the Turks in Europe. CACI Analyst. [Online]. Available at: https://www.turkeyanalyst.org/publications/turkey-analyst-articles/item/579-weaponizingthe-diaspora-erdo%C4%9Fan-and-the-turks-in-europe.html

the Gezi protests received attention from host-country policymakers of Turkish descent (Baser 2015), pro-regime mobilisation and co-optation efforts abroad, and the surveillance efforts by embassy and consular personnel, were over-looked.[16] A minor change in host-state responses towards transnational repression only occurred after Turkey's decision to grant extraterritorial voting rights to citizens abroad, which resulted in the transnationalisation of electoral campaigns and rallies. Starting with the 2014 parliamentary elections, the AKP, as well as opposition parties, have been increasingly active in competing for votes in the diaspora. In this context, repression by the regime has been largely limited to covert and soft coercive methods, such as monitoring the activities of the opposition parties and their supporters, intimidating targeted campaign activities and organising counter-rallies.[17] While such forms of repression received some attention from host-country policymakers, host-country responses have been limited to raising questions around the legality of campaigning rather than acknowledging the regime's efforts to silence transnational opposition forces.[18] Several governments, including those of the Netherlands and Germany, for instance, have thus banned electoral campaigning by foreign leaders in their national territories to counter the AKP's popular mobilisation efforts during elections.[19]

A slight turn in host-state responses towards transnational repression only took place in the aftermath of the coup attempt in Turkey, which resulted in hard and overt repression in the diaspora. In this regard, as our interviewees stated, most of the European host countries have been implementing both overt and covert security measures to counter Turkey's efforts to intimidate members of the diaspora. For instance, during the interview, Ragip Duran, an award-winning journalist who has been living in Germany, underlined that Germany and other European countries have realised after 2017 and 2018 that the threats by the Erdoğan regime are real, which is why they have started to

---

[16] Interview of first author with German-Turkish policymaker in 2020.

[17] Interview of first author with members of transnational party representatives of the Republican People's Party (CHP) and the People's Democratic Party (HDP) in 2019.

[18] Der Spiegel. 2017. Darf Erdogan in Deutschland Wahlkampf machen? 20.02.2017. [Online]. Available at: https://www.spiegel.de/politik/deutschland/recep-tayyip-Erdoğan-in-deutschland-darf-erhier-wahlkampf-machen-a-1135434.html

[19] Rallies have been banned in Germany: https://www.welt.de/politik/deutschland/article 166067627/Bundesregierung-verbietet-Auftritt-von-Erdoğan-in-Deutschland.html and the Netherlands due to security concerns: https://www.bbc.com/news/world-europe-39242707

take security issues more seriously. Some public figures we have interviewed highlighted that the police and intelligence services in their country of residence protect them from potential attacks by Turkish intelligence or co-opted diaspora members who are loyal to the regime. In particular, Turkish-origin policymakers who live and work in democratic countries, but who are covertly and (at times) overtly targeted by the agents of the regime, also reported the implementation of such forms of host-country protection. A policymaker in the German parliament who has been verbally harassed by the regime during multiple public appearances, highlights that 'the security forces reacted quickly and provided adequate protection from then on'.[20]

Yet, another policymaker from the German Left Party (*Die Linke*) who was physically attacked on the street by supporters of the regime due to his criticism of the AKP and his open co-operation with the Kurdish opposition, explains that police forces guarantee his security regularly, but that protection alone has been insufficient as 'the legal persecution of agents of the regime has been rather difficult due to the hit-and-run nature of incidents'.[21] He further noted that host countries provide protection to only a small segment of the Turkish diaspora, while the majority of activists continue to live with the fear of potential physical or verbal assault. Therefore, diaspora members who are not public intellectuals or former politicians could be said to feel more vulnerable with regard to protection by the host state, but less vulnerable when it comes to random attacks on the streets, as they are not easily recognised by regime loyalist diaspora members.

Even though the regime has been trying to target all opposition groups in the diaspora, its current arch-enemy continues to be the Gülen Movement. During the interview, Hayko Bağdat, for instance, underlined that the Turkish state has been much more brutal to the members of the GM than other opposition groups, thus necessitating a response from host-country governments. The regime's efforts to extradite and coerce the return of members of the GM were largely undermined by host countries. Already in 2017, German policymakers raised concerns about Turkey's efforts to persuade the German government to support its global fight against the GM. According to official records of the German government, the head of Turkey's National Intelligence Service (*Milli İstihbarat Teşkilatı*) presented a dossier listing the names and activities of the GM

---

[20] Interview of first author with German-Turkish policymaker in 2020.

[21] Interview of first author with German-Turkish policymaker in 2019.

in Germany in an attempt to co-ordinate its repression efforts with the German authorities.[22] However, the response of the German government towards extradition requests of individuals associated with the GM or the coup were rejected by the authorities, who stated that Germany would only consider legal co-operation in cases involving murder.[23] Similar host-countries refusing to adhere to Turkey's extradition efforts include Austria and Switzerland.[24]

Thus, European host-country governments have largely neglected any co-operation with the regime and moved towards limiting its efforts to surveil, repress and coerce dissidents abroad.[25] Restrictive responses have been further fuelled by the controversial involvement of several mosque communities associated with Turkey's Diyanet as well as diplomatic personnel in collecting intelligence on the GM and other dissident groups across Europe.[26] In response to espionage activities on behalf of the regime, the German police raided the homes of involved individuals, and launched a large-scale investigation.[27] The scandal further resulted in significant cuts of funding for religious associations associated with Turkey,[28] and the questioning of state-level co-operation on matters related to Islamic education in Germany.[29] In the aftermath of the

[22] Deutscher Bundestag. 2017. Antwort der Bundesregierung: Drucksache 18/12498. auf die Kleine Anfrage der Abgeordneten Ulla Jelpke, Jan van Aken, Christine Buchholz, weiterer Abgeordneter und der Fraktion DIE LINKE. Drucksache 18/12008 [Online]. Available at: http://dipbt.bundestag.de/doc/btd/18/124/1812498.pdf

[23] Sabah. 2016. Almanya'dan skandal 'iade' açıklaması. 1.11.2016 [Online]. Available at: https://www.sabah.com.tr/dunya/2016/11/02/almanyadan-skandal-iade-aciklamasi

[24] For the Swiss case: https://www.luzernerzeitung.ch/schweiz/diplomatie-schweiz-bewilligt-kaum-auslieferungen-an-tuerkei-ld.82138 and for Austria: https://www.derstandard.at/story/2000127940808/entscheidung-in-wien-ueber-einen-dicken-fisch-der-auch-mit

[25] The response of European host-country governments stands in stark contrast with other authoritarian states around the globe that have largely co-operated with the extradition efforts of the regime.

[26] In France, the Netherlands, Austria and Germany, the AKP regime co-ordinated efforts to gather information and surveillance on dissidents.

[27] DW. 2017 Turkish imam spy affair in Germany extends across Europe. 02/16/2017.[Online]. Available at: https://www.dw.com/en/turkish-imam-spy-affair-in-germany-extends-across-europe/a-37590672

[28] DW. 2017. German government to cut Islamic DITIB funding. 10/05/2017.[Online]. Available at: https://www.dw.com/en/germany-to-slash-funding-for-islamic-organization-ditib/a-40810472

[29] DW.2016. German state distances itself from Islamic group. 09/06/2016.[Online]. Available at: https://www.dw.com/en/north-rhine-westphalia-distances-itself-from-islamic-group-ditib/a-19528476

espionage scandal, which disrupted relations between Turkey's mosque networks across Europe with policymakers in host countries,[30] other groups associated with the regime such as the ultra-nationalist Grey Wolves and their diasporic associations also became the subject of debate.[31] Concerns about the growing influence of the regime on diaspora groups such as the Grey Wolves, and related concerns about their involvement in repressing ethnic minorities in the diaspora, ultimately resulted in the ban of the group in France.[32]

Simultaneously, European host-country governments have also moved to increasingly protect groups targeted by the regime in the aftermath of the coup attempt by granting political asylum. However, the number of applications varied widely across Europe.[33] According to the German Federal Foreign Office (*Auswärtiges Amt*), the number of asylum applications to Germany grew significantly after the coup attempt in 2016, while the number of applications by Turkish rather than Kurdish asylum seekers constituted the majority of requests.[34] Regional Courts in Germany who decide over asylum applications case-by-case, have primarily ruled in favour of asylum applicants who are persecuted in Turkey due to their membership in the GM being protected

[30] In the Netherlands, espionage allegations against imams from Turkey resulted in requests to expel members of mosque communities who helped collect intelligence on behalf of the regime: https://www.ad.nl/binnenland/cda-leider-buma-wil-voorzitter-diyanet-het-land-uit-zetten~a5f30555/?referrer=https%3A%2F%2Fwww.google.com%2F Furthermore, policymakers from the Christian Democratic Party (CDA) passed a bill in the Dutch parliament demanding that the salaries of clerics should be paid by local communities in the Netherlands: https://www.trouw.nl/nieuws/Erdoğan-beheerst-turkse-moskeeen-daar-verandert-den-haag-niets-aan~b06ca689/?referrer=https%3A%2F%2Fwww.google.com%2F

[31] DW.2020. German lawmakers urge ban on extreme-right Gray Wolves. 11/07/2020November 7, 2020. [Online]. Available at: https://www.dw.com/en/german-lawmakers-urge-ban-on-extreme-right-turkish-graywolves/a-55528032

[32] DW. 2020. France bans Turkish ultra-nationalist Grey Wolves. 11/04/2020. [Online]. Available at: https://www.dw.com/en/france-bans-turkish-ultra-nationalist-grey-wolves-group/ a-55503469

[33] European Commission. Migration and Home Affairs. [Online]. Available at: https://ec.europa.eu/home-affairs/sites/homeaffairs/files/2017.1172_no_claims_from_turkish_asylum_seekers.pdf

[34] Welt. 2020. Mehr Asylbewerber aus der Türkei – Bundesregierung kritisiert "Missbrauch der Justiz". 10.01.2020. [Online]. Available at: https://www.welt.de/politik/deutschland/article204891706/Asylbewerber-aus-der-Tuerkei-Bundesregierung-kritisiert-Missbrauch-der-Justiz.html

in Germany.[35] Other host-country governments, including Switzerland and Austria, have equally indicated support for asylum applications by dissidents after the failed coup attempt.[36] In addition to granting asylum, host-country policymakers in Germany told us that they pay 'attention to insights gained from Kurdish and Alevite activists who have been facing repression by the regime since the 1980s'.

Overall, some European governments who host a relatively large population of Turkey's diaspora, such as Germany, France and the Netherlands, appeared to gradually reformulate their approach in accordance with Turkey's increased involvement in its diasporas, and moved to restrict or control the impact of transnational state apparatuses and related proxies on the ground over time. Yet, policy responses have been largely reactive and have particularly addressed high-intensity and overt repression efforts of the regime. Thus, low-intensity and covert types of repression and its everyday impacts on immigrant communities from Turkey remain largely unaddressed by host-country governments. The relative silence of host countries towards low-intensity and everyday dynamics of repression, however, is perceived sceptically by members of the diaspora. Our interlocutors who were affected by repression, for instance, highlighted that despite the protection that democratic host countries provide to members of society, it remains hard to predict the limits of the Turkish state, thus invoking an atmosphere of ongoing fear and silence across the diaspora. Therefore, the wider and less visible effects of repression, and the need for a long-term solution, was one of the pressing concerns among our interview partners. This situation not only affected diasporas' interactions with Turkey, but also had an impact on how diasporas perceived their host states' position on these issues, which in the long run may affect integration prospects and the overall sense of belonging of immigrants from Turkey.

---

[35] This stance is illustrated by the ruling of a court in Baden-Württemberg which ruled in favour of a former teacher's application to seek asylum in Germany: http://www.landesrecht-bw.de/jportal/?quelle=jlink&docid=MWRE180000681&psml=bsbawueprod.psml&max=true&doc.part=L&doc.norm=all In addition, there are several other examples of court rulings from Augsburg, Cologne and Düsseldorf.

[36] In the context of Austria, see: https://www.diepresse.com/5062311/asyl-fuer-tuerkische-fluechtlinge-oesterreichs-eu-mandatare-mehrheitlich-dafuer and in the context of Switzerland, see: https://www.srf.ch/news/schweiz/Erdoğans-arm-reicht-bis-in-die-schweiz

Everyday Dynamics of Transnational Repression on Diaspora Groups

Besides triggering varying host-country reactions in Europe, Turkey's transnational repression strategies have also had a varying impact on Turkey's diaspora populations in Europe. In this context, our fieldwork shows that Turkey's growing authoritarian practices have created an atmosphere of mistrust across different groups within the diaspora. Most of our interlocutors and long-term ethnographic observations reveal that solidarity and collective action across diaspora organisations from different ideological or generational backgrounds have been difficult as a result of the current political dynamics at play in diaspora spaces. Among those who have been affected the most in the post-2016 waves of repression are unquestionably members of the GM. To date, members of the GM continue to feel insecure, although they reside in democratic host countries. Those who belong to the GM admitted that the level of insecurity affects their everyday life, as they are not only aware of the threat of punishment which awaits them upon return in Turkey, which is why they cannot go back, but they also fear that Turkey's transnational state apparatuses may harm them *in the future*. As a result of these insecurities, they are unable to proceed with their lives. Often their passports have been cancelled, while they avoid interactions with embassies and consulates due to fears of being captured or harmed by the regime upon entering official Turkish premises.

In the long run, these incidents caused a feeling of 'statelessness', and several interviewees stated that they feel like they are destined to a 'civil death'. In addition, members of the GM were also intimidated by the reputation of the GM, which was often associated with terrorism and an anti-democratic stance in state-sponsored rhetoric. Scared of 'snitching' on the part of other Turkish community members, our informants told us that they avoid interaction with the rest of the diaspora and live an overall isolated life. Two interviewees said that they were not going to the mosque anymore, to avoid meeting other members of the diaspora, and instead gather at each other's houses for prayers. Other less-known individuals did not necessarily worry about being identified as a member of the GM. However, as one interviewee noted, they still avoided interactions because of the psychological stress associated with being a member of the GM.[37]

---

[37] Interview of second and third authors with several members of the GM.

The relative retreat of members of the GM from the diaspora has also been noted by host- country policymakers and members of the diaspora. In Germany, for instance, interlocutors explained that existing education platforms of the GM 'disappeared from the landscape overnight after the coup attempt', and that 'known members of the movement have been excluded from official political and social events in the diaspora ever since'.[38] This exclusionary stance is not only evident in the states' approach towards members of the GM, but is also reflected in the stance that other groups in the diaspora have taken. Most groups within the diaspora, such as Leftists, Kemalists, Alevites and Kurds, despised the GM for a variety of reasons, and therefore chose not to interact with members of the movement. One leftist activist described the GM as 'the former big brother of the current regime' and noted that 'no one should ever trust them', revealing the overall sentiment in these circles that despise the GM due to its complicity in the regime's anti-democratic stance and numerous human rights violations before the GM–AKP dispute.[39]

While our interviewees generally acknowledged that members of the GM have faced high-intensity repression by the Turkish state, the usual suspects of state repression from Turkey, namely Leftist, Kurdish and Alevite actors in the diaspora, also continued to face *constant* levels of repression by the state to which they have 'grown accustomed', as one of our interlocutors stated in an interview. Kurdish activists further noted that 'the Kurdish diaspora community is immune to living under pressure by the Turkish state, and that recent measures did not create additional fear of repression among Kurds'.[40] Alevi activists, however, reported renewed attempts of surveillance and intimidation against members of the Alevi community, especially religious figures and leaders. According to the leader of a regional Alevi association, 'repression against the Alevite community and its leaders is growing', largely due to its 'great potential to mobilize against the regime and its involvement in electoral campaigns'.[41] Thus, it appears that often those who oppose the regime abroad openly and harshly, also receive the highest levels of repression by the regime.

---

[38] Interview of first author with German-Turkish expert in 2020.
[39] Interview of first author with a Leftist activist in 2020.
[40] Interview of second and third authors with Kurdish activist in 2019.
[41] Interview of first author with a leader of an Alevi association in 2019.

Public figures in exile, such as prominent journalists, politicians and well-known diaspora activists, report of being increasingly exposed to transnational repression on a daily basis. For instance, our interview with Hayko Bağdat, an exiled Turkish-Armenian journalist currently based in Germany, revealed that death threats and harassment on social media platforms are frequent forms of repression that public intellectuals who fled Turkey face. Other public figures who openly campaigned against the regime stated that they regularly felt very insecure on a daily basis, constantly fearing verbal or physical attacks by regime loyalists who might be able to recognise them on the street. Those fears were often accompanied by the feeling of being constantly monitored by the state, as an interview with Faysal Sarıyıldız, a Kurdish politician in exile, revealed. Despite these experiences, others highlighted that networks such as family and friends could serve as a form of community protection. Hasip Kaplan, a Kurdish politician in exile, for instance, explained that he has not felt the long arm of Turkey in Germany as an immediate threat because he was always surrounded by family members and other networks which protected him from everyday forms of repression. However, rumours have been reported by Kurdish media outlets that his name placed on an execution list which contained names of dissidents in exile from different shades of opposition movements in Turkey.[42]

In stark contrast with the everyday dynamics of repression faced by selective members of the diaspora community there were relatively low experiences of transnational repression by new Turkish migrants who left the country voluntarily, mainly for economic reasons. They remain largely unaffected by the regime's repression efforts as they do not fall into the traditional category of 'enemies of the state'. A white-collar migrant who recently immigrated to the Netherlands, for instance, visited a civil association affiliated with Turkey's Diyanet 'out of curiosity', and did not feel threatened or undermined by their personnel, even though he was not a supporter of their policies. Others who migrated to European host countries had a simmilar experience and noted that those 'who already feel under pressure are those who left Turkey due to their political activities', while others were unaffected by transnational

---

[42] ANF News 2020. German government confirms existence of execution lists.27.07.2020. [Online]. Available at: https://anfenglish.com/features/german-government-confirms-existence-of-executionlists-53751

repression. Yet, they remained concerned with developments at home. Some of our interviewees, for instance, point out that they are worried about 'what happens in Turkey rather than what happens in diaspora spaces'.[43]

In line with these observations, some white-collar immigrants organised themselves in alternative spheres of contention, and sought to influence politics in Turkey through intellectual or community activism. However, as one of our interlocutors from a new migrant association in Germany explained they primarily 'remain amongst themselves'.[44] Not necessarily out of fear, but because they wanted to provide an alternative image of Turkey in their host countries. Ultimately, these groups repeatedly voiced their concern about being perceived as part of Turkey's conflict-laden immigrant community, which was often associated with growing negative connotations in host countries' integration debates. Thus, it appears that Turkey's coercive activities in Europe are also increasingly affecting the integration debates about Turkey-originated migrants, and feeding into xenophobic stereotypes and affecting diaspora members' positionality in Europe in a negative way.

Overall, our analysis shows that different groups in the diaspora seem to face varying levels of repression from Turkey, which further affects their everyday lives and activism in different ways. While some groups in the diaspora can, at times, escape the ever-growing web of repression by the Turkish state, others appear to be trapped at the centre of the state's focus, and thus face continued repression. These nuances often go unnoticed by policymakers of host countries, who are primarily concerned with tackling high-intensity and overt forms of repression originating from the Turkish state. However, on the ground, these everyday dynamics of repression create distance, shame and fear among members of the diaspora. Furthermore, they seem to have behavioural implications and yield processes of mutual exclusion and fragmentation, which can hamper solidarity networks and potential collective action against authoritarianism over time. Many interviewees confirmed that activism against the regime, especially collective efforts, were difficult and declined as a consequence of repression which affects different groups to varying degrees. While we cannot confirm whether resistance against the regime has declined

---

[43] Interview of second and third authors with recent emigrants and activists.
[44] Interview of first author with recent emigrants and activists in 2020.

due to increased employment of transnational repression by the AKP regime, the findings indicate an interesting trend which needs to be further explored.

Conclusion

This chapter has reflected on the ongoing transformations of Turkey's diaspora governance under growing authoritarianism at home by paying close attention to the changes in Turkey's approach to repression of anti-regime groups abroad. We have shown that Turkey has not only extended its set of repression repertoires since 2013, which it applies across its diasporas in Europe and beyond, but that over time, repression tactics have become more sophisticated. In this context, we observe that Turkey's transnational state institutions or organisations, which were ostensibly established for the purposes of outreach, soft power or diplomacy aimed at empowering certain parts of the diaspora, are increasingly being used to coerce and repress opponents of the regime. Our study shows that Turkey's transnational repression efforts must be evaluated in the context of host-country responses, and the effects they produce on the ground. Thus, our analysis revealed that host-country responses to transnational repression have been largely positive, especially during the height of repression in the post-coup period, which included the use of high-intensity repression strategies against dissidents. In this context, some European host countries have been favourable towards applications for asylum. Furthermore, we found that host-state protection by police or other security forces has been granted selectively to those severely affected by transnational repression – in particular, elite or well-known figures within the diaspora.

At the same time, however, lower-intensity repression or newly employed forms of digital transnational repression, as well as the varying effects they produce within the diaspora, have gone unnoticed and unaddressed by European host-country policymakers. Thus, our analysis suggests that host-country responses have been mainly reactive and formulated retroactively to Turkey's repression efforts. Host-country responses also have been largely focused on short-term security provision for those affected acutely by repression, without acknowledging the need for long-term solutions such as offering reporting mechanisms that hold perpetrators of repression accountable or forming much-needed co-operation and alliance platforms between host countries and democratic forces in the diaspora. Moreover, host countries do not acknowledge the varying levels of repression faced by different groups within the diaspora.

Furthermore, the second part of our analysis shows that group-level dynamics and differences between intradiasporic groups not only determine the framing and targeting by the regime, but are of relevance to how different members of the diaspora navigate the everyday realities of repression. Our analysis suggests that diasporas which are fragmented across political, ideological, class, religious and ethnic cleavages may be framed differently by the state, and as a result may experience repression from their home states differently. Those framed as the *enemies of the state* who are visible and in open opposition to the state, such as the GM or Kurdish activists, experience higher levels of repression, and therefore may have the ability to escape the web of transnational repression targeting them by way of using host-country protection, among other strategies. Others, who are not explicit or visible opponents of the regime, but engage in ways of resistance against the AKP, must risk repression or remain in the shadows of their democratic engagement. Most interestingly, our interlocutors have highlighted that the majority of the members of the diaspora remain largely undisturbed by transnational repression, and therefore do not perceive the presence of repressive structures and agents in the diaspora as a threat to their livelihoods. While our study does not explore whether repression deters resistance to or opposition against authoritarian regimes, future studies should focus on the effects of repression on political mobilisation against the regime. In particular, additional focus is needed to understand why the political activism of certain intradiasporic groups such as Kurds and Alevites remains strong despite ongoing threats by the regime, while other groups who also face high threats from the regime, such as members of the GM, have largely ceased their activities, thus inviting an intradiasporic exploration of the effects of transnational repression.

References

Adamson, F. B. 2005. 'Globalisation, transnational political mobilisation, and networks of violence'. *Cambridge Review of International Affairs* 18(1): 31–49.

——. 2018. 'Sending states and the making of intra-diasporic politics: Turkey and its diaspora(s)'. *International Migration Review* 1–27.

Akçay, Ü. 2021. 'Authoritarian consolidation dynamics in Turkey'. *Contemporary Politics* 27(1): 79–104.

Baser, B. 2015. *Diasporas and Homeland Conflict: A Comparative Perspective*. London: Routledge.

Baser, B. and Féron, É. 2022. 'Host state reactions to home state diaspora engagement policies: Rethinking state sovereignty and limits of diaspora governance'. *Global Networks* 22(2): 226–41.

Baser, B. and Öztürk, A. E. 2020. 'Positive and negative diaspora governance in context: From public diplomacy to transnational authoritarianism'. *Middle East Critique* 29(3): 319–34. doi: 10.1080/19436149.2020.1770449

Böcü, G. 2022. 'Home and host country policy interaction in the making of Turkey's diasporas. *Middle East Critique* 31(4): 355–70.

Böcü, G. and Baser, B. 2022. 'Transnational mobilization of future generations by non-democratic home states: Turkey's diaspora youth between empowerment and co-optation'. *Ethnopolitics*.

Böcü, G. and Nidhi, P. 2022. 'Populist diaspora engagement: Party-led outreach under Turkey's AKP and India's BJP'. *Diaspora Studies*.

Bruneau, M. 2010. 'Diasporas, transnational spaces and communities'. *Diaspora and Transnationalism: Concepts, Theories and Methods* 3(1): 35–50.

Butler, K. D. 2001. 'Defining diaspora, refining a discourse'. *Diaspora* 10: 189–218.

Cooley, A. A. and Heathershaw, J. 2017. *Dictators without Borders: Power and Money in Central Asia*. New Haven, CT: Yale University Press.

Dagi, I. 2008. 'Islamist parties and democracy: Turkey's AKP in power'. *Journal of Democracy* 19(3): 25–30.

Esen, B. and Gumuscu, S. 2016. 'Rising competitive authoritarianism in Turkey'. *Third World Quarterly* 1–26.

——. 2017. 'Turkey: How the coup failed'. *Journal of Democracy* 28(1): 59–73.

Gumuscu, S. and Sert, D. 2009. 'The power of the devout bourgeoisie: The case of the Justice and Development Party in Turkey'. *Middle Eastern Studies* 45(6): 953–68.

Lemon, E. 2019. 'Weaponizing Interpol'. *Journal of Democracy* 30(2): 15–29.

Maritato, C., Öktem, K. and Zadrożna, A. 2021. 'Introduction: A state of diasporas: The transnationalisation of Turkey and its communities abroad'. *DIASPORA* 21(2): 105–20.

Michaelsen, M. 2017. 'Far away, so close: Transnational activism, digital surveillance and authoritarian control in Iran'. *Surveillance & Society* 15(3/4): 465–70.

Moss, D. M. 2016. 'Transnational repression, diaspora mobilization, and the case of the Arab Spring'. *Social Problems* 63: 480–98.

——. 2022. *The Arab Spring Abroad: Diaspora Activism against Authoritarian Regimes*. New York: Cambridge University Press.

Mügge, L. 2013. 'Ideologies of nationhood in sending-state transnationalism: Comparing Surinam and Turkey'. *Ethnicities* 13(3): 338–58. doi: 10.1177/1468796812451096

Østergaard-Nielsen, E. 2003. *Transnational Politics: Turks and Kurds in Germany*. London and New York: Routledge.

Öztürk, A. E. and Baser, B. 2021. 'New Turkey's new diasporic constellations: The Gezi generation and beyond'. Hellenic Foundation for European and Foreign Policy (ELIAMEP) Policy Paper No. 84.

Öztürk, A. E. and Sözeri, S. 2018. 'Diyanet as a Turkish foreign policy tool: Evidence from the Netherlands and Bulgaria'. *Politics and Religion* 11(3): 624–48. doi: 10.1017/S175504831700075X

Saatçioğlu, B. 2010. 'Unpacking the compliance puzzle: The case of Turkey's AKP under EU conditionality'. KFG Working Paper Series No. 14, Kolleg-Forschergruppe (KFG), 'The transformative power of Europe', Freie Universität Berlin.

Senay, B. 2012. *Beyond Turkey's Borders: Long-Distance Kemalism, State Politics and the Turkish Diaspora*. Bloomsbury Publishing.

Shain, Y. 1994. 'Marketing the democratic creed abroad: US diasporic politics in the era of multiculturalism'. *Diaspora: A Journal of Transnational Studies* 3(1): 85–111.

——. 2002. 'The role of diasporas in conflict perpetuation or resolution'. *SAIS Review of International Affairs* 22(2): 115–44.

Shain, Y. and Barth, A. 2003. 'Diasporas and international relations theory'. *International Organization* 57(3): 449–79.

Sökefeld, M. 2006. 'Mobilizing in transnational space: A social movement approach to the formation of diaspora'. *Global Networks* 6(3): 1470–2266.

Topak, O. 2017. 'The making of a totalitarian surveillance machine: Surveillance in Turkey under AKP rule'. *Surveillance & Society* 15(3/4): 535–42.

Tsourapas, G. 2020. 'Global autocracies: Strategies of transnational repression, legitimation, and co-optation in world politics'. *International Studies Review* viaa061. doi: 10.1093/isr/viaa061

Turam, B. 2007. *Between Islam and the State: The Politics of Engagement*. Redwood City, CA: Stanford University Press.

Updegraff, R. 2012. 'Turkey under the AKP: The Kurdish Question'. *Journal of Democracy* 23(1): 119–28.

Van Hear, N. 2014. 'Diaspora formation'. In Anderson, B. and Keith, M., *Migration: A COMPAS Anthology*. Oxford: ESRC Centre on Migration, Policy and Society, University of Oxford, pp. 196–7.

Yanasmayan, Z. and Kaşlı, Z. 2019. 'Reading diasporic engagements through the lens of citizenship: Turkey as a test case'. *Political Geography* 70: 24–33.

Yavuz, M. H. 2013. *Toward an Islamic Enlightenment: The Gülen Movement*. Oxford: Oxford University Press.

11

TRANSNATIONAL REPRESSION AND MIGRATION DIPLOMACY: THE CASE OF ITALIAN–EGYPTIAN RELATIONS

Saipira Furstenberg, Alessandra Russo and Gillian Kennedy

On 7 February 2020, Patrick Zaky, an Egyptian graduate student at the University of Bologna, was arrested upon his arrival at Cairo airport. Zaky was a researcher on gender and human rights at the Cairo-based Egyptian Initiative for Personal Rights as well as a women and gender studies Erasmus Mundus Master's Degree student in Italy, which is a programme supported by the European Commission. At the time of his arrest, Zaky faced charges including harming national security, inciting illegal protests and intent to overthrow the state. While in prison, he was tortured, and his detention was renewed in December 2020. Egyptian officials refused to respond to torture allegations, and provided few details about his arrest. Nevertheless, given the increasingly autocratic political climate in Egypt since the wave of uprisings that began during the 2011 Arab Spring, it is highly likely that Zaky was arrested because of his association with EIPR and his human rights work. Although Zaky was released from prison in December 2021, at the time of writing he is yet to be tried, as his trial has been adjourned several times without valid explanation.

The arrest of Patrick Zaky in Cairo represents a case of transnational repression, as international students constitute a substantial and growing mobile population of concern to sending states (Glasius 2018). International students also encompass networks and activities that are associated to both their host and home societies (Gargano 2009). Between 2015 and 2019, more than 3,200 Egyptian students, professors and university staff moved to Europe.[1] International students are not only surveilled while abroad, but also subjected to heightened risks and violence upon returning home, despite their affiliations with institutions and universities located in democracies (Rotella 2021; Human Rights Watch 2021; Allen-Ebrahimian 2018; Scholars at Risk 2019; Furstenberg et al. 2020). The imprisonment and torture of Patrick Zaky not only reflects the erosion of democratic rights in Egypt, but also the long arm of the authoritarian state to silence its regime challengers from abroad.

In recent years the Egyptian government has taken unprecedented measures of censorship, surveillance and repression against activists and academics living in exile (Moss et al. 2022; Michaelsen 2020; Tsourapas 2021; Hamzawy 2019; Schenkkan and Linzer 2021). Against this background, this chapter aims to understand what political capacity and will, if any, the European Union and its member states have against authoritarian states perpetuating transnational repression. The chapter begins by describing the political context in Egypt. It then examines European Union (EU) responses to transnational repression incidents, through the case study of Italy. Using the theoretical framework of 'migration diplomacy', this chapter shows that (1) economic trade linkages and (2) the density of diplomatic ties in the fields of security and migration, shape receiving-state responses to transnational repression. Specifically, we argue that the strength of trade linkages and high density of diplomatic ties between Egypt, Italy and the EU severely limit the capacities of European states to engage against Egypt's state repression, both domestically and transnationally. As Quinsaat's chapter on US–Philippines linkages in this volume also shows (see Chapter 8), Western states' economic and security interests not only enable authoritarian states to perpetuate transnational repression, but these linkages often make democracies *complicit* in the perpetuation of transnational repression. The chapter concludes with a discussion and recommendations for future research on the topic.

---

[1] European Commission, European Neighbourhood Policy and Enlargement Negotiations, Egypt. [Online]. Available at: https://ec.europa.eu/neighbourhood-enlargement/neighbourhood/countries/egypt_en

Political Context in Egypt

As mentioned above, the imprisonment of Patrick Zaky reflects the worsening of democratic norms in Egypt. Since the removal of the Muslim Brotherhood's presidential ruler, Muhamed Morsi, in 2013, Egypt has witnessed the most brutal incidences of state repression since the nation's military coup. On 14 August 2013, armed security forces coercively removed Muslim Brotherhood protesters from the Rabi'a 'Adawiya and Nahda squares in Cairo, simultaneously, resulting in the deaths of over 850 people according to independent reports by Amnesty International and Human Rights Watch (Human Rights Watch 2014). Subsequently, the ruling regime, led by former defence minister, General Abdel Fattah Abdel al-Sisi, has escalated the repressive violence against his opponents, seeking to consolidate regime control by suppressing opposition groups at home, while seeking to annihilate political opponents in exile by transnational repressive practices. These methods include draconian legislation to curtail NGOs and their partnerships outside of Egypt, alongside a persistent set of repressive tools to deter and eliminate all diaspora activism deemed to be anti-regime, including the introduction of visa restrictions, Interpol arrest warrants and intelligence surveillance of Egyptians abroad via embassy functions, alongside a persistent climate of coercively threatening diaspora activists by informal notification through phone calls from intelligence services to make dissidents aware that their activities abroad have consequential oppressive responses. These tactics have increased in regularity particularly since May 2014, when al-Sisi was elected.

In light of this growing authoritarianism, Egyptian students residing abroad have been subject to transnational repression perpetrated by Sisi and his government. This is because students and scholars abroad have been perceived by the regime as a security threat. As described by Egypt's Minister of Immigration and Expatriate Affairs, Nabila Makram, 'Egyptian students abroad are the most dangerous group of emigrants.'[2] On another occasion, the minister further stated that 'anyone speaking against Egypt abroad' will be 'punished'.[3]

---

[2] Quote retrieved from Open Democracy, Nora Noralla (2021). 'Egyptian researchers must choose between forced exile and arrest'. [Online]. Available at: https://www.opendemocracy.net/en/north-africa-west-asia/egyptian-researchers-must-choose-between-forced-exile-and-arrest/

[3] Steven Zhou, CBC News, 26 July 2019. 'Critics of Egypt abroad will be "punished", Egyptian minister says in Canada'. [Online]. https://www.cbc.ca/news/canada/toronto/egypt-nabila-makram-threat-1.5225059

In May 2018, the security forces detained Walid al-Shobaky, an Egyptian doctorate student at the University of Washington in the US, after he conducted a number of interviews related to his field research on the judiciary's role in the political changes in Egypt in recent years. He was also charged with spreading false news and being affiliated with a terrorist group. In 2021 another international student, Ahmed Samir Santawy, enrolled as a Master's student in Sociology and Social Anthropology at the Central European University in Vienna, Austria, was detained by Egyptian security forces. Santawy's academic work focuses on women's rights in Egypt, particularly on the history of reproductive rights. On 1 February 2021, the State Security Prosecutor formally charged Santawy with 'joining a terrorist organization', 'deliberately spreading false news and data' and 'use of a private account on the Internet to spread false news or data' (FIDH 2021).

Such trends reflect broader tendencies among authoritarian states to repress scholarly voices. As pointed out by a Scholars at Risk report (2020), attacks against researchers, students and academics have been on the rise in recent years, particularly across authoritarian countries. As argued by Glasius (2018: 190), student mobility is increasingly seen as a threat for an authoritarian government, as 'students [. . .] may exercise transnational voice criticizing the home government during their stay abroad'. In this sense, as noted by Tsourapas (2019), cross-border mobility poses a challenge for authoritarian states. On the one hand, migrants' actions abroad can, at times, bolster authoritarian practices and regime stability by promoting long-distance nationalism and loyalty (see Hirt and Mohammad, this volume, on the role of taxes and Brand 2010 on out-of-country voting). On the other hand, as demonstrated during the Arab Spring, they can challenge non-democratic practices by engaging in activism, human rights mobilisation and lobbying (Moss 2016, 2022). In this respect, students abroad may play a key role in promoting change at home, learning and adapting democratic norms of their host states, seeking to change the politics of their home states, and demanding reforms from their government as a result. Such actions represent a potential threat to the regime's stability. Hence, authoritarian states resolve to confine citizens' mobility, tighten travel policies or impose travel bans, including on scholars and academics, and use various tactics of transnational repression to surveil, threaten and suppress dissent among their citizens living abroad, including students (see also Tsourapas 2019).

However, while the emerging literature on transnational repression has extensively examined methods of transnational repression and their detrimental effects on the fundamental rights of targeted individuals, we still have little understanding of how transnational repression practices are dealt with in democratic states hosting the affected individuals. In particular, how density of diplomatic ties and strategic interests between authoritarian countries perpetuating transnational repression and democracies hosting the exiles affect transnational repression dynamics. In the following sections we examine cross-border co-operation between Egypt, Italy and the EU to understand how the density of diplomatic ties influences Western responses to transnational repression. We argue that strategic linkages tied to migration condition how Italy and the EU respond to Egypt's transnational repression.

Migration Diplomacy and Interstate Relations

Our analysis draws upon scholarly work exploring interstate foreign policy relations driven by migration policy choices (Thiollet 2011; Norman 2020; Tsourapas 2017). In recent years, researchers have identified how states' diplomatic agendas are influenced by international migration and its management, with migration taking a more prominent place in the foreign policy of states (Tsourapas 2019; Geddes and Maru 2020; Tsourapas and Zartaloudis 2021). This research offered important insights into understanding states' foreign policy decisions and how these are tied to migration dynamics. For instance, the works of Greenhill (2003), Hollifield (2000) and Thiollet (2011) show the strategic use of migration flows as a critical negotiating instrument in international politics. This line of work typically examines migration diplomacy, a concept that aims to understand the nexus between foreign and migration policies and concerns (Tolay 2023: 2; Tsourapas and Zartaloudis 2021: 4).

In this view, scholars have identified ongoing processes of how states use migrants and refugees in their migration diplomacy strategies, pointing out on the nature of migration relations (Adamson and Tsourapas 2019; Norman 2020; Ceccorulli 2022). Adamson and Tsourapas (2018: 115–16), for instance, explore how strategies of migration diplomacy are shaped by states' economic and security interests, as well as the diplomatic tools, processes and procedures to manage cross-border population mobility. Their work sheds light on the policy decisions and migration-related strategies that receiving, sending and transit states use to achieve goals related to migration, or to obtain economic and political gains (Adamson and Tsourapas 2018).

Migration diplomacy is a useful tool to understand the interplay between migration and power politics between states. A key element of migration diplomacy is the tactical use of 'issue linkage', namely, the simultaneous discussion of two or more issues for joint settlement (Poast 2012), which allows some actors to extract positive gains on one issue in return for the favours expected on another (Weber and Wiesmeth 1991). 'Issue linkage' is an essential instrument in international relations, by which states secure agreement as a means to pursue other goals, such as enhancing their security or achieving economic interests and improving their public diplomacy (Adamson and Tsourapas 2018; Haas 1980). For the purposes of our analysis, we examine how migration diplomacy affects autocratic states' transnational repression dynamics. In the following sections, we identify how strategic linkages tied to migration, trade and security between Egypt and Italy and the EU reduce Italy's will and capacity to counter Egyptian state repression against its population abroad, including its students.

Egypt–Italy–EU Trajectories of Co-operation Agreements and Issue Linkages

Economic Ties and Trade

The Mediterranean and Middle Eastern countries, particularly Egypt and Libya, have historically been important for Italian foreign policy affairs owing to their geographical proximity and Italy's vested interests in the region, including energy security, trade and migration, among others matters (Del Sarto and Tocci 2008; Paoletti 2010; Brighi 2013; Ceccorulli 2022). Since 2014, following the nomination of Matteo Renzi as the Italian Prime Minister, diplomatic relations between Italy and Egypt have intensified (NENA 2018). The year 2014 was marked by several rounds of official visits paid by Italian ministers (Minister of Foreign Affairs Federica Mogherini, as well as Minister of Internal Affairs Angelino Alfano) to Cairo, including Renzi's visit in August 2014 – incidentally, during the Italian six-month rotating Presidency of the Council of the European Union. All this culminated in al-Sisi's visit to Rome in November 2014,[4] the first official trip of his tour of European capitals, followed by a further visit of a representative of Renzi's government to Cairo a few days after. During the visit, the Minister of Defence, Roberta Pinotti, discussed with the Sisi government issues of common interest, such as the Libyan crisis, international terrorism and irregular migrations, and plans for co-operation, including transfers of security technologies, as well as joint military training and intelligence sharing (see also Meringolo 2016).

In 2015 co-operation between Egypt and Italy continued along the same lines. In January 2015 the Minister of Agriculture, Food and Forestry Policies, Maurizio Martina, visited Cairo to strengthen Italian initiatives in the field of agriculture and rural development co-operation in Egypt. Italy is the most important market for Egyptian products of the primary sector, and Italian exports to Egypt skyrocketed in 2013–14 (Ministero delle politiche agricole alimentari e forestali 2015). A month later, a delegation of Italian entrepreneurs led by the Deputy Minister of Economic Development, Carlo Calenda, flew to Egypt to explore investment opportunities linked to the infrastructure project of the enlargement of the Suez Canal (Panarella 2015). Shortly afterwards, in March 2015, Renzi attended Egypt's Economic Development Conference in Sharm El-Sheikh, where he reiterated that he considered al-Sisi a strategic partner for Italy.

An explosion that hit the Italian consulate in Cairo in July 2015, which was perpetuated by Islamic State (BBC 2015), intensified the declaration of proximity and solidarity between the two countries, as restated on the occasion of a new visit of the Minister of Foreign Affairs, Paolo Gentiloni, to Cairo (Accorsi 2015). The strengthening of cordial relations between the two countries was professed by Renzi during an interview with *Al-Jazeera* in 2015, in which the Italian leader praised the al-Sisi government:

> I think al-Sisi is a great leader [. . .] Egypt invested in the future on the leadership of al-Sisi. [. . .] Egypt will be saved only with the leadership of al-Sisi, this is my personal position and I am proud of my friendship with him and I will support him in the direction of peace because the Mediterranean without Egypt will be absolutely a place without peace. (Serra 2015)

---

[4] Egypt's president met with Italy's head of state Napolitano, with the Ministry of Foreign Affairs' Gentiloni being present, followed by the Pope in the Vatican, the Chairman of the Senate, Pietro Grasso, and finally, President of the Council of Ministers, Renzi.

This statement was not only made in light of the attack, but also in the midst of a new Italy–Egypt energy agreement. The Italian oil and gas company Eni announced the discovery of the Zohr gas field, which represents the largest-ever discovered gas field in the Mediterranean Sea (SRM 2014). North Africa has historically been a preferred source for Italy's energy supplies due to the strong presence of Eni in the region (Brighi and Musso 2017). For Egypt, Italy represents its most important exporting nation, with oil and gas being its most crucial products. It is worth noting, however, that Eni is not the only major Italian industrial group having extensively invested in Egypt. Edison, the Italian electricity company, also exploits gas and oil reserves along the Mediterranean coast through a joint venture with the Egyptian Petroleum Company. Furthermore, in the banking sector, Intesa Sanpaolo acquired the largest share of Bank of Alexandria, the latter being also part of an agreement with the Egyptian government and Naples-based university Federico II (SRM 2014). As of 2014, there were almost nine hundred Italian enterprises operating in Egypt, generating a total revenue of €3.5 billion and creating employment opportunities for almost thirty thousand people (ibid.). Italy is the second EU country after Germany in the total of businesses operating in Egypt.

Egypt's influence in the EU economy is also significant, as the country has signed lucrative deals with many of the EU countries. In 2014 alone, EU states authorised 290 licences for military equipment to Egypt, totalling more than €6 billion (US$6.77 billion) (Amnesty International 2016). The main EU countries supplying arms to Egypt were Bulgaria, Cyprus, Czech Republic, France, Germany, Hungary, Italy, Poland, Romania, Slovakia, Spain and the UK. Additionally, according to a Privacy International report (2017), several companies from EU countries, including Germany, Italy and the UK, have also supplied the Egyptian authorities with sophisticated equipment or technologies aimed at state surveillance that may have been used to suppress peaceful dissent and violate the right to privacy at home and abroad (Privacy International 2016). The intensification of such economic linkages has, therefore, been taking place against the backdrop of the Egyptian government's crackdown on human rights and political dissent.

Border Control and Security

Italy's relationship with Egypt is not limited to the economic field. Rather, it also encompasses further military, security, justice and home affairs dimensions.

Much of these matters revolve around Italy's concerns vis-à-vis regular migration management and irregular migration containment. Egypt is one of the North African countries of departure for the Central Mediterranean Sea route to Italy, and thus a key partner for co-operation agreements on migration management and readmission agreements. Efforts to stave off migration are funded by Italy's Official Development Assistance and, more recently, by the Italian Fund for Africa (Colombo and Palm 2019). Repatriations of clandestine migrants have been centre stage in bilateral negotiations. The War on Terror and the events which followed the Arab Spring in 2011 have placed the Mediterranean and the Middle East at the forefront of Italy's foreign policy in the region (Brighi and Musso 2017). In this sense, Egypt has become a key partner for Italy and Europe in terms of so-called security and migration policies.

The emphasis of EU policymaking on irregular migration across the Mediterranean over the past two decades has turned Egypt into a significant player in the Euro-African migration system. Relations between the EU and Egypt on migration have been historically governed through the EU Global Approach to Migration and Mobility, which has been in place since 2005 (European Commission 2011). This framework is further complemented by the European Neighbourhood Policy, Valletta, and regional co-operation agreements, such as the EU–Africa Migration & Mobility Dialogue and the 2013 EU–Horn of Africa Migration Route Initiative (IOM Khartoum Process). In addition, the European Commission has also established the EU–Egypt dialogue on migration in the context of the EU–Egypt Partnership Priorities 2017–20 (EEAS 2019). The post-2011 refugee and migration crisis across the Mediterranean has been a driving force behind closer European co-operation with Egypt's military regime on migration and border control. The perception of Egypt as a potential emigration 'hot spot' towards Europe made the EU more inclined to co-operate with the Egyptian government to prevent refugee arrivals from this new point of departure. Essentially this co-operation revolves around two elements: to secure the borders of the EU to prevent entry, and to return so-called 'illegal migrants' to their country of origin or transit state.

From the Egyptian point of view, as argued by Völkel (2020), the EU's fear of irregular migration has led many autocrats in the southern Mediterranean, and the Egyptian government in particular, to forge new alliances with the EU (ibid.): 'It was only in the course of the 2015 migration "crisis" in Europe that the Egyptian government understood that the existence of refugees and irregular migrants in its country is an important ace in its own hands' (Völkel 2022: 177). In this sense, migration diplomacy and border control policies rapidly gained importance for both sides.

The rise of irregular migration flows across the Mediterranean from the Middle East and North Africa (MENA) region to Europe after the Arab uprisings propelled the issues of refugees, migration and border controls to the top of EU priorities. To tackle the plight of refugees and migrants, the EU is increasingly outsourcing its external border management to third countries in the Mediterranean region, principally Libya, Morocco and Egypt (European Parliament 2015). In this sense, as argued by Tsourapas (2020: 10), 'from the EU side, there is a growing need to recruit Egyptian help in taming the rise of irregular migration and refugee flows across the Mediterranean'. The EU support to Egypt resulted in a deal worth €60 million aimed at enhancing the country's response to irregular migration challenges (European Commission 2017). Additionally, various EU projects and bodies also provide capacity support in border controls to third countries, like Egypt (Privacy International 2020). These efforts are co-ordinated with individual member states.

In this respect, Italy plays an important role in facilitating the EU's efforts to curb irregular migration flows. Egypt is one of the recipients of the Regional Development and Protection Programme for North Africa, jointly funded by the EU (Asylum, Migration and Integration Fund, European Neighbourhood Instrument and Trust Fund for Africa), and a consortium of EU member states led by Italy (Ministry of Interior), and implemented in partnership with UNHCR, IOM and NGOs such as Coopi, Save the Children and StARS. The programme aims to improve local life conditions as an alternative to migration as well as assisting voluntary returnees and providing capacity building to national authorities dealing with refugees and vulnerable migrants.[5]

Moreover, under the EU's operations of patrolling and search-and-rescue, Italy is also committed to curb irregular migration across the Central Mediterranean route. Operation Themis, launched in 2018 under the European

---

[5] See Ministry of Internal Affairs, 2020. Programma Regionale di Sviluppo e Protezione per il Nord Africa (RDPP NA). [Online]. Available at: http://www.libertaciviliimmigrazione.dlci. interno.gov.it/it/notizie/programma-regionale-sviluppo-e-protezione-nord-africa-rdpp-na; Gazetta Officiale. MINISTERO DELL'ECONOMIA E DELLE FINANZE. (28.01.2019). Online. Available at: https://www.gazzettaufficiale.it/eli/id/2019/03/12/19A01649/sg

Border and Coast Guard Agency (Frontex), covers the flows coming from Egypt, among other countries. The programme aims to support Italian authorities in border control activities and tackle drug smuggling as well as possible terrorist threat in the Central Mediterranean.[6] Through the collection and sharing of intelligence and security measures, the programme aims to prevent possible criminal or terrorist groups entering the territory of the EU (Dibenedetto 2018). Italy further engages with Egyptian border authorities through capacity-building initiatives, in the framework of the EU's externalisation of border management. In return, the Egyptian authorities have publicised their efforts by adopting laws and initiatives to demonstrate their engagement with EU policies. In this regard, the government has consolidated its domestic legal framework on migration, reinforced border controls and enacted the criminalisation of smuggling (Völkel 2020). Such efforts were quickly praised by EU authorities, who described the Egyptian authoritarian government as a reliable partner in the fight against illegal migration flows (Nielsen 2016).

In reality, however, such efforts are largely cosmetic, as their actual impact on refugees and undocumented migrants in Egypt so far is limited (Völkel 2020). From the Egyptian point of view, such initiatives are largely designed to attract further financial funding from the EU and international donors such as the IMF (ibid.). In this sense, as argued by Völkel (2020: 174), given economic and political incentives from the EU, the Egyptian authorities have discovered migration and border control policies to be a convenient way to reach a better position in their relations with the EU and its member states.

Counterterrorism and Security Ties

The bilateral relations between Egypt, Italy and the EU further cover various internal security matters, ranging from terrorism to law enforcement co-operation. Due to its geostrategic location, Egypt has been considered a key player in Middle East politics, both in terms of its continued role of mediation within the Arab–Israeli conflict and for its commitment to the fight against Islamic terrorism (Brighi and Musso 2017: 76). The Egyptian President used

---

[6] See European Council and the Council of the European Union. 'Saving lives at sea and targeting criminal networks'. [Online]. Available at: https://www.consilium.europa.eu/en/policies/migratory-pressures/saving-lives-at-sea/

emigration diplomacy to exploit European fears of radicalisation via irregular immigration. As noted by Al-Kashef and Martin (2019), in Cairo's understanding there is a direct link between the influx of migration and the increase in terrorist attacks on its territory. The implementation of the activities under the EU–Egypt counterterrorism agreement includes four elements: training of prosecutors in examine digital evidence; Internet Referral Units; exchange of experiences with EU agencies and member states on counterterrorism; and strategic communications and financing of terrorism.

In relation to the aforementioned initiatives, in 2000 Italy and Egypt signed a police co-operation agreement (in force from January 2007) which paved the way to direct deportations, in the absence of an actual extradition treaty. It has also contributed to the increase in asylum denial requests (see Table 11.1).

Table 11.1 Results of Egyptian asylum requests – number and percentage – approved by Italy: approval made during the year indicated in the first column, independently of the request date[1]

	Refugee status granted	Subsidiary protection granted	Humanitarian protection granted	Asylum denied	Unreachable	Other	Total
2012	114 (21%)	23 (4%)	245 (46%)	63 (12%)	5 (1%)	88 (16%)	538
2013	102 (22%)	50 (11%)	182 (38%)	56 (12%)	78 (16%)	6 (1%)	474
2014	79 (10%)	58 (8%)	437 (57%)	164 (21%)	28 (4%)	1 (>1%)	767
2015	27 (4%)	31 (4%)	200 (29%)	303 (44%)	132 (19%)	2 (>1%)	695
2016	33 (6%)	37 (7%)	214 (40%)	229 (42%)	27 (5%)	0 –	540
2017	34 (5%)	12 (2%)	295 (46%)	210 (33%)	94 (15%)	0 –	645
2018	47 (6%)	4 (>1%)	240 (30%)	434 (55%)	62 (8%)	3 (>1%)	790
2019	61 (7%)	12 (~1%)	8 (1%)	691 (76%)	97 (11%)	35 (4%)	904

[1]*Source:* Ministero de L'Interno. Dipartimento per le libertà civil ed immigrazione. http://www.libertaciviliimmigrazione.dlci. interno.gov.it/it/documentazione/statistica (authors' elaboration)

The table shows how many Egyptian citizens, having applied for international protection in Italy, managed to be granted refugee status or other forms of protection; and how many have been denied the request or have not been reached by the Italian authorities. It is interesting to note that the number of denied asylum applications between 2012 and 2019 increased significantly.

In 2018, Italian authorities arrested Egyptian-Italian politician Mohamed Mahsoub, a former leading member of the Muslim Brotherhood group, under the Interpol Red Notice system (see Chapter 9 by Grossman and Hobbins, Chapter 12 by Lemon, and Lemon [2019] for details of how states use Interpol as a tool of transnational repression). The arrest of Mahsoub further demonstrates the strategic role played by energy deals between Egypt and its European partners. A former Al Wasat politician, Mahsoub was detained for twelve hours in Sicily in August 2018, but then released. Italian police held Mahsoub at the request of Egyptian authorities for an alleged fraud charge. He had been on the Interpol list since 2013. However, it was only with the ascent of Giuseppe Conte's populist government and its subsequent closer ties to the Egyptian state, accompanied by the signing of an energy deal between the Italian company Eni and the Egyptian Tharwa company, worth about $105 million in August 2018, that Mahsoub's status altered significantly (Nowar 2018). Although Mahsoub had been resident in Italy since 2013 and held Italian citizenship since 2016, his arrest came only after the signing of the energy deal.

The commitment of the Italian government in supporting the Egyptian regime has also been visible in military and counterterrorism collaboration. In 2015 Italy also endorsed Egypt's fight against the so-called Islamic State, or ISIS, Islamist terrorist organisation by signing a new defence co-operation agreement and by increasing its sales of military supplies, including small arms and counterterrorism software (Brighi and Musso 2017: 76). In June 2016, the Italian Ministry for Economic Development gave the go-ahead to sell surveillance software to the National Defence Council, Egypt's main counterterrorism body (La Stampa 2016). In the following year, the Egyptian police academy signed a new protocol, ITEPA Programme, with the Italian Interior Ministry to establish an International Training Centre funded by Italy and Europe at the police academy in Cairo (Egypt Today 2017). As part of this agreement, Italian police have trained Egyptian security agents from 2016 until the present (Egyptwide 2022). While this co-operation agreement has been widely acclaimed among Italian officials and the EU in fighting illegal migration and human trafficking,[7] the arrangement is likely to pose serious challenges to human rights in Egypt by strengthening the coercive apparatus of a totalitarian-like regime.

For decades, the police academy in Egypt has been perceived as a tool of repression used by the regime to crack down on dissent and human rights defenders. Under al-Sisi, the government has intensified repression practices by empowering the military and intelligence and security services to control civil society groups.[8] As noted by Hamzawy (2017: 1), Sisi's government has effectively institutionalised its authoritarian governance doctrine by implementing undemocratic laws – such as the Protest Law, NGO Law, Penal Code, Terrorism Law and Military Court Law – that enable the regime to criminalise activities or make terrorism accusations without restraints. As Brighi and Musso (2017: 77) further note, 'al-Sisi's anti-terrorism campaign has notoriously refused to distinguish between followers of ISIS and Egypt's own internal political opposition'. In essence, the government is using lawmaking to legalise and legitimise its oppressive behaviour. In this context, the securitisation of border controls has been used as a strategy by the regime to instigate an atmosphere of fear that Egypt might be threatened from outside as well as inside (see also Völkel 2020). EU initiatives such as ITEPA inevitably benefit the Egyptian Ministry of Interior and enhance police co-ordination and intelligence power. Yet, without strong accountability and monitoring, such programmes could have further negative consequences by legitimising abuses of power that are already taking place in the country.

Conclusion

International cross-border ties between Egypt and Italy across political, economic and security dimensions embedded within the broader EU agenda to

---

[7] A 2019 article on the Polizia di Stato (Italian State Police) website reported that Italy and Egypt would sign a memorandum of understanding to extend the validity of the protocol signed in 2017, thus launching a further edition of the project. This edition, which will be called ITEPA 2, will be financed by the EU and last for two years (see https://www.europarl. europa.eu/doceo/document/E-9-2020-002252_EN.html)

[8] In Italy, the case of Patrick Zaky discussed in this chapter's introduction resonates with the brutal murder of Giulio Regeni, a Cambridge University doctoral student who was murdered while carrying out his fieldwork research on trade unions in Cairo.

curb illegal migration have enabled the Egyptian government to ignore and bypass democratic norms. Overall, the EU appears to prioritise its security agenda related to migration and border controls without accounting for human rights abuses under al-Sisi's regime. In this view, our analysis highlights the role played by external actors in encouraging and strengthening authoritarian practices, including the targeting of international students and transnational repression. Through specific targeted actions, such as an increase of financial resources or providing material support for capacity-building matters, EU institutions and its governments have effectively strengthened the political resources capabilities of the Egyptian government. As argued by Vanderhill (2014: 258), external assistance can empower individuals and groups in the recipient country. However, if they 'are pro-democratic, then this helps the development of democracy; if they are non-democratic, then this aids the development of autocratic regimes' (ibid.).

International assistance in the form of weapons or financial resources can increase the internal security apparatus of authoritarian leaders or enable governments to purchase weapons and strengthen internal security forces (Vanderhill 2013). As a result, this improves the ability of authoritarian governments to repress pro-democratic opponents. Financial investments of the EU into the Egyptian state, and the EU's technical assistance to the Sisi regime in the domains of security and migration, have provided additional resources that enable the Egyptian government to increase its repressive capacity.

Additionally, our analysis demonstrates that the nature of the linkages between the recipient state and the external actors further conditions the promotion of authoritarian practices. As demonstrated in this chapter, both Italy and the EU have vested economic and geopolitical interests in Egypt. Egypt is a key strategic partner in the energy and trade sectors. The discovery of a gas field on the Egyptian coast places Egypt as a key partner of the Italian energy security strategy, particularly in light of Europe's oil embargo on Russia. Moreover, the country is also an important ally on matters of irregular migration and border controls. As our analysis shows, besides the provision of natural resources and the fight against terrorism, migration diplomacy has become one of the key strategic policy fields. Such dynamics put the EU and Italy in a vulnerable position, with little leverage to put pressure on the Egyptian state. Clearly, given the EU's and Italy's strong economic and security ties with the Egyptian government and the EU's dependency on Egypt to curb illegal migration flows transiting through the Mediterranean from Africa and the Middle East, Egypt's respect for democracy and human rights has been worsening and has allowed al-Sisi's regime to further increase political repressive practices.

The arrest of Patrick Zaky triggered an immediate reaction from academics as well as human rights and policy circles, both locally and globally. A number of European politicians and MEPs, including the President of the European Parliament, David Sassoli,[9] made statements about the need to immediately free Zaky and drop the charges against him. The European Parliament also called on the EU and its member states to use all foreign policy instruments possible to release Patrick Zaky and to continue monitoring Zaky's pre-trial hearings from the delegations in Egypt (The European Parliament 2020). The unlawful detention of the Egyptian student generated strong protests and mobilisation in Italy. In particular, his story alarmingly resonated with the brutal murder of Giulio Regeni, a Cambridge University doctoral student who was murdered in Cairo in 2016 while carrying out his fieldwork research on trade unions. In April 2021, the Italian Senate voted through a motion calling upon the government to activate the institutional procedures to grant Patrick Zaky Italian citizenship, as well as urging Italian diplomatic representatives in Cairo to attend the judicial hearings. In July 2021, the Chamber of Deputies, following in the steps of the Senate, passed by a vast majority a motion urging the government to take all the measures within its competence in order to confer Italian nationality on the activist and to continue advocating for his release (Minervini 2021: 444). By law, these motions have had no immediate legal fallouts on Zaky's citizenship award.[10] Yet his arrest represents a legitimate matter of national and international concern.

Despite the appeal of the Italian government and the international community to release Patrick Zaky, our analysis demonstrates that in the context

---

[9] David Sassoli, 2020. Chiedo che Patrick Zaky, arrestato in Egitto, venga immediatamente rilasciato e restituito all'affetto dei suoi cari e ai suoi studi. Facebook Page Video [Online]. Available at: https://www.facebook.com/pagina.DavidSassoli/videos/1486686031494343

[10] According to Law No. 91 of 1992 (article 9), Italian citizenship could be awarded for special reasons via a decree of the head of state (Presidente della Repubblica) after having consulted the Council of State (the legal-administrative consultative body that checks for public administration acts) and after a deliberation of the Council of Ministers, upon a proposal put forward by the Minister of Interior in agreement with the Minister of Foreign Affairs.

of the EU, responses to transnational repression are conditioned by strategic interests that outweigh democratic normative commitments and human rights norms. The EU and the Italian government have clearly privileged dealing with Egypt based on key strategic interests to the detriment of human rights values. There is a high level of co-operation and integration between Egypt, the EU and Italy on migration, security and energy issues, providing Egypt with greater leverage. In such context, the EU and its member states lack the capacity to condemn the Egyptian government and its human rights violations. Furthermore, the alliance between Egypt and the EU in the above strategic areas has insulated Sisi's government from pressure to adopt political and democratic reforms. Despite reports from civil society actors which denounce human rights abuses in Egypt, there has not been any united and co-ordinated response from the EU and its member states to put real pressure on al-Sisi and his government to prevent widespread abuse and repression practices taking place both at domestic and transnational levels. In this environment, there is a high likelihood that cases of transnational repression – as what happened to Patrick Zaky – will reoccur and remain unchallenged.[11]

References

Accorsi, A. 2015. 'Egitto, la strategia del terrore: "Consolato italiano obiettivo semplice e vicino ad al Sisi"'. *La Repubblica*, 13 July. [Online.] Available at: https://www.repubblica.it/esteri/2015/07/13/news/egitto_attentato_consolato_italiano_strategia_terrorismo-118995392/

Adamson, F. and Tsourapas, G. 2018. 'Migration diplomacy in world politics'. *International Studies Perspectives* 20(2): 113–28.

Al-Kashef, M. and Martin, M. 2019. 'EU–Egypt migration cooperation: At the expense of human rights'. EuroMedRights. [Online.] Available at: https://euromedrights.org/publication/eu-egypt-migration-cooperation-where-are-human-rights/

Allen-Ebrahimian, B. 2018. 'China's long arm reaches into American campuses'. *Foreign Policy*, 7 March. [Online.] Available at: https://foreignpolicy.com/2018/03/07/chinas-long-arm-reaches-into-american-campuses-chinese-students-scholars-association-university-communist-party/

al-Salam, M. abd. 2016. 'On the prevention of foreign academics and researchers from entering Egypt', 12 February. Freedom of Thought and Expression

---

[11] On 19 July 2023 the Egyptian President, Abdel Fattah al-Sisi, pardoned the human rights researcher Patrick Zaki, who was subsequently released from prison.

Law Firm. [Online.] Available at: https://afteegypt.org/en/afte_publications/2016/02/12/11773-afteegypt.html

Ambrosio, T. 2009. *Authoritarian Backlash: Russian Resistance to Democratization in the Former Soviet Union*. London: Ashgate.

Amnesty International. 2014. 'Egypt: Rampant torture, arbitrary arrests and detentions signal catastrophic decline in human rights one year after ousting of Morsi', 3 July. [Online.] Available at: https://www.amnesty.org/en/latest/news/2014/07/egypt-anniversary-morsi-ousting/

——. 2015. Egypt: Generation Jail: Egypt's youth go from protest to prison'. [Online.] Available at: https://www.amnesty.org/en/documents/mde12/1853/2015/en/

——. 2016. 'EU: Halt arms transfers to Egypt to stop fuelling killings and torture'. [Online.] Available at: https://www.amnesty.org/en/latest/news/2016/05/eu-halt-arms-transfers-to-egypt-to-stop-fuelling-killings-and-torture/

——. 2022. 'Egypt: Human rights crisis deepens one year after national human rights strategy launched', 21 September. [Online.] Available at: https://www.amnesty.org/en/latest/news/2022/09/egypt-human-rights-crisis-deepens-one-year-after-national-human-rights-strategy-launched/

ANSA. 2022. 'Egypt's trial against researcher Zaki adjourned to 27/9', 21 June. [Online.] Available at: https://www.ansa.it/english/news/general_news/2022/06/21/egypts-trial-against-researcher-zaki-adjourned-to-27/9_6a701c21-49c9-4272-bfbb-85e35265e641.html

Asharq Al-Awsat. 2017. 'Egypt repeats call on Interpol to arrest fugitives in Qatar and Turkey', 4 July. [Online]. Available at: https://eng-archive.aawsat.com/theaawsat/news-middle-east/egypt-repeats-call-interpol-arrest-fugitives-qatar-turkey

BBC. 2015. 'Islamic State "behind blast" at Italian consulate in Cairo', 11 July. [Online.] Available at: https://www.bbc.com/news/world-middle-east-33491512

BP. 2019. 'BP to divest mature oil assets in Egypt to Dragon Oil'. [Online.] Available at: https://www.bp.com/en/global/corporate/news-and-insights/press-releases/bp-to-divest-mature-oil-assets-in-egypt-to-dragon-oil.html

Brighi, E. and Musso, M. 2017. 'Italy in the Middle East and the Mediterranean: The evolving relations with Egypt and Libya'. *Italian Politics* 32(1): 70–89.

Ceccorulli, M. 2022. 'Triangular migration diplomacy: The case of EU–Italian cooperation with Libya'. *Italian Political Science Review* 52: 328–45.

Colombo, S. and Palm, A. 2019. 'Italy in the Mediterranean: Priorities and perspectives of a European Middle Power'. Foundation for European Progressive Studies (FEPS).

Council of the European Union. 2013. Foreign Affairs Council meeting, Brussels, 21 August. [Online.] Available at: https://www.sipri.org/sites/default/files/2016-03/EU-Council-conclusions-on-Egypt.pdf

Dahinden, J. 2010. 'The dynamics of migrants' transnational formations: Between mobility and locality'. In Bauböck, R. and Faist, T. (eds), *Diaspora and Transnationalism: Concepts, Theories and Methods*. Amsterdam: Amsterdam University Press.

Sassoli, D. 2020. Chiedo che Patrick Zaky, arrestato in Egitto, venga immediatamente rilasciato e restituito all'affetto dei suoi cari e ai suoi studi. Facebook Page Video [Online]. Available at: https://www.facebook.com/pagina.DavidSassoli/videos/1486686031494343

Del Sarto, R. A. and Tocci, N. 2008. 'Italy's politics without policy: Balancing Atlanticism and Europeanism in the Middle East'. *Modern Italy* 13(2): 135–53.

Dibenedetto, A. 2018. 'Operation Themis and its meaning to Italy'. CESI. [Online.] Available at: https://www.cesi-italia.org/contents/Operation%20Themis%20impaginato%20Eng.pdf

Dunne, M. and Hamzaw, A. 2019. 'Egypt's political exiles going anywhere but home'. Accessed 8 July 2020. Available at: https://carnegieendowment.org/2019/03/29/egypt-s-political-exiles-going-anywhere-but-home-pub-78728

EEAS. 2019. Second meeting of the Migration Dialogue between the European Union and Egypt. 11 July. [Online.] Available at: https://eeas.europa.eu/headquarters/headquarters-homepage/65317/second-meeting-migration-dialogue-between-european-union-and-egypt_en

Egyptwide. 2022. 'Official violators: Egypt–Italy police cooperation in human rights violations'. [Online.] Available at: https://www.egyptwide.org/publication/report-official-violators

Egypt Today. 2017a. 'Egypt to resend list of wanted MB elements to Interpol'. 2 July. [Online.] Available at: https://www.egypttoday.com/Article/1/9919/Egypt-to-resend-list-of-wanted-MB-elements-to-Interpol

——. 2017b. 'Italy to establish training center at Egyptian police academy'. 21 September. [Online.] Available at: https://www.egypttoday.com/Article/1/23961/Italy-to-establish-Training-Center-at-Egyptian-police-academy

Euromed Rights. 2019. 'EU–Egypt migration cooperations: Where are human rights?' [Online.] Available at: https://euromedrights.org/publication/eu-egypt-migration-cooperation-where-are-humanrights/#:~:text=While%20Egypt%20does%20not%20constitute%20a%20major%20country,policy%20and%20obtain%20funds%20for%20its%20domestic%20projects

European Commission. 2011. 'The global approach to migration and mobility'. [Online.] Available at: https://eur-lex.europa.eu/legal-content/EN/TXT/PDF/?uri=CELEX:52011DC0743&from=en

——. 2017a. 'EU Emergency Trust Fund for Africa: Enhancing the response to migration challenges in Egypt (ERMCE)'. [Online.] Available at: https://ec.europa.

eu/trustfundforafrica/region/north-africa/egypt/enhancing-response-migration-challenges-egypt-ermce_en

——. 2017b. Recommendation for a COUNCIL DECISION. COM(2017) 809 final. [Online.] Available at: https://eur-lex.europa.eu/resource.html?uri=cellar:dda74421-e56a-11e7-9749-01aa75ed71a1.0001.02/DOC_1&format=PDF

——. 2021. 'European Union, trade in goods with Egypt'. [Online.] Available at: https://webgate.ec.europa.eu/isdb_results/factsheets/country/details_egypt_en.pdf

European Commission. 'European Neighbourhood Policy and Enlargement Negotiations, Egypt'. [Online.] Available at: https://ec.europa.eu/neighbourhood-enlargement/neighbourhood/countries/egypt_en

European Council and the Council of the European Union. 'Saving lives at sea and targeting criminal networks'. [Online.] Available at: https://www.consilium.europa.eu/en/policies/migratory-pressures/saving-lives-at-sea/

European Parliament. 2015. 'EU cooperation with third countries in the field of migration'. [Online.] https://www.europarl.europa.eu/RegData/etudes/STUD/2015/536469/IPOL_STU%282015%29536469_EN.pdf

European Parliament. 2020a. MOTION FOR A RESOLUTION On the deteriorating situation of human rights in Egypt, in particular the case of the activists of the Egyptian Initiative for Personal Rights (EIPR)(2020/2912(RSP)). [Online]. Available at: https://www.europarl.europa.eu/doceo/document/B-9-2020-0426_EN.html

European Parliament. 2020b. MOTION FOR A RESOLUTION On the deteriorating situation of human rights in Egypt, in particular the case of the activists of the Egyptian Initiative for Personal Rights (EIPR)(2020/2912(RSP)). [Online]. Available at: https://www.europarl.europa.eu/doceo/document/B-9-2020-0430_EN.html

European Parliament. 2020c. 'EP-President Sassoli calls for immediate release of Patrick Zaky'. [Online.] Available at: https://the-president.europarl.europa.eu/en/newsroom/ep-president-sassoli-calls-for-immediate-release-of-patrick-zaky

Eurostat Asylum Database [Online.] Accessed 4 September 2020. Available at: https://ec.europa.eu/eurostat/web/asylum-and-managed-migration/data/database

FIDH. 2021. 'Egypt: Arbitrary detention and ill-treatment of women's rights student Ahmed Samir Santawy'. [Online.] Available at: https://www.fidh.org/en/issues/human-rights-defenders/egypt-arbitrary-detention-and-ill-treatment-of-women-s-rights-student

Front Line Defenders. 'Judicial harassment of Gamal Eid'. [Online.] Available at: https://www.frontlinedefenders.org/en/case/judicial-harassment-gamal-eid

Furstenberg, S., Prelec, T. and Heathershaw, J. 2020. 'The internationalization of universities and the repression of academic freedom'. Freedom House Special Report 2020. [Online.] Available at: https://freedomhouse.org/report/special-report/2020/internationalization-universities-and-repression-academic-freedom#footnote4_tahwh28

Gargano, T. 2009. '(Re)conceptualizing international student mobility: The potential of transnational social fields'. *Journal of Studies in International Education* 13(3): 331–46.

Glasius, M. 2018. 'Extraterritorial authoritarian practices: a framework'. *Globalisations* 15(2): 179–97.

Geddes, A. and Maru, M. T. 2020. 'Localising migration diplomacy in Africa? Ethiopia in its regional and international setting (September 2020)'. Robert Schuman Centre for Advanced Studies Research Paper No. RSCAS 2020/50. Available at: https://ssrn.com/abstract=3712282

Greenhill, K. 2003. 'The use of refugees as political and military weapons in the Kosovo conflict'. In Thomas, R. G. C. (ed.), *Yugoslavia Unraveled: Sovereignty, Self-Determination, Intervention.* Lanham, MD: Lexington Books.

Guardian, The. 2020. 'Giulio Regeni's parents urge Italy to help student held in Egypt'. 14 February. [Online.] Available at: https://www.theguardian.com/world/2020/feb/14/giulio-regenis-parents-urge-italy-to-help-student-held-in-egypt

Haas, E. B. 1980. 'Why collaborate? Issue-linkage and international regimes'. *World Politics* 32(3): 357–405.

Hamzawy, A. 2017. 'Legislating authoritarianism: Egypt's new era of repression'. Carnegie Endowment for Peace. [Online.] Available at: https://carnegieendowment.org/2017/03/16/legislating-authoritarianism-egypt-s-new-era-of-repression-pub-68285

Hollifield, J. F. 2000. 'The politics of international migration: How can we "Bring the state back in"?' In Hollifield, J. F. and Brettell, C. F. (eds), *Migration Theory: Talking across Disciplines*, 2nd edn. New York and London: Routledge, pp. 183–237.

Human Rights Watch. 2014. 'All according to plan. The Rab'a Massacre and mass killings of protesters in Egypt'. [Online.] Available at: https://www.hrw.org/report/2014/08/12/all-accordingplan/raba-massacre-and-mass-killings-protesters-egypt

——. 2021. '"They don't understand the fear we have". How China's long reach of repression undermines academic freedom at Australia's universities'. [Online.] Available at: https://www.hrw.org/report/2021/06/30/they-dont-understand-fear-we-have/how-chinas-long-reach-repression-undermines

——. 2022. 'Egypt events of 2021'. World Report 2022. [Online.] Available at: https://www.hrw.org/world-report/2022/country-chapters/egypt

Kashef, M. al- and Martin, M. 2019. 'EU–Egypt migration cooperation: At the expense of human rights'. EuroMedRights.

Kilani, F. 2014. 'Qatar's Al-Araby Al-Jadeed: Will new media venture silence suspicions?' BBC, 28 November. [Online.] Available at: https://www.bbc.co.uk/news/world-middle-east-30141659

Kirkpatrick, D. and Harris, G. 2017. 'Saudis and Emiratis list dozens linked to Qatar as aiding terrorism'. *New York Times*, 9 June. [Online.] Available at: https://www.nytimes.com/2017/06/09/world/middleeast/saudi-arabia-united-arab-emirates-qatar-terrorism-list.html

Knight, B. 2015. 'Germany frees Al-Jazeera journalist Ahmed Mansour'. *The Guardian*, 23 June. [Online.] Available at: https://www.theguardian.com/world/2015/jun/22/egyptian-journalist-ahmed-mansour-released-germany-al-jazeera

La Stampa. 2016. 'L'Italia esporterà software di sorveglianza in Egitto'. 29 June. Available at: https://www.lastampa.it/cronaca/2016/06/29/news/l-italia-esportera-software-di-sorveglianza-in-egitto-1.34994393

Memorandum of understanding between The Italian Ministry of Labour and Social Policies and the Egyptian Ministry of Manpower and Migration concerning the implementation of the agreement on cooperation on Bilateral labour migration. 28 November 2005. [Online.] Available at: http://www.lavoro.gov.it/temi-e-priorita/immigrazione/focus-on/accordi-bilaterali/Documents/EGAccordo BilateraleEgitto.EN.pdf

Meringolo, A. 2016. 'Egitto'. In Greco, E. and Ronzitti N., *Rapporto sulla Politica Estera Italiana: il Governo Renzi*. Rome: Istituto Affari Internazionali/Edizioni Nuova Cultura, pp. 101–5.

Michaelson, R. 2018. 'Politician who fled Egypt arrested in Sicily'. *The Guardian*, 2 August. [Online.] Available at: https://www.theguardian.com/world/2018/aug/02/arrest-highlights-growing-ties-between-egypt-and-italy

Middle East Monitor. 2020. 'Germany signs $43m gas deal with Egypt despite appalling human rights crisis'. 11 February. [Online.] Available at: https://www.middleeastmonitor.com/20200211-germany-signs-43m-gas-deal-with-egypt-despite-appalling-human-rights-crisis/

Ministero de l'Interno. Dipartemento per le liberta civil ed immigrazione. [Online.] Available at: http://www.libertaciviliimmigrazione.dlci.interno.gov.it/it/notizie/programma-regionale-sviluppo-e-protezione-nord-africa-rdpp-na

Ministero de l'Interno. Dipartemento per le liberta civil ed immigrazione. [Online.] Available at: http://www.libertaciviliimmigrazione.dlci.interno.gov.it/it/documentazione/statistica

Ministero delle politiche agricole alimentari e forestali. 2015. Martina in Egitto: firmato memorandum collaborazioni agro-alimentari. [Online.] Available at: https://www.politicheagricole.it/flex/cm/pages/ServeBLOB.php/L/IT/IDPagina/8286

Minervini, G. 2022. 'Italian citizenship attribution to Patrick Zaki'. *The Italian Review of International and Comparative Law* 1(2): 443–53.

Muhammad al-Kashef and Martin, M. 2019. 'EU—Egypt migration cooperation: At the expense of human rights'. EuroMedRights.

Near East News Agency (NENA). 2018. 'Helmy Regeni un ricordo,con Renzie Eni salvati i rapporti Italia-Egitto'. 5 March. [Online.] Available at: https://nena-news.it/helmy-regeni-un-ricordo-con-renzi-e-eni-salvati-i-rapporti-italia-egitto/

Nielsen, N. 2016. 'Egypt blames EU—Turkey deal for refugee spike'. *The Observer*, 31 August. Available at: https://euobserver.com/migration/134829

Norman, K. P. 2020. 'Migration diplomacy and policy liberalization in Morocco and Turkey'. *International Migration Review* 54(4): 1158–83le.

Nowar, N. 2018. 'Natural gas galore: Egypt's high hopes'. *Ahram*, 5 July. [Online.] Available at: http://english.ahram.org.eg/NewsContent/3/12/306284/Business/Economy/Natural-gas-galore-Egypts-high-hopes-.aspx

Panarella, E. 2015. 'Egitto, il canale di Suez chiama l'Italia: "Venite ad investire qui"'. *Il Messagero*, 26 February. [Online.] Available at: https://www.ilmessaggero.it/primopiano/esteri/egitto_canale_suez_italia_venite_investire_qui-886869.html

Poast, P. 2012. 'Does issue linkage work? Evidence from European alliance negotiations, 1860 to 1945'. *International Organization* 66(2) (Spring 2012): 277–310.

Privacy International. 2016. 'The President's men? Inside the Technical Research Department'. [Online.] Available at: https://privacyinternational.org/sites/default/files/2017-12/egypt_reportEnglish.pdf

——. 2020. 'Borders without borders: How the EU is exporting surveillance in bid to outsource its border controls'. [Online.] Available at: https://privacyinternational.org/long-read/4288/borders-without-borders-how-eu-exporting-surveillance-bid-outsource-its-border

Qing, G. and Schweisfurth, M. 2015. 'Transnational connections, competences and identities: Experiences of Chinese international students after their return home'. *British Educational Research Journal* 41(6) (December 2015): 947–97.

Rai Uno. 2020. 'Patrick George Zaki – Erasmo Palazzotto, presidente Commissione parlamentare d'inchiesta sulla morte di Giulio Regeni'. 11 February. [Online.] Available at: https://www.raiplayradio.it/audio/2020/02/Patrick-George-Zaki---Erasmo-Palazzotto-presidente-Commissione-parlamentare-dinchiesta-sulla-morte-di-Giulio-Regeni-1f79404e-2367-4677-b7ac-42e9827251f3.html?wt_mc=2.social.tw.radio1_vivavoce.&wt

Reporters without Borders. 2018. 'Baromètre des violations de la liberté de la presse'. [Online.] Available at: https://rsf.org/fr/barometre?year=2018&type_id=235#list-barometre%20,%20https://www.frontlinedefenders.org/en/case/judicial-harassment-gamal-eid

Rotella, S. 2021. 'Even on US campuses, China cracks down on students who speak out'. *Propublica*, 30 November. [Online.] Available at: https://www.propublica.org/article/even-on-us-campuses-china-cracks-down-on-students-who-speak-out

Saied, M. 2020. 'Germany concludes major naval arms package to Egypt, despite opposition'. *Al-Monitor*, 9 November. [Online]. Available at: https://www.al-monitor.com/originals/2020/11/egypt-germany-deal-naval-equipment-tensions-east-med.html#ixzz79jzzr2Rv

Schenkkan, N. and Linzer, I. 2021. 'Out of sight, not out of reach'. [Online.] Available at: https://freedomhouse.org/sites/default/files/2021-02/Complete_FH_TransnationalRepressionReport2021_rev020221.pdf

Scholars at Risk. 2019. 'Free to Think 2019'. Academic Freedom Monitoring Project, November. [Online.] Available at: https://www.scholarsatrisk.org/resources/free-to-think-2019/

——. 2020. 'Free to Think 2020'. [Online.] Available at: https://www.scholarsatrisk.org/wp-content/uploads/2020/11/Scholars-at-Risk-Free-to-Think-2020.pdf

Serra, B. 2015. 'Q&A with Italian PM: "I think Sisi is a great leader"'. *Al-Jazeera*, 12 July. [Online.] Available at: https://www.aljazeera.com/features/2015/7/12/qa-with-italian-pm-i-think-sisi-is-a-great-leader

SRM Centro Studi. 2014. 'Egitto paese chiave per l'economia mediterranea'. [Online.] Available at: https://www.sr-m.it/egitto-paese-chiave-per-leconomia-mediterranea/

Thiolett, H. 2011. 'Migration as diplomacy: Labor migrants, refugees, and Arab regional politics in the oil-rich countries'. *International Labor and Working-Class History* 79: 103–21.

Tolay, J. 2023. 'Interrogating and broadening the emerging narrative on migration diplomacy: A critical assessment'. *Millennium* 51(1): 354–75.

Tsourapas, G. 2017. 'Migration diplomacy in the Global South: Cooperation, coercion and issue linkage in Gaddafi's Libya'. *Third World Quarterly* 38(10): 2367–85.

——. 2019. 'A tightening grip abroad: Authoritarian regimes target their emigrant and diaspora communities'. Migration Information Source. [Online.]. Available at: https://www.migrationpolicy.org/article/authoritarian-regimes-target-their-emigrant-and-diaspora-communities

——. 2020. 'The EU–Egypt Partnership priorities and the Egyptian migration state'. MAGYC Policy report paper. [Online.] https://www.magyc.uliege.be/wp-content/uploads/2020/04/D2.4-v1April2020.pdf

——. 2021. 'Global autocracies: Strategies of transnational repression, legitimation, and co-optation in world politics'. *International Studies Review* 23(3) (September 2021): 616–44. https://doi.org/10.1093/isr/viaa061

Tsourapas, G. and Zartaloudis, S. 2021. 'Leveraging the European refugee crisis: Forced displacement and bargaining in Greece's bailout negotiations'. *Journal of Common Market Studies*: 1–19.

United Nations. 2021. 'Egypt urged to remove activists from "terrorist" list'. *UN News*, 11 February. [Online.] Available at: https://news.un.org/en/story/2021/02/1084422

University of Bologna. 2020. 'Patrick George Zaki's arrest: The motion of the University of Bologna'. 12 February. [Online.] Available at: https://www.unibo.it/en/notice-board/patrick-george-zakys-arrest-the-motion-of-the-university-of-bologna

Völkel, J. C. 2022. 'Fanning fears, winning praise: Egypt's smart play on Europe's apprehension of more undocumented immigration'. *Mediterranean Politics* 27(2): 170–91.

Vanderhill, R. 2013. *Promoting Authoritarianism Abroad*. Boulder, CO: Lynne Rienner.

——. 2014. 'Promoting democracy and promoting authoritarianism: Comparing the cases of Belarus and Slovakia'. *Europe-Asia Studies* 66(2): 255–83.

Weber, S. and Wiesmeth, H. 1991. 'Issue linkage in the European Community'. *Journal of Common Market Studies* 29(3): 255–67.

PART IV

TRANSNATIONAL REPRESSION AND
THE ROLE OF INTERNATIONAL
INSTITUTIONS AND LAW

12

INTERNATIONAL ORGANISATIONS AS TOOLS OF TRANSNATIONAL REPRESSION: STRATEGIES OF INSTITUTIONAL MANIPULATION AND RESISTANCE

Edward Lemon

In October 2017, Mirzorahim Kuzov, leading member of Tajikistan's Islamic Renaissance Party, a political party that had been banned by the Tajik government in 2015, was detained at Athens International Airport. He was returning from a human rights conference organised by the Organisation for Security and Cooperation in Europe (OSCE) in Warsaw. When he arrived at the airport in Greece to catch a connecting flight, his name flashed up on Interpol's database; the government of Tajikistan had issued a request for his detention, or Red Notice, accusing him of 'extremism'. After one month in detention, the Greek government denied the government of Tajikistan's request to extradite Kuzov on the grounds that he would be mistreated if he returned to Tajikistan.

Although Kuzov was freed by the Greek government's refusal to comply with Tajikistan's wishes, his persecution via a Red Notice is not an isolated occurrence. Despite accounting for just 0.12 per cent of the world's population, Tajikistan had 2,528 Red Notices in circulation via Interpol by 2017, amounting to 2.3 per cent of the total Notices in circulation at the time. In many cases, these Notices are used not to target legitimate criminals, but rather to repress political dissidents – and the Tajik government's use of Interpol to repress human rights advocates is not unique. Authoritarian regimes from

Russia to Iran, China and Venezuela have and continue to use Interpol, the world's police co-operation body, to pursue their opponents (Lemon 2019).

When governments enact transnational repression to target opponents living abroad, they rarely do so alone. In most cases, they *collaborate bilaterally* with the host government or multilaterally through international organisations. Authoritarian governments have established regional organisations built around autocratic norms, codifying rules that bypass human rights norms, facilitate swift extraditions and bolster regime protections against threats to their hold on power (Cooley and Schaaf 2017). In 2010 UHRP Executive Director Omer Kanat attempted to travel to Kyrgyzstan and Kazakhstan as a representative of the World Uyghur Congress. In advance of his trip, Kanat learned that he would not be allowed to enter Kyrgyzstan due to his presence on a list of people banned from entering the country. As a result, Kanat decided to continue to Kazakhstan, but he was detained there upon arrival. After being interrogated in the airport in Almaty, he was informed that he would not be allowed to enter Kazakhstan or any other member state of the Shanghai Cooperation Organisation (SCO), including Russia, because he was on the organisation's blacklist of wanted terrorists (Jardine, Hall and Lemon 2021). He was then deported to Turkey.

This chapter examines two types of relationship between transnational repression and international organisations, illustrated by the examples above. First, it demonstrates how Eurasian regimes are *manipulating* Interpol, which is an international organisation that professes to have a commitment to working in the 'spirit of the UN Declaration on Human Rights' (Interpol 1956). Although purported to be politically neutral, the world's police co-operation body has been increasingly manipulated by authoritarian regimes to pursue opponents abroad. Regimes have taken advantage of its systems of communication, opaqueness, guiding principles of respect for sovereignty and sovereign equality between states, and its limited capacity to ensure the validity of Notices, to turn it into a tool of transnational repression. Interpol has not been used as effectively at rendering exiles back as organisations as the SCO and Commonwealth of Independent States (CIS) have been within their member states over the past two decades. Nevertheless, it has led to exiles being detained, hampered their mobility, and led to reputational damage. As an international organisation with 194 members, authoritarian governments try to signal that ending up in an Interpol database signals 'international consensus' that a 'flagged' person is a criminal.

Second, this chapter examines, as illustrated in Omer Kanat's case, how regimes have *co-operated* through two 'authoritarian regional organisations', the SCO and the CIS, which support members by enforcing regime 'stability' and 'authority', as well as offering material assistance to weaker members (Kneuer et al. 2016; Obydenkova and Libman 2018; Lemon and Antonov 2020). These organisations have developed legal frameworks and activities created in the name of the new norms of regional security, stability or counterterrorism. They give governments a number of extraterritorial powers, bypassing traditional domestic legal checks and international norms that support human rights. Members of these authoritarian regional organisations share information about suspects and may conduct investigations on each other's territory. This system privileges regional security co-operation over international human rights obligations, and puts regimes' political opponents, journalists and other civil society members at risk.

This chapter draws its analysis from examples in Central Asia and Russia. This area is especially suited to studies of regional organisations, given it has a shared language (Russian), post-colonial hegemony (Russia), cultural, political and economic linkages, common Soviet legacy and a range of regional organisations that have facilitated transnational repression. At the time of writing in the summer of 2022, Russia's invasion of Ukraine continues to reverberate around the region and could shape the use of transnational repression. The chapter starts by offering an overview of the literature on transnational authoritarianism and authoritarian institutions before discussing the two authoritarian regional organisations mentioned above: the SCO and CIS. In the final section, I discuss what features of Interpol have made it susceptible to manipulation, the effects of targeting an individual through Interpol, and how it has been reforming over the past five years since receiving criticism from policymakers, NGOs and researchers of transnational repression.

Transnational Repression, Authoritarianism and International Organisations

The volume within which this chapter is embedded stands testament to the wealth of scholarship on what has variously been termed 'counter-exile strategies' (Shain 2005), 'extraterritorial security practices' (Lewis 2015), 'transnational repression' (Moss 2016) and 'transnational authoritarianism' (Tsouparas 2020) that has developed over the past few years. Scholars such as Tsourapas in this volume (see also Öztürk 2020) have developed typologies of the 'repertoires' of transnational repression and examined case studies ranging from Tajikistan (Lemon 2018) to Central Asia (Lewis 2015; Furstenberg et al. 2021; Del Sordi 2018), Iran (Michaelsen 2018), Libya and Syria (Moss 2016, 2022). But less attention has been paid to the mechanisms through which transnational repression operates, specifically the role of international organisations.

This chapter uses insights from the literature on transnational authoritarianism and authoritarian regional organisations to overcome this gap. Over the past two decades, scholars have turned their attention to the ways in which international factors can explain the persistence of authoritarian regimes (Tansey 2017). Scholars examining how actors learn from each other to strengthen authoritarian regimes or hinder democratisation have labelled this phenomenon 'autocracy promotion' (Burnell 2010), 'democracy resistance' (Nodia 2014), 'autocracy support' (Yakouchyk 2019), 'authoritarian collaboration' (von Soest 2015), 'authoritarian learning' (Heydermann and Leenders 2011) or 'authoritarian diffusion' (Ambrosio 2010).

International organisations form a central part of these illiberal processes – a topic that has only become the subject of sustained academic research in recent years. (See also Chapter 9 by Grossman and Hobbins, this volume.) A large literature on institutions and authoritarianism has emerged (Pepinsky 2014) to examine how elections, political parties, courts, legislatures and civil society shape authoritarian durability (Cox 2009; Magaloni 2006; Gandhi and Przeworski 2007; Brownlee 2007; Blaydes 2010; Hess 2010). Andreas Schedler highlights two strands of thinking about these institutions (Schedler 2009). *Probabilistic* theories view them as constraints on behaviour, while *possibilistic* theories consider them to be enabling devices. For example, where the International Criminal Court *constrains* behaviour by punishing those that abuse human rights, Interpol, as discussed later, *enables* regimes to pursue opponents abroad.

More recently, scholars have examined the influence of international institutions on dynamics of authoritarianism. While democratic states seek to use international institutions to open borders, facilitate the flow of capital and spread democracy by locking in commitments to liberal reform in exchange for the benefits of membership, the goals of autocratic states are quite different. In their groundbreaking work on authoritarian regionalism, Libman and Obydenkova (2019) adopt a possibilistic logic to examine how non-democratic regional organisations enable authoritarian consolidation at the national level. Using case studies from Eurasia, they argue that what they call 'non-democratic regional organizations' do shape domestic regimes, both materially and symbolically. Such organisations are often created and sustained from the top down by great powers seeking to increase their influence. Powerful states are what Kneuer and Demmelhuber (2016) call 'authoritarian gravity centres'. These centres are both *transmission belts* for the active promotion of autocratic policies and *learning rooms*, where 'worst' practices are shared (Kneuer, Peresson and Zumbrägel 2019; Hug 2016).

What drives co-operation? Most would agree with the assertion that '[a]uthoritarian governments' primary concern is to stay in power' (Von Soest 2015: 626). Beyond this common concern about regime security, Ambrosio divides the motivations for collaboration into two complementary logics: a logic of consequences and a logic of appropriateness (Ambrosio 2010). According to the logic of consequences, regimes adopt or promote policies based on their perceived effectiveness and the expected risks of non-action. Autocrats support other regimes during crises if they perceive the situation as similar to their own, such as Russia's fear of contagion during the 'colored revolutions' where authoritarian regimes were overthrown in Georgia and elsewhere. Accordingly, Libman and Obydenkova (2018: 155) argue that regional organisations can provide powerful autocratic states with 'redistribution mechanisms' to provide economic benefits (energy subsidies, cheaper arms exports, labour-market access, loans, aid, Foreign Direct Investment) and legitimisation (election monitoring, rhetorical support) to weaker member states in return for their continued membership.

Others have examined the way regional organisations help bolster repressive capacities through security assistance and intelligence sharing (Debre 2021; Cooley and Heathershaw 2017). This process is not purely based on material linkages. The logic of appropriateness refers to the perceived normative value of a policy and the desire by promoters and adopters to be part of the same community. For example, rising powers have stressed the need for 'civilizational diversity', and in doing so have questioned the universal applicability of democratic governance, human rights and liberal norms (Acharya 2020). At the same time, regional organisations have been conduits through which regimes can seek what Maria Debre (2021) has called 'international appeasement', helping governments frame themselves as democratically elected and committed to international norms of good governance without actually enforcing them. Roy Allison and Alexander Libman refer to the normative bonding of post-Soviet states motivated by 'protective integration', bandwagoning with Russia and China to increase the likelihood of incumbent survival through the redistribution mechanisms discussed above (Allison 2008; Libman 2007).

Two gaps remain, however. First, the literature on transnational repression has not fully accounted for how international organisations have become tools of transnational repression, which comprises an essential part of the 'menu of autocratic innovation' (Morgenbesser 2020: 1059). Neither has the literature on authoritarian regionalism fully engaged with transnational repression as a method of protective integration. By targeting opponents abroad, authoritarian regimes achieve two goals that have the potential to strengthen their domestic power. First they directly punish dissenters in an effort to silence them, subjecting them to surveillance, harassment, detention, rendition, proxy punishment (also referred to as 'coercion-by-proxy') of their relatives at home (Moss 2016; Adamson and Tsourapas 2020) and assassination. Second, they signal to society and other members of social movements or political parties the cost of going against the regime.

A second gap in the literature on authoritarianism is related to the way it has largely neglected how authoritarian actors manipulate international organisations that have some commitment to democracy or human rights, such as the Council of Europe, UN Human Rights Council and Interpol. While regimes' abilities to shape these pre-existing organisations are more constrained, the symbolic pay-offs of doing so are greater in light of the organisations' democratic members and purported commitment to human rights, as I argue with regard to Interpol. For these reasons, understanding the relationship between regional organisations designed to facilitate transnational repression, international organisations and authoritarian regime endurance is essential for understanding the character and evolution of governance in the contemporary world.

Transnational Repression in Eurasia

Referring to post-Soviet space, David Lewis (2016) argues that a 'Moscow Consensus' has emerged. As Lewis argues, 'across the Eurasian region, authoritarian states increasingly band together to resist liberal values and pro-democracy initiatives' (ibid.: 13). Instead of exporting an entire political model in the way Western states have promoted democracy, they constitute a loose set of ideas and values that resonate among the authoritarian regimes in Eurasia. Lewis lists four overlapping areas of convergence. First, governments view the state of nature as a Hobbesian anarchy, a war of all against all. Faced with the chaos produced by more open, democratic forms of rule, authoritarian power holders believe that a strong, centralised state is required to provide political order. Second, governments have been able to take advantage of 'à-la-carte regionalism' (Libman and Vinokurov 2007) to pick and choose whether to participate in a range of co-operative structures and initiatives led by Russia, China, the US and the EU (Russo 2017). Third, they view their populations as a potential source of threat to their authority, and fertile ground for recruitment by so-called extremists. Lastly, although the governments remain committed to economic growth and integration into the global financial system, the political economy in each state remains deeply corrupt and the elite remains resistant to market reform in so far as it cuts into their access to rents through their kleptocratic practices. Each government has prioritised economic reform over political liberalisation, insisting on a gradualist approach to political transition. In addition to the areas outlined by Lewis, authoritarian governments have adopted a loose definition of terrorism and extremism, capitalising on the Global War on Terror to crack down on domestic dissent (Horsman 2005). Equipped with such an all-encompassing definition, 'the "terrorist" designation has become a weapon that authoritarians can wield against political foes' (Cooley 2015: 51).

The Moscow consensus relies on material linkages. While police forces, diaspora groups, embassies, ministries of justice and other branches of government are often involved in transnational repression, in many cases it is the intelligence services that are the leading actor. After the collapse of the Soviet Union in 1989, newly independent states developed their own government institutions, including security services. Despite these cosmetic changes, intelligence agencies continue to mirror, in structure, recruiting and training, their former KGB selves. Mark Galeotti describes these enduring ties as 'Repressintern', a name derived from the Comintern, the communist organisation advocating for world revolution. According to Galeotti, since the Soviet Union, Russia has developed 'a strong commitment to [. . .] mutually-supportive intelligence-sharing understandings that also extend to direct "active measures" intended to maintain friendly authoritarian regimes in its so-called "near abroad"' (Galeotti 2016: 12). Many KGB-trained intelligence officers remain in Eurasia's security services (Lefebvre and McDermott 2008). Galeotti is correct that these informal links form 'one more instrument in its [Russia's] campaign to dominate post-Soviet Eurasia through a mix of coercion and assistance' (Galeotti 2016: 13). They have taken advantage of these links to pursue their own agendas and silence dissidents living abroad.

Regional organisations have codified these linkages. Libman and Vinokurov describe Eurasian regionalism as a very specific form of 'holding-together' regionalism (Libman and Vinokurov 2012). After the collapse of the Soviet Union, Russia sought to retain hegemony over the Near Abroad by establishing a series of regional organisations which it dominated. These included the Commonwealth of Independent States (Armenia, Azerbaijan, Belarus, Kazakhstan, Kyrgyzstan, Moldova, Russia, Tajikistan, Uzbekistan) and Collective Security Treaty Organisation (Armenia, Belarus, Kazakhstan, Kyrgyzstan, Russia, Tajikistan). With the establishment of the Shanghai Cooperation Organisation in 2001, China became more closely involved in Eurasian security governance. Both of these organisations have adopted regulations to enable and normalise transnational repression.

Co-operating through International Organisations

Commonwealth of Independent States: 'Virtual Regionalism?'

Established in April 1992 at a meeting in Almaty, Kazakhstan, the Commonwealth of Independent States (CIS) brought together the states of the former Soviet Union (with the exception of the Baltic states, which consider Soviet rule to have been occupation). The CIS was designed to manage the Soviet break-up and preserve many of the pre-existing economic, political and military ties among the Soviet republics. But it has experienced limited success in creating regional ties. Disillusioned with the organisation and driven by domestic politics, the number of member states has dwindled. Turkmenistan, which never ratified the founding charter, became an associate member in 2005. Georgia withdrew from the organisation altogether following war with Russia in August 2008; Ukraine followed suit in 2018. This leaves Russia, Kazakhstan, Kyrgyzstan, Tajikistan, Turkmenistan, Armenia, Azerbaijan, Belarus and Moldova as current members of the CIS.

The CIS formally brings together representatives from Eurasia on a regular basis, including at least one annual meeting of heads of state. Security co-operation has formed a central role in the organisation since its inception, when member states agreed to share intelligence and co-operate in the conduct of investigations and operations. The 1999 CIS Agreement on Cooperation in the Fight against Terrorism envisages intelligence sharing, streamlined extraditions, extraterritorial policing, legal harmonisation and joint training sessions. But in doing so it is at odds with international human rights standards by guaranteeing diplomatic immunity for members of the law enforcement agencies and defining terrorists broadly as 'individuals who represent a threat to the security of the State', potentially including members of the opposition or representatives of civil society (Russo 2017: 216). Under the auspices of the CIS Council of Directors of Security Agencies and Special Services, representatives from the security services of each state meet every year. In June 2000, CIS member states agreed to set up an Anti-Terrorism Centre (ATC) in Moscow to co-ordinate intelligence activities. Since 2002 the ATC has operated a local office in Bishkek, Kyrgyzstan to co-ordinate activities in Central Asia. Although the organisation has organised a series of conferences and published papers, its role in countering terrorism in Eurasia has remained limited. In a potential move to revitalise the organisation, it held its first joint counter-terrorism exercises in May 2017. But since then, little progress has been made to enhance joint counterterrorism operations.

Analysts have been quick to dismiss the CIS as ineffective, arguing that suspicion towards Russia by many member states has hampered co-operation (Sakwa and Webber 1999; Kubicek 2009, 1999). Although some member states, particularly Tajikistan and Kyrgyzstan, remain dependent on Russia, most members are suspicious towards the Kremlin's motives and resist its attempts to reassert control in its Near Abroad. What has emerged in Eurasia, Roy Allison argues, is 'virtual regionalism', offering leaders in the region symbolic political legitimacy (Allison 2008). Rather than harbouring a genuine desire to co-operate for the greater good, the primary motivation for smaller states in Eurasia (Central Asia, Armenia, Belarus) to engage in regionalist projects has been what he terms 'protective integration', or 'the reinforcement of domestic regime security and the resistance of "external" agendas of good governance or democracy promotion' (Allison 2008: 185).

While the CIS itself has not been particularly effective as a 'redistribution mechanism' in providing material and symbolic benefits to members, one of the more effective areas of co-operation between CIS member states has been in the sphere of transnational repression (Libman and Obydenkova 2019). Within the CIS, extradition is governed by the 1993 Convention on Legal Assistance and Legal Relations in Civil, Family and Criminal Matters, also known as the Minsk Convention. Although the convention guarantees the rights of those detained under national law and lists four technical reasons why a person cannot be extradited, the document makes no mention of the principle of non-refoulement, the norm of not sending refugees back to a country where they are liable to be mistreated as enshrined in Article 33 of the 1951 Refugee Convention. Article 58 (1b) of the convention states that an extradition demand must contain a 'description of the actual circumstances of the action and the text of the law of the requesting contracting party, after which the action is considered a crime'. The Minsk Convention codified the fraternal culture of the CIS, which demanded that extradition be handled in an informal manner, subject to relatively few constraints (Ginsburgs 1993: 331). Accusations are taken at face value and diplomatic assurances from the requesting state that torture will not be used against those who return are often unquestioningly accepted. In short, the document places the principle of co-operation in criminal investigation over human rights obligations.

Transnational repression via the CIS has manifested itself most prominently through the transfer of terrorist and extremist suspects between member states. The CIS Anti-Terrorism Centre (ATC) holds a centralised database of wanted terrorists. According to Police Col. Gen. Andrey Novikov, head of the CIS Anti-Terrorism Centre, by December 2019 there were 10,000 terrorists on the list (TASS 2019). Yet, inclusion on the list can be arbitrary. According to a family member of Muhiddin Kabiri, the leader of the opposition Islamic Renaissance Party in Tajikistan, the blacklist still includes Kabiri's mother, who died in 2012, as well as his niece and his father, who died in 2016. The last two ended up on the list simply because they were present at the family's residence in the town of Faizobod when officers from Tajikistan's security services visited in July 2015. Between 2015 and 2019, according to the CIS, five hundred individuals on the list were apprehended (TASS 2019). These efforts coincide with legal harmonisation processes that aim to standardise understandings of terrorism and extremism in the region. To date, the CIS has published over six hundred model laws on issues ranging from trade to tourism and extremism. Using document comparison software, Antonov and Lemon compared laws on terrorism and extremism across CIS member states, finding that, when compared with the CIS model law, Russia's law on terrorism was 42 per cent the same as those proposed by the CIS; Kyrgyzstan's proportion of overlap was 38 per cent, and Tajikistan's 29 per cent (Antonov and Lemon 2020).

While it is impossible to measure the precise number of times extraditions have been facilitated by the Minsk Convention due to the CIS and member states not publishing statistics, there are numerous cases where we can document its use. For example, in February 2006, eleven Uzbek asylum seekers were forcibly returned from Ukraine to Uzbekistan. In 2007 Kazakhstan extradited twenty-eight Uzbek asylum seekers, the largest such incident up to that time among former Soviet republics (Human Rights Watch 2011). In 2010 Kazakhstan extradited twenty-nine asylum seekers fleeing persecution in Uzbekistan for 'involvement in illegal organisations' and 'attempting to overthrow the constitutional order' (Human Rights Watch 2010). The judge justified the ruling using the 1993 CIS Minsk Convention and 2001 Shanghai Convention (discussed below). While counterterrorism is one of the many areas of focus for the CIS, for the Shanghai Cooperation Organisation, which I turn to now, it is the central focus.

SCO: A League of Authoritarian Gentlemen

Originating from efforts to demarcate national borders after the collapse of the Soviet Union, the Shanghai Cooperation Organisation (SCO) was established by member states in 2001. The organisation initially brought together China, Russia, Tajikistan, Uzbekistan, Kyrgyzstan and Kazakhstan, with Pakistan and India joining in 2017. Although the organisation has established mechanisms to foster economic and cultural co-operation, its primary mandate is to fight the 'three evils' of terrorism, extremism and separatism (Aris 2011). Operating on the assumption that 'security problems in Central Asia are generally more transnational than interstate', the SCO's approach to security acknowledges that collaborative approaches are needed to govern borderless security threats (Allison 2004: 482).

As political scientist Thomas Ambrosio argues, 'the SCO is not meant to be just another intergovernmental "talking shop", but rather the embodiment of a new set of values and norms governing the future development of Central Asia' (Ambrosio 2010: 1322; see also Seiwert 2021). None of the member states of the SCO meet the basic conditions for being a liberal democracy. In its charter, the organisation makes no reference to 'democracy' as a political goal at the domestic level or 'human rights' as something in need of protecting. As Stephen Aris argues, protecting the regimes of the group's member states lies at the heart of the SCO's 'state-centric regional security governance' (Aris 2011).

The SCO's core focus is counterterrorism. The organisation's 2005 Concept of Cooperation requires members to mutually recognise terrorist, extremist and separatist acts, regardless of whether their own legislation would classify them as such. Put simply, the law of one member becomes the law of all members. With many member states offering amorphous definitions of these acts and Article 2 of the 2009 SCO Convention on Counter-Terrorism defining extremism as 'any deed aimed at a violent seizure of power or violent holding of power, and at violent change of the constitutional order of the state', space is opened for member states to take advantage of the system to pursue political opponents (Cooley 2012: 98–108). These definitions exhibit a clear preoccupation with safeguarding the security of the government, rather than the population. Mutual recognition prevents those formally accused or suspected of participating in one of these events to seek asylum in another member state. Under Article 23 of the aforementioned Convention, SCO member states 'shall take the necessary measures to prevent the granting of refugee status and corresponding documents to persons complicit in offenses'. Accordingly, a state's jurisdiction is not confined to its own territory, facilities or citizens. Rather, the Convention permits member states to claim jurisdiction whenever the alleged offence is 'aimed at or resulted in the commission of a terrorist act for the purpose of compelling that Party to do or abstain from doing any act' (Article 5, par 2.3). In other words, states can pursue their citizens within the entire SCO region.

The SCO works through two administrative bodies: the Secretariat based in Beijing, and the Regional Anti-Terrorism Structure (RATS), established in Bishkek in 2002 and moved to Tashkent in 2004. RATS organises joint military exercises and facilitates co-operation between security services and law enforcement officers in member states by assisting international searches for individuals. It therefore performs a similar function to the CIS Anti-terrorism Centre, although it has been more active than its counterpart. Like Interpol, RATS cannot enforce laws or issue arrest warrants itself. Instead, it co-ordinates activities among the internal security services of its member states. To help share information, RATS keeps a consolidated list of extremist, terrorist and separatist individuals and groups. In 2010 the list had forty-two organisations and 1,100 individuals (OHCHR 2011). By September 2016, the list had reportedly grown to include 2,500 individuals and 769 groups, including political opposition parties (e.g. the Islamic Renaissance Party of Tajikistan and the Democratic Choice of Kazakhstan) and religious groups (e.g. Tablighi Jamaat, Salafis and Jehovah's Witnesses). Members can transmit arrest requests for individuals on the wanted list. A request includes the name of the individual, the requesting state, alleged crimes and the action required. The request must be signed by the head or deputy head of the relevant authority, such as the local prosecutor or intelligence services. In urgent cases, requests can be transmitted orally. SCO agreements do not set forth any required procedural safeguards for the conduct of extradition co-operation. The receiving state has no means of verifying the quality of the evidence used by the requesting state to pursue a suspect. These legal provisions and norms run counter to each state's obligation under international human rights and refugee law (FIDH 2012; HRIC 2011).

The scale of the use of SCO agreements remains unclear. A report by Human Rights in China documents 307 cases of extradition between SCO member states between 2001 and 2011 (Human Rights in China 2011). Between 2011 and 2015, RATS announced that it facilitated the extradition of 213 individuals between member states (UN 2017). Extraditions among member states surged to 150 in 2017 alone (UN 2018). Combining these data points gives us an estimate of 770 individuals extradited through the SCO by 2017. It remains unclear how many of these individuals were actually members of terrorist organisations and how many are activists pursued in the name of counterterrorism and extremism.

The main initial vectors of transnational repression appear to be between Russia and China and from Russia to Uzbekistan (Cooley 2012). For example, FSB director Nikolai Patrushev reported at a RATS meeting in March 2006 that Russia had handed over nineteen people suspected of membership in Hizb-ut-Tahrir to Uzbekistan (Borogan and Soldatov 2010: 429). In November 2006, Russian Minister of Internal Affairs, Rashid Nurgaliyev, announced the extradition of 'more than 370 emissaries of Hizb-ut-Tahrir' in that year alone (FIDH 2010: 17). In some cases, these individuals were linked to other groups and *rebranded* as Hizb-ut-Tahrir, which has been banned in Russia since 2003, to facilitate their deportation. For example, in 2005 thirteen citizens of Uzbekistan, known as the 'Ivanovo Uzbeks', were arrested in Russia. The Uzbek government accused them of membership of the Akromiya movement, a group created by the Uzbek security services to justify cracking down on civil society. Since the group was not banned in Russia, the Prosecutor General accused them all of membership of Hizb-ut-Tahrir. They were later released but denied asylum in Russia and forced to move to Europe.

Manipulating International Organisations: Weaponising Interpol

In addition to co-operating through regional organisations, autocratic governments have manipulated international organisations, most notably Interpol, to pursue opponents abroad. Founded in 1923 as the International Criminal Police Commission (ICPC), and renamed Interpol in 1956, the organisation brings together police forces from 194 countries. Interpol was not created by a treaty or founded by states. Rather than being an international organisation as defined by Article 57 of the UN Charter, Interpol is more of a 'policeman's club' with police forces rather than states constituting its membership (Bresler 1992; Calcara 2020). Article 3 of the Interpol Constitution states that member states are 'strictly prohibited' from using the system to pursue criminals facing charges of a 'political, racial, religious or military character' (Interpol 1956). The vaguely worded Article 2 of its Constitution states it is committed to working 'in the spirit of the "Universal Declaration of Human Rights"'.

As a platform for the exchange of information between 194 police forces worldwide, Interpol is best understood as a 'sophisticated electronic bulletin board' where police forces can post wanted notices and share information (Bromund 2020). As mentioned by Hobbins and Grossman in this volume, Interpol does not issue arrest warrants itself or employ its own agents to conduct arrests, but distributes arrest requests, or Red Notices, issued by member states among law enforcement bodies worldwide. A Red Notice is an electronic alert published by Interpol at the request of a member state. To be clear, it is *not* an international arrest warrant, as is commonly believed. Its function is to 'seek the location of a wanted person and his/her detention, arrest or restriction of movement for the purpose of extradition, surrender or similar lawful action' (Interpol 2020). States have also used a second type of notice to pursue opponents abroad: diffusions. Like Red Notices, diffusions are often described as 'all-points bulletins' that seek to locate and arrest a wanted individual. But unlike the more formal review process that Red Notices go through, diffusions are sent directly to member states through Interpol's web-based information-sharing system without undergoing any oversight.

To date, only a handful of academic articles have examined how Interpol has become a tool of transnational repression (e.g. Stalcup 2013; Lemon 2019; Cooley 2015). As these works point out, a number of issues make Interpol susceptible to manipulation by authoritarian regimes. Interpol operates on the basis of mutual trust between members and the erroneous assumption that each member upholds the rule of law without politicising their justice system. Like other organisations, Interpol abides by the principle of sovereign equality, the idea that every sovereign state possesses the same legal rights as any other sovereign state, placing limitations on its ability to determine whether accusations are political. Instead, the organisation operates under the assumption that all Red Notices and diffusions are legitimate. Although checks exist, the process is largely based on faith in the good intentions of the requesting country. On its website, the organisation notes that those against whom Red Notices are issued 'are suspected of committing a crime but have not yet been prosecuted and so should be considered innocent until proven guilty'. But it remains unclear how it puts these words into action.

The task of checking the validity of warrants is becoming even more challenging as the organisation continues to accept an increasing number of notices. To increase efficiency, police agencies since 2002 have been able to enter the Red Notice request directly into Interpol's system through the I-24/7 platform.[1] Before Interpol launched this web-based communication system, it took an average of four to six months for a physical copy of a Red Notice to be delivered to member states (Stalcup 2013). Now distribution is almost instantaneous. This move has created a dramatic increase in the number of entries in Interpol's database. In 1998 Interpol published only 737 Red Notices; by 2007 that figure was 3,131; in 2019 it published 13,377 Red Notices. At present, Interpol's database contains over 217,000 entries. Of these Red Notices in circulation, just 7,498 were accessible on Interpol's website at the time of writing in early 2022. Those Red Notices issued through, but not reviewed by, Interpol appear instantly and contain information about the accused while denoting 'request being processed'. Moreover, by the end of 2019 there were 100,811 diffusions in circulation, up from just 7,500 in 2002. While Interpol argued that these moves have boosted efficiency and enhanced the capacity of police forces to respond to urgent cases, the new system has made it easier for authoritarian regimes to quickly circulate incomplete and inaccurate information about their political opponents, including journalists and peaceful human rights activists.

Interpol lacks the capacity to deal with this surge. The organisation has seven hundred employees, and only forty at the body responsible for overseeing Red Notices and diffusions, the Commission for the Control of Interpol's Files (CCF). Its €1.144 million budget in 2020 is just 0.7 per cent of the total for the organisation. As a result, implementing the necessary checks remains problematic (Fair Trials 2013). Such an increase in the number of Red Notices is concerning, given that global criminal justice watchdog Fair Trials International estimates that approximately 30 per cent of the organisation's membership consider a Red Notice to be a valid request for provisional arrest, regardless of which country issues the request (Tinsley 2014: 33).

In addition, Interpol has not established a sufficient appeal system through which those targeted can refute the charges against them. The CCF remains opaque, overburdened and slow to process requests. Given that not all Red Notices are published on the organisation's website, many who are subject to them only realise they are on the list once they are detained. Those wishing to challenge their Red Notice on the basis that it violates Interpol's Constitution

---

[1] More information can be found here: https://www.interpol.int/en/How-we-work/Databases

must apply to the CCF. Disclosure of information by the CCF is not automatic, however. Interpol itself does not own the information it stores on its database. For it to disclose information about the subject of a Red Notice, the issuing country needs to agree, and authoritarian governments almost never respond to these requests. Interpol's system therefore violates the principle of due process because the organisation cannot notify individuals of a notice against them without the issuing country's permission.

Complaints of abuse are correspondingly rising. In 2018 the CCF received 1,594 requests for access to, correction or deletion of entries. This is an eightfold increase from 2010, when it received 201 requests. Decisions can take up to nine months, during which time the diffusion or Red Notice remains active. Challengers bear the burden of proof and cannot take Interpol to court, as it is legally immune. The CCF still groundlessly refuses to release information about the countries that are receiving the most complaints. Based on Interpol figures from 2016, Theodore Bromund from the Heritage Foundation concluded that the deletion rate of Red Notices was 1.3 per cent (Bromund 2018). Estimating the scale of the abuse is therefore difficult. The Freedom House (Schenkkan and Linzer 2021) report 'Out of Sight, Not Out of Reach' on transnational repression found at least twelve countries abused Interpol to pursue political opponents between 2014 and 2020, including all five Central Asian republics and Russia.

Part of the problem certainly lies within the strategic culture of Interpol itself (Stalcup 2013). Interference by human rights groups and diplomats was viewed as a barrier to efficient work by Interpol employees (Bresler 1992: 366–8). While Interpol seems to recognise the need for reform, this is not its main priority. Its Strategic Framework 2017–20 lists five objectives related to enhancing and streamlining co-operation to prevent crime, but makes no mention of upholding human rights.

Funding has also become a tool for influence over the organisation. While most members are required to make statutory contributions, some have made further donations in order to further their influence. The United Arab Emirates, for example, has donated $54 million through a charity called the Interpol Foundation for a Safer World, equalling the statutory contributions of all of the other 193 members combined. In a sign of its growing influence, the UAE hosted the 2018 General Assembly and was slated to host the 2020 version before the Covid-19 pandemic. At the 2021 General Assembly, former general inspector of the Ministry of Interior of the UAE, Ahmed Naser Al-Raisi, became President of Interpol. Talk of the UAE 'taking over' Interpol is exaggerated; the president has a limited role in the day-to-day operations of the organisation. That said, authoritarian regime-based governance of the organisation remains a concern.

Criticism of Interpol has grown in recent years. Since Fair Trials International and other organisations started working to highlight the misuse of Interpol in 2012, the organisation has taken steps towards reform (Fair Trials 2018). It announced in June 2014 that it would not publish Red Notices for those who had refugee status and that it would remove existing entries for refugees, introducing a formal policy on this in 2017. At the same time, it announced that it would be subjecting Red Notices to increased scrutiny, only publishing them after they had been formally reviewed. A new structure and set of operating rules, approved by the General Assembly in 2016, went into effect in March 2017. It restructured the CCF into two chambers. The Supervisory and Advisory Chamber ensures that Interpol complies with its rules on data security. The Requests Chamber deals with applications for information and deletions by those subject to Red Notices.

As discussed by Hobbins and Grossman in this volume, member states have also taken steps to insulate themselves against Interpol abuse within their jurisdiction. A bill called the Transnational Repression Accountability and Prevention Act was passed by congress in December 2021.[2] The TRAP Act commits the US to taking steps to 'improv[e] the transparency of INTERPOL and ensur[e] its operation consistent with its Constitution' by seeking to 'impose penalties on countries for regular or egregious violations of INTERPOL's Constitution'. Section 6(a) reaffirms the Department of Justice's position that US law does not allow the US government to arrest an individual based solely on a Red Notice unless an extradition treaty is in place, or unless the other state sends a diplomatic request and the US issues its own arrest warrant.

But despite this progress, problems remain. Interpol remains opaque, secretive and lacks accountability. The new refugee policy is being unevenly enforced. There have been some successful applications under the new rules.

---

[2] For more detail on how autocratic regimes manipulate the US immigration system to persecute dissidents, see the chapter by Grossman and Hobbins in this volume.

President of the World Uyghur Congress Dolkun Issa had his Chinese-issued Red Notice deleted in early 2018 (Reuters 2018). Muhiddin Kabiri, the leader of the Islamic Renaissance Party, successfully had his Red Notice removed in early 2018, having been granted asylum in the EU (Pannier 2018). Yet the policy does not seem to be being consistently implemented. Turkish journalist Hamza Yalcin, for instance, was detained in Spain in August 2017 on a Red Notice, despite having been granted asylum in Sweden.

There are mechanisms in place to punish states found to be violating Interpol's rules. According to Articles 17(5), 131(1) and 131(3) of Interpol's Rules on the Processing of Data, the organisation can ban a state from using its information system if it violates the rules by, for example, being found to be using Interpol to pursue political opponents. Interpol has blocked members in the past, with Syria losing access from 2012 to 2021 and Afghanistan losing access after the Taliban takeover in August 2021. However, Syria has since been readmitted to the organisation, despite President Bashar al-Assad's egregious human rights record. This mechanism could be invoked against serial abusers of Interpol, like Turkey and Russia; thus far, however, abusers have not been sanctioned for using Interpol as a weapon of transnational repression.

The Symbolic and Punitive Effects of Interpol Abuse

Manipulating the Interpol system serves both a punitive and a symbolic function. Interpol very clearly states that individuals are not wanted by Interpol and that the organisation does not issue arrest warrants. Yet the mere transmission of data through Interpol gives accusations credibility in other jurisdictions and among the broader public (Lewis 2015). Inclusion on an Interpol list in and of itself lends legitimacy to the notion that opposition activists are in fact criminals and terrorists. In Tajikistan, having opposition leader Muhiddin Kabiri included on Interpol's wanted list in 2016 was widely mentioned in state media. As with other 'authoritative' regional organisations like the SCO and CIS, state media frequently mention political opponents being on Interpol's wanted lists as proof that the groups are 'international criminal and terrorist organisations' that threaten stability not only in Tajikistan, but in the countries where they reside (Jumhuriyat 2017).

If stopped at the border, those subject to Red Notices have been detained without trial, and without any evidence being brought against them, for up to nine months. As noted by Hobbins and Grossman in this volume, once released problems have not ended for those subject to a Red Notice. It restricts the ability of those accused to open a bank account, find employment and to travel. Being an internationally wanted criminal also has a detrimental impact on the reputation of those targeted. One Turkish journalist argued that the use of a Red Notice damaged his reputation:

> The Turkish media widely reported my Red Notice, labelling me a terrorist. It does not only discredit me, it discredits the news agency I work with. How can we persuade doubters to trust us if we are labelled terrorists?[3]

Many refugees remain on Interpol wanted lists long after they have been granted refugee or asylum status. Although Interpol is reforming gradually, it often takes years to achieve the removal of their names from the Interpol wanted list. Hikmatullo, an associate of Tajik opposition movement Group 24 now living in Germany, is unsure about his situation:

> I think I am on the Interpol list. I went to open a bank account when I arrived in Poland, but was told that I did not pass the security clearance. My lawyer has written to Interpol requesting information about whether I am in their database. It has been three months and I have not heard. I was recently granted asylum. But I do not want to travel beyond Europe without knowing my status.[4]

Interpol's lack of transparency creates an uncertain situation for many political exiles, who remain in the dark as to their status. Fear of being on the Interpol list causes many to restrict their own freedoms and act with caution even after they are granted asylum.

Conclusion

The practice of the extraterritorial targeting of dissidents and opposition groups is not a new phenomenon. In the twentieth century, many non-democratic countries used strategies of infiltration, secret policing and assassinations to control opposition movements and individuals in exile (Shain 2005). Yet there

---

[3] Interview with Turkish journalist, Washington, DC, November 2018.
[4] Interview with Group 24 activist, Warsaw, June 2017.

is evidence that the scale has increased in recent years as mobility has increased and new technologies have facilitated digital activism across borders (Schenkkan and Linzer 2021). As this chapter has argued, the proliferation of bilateral and multilateral mechanisms of co-operation to target opponents abroad, such as regional organisations like the Shanghai Cooperation Organisation and Interpol, has also played a key role in the spread of transnational repression. Combined, these developments have increased regimes' perception of the threat that exiles pose and provided greater opportunities for governments to target their subjects abroad.

While authoritarian regimes in Eurasia have had mixed success in using the three organisations profiled here to render wanted persons back to their home country, international organisations nonetheless comprised an important mechanism of transnational repression. These practices form part of a broader strategy of 'protective integration' that help to bolster regime security, stability and legitimacy (Allison 2018) in several ways. First, international organisations offer members the means to harass and intimidate exiles, signalling to them and a broader audience the high costs of dissent. Second, they offer important symbolic benefits, conferring legitimacy on campaigns against domestic opponents by signalling that there is an international consensus that they are illegitimate actors. Third, they embolden authoritarian regimes by creating a normative space that prioritises domestic stability over human rights, giving authoritarian regimes greater leeway to operate transnationally.

Together, these developments point towards a continuing intensification of transnational repression in the coming years. As the world becomes more multipolar with the rise of new powers and the relative decline of the United States, we can expect China and Russia to continue to develop parallel institutions and support norms that bolster authoritarianism (Cooley and Nexon 2020). While Russia's standing in the region is being undermined by its invasion of Ukraine, there is reason to believe that the authoritarian regimes of the region will continue to collaborate with Russia and Russian-led organisations to deploy transnational repression. Neighbouring countries may make efforts to decouple their economies from Russia and develop alternative trade routes to bypass its territory. But their concern over regime stability will lead them to continue to work with Russia in the security sector and utilise the SCO and CIS to practise transnational repression in the name of countering extremism and terrorism. We can also expect authoritarian states to continue to abuse Interpol, given the organisation's relatively weak capacity to enact reforms, increase transparency and use its own rules to punish abusers.

But there are still crucial knowledge gaps that require future research. Despite various new datasets on transnational repression (CAPE 2019; Lemon, Jardine and Hall 2021; Schenkkan and Linzer 2021), we still do not have estimates as to the scale of transnational repression through international organisations, including the number of reported cases of detentions and renditions based on use of their databases. Such mapping would help us further understand geographical patterns and common practices. Future studies could adopt ethnographic methods to embed themselves within organisations like Interpol, as Meg Stalcup has done before (Stalcup 2013). Such research could uncover the culture of the organisation, and help explain both why it has become susceptible to manipulation and why it is so resistant to change. In sum, there is fertile ground for further research on the mechanisms of transnational repression, including the use of regional and international organisations.

References

Acharya, A. 2020. 'The myth of the "Civilization State": Rising powers and the cultural challenge to world order'. *Ethics & International Affairs* 34(2): 139–56.

Adamson, F. B. and Tsourapas, G. 2020. 'The migration state in the Global South: Nationalizing, developmental, and neoliberal models of migration management'. *International Migration Review* 54(3): 853–82.

Alcara, G. 2020. 'A transnational police network co-operating up to the limits of the law: Examination of the origin of INTERPOL'. *Transnational Legal Theory* 11(4): 521–48.

Alimov, R. 2017. 'The role of the Shanghai Cooperation Organization in counteracting threats to peace and security'. *Prevention* 3(15).

Allison, R. 2004. 'Regionalism, regional structures and security management in Central Asia'. *International Affairs* 80(3): 463–83.

——. 2008. 'Virtual regionalism, regional structures and regime security in Central Asia'. *Central Asian Survey* 27(2): 185–202.

Ambrosio, T. 2010. 'Constructing a framework of authoritarian diffusion: Concepts, dynamics, and future research'. *International Studies Perspectives* 11(4): 375–92.

Aris, S. 2011. *Eurasian Regionalism: The Shanghai Cooperation Organisation*. London: Palgrave.

Blaydes, L. 2010. *Elections and Distributive Politics in Mubarak's Egypt*. New York: Cambridge University Press.

Borogan, I. and Soldatov, A. 2010. *The New Nobility: The Restoration of Russia's Security State*. London: PublicAffairs.

Bresler, F. 1993. *Interpol: A History and Examination of 70 Years of Crime Solving*. London: Mandarin.

Bromund, T. 2020. 'The US must promote democratic leadership in Interpol'. *Heritage Foundation*, 10 November. Accesssed at: https://www.heritage.org/global-politics/report/the-us-must-promote-democratic-leadership-interpol

Brownlee, J. 2007. *Authoritarianism in an Age of Democratization*. Cambridge: Cambridge University Press.

Burnell, P. 2010. 'Is there a new autocracy promotion?' *Working Paper 96*.

CAPE. 2019. The Central Asia Political Exiles Codebook. https://excas.net/wp-content/uploads/2020/09/CAPE_Codebook.pdf

Cooley, A. 2012. *Great Games, Local Rules: The New Great Power Contest in Central Asia*. Oxford: Oxford University Press.

——. 2015. 'Authoritarianism goes global: Countering democratic norms'. *Journal of Democracy* 26(3): 49–63.

Cooley, A. and Heathershaw, J. 2017. *Dictators Without Borders: Power and Money in Central Asia*. London: Yale University Press.

Cooley, A. and Schaaf, M. 2017. 'Grounding the backlash: Regional security treaties, counternorms, and human rights in Eurasia'. In Hopgood, S., Snyder, J. and Vinjamuri, L. (eds), *Human Rights Futures*. Cambridge: Cambridge University Press, pp. 159–88.

Cox, G. 2009. 'Authoritarian elections and leadership succession, 1975–2004'. *APSA 2009 Toronto Meeting Paper*.

Debre, M. 2022. 'Clubs of autocrats: Regional organizations and authoritarian survival'. *Review of International Organizations* 17: 485–511.

Del Sordi, A. 2018. 'Sponsoring student mobility for development and authoritarian stability: Kazakhstan's Bolashak Programme'. *Globalizations* 15(2): 215–31.

Fair Trials. 2018. 'Strengthening INTERPOL: An update'. Accessed at: https://www.fairtrials.org/articles/publications/strengthening-interpol-an-update/

FIDH. 2010. 'Russian society under control'. Accessed at: https://www.fidh.org/IMG/pdf/Russian_society_under_control.pdf

——. 2012. 'Shanghai Cooperation Organisation: A vehicle for human rights violations'. Accessed at: https://www.fidh.org/IMG/pdf/sco_report.pdf

Furstenberg, S., Lemon, E. and Heathershaw, J. 2021. 'Spatialising state practices through transnational repression'. *European Journal of International Security* 6(3): 358–78.

Galeotti, M. 2016. '"RepressIntern": Russian security cooperation with fellow authoritarians'. 21 November. Accessed at: https://fpc.org.uk/repressintern-russian-security-cooperation-fellow-authoritarians/

Gandhi, J. and Przeworski, A. 2007. 'Authoritarian institutions and the survival of autocrats'. *Comparative Political Studies* 40(11): 1279–1301.

Ginsburgs, G. 1999. 'Extradition of fugitive criminals under the CIS Convention on Legal Assistance in Russia's law and practice'. *Criminal Law Forum* 10: 317–57.

Hess, S. 2010. 'Protests, parties, and presidential succession'. *Problems of Post-Communism* 57(1): 28–39.

Heydemann, S. and Leenders, R. 2011. 'Authoritarian learning and authoritarian resilience: Regime responses to the "Arab Awakening"'. *Globalizations* 8(5): 647–53.

Horsman, S. 2005. 'Themes in official discourses on terrorism in Central Asia'. *Third World Quarterly* 26 (1): 199–213.

HRIC. 2011. 'Counter-terrorism and human rights: The impact of the Shanghai Cooperation Organization'. Accessed at: https://www.hrichina.org/sites/default/files/publication_pdfs/2011-hric-sco-whitepaper-full.pdf

Hug, A. 2016. *Sharing Worst Practice: How Countries and Institutions in the Former Soviet Union Help Create Legal Tools of Repression*. London: Foreign Policy Centre.

Human Rights Watch. 2010. 'Kazakhstan: Letter to the Prosecutor General regarding 29 asylum seekers'. 2 December. Accessed at: https://www.hrw.org/news/2010/12/02/kazakhstan-letter-prosecutor-general-regarding-29-asylum-seekers

——. 2011. 'Kazakhstan: Forced returns to Uzbekistan illegal'. 10 June. Accessed at: https://www.hrw.org/news/2011/06/10/kazakhstan-forced-returns-uzbekistan-illegal

Interpol. 1956. 'Constitution of the ICPO-INTERPOL'.

——. 2022. 'Toolkit: INTERPOL Red Notices and diffusions'. Accessed at: https://www.fairtrials.org/articles/information-and-toolkits/interpol-red-notices-and-diffusions/

Jardine, B., Hall, N. and Lemon, E. 2021. 'No space left to run: China's transnational repression of Uyghurs'. *Uyghur Human Rights Project*.

Jumhuriyat. 2017. 'HNIT va Davlati Islomi. Isboti Amali Yak Budani Ta'limot, Fa'liyat va Maksadi Du Tashkiloti Ekstremisti' [IRPT and Islamic State: Their purpose, activities and education are both extremist]. 9 November. Accessed at: http://jumhuriyat.tj/index.php?art_id=31449

Kneuer, M. and Demmelhuber, T. 2016. 'Gravity centres of authoritarian rule: A conceptual approach'. *Democratization* 5: 775–96.

Kneuer, M., Demmelhuber, T., Peresson, R. and Zumbrägel, T. 2019. 'Playing the regional card: Why and how authoritarian gravity centres exploit regional organisations'. *Third World Quarterly* 40(3): 451–70.

Kubicek, P. 1999. 'The end of the line of the Commonwealth of Independent States'. *Problems of Post-Communism* 46(2): 15–24.

——. 2009. 'The Commonwealth of Independent States: An example of failed regionalism?' *Review of International Studies* 35: 237–56.

Lefebvre, S. and McDermott, R. 2008. 'Russia and the intelligence services of Central Asia'. *International Journal of Intelligence and Counter-Intelligence* 21(2): 251–301.

Lemon, E. 2018. 'From Moscow to Madrid: Governing security threats beyond Tajikistan's Borders'. In Laruelle, M. (ed.), *Tajikistan on the Move.* Lanham, MD: Lexington Books.

——. 2019. 'Weaponizing Interpol'. *Journal of Democracy* 30(2): 15–29.

Lemon, E. and Antonov, O. 2020. 'Authoritarian legal harmonization in the post-Soviet space'. *Democratization* 27(7): 1221–39.

Lewis, D. 2015. '"Illiberal spaces": Uzbekistan's extraterritorial security practices and the spatial politics of contemporary authoritarianism'. *Nationalities Papers* 43: 140–59.

——. 2016. 'The "Moscow Consensus": Constructing autocracy in post-Soviet Eurasia'. Foreign Policy Centre, 24 May. Accessed at: https://fpc.org.uk/moscow-consensus-constructing-autocracy-post-soviet-eurasia/

Libman, A. 2007. 'Regionalisation and regionalism in the post-Soviet space: Current status and implications for institutional development'. *Europe-Asia Studies* 59(3): 401–30.

Libman, A. and Vinokurov, E. 2012. A. *Holding-Together Regionalism: Twenty Years of Post-Soviet Integration*. London: Palgrave.

Magaloni, B. 2006. *Voting for Autocracy: Hegemonic Party Survival and Its Demise in Mexico*. Cambridge: Cambridge University Press.

Michaelsen, M. 2018. 'Exit and voice in a digital age: Iran's exiled activists and the authoritarian state'. *Globalizations* 15(2): 248–64.

Morgenbesser, L. 2020. 'The menu of autocratic innovation'. *Democratization* 27(6): 1053–72.

Moss, D. 2016. 'Transnational repression, diaspora mobilization, and the case of the Arab Spring'. *Social Problems* 63(4): 480–9.

——. 2022. *The Arab Spring Abroad: Diaspora Activism Against Authoritarian Regimes*. Cambridge: Cambridge University Press.

Nodia, G. 2014. 'The revenge of geopolitics'. *Journal of Democracy* 25(4): 139–50.

Obydenkova, A. and Libman, A. 2019. *Authoritarian Regionalism in the World of International Organizations: Global Perspective and the Eurasian Enigma*. Cambridge: Cambridge University Press.

Öztürk, A. 2020. 'The repertoire of extraterritorial repression: Diasporas and home states'. *Migration Letters* 17(1).

Pannier, B. 2018. 'Rare triumph for Tajikistan's IRPT, as leader removed from Interpol's "Red Notice"'. *Radio Free Europe*, 3 March. Accessed at: www.rferl.org/a/tajikistan- islamic-renaissance-party-leader-kabiri-interpol/29076658.html.

Pepinsky, T. 2014. 'The institutional turn in comparative authoritarianism'. *British Journal of Political Science* 44(3): 631–53.

Reuters. 2018. 'China upset as Interpol removes wanted alert for exiled Uighur leader'. 24 February. Accessed at: https://www.reuters.com/article/us-china-xinjiang/china-upset-as-interpol-removes-wanted-alert-for-exiled-uighur-leader-idUSKCN1G80FK

Sakwa, R. and Webber, M. 1999. 'The Commonwealth of Independent States, 1991–1998: Stagnation and survival'. *Europe-Asia Studies* 51(3): 379–415.

Schedler, A. 2009. 'The new institutionalism in the study of authoritarian regimes'. *APSA 2009 Toronto Meeting Paper*.

Schenkkan, N. and Linzer, I. 2021. 'Out of sight, not out of reach'. *Freedom House*. Accessed at: https://freedomhouse.org/report/transnational-repression

Seiwert, E. 2021. 'The Shanghai Cooperation Organisation and China's strategy of shaping international norms'. PhD dissertation. Free University Berlin.

Shain, Y. 2005. *The Frontier of Loyalty: Political Exiles in the Age of the Nation-State*. Ann Arbor: University of Michigan Press.

Stalcup, M. 2013. 'Interpol and the emergence of global policing'. In Garriott, W. (ed.), *Policing and Contemporary Governance: The Anthropology of Police in Practice*. New York: Palgrave Macmillan.

Tansey, O. 2017. *The International Politics of Authoritarian Rule*. Oxford: Oxford University Press.

TASS. 2019. 'Some 10,000 individuals wanted for terrorism, extremism in CIS'. 3 December. Accessed at: https://tass.com/world/1094987

Tsourapas, G. 2020. 'Global autocracies: Strategies of transnational repression, legitimation, and co-optation'. *International Studies Review* 1–29.

Von Soest, C. 2015. 'Democracy prevention: The international collaboration of authoritarian regimes'. *European Journal of Political Research* 54(4): 623–38.

Yakouchyk, K. 2019. 'Beyond autocracy promotion: A review'. *Political Studies Review* 17(2): 147–60.

13

CONFRONTING TRANSNATIONAL REPRESSION USING INTERNATIONAL LAW

Don Picard and Dana M. Moss

When foreign governments repress journalists, activists, political opponents, ethnic and racial groups and diaspora communities residing
outside of their territory, they commit acts of transnational repression. The
United States' Federal Bureau of Investigation lists a range of forms that transnational repression may take, including 'Stalking, Harassment, Hacking,
Assaults, Attempted kidnapping, Forcing or coercing the victim to return to
the home country, Threatening or detaining family members in the home
country, Freezing financial assets, [and] Online disinformation campaigns'.[1]
Other methods of coercion, as illustrated by Hirt and Mohammad (this
volume), Adamson (this volume) and Moss (2016), include forced taxation, surveillance and the denial of passport renewal. These tactics are often
extremely effective in silencing regime critics, undermining political organising abroad and forcing diasporas to perform loyalty to home-country regimes.

These acts of transnational repression, illustrated across the various chapters of this volume, are almost always illegal under the national law of the residence state where they are committed. Moreover, when they are committed by
a *foreign* state, they may also become *internationally wrongful acts* subject to

---

[1] *See* the official website of the United States Government on the topic here: https://www.fbi.
gov/investigate/counterintelligence/transnational-repression#:~:text=When%20foreign%20
governments%20stalk%2C%20intimidate,get%20help%20to%20stop%20it

sanctions under international law. Such actions require redress, both to protect individuals' rights and the sovereignty of victims' states of residence. It is therefore important to understand how international law and international institutions provide states, victims and the international community with means to act against transnational repression.

As shown in this chapter, the practice of transnational repression is incompatible with provisions of the United Nations (UN) Charter and numerous widely ratified international human, civil and political rights treaties. It also seriously threatens existing norms of interstate relations. Because transnational repression violates the human rights of diaspora members, its practice may invoke residence states' *international legal obligations* to protect diaspora members – including migrants, international students, asylum seekers, refugees and permanent residents – living in their territories. (It must be noted that the strength of the residence state's international legal obligation varies somewhat depending upon the legal status of the resident pursuant to both national and international law applicable to the residence state.) Moreover, when a residence state allows transnational repression to be practised by authoritarian governments against its residents with impunity, that residence state undermines the rule of law in its own territory as well as weakening relevant international agreements to which the residence state is a party.

As the chapters in this volume by Böcü et al., Furstenberg et al. and Quinsaat demonstrate, some national policymakers and law enforcement organisations have responded in constructive ways to the threats posed by transnational repression. Such responses signal the beginning of a welcome shift in governmental responses to transnational repression. Yet, despite alarms from academics, the media, think tanks and diaspora members themselves, most residence states have been slow to recognise and respond to the extensive use of these practices against their residents – residents who, as we argue, they are obligated to protect.

This chapter argues that international law – including human rights law, state responsibility law, the law of diplomatic protection and the law of reparations – provides residence states with both the authority and incentive to protect their residents from authoritarian governments' uses of transnational repression. We show that a wide range of international governmental institutions are available to victims of human rights violations and their residence states. These institutions include regional human rights tribunals, administrative bodies established by international human rights treaties, the UN Human Rights Council and the UN High Commissioner for Human Rights, among others. In addition, a number of country-specific and international non-governmental organisations (NGOs) are active in supporting victims of human rights abuses, including transnational repression.[2]

This chapter critically examines existing legal instruments, both at the national and international levels, that may be used by host states to protect individuals subjected to transnational repression. In so doing, this chapter is designed to inform policy and practice at local, national and international levels to bolster diaspora protection. In addition to strengthened action by residence states at the national and local levels, we also propose that policy-makers and practitioners should recognise the role that other kinds of actors, including civil society advocates and diaspora members, can play in combating transnational repression.

The chapter is structured as follows: the first section examines international law, focusing on treaties currently in force, and international institutions that provide protection for individuals subject to acts of transnational repression. Section 2 focuses on the role of residence states and relevant elements of the law of state-to-state relations. The conclusion proposes ways that states, victims, international institutions and NGOs can strengthen their opposition to transnational repression, including some encouraging examples.

1. International Law Most Applicable to Transnational Repression

At the time of this writing, there is no single treaty or legal regime devoted exclusively to the control of transnational repression. Instead, elements of the applicable international law are found in a wide range of provisions within international human rights treaties, the UN Charter and the international law of state-to-state relations that allow, or even compel, national governments to act against acts of transnational repression. This law is interpreted and

---

[2] For example, see Crowd Justice (crowdjustice.com); Democracy for the Arab World Now (dawnmena.org); Fair Trials International (fairtrials.org); Global legal Action Network (glanlaw. org); Hivos People Unlimited (hivos.org); Privacy International (privacyinternational.org). This list is not comprehensive, nor is it an endorsement.

implemented by a variety of international institutions. These include regional human rights tribunals, the UN's International Court of Justice, the quasi-judicial treaty bodies established by human rights treaties and various UN Human Rights agencies.

A. International Human Rights Treaties and Implementing Institutions

Acts of transnational repression violate fundamental human rights, which are protected by a number of international and regional treaties. These rights include freedom of belief and conscience, freedom of expression (including via social media and peaceful demonstrations), freedom of association with like-minded people and protection from unjustified invasions of privacy and arbitrary arrest and detention.

In the past, the granting and protection of such rights were considered the exclusive prerogative of an individual's state of residence. Changes to such exclusivity accelerated after World War II. The UN Charter, which came into effect in October 1945, states among its aims: 'Promoting and encouraging respect for human, civil and political rights and for fundamental freedoms for all without distinction as to race, sex, language or religion' in Article 1, Paragraph 3. In December 1948, the UN General Assembly adopted Resolution 217A, The Universal Declaration of Human Rights.[3] Numerous (and more specific) multilateral treaties followed.

Beginning in December 1966 with the International Covenant on Civil and Political Rights (ICCPR) and the International Covenant on Economic, Social and Cultural Rights, nine separate human rights treaties (many with additional protocols) were adopted by large numbers of states. The most recent of these, adopted in 2006, is the International Convention for the Protection of all Persons from Enforced Disappearance (CED). A list of these 'core' human rights treaties and their dates of adoption is available at the United Nations High Commissioner for Human Rights website (https://www.ohchr.org/en/instruments-listings). Of particular note is the fact that the ICCPR made human, civil and political rights of the citizens of treaty parties a

---

[3] The United Nations High Commissioner for Human Rights provides an English translation of the full text here: https://www.ohchr.org/sites/default/files/UDHR/Documents/UDHR_Translations/eng.pdf

matter of responsibility for *all* state parties to this treaty, not only the government of a person's state of residence.[4] A total of 173 states are parties to the ICCPR, 116 states are party to the ICCPR's First Optional Protocol (known as the First Protocol) and 193 states are members of the UN, and thus parties to the UN Charter.

As early as 1948, many states in Europe and the Americas agreed among themselves to further protect the human rights of their citizens and residents. They did so by ratifying treaties binding their governments to provisions resembling some of the later UN agreements. States in the African region followed suit beginning in 1981. These additional regional human rights treaties expanded the scope of human rights protections beyond the state parties to the treaties described above. While these regional agreements differ from each other in various ways, all of them protect the fundamental rights of individuals to freely express their opinions and beliefs and to associate with others of like mind. They ban member-state governments from arbitrary punishments and discrimination based on the exercise of such actions and opinions. They also prohibit arbitrary arrest, confinement and torture, among other forms of cruel punishment. Individuals may file claims for violations of protected rights pursuant to the rules of each of these tribunals. As of 2018, there were some twenty international courts and even more quasi-judicial bodies providing standing for individual complaints and claims for relief (Shikhelman 2018).

But which human rights protect victims of transnational repression? It is important to be specific. We do this by examining the International Covenant on Civil and Political Rights, the most comprehensive of the UN-sponsored human rights treaties. Many of the same rights are also protected by similar provisions of regional human rights agreements and by other core UN human rights treaties. The ICCPR provisions that are particularly relevant to controlling acts of transnational repression are summarised and paraphrased here:

- All individuals within a party's territory and subject to its jurisdiction have all the rights recognised in the Covenant without distinction of any

[4] See, for example, Human Rights Committee, General Comment 31, on 'the Nature of the General Legal Obligations Imposed on States Parties to the Covenant': https://www.refworld.org/docid/478b26ae2.html

kind, such as race, colour, sex, language, religion, political or other opinion, national or social origin, property, birth or other status. Any person whose rights or freedoms are violated must have an effective remedy and may have his case determined by competent judicial, administrative or legislative authorities; competent authorities shall enforce such remedies.

- Every human being has the inherent right to life. No one shall be arbitrarily deprived of their life.
- No one shall be subjected to torture or to cruel, inhuman or degrading treatment or punishment.
- All persons are free from arbitrary arrest or detention; any victim of unlawful arrest or detention must have an enforceable right to compensation.
- Everyone has the right to leave any country, including his own; no one shall be arbitrarily exiled from his own country.
- An alien lawfully in the territory of a State Party may be expelled only by a lawful process, where he has been allowed to submit the reasons against expulsion, and is competently represented before the authorised decision maker.
- No one is subject to interference with his privacy, family, home or correspondence, nor to unlawful attacks on his honour and reputation.
- Freedom of thought, conscience and religion, including the right to manifest one's belief in worship, observance, practice and teaching, is required.
- The right to hold opinions without interference and the freedom to seek, receive and impart information and ideas of all kinds, regardless of frontiers, either orally, in writing, or in print, is required.
- The right of peaceful assembly and freedom of association with others is required. Protection against discrimination on any ground such as race, colour, sex, language, religion, political or other opinion, national or social origin, property, birth or other status is required.[5]

In addition to the ICCPR, there are eight other core human rights treaties. Some deal with the rights applicable to specific classes of people, for example

---

[5] The full text of the ICCPR, to which there are 173 state parties, may be found at the website of the UN High Commissioner for Human Rights: https://www.ohchr.org/EN/ProfessionalInterest/Pages/CCPR.aspx

the rights of women, children, the disabled and migrant workers. Others prohibit specific actions relevant to repressive practice of proxy punishment by prohibiting actions that regimes are known to take against dissidents' family members who reside in the home country, including arbitrary arrest, enforced disappearance and torture. Each of these eight treaties binds only the states that have ratified that treaty. We suggest that advocates for victims of transnational repression examine all these treaties, as well as the applicable regional treaties, when developing a strategy for confronting transnational repression in specific cases. Many states identified by the US State Department as practising transnational repression, for instance, are parties to several of these treaties, as well as the relevant regional treaties. For example, known practitioners of transnational repression, such as Russia, Turkey, Pakistan and Libya, are among parties to a number of human rights treaties, including the ICCPR. Russia and Turkey are also parties to the European Convention on Human Rights. Each of these treaties may provide useful leverage when pursuing legal cases against offending regimes and their agents accused of enacting transnational repression.

B. Treaty Bodies

An important means of implementing treaty-based rights protected by the nine core human rights treaties mentioned above is through the use of the standing administrative mechanisms of each treaty, which are known as 'treaty bodies'. Treaty bodies clarify and develop the meaning and application of each treaty's provisions and seek to resolve complaints by state parties and individual victims regarding violations. The extensive body of case decisions and general commentary produced by the treaty bodies may be used by victims and advocates to authoritatively interpret and apply treaty provisions to individual cases. Additionally, the treaty bodies monitor state parties' compliance with the treaties and produce reports of their periodic reviews. They also publish most of their decisions issued in response to claims of individuals asserting treaty violations. The treaty bodies who hear these claims use their own prior decisions and commentary, as well as the relevant decisions of other treaty bodies, as guides to their decision-making. They also refer to the jurisprudence of the International Court of Justice of the UN and regional human rights tribunals.

The most well-known and respected of the treaty bodies is the Human Rights Committee (HRC) of the ICCPR,[6] which acts in two distinct ways. It does so first by monitoring and seeking to improve state parties' compliance, and second, by acting on claims of individual victims seeking relief from a state's violations of treaty provisions. The HRC implements monitoring by requiring periodic reports from each state party based upon questions from the HRC.[7] During this process, national human rights institutions, interested civil society organisations and other state parties may participate in the proceedings. Such proceedings conclude with a report issued by the HRC to the state party that includes recommendations for improvement. The final written report on each state is made public. The HRC also provides training for state parties to assist in the preparation of their national reports. The second mechanism for HRC action is through resolving claims of individuals seeking relief from state parties' violations of the treaty. The HRC is empowered by the ICCPR's First Protocol to hear complaints by individuals of state parties' treaty violations. While not all parties to the ICCPR have ratified the First Protocol, 116 of the Covenant's 173 parties have done so, thus providing their residents with access to the HRC's 'individual procedures'.

Scholars and practitioners have understandably expressed scepticism as to whether the process of state party self-reporting could have an impact on state compliance. Although there is only limited empirical research on this topic, studies have shown that reporting states improve their rights practices when they engage in ongoing dialogue with the treaty bodies (Creamer and Simmons 2020). The quasi-public process also mobilises civil society organisations and legislative institutions within state parties to pressure state institutions into treaty compliance.

---

[6] Current information as to the HRC's current activities and cases may be found at the website of the Office of the UN High Commissioner for Human Rights: https://www.ohchr.org/en/treaty-bodies/ccpr

[7] An illustrative example is one such question issued to the US in connection with the ICCPR examination in 2019 during Donald Trump's presidency. Referring to ICCPR Article 19 on freedom of expression, the HRC asked the US: 'Please comment on reports of a pattern of threats and intimidation by some government authorities, including the President himself, against journalists and media outlets.' The full request is available at the UN Human Rights Committee, 'List of issues prior to submission of the fifth periodic report of the United States of America', 18 April 2019 (CCPR/C/USA/QPR/5).

Regarding the value of individual procedures, research by Shikhelman (2018) notes that since individual petitioning became available in 1977, some 2,371 petitions have been brought before the HRC through March 2014. Analysis of decisions in these cases, as well as interviews with a number of petitioners and their counsel and advisors, provides considerable insight into the successes and failures of this forum for those seeking relief. Shikhelman (2018) finds that there was substantial satisfaction on the part of claimants. They generally perceived the system as fair, and three-quarters of claimants felt their case had a wider impact on human rights compliance. A whopping 93.5 per cent of those interviewed would consider filing another case or recommending that others do so. Shikhelman also finds, however, that there is inadequate information available to potential claimants about *how* to access the claims system, especially in countries with poor human rights records. There was also considerable frustration among claimants in trying to contact HRC staff in connection with their filed claims.

Another finding is that the HRC staff has an extremely limited budget and received far more claims than could be processed efficiently; the average time from claim filing to decision was three and a half years. Most claimants had help with the process from NGOs or private lawyers. Unsurprisingly, states with poor human rights records were slow to comply with HRC decisions and often compliance was inadequate (ibid.: 482–512; David 2014a, 2014b). While more empirical research is needed on the promise and pitfalls of this process, the HRC may provide a fruitful (albeit imperfect) path forward to pursue victims' claims.

C. Implementation and Enforcement of Human Rights by Institutions of the United Nations

In addition to the systems of law and institutions established by the nine core human rights treaties, their protocols, regional human rights agreements and their tribunals, there are also important human rights institutions established by the United Nations General Assembly pursuant to the UN Charter. Prominent among these are the High Commissioner for Human Rights (HCHR) and the Human Rights Council (hereafter referred to as the Council, so as not to confuse it with the HRC discussed above).

The UN institutions act with authority applicable to all UN member states, and HCHR acts on a variety of subjects, including by conducting a broad assessment of the human rights situation of each UN member state through a process analogous to the treaty bodies' monitoring and reporting processes described above. This assessment, which began in 2006, is known as the Universal Periodic Review (UPR), and is performed by a working committee of all members of the UN Human Rights Council. Current information on the UPR process can be found at the HCHR website, including how public interventions are processed.[8] We strongly recommend that transnational repression should be one of the factors assessed in the UPR process for all states.

The HCHR also supports the other work of the Council, whose mandate is to prevent abuses, inequity and discrimination, to protect the most vulnerable and to expose perpetrators. It is composed of forty-seven elected UN member states, each serving three-year terms. The Council meets in Geneva for ten weeks each year, addressing human rights either in specific countries or regarding issues of general international concern.[9]

Civil society groups that are active on human rights issues can make a significant contribution to controlling transnational repression by urging treaty bodies, the HCHR and the Council to focus upon transnational repression as a continuing issue of concern in all of their activities.

D. Special Procedures: Thematic Mandates

One of the most important activities of the HCHR and the Council is to support the work of UN-appointed independent experts focusing on various specific issues in the human rights arena. The Council establishes mandates on particular subjects and appoints Working Groups and Special Rapporteurs to investigate and report on these subjects, including by proposing actions that may be recommended to the Council or other UN bodies and UN member states.[10]

The current mandates include a number of subjects highly relevant to transnational repression, for example: preventing arbitrary detention and

---

[8] See United Nations Human Rights Council. Basic facts about the UPR. [Online]. Available at: https://www.ohchr.org/en/hrbodies/upr/pages/basicfacts.aspx

[9] For more information about this process, see United Nations Human Rights Council. [Online]. Available at: https://www.ohchr.org/en/hr-bodies/hrc/about-council

[10] A list of the current mandates may be found at United Nations Human Rights Office of the High Commissioner. [Online]. Available at: https://spinternet.ohchr.org/ViewAllCountry-Mandates.aspx?Type=TM&lang=en

enforced disappearances and supporting freedom of opinion, expression, assembly and privacy. Residence states, civil society organisations and diaspora communities suffering from or concerned about controlling transnational repression should reach out to the holders of relevant mandates to inform their work and provide evidence for their reports. While the thematic mandate holders cannot act upon claims of individuals or groups directly, their reports and informal activities do address specific cases and can thus add pressure upon and provide evidence to treaty bodies, the Council and other UN agencies that are authorised to respond to specific claims.[11]

The problem of what Aljizawi and Anstis (2022), Michaelsen (2017 and in this volume) and others have dubbed as 'digital transnational repression' is currently being addressed through the Council's Special Procedures. The Special Rapporteur on the promotion and protection of the right to freedom of opinion and expression has called for renewed attention by the UN to digital surveillance practices and their impact on human rights. His report, published in May 2019, recommends establishing a cross-mandate UN task force or mechanism to address specific cases of human rights abuses facilitated by digital surveillance.[12] As noted in his report, the 'democratization' of digital surveillance tools increasingly facilitates the violation of individuals' human rights *across borders*. Private industry has bridged the capacity gap that made these technologies the preserve of only a few countries. Digital surveillance tools require particular attention, since even the attempt to use them against an individual (whether or not the subject has knowledge of it) constitutes an interference with fundamental human rights.[13]

[11] See, for example, the Human Rights Council report, published on 4 October 2019, on the execution of Jamal Khashoggi and related recommendations: 'A/HRC/41/36: Investigation of, accountability for and prevention of intentional State killings of human rights defenders, journalists and prominent dissidents – Report of the Special Rapporteur on extrajudicial, summary or arbitrary executions': https://www.ohchr.org/en/documents/thematic-reports/ahrc4136-investigation-accountability-and-prevention-intentional-state

[12] United Nations Human Rights Council, 2019, 'Report of the Special Rapporteur on the promotion and protection of the right to freedom of opinion and expression', p. 19, A/HRC/41/35.

[13] United Nations Human Rights Council, 'Report of the United Nations High Commissioner for Human Rights on the right to privacy in the digital age', p. 3, 3 August 2018 (A/HRC/39/29).

E. The International Court of Justice

The International Court of Justice (ICJ) is the principal judicial organ of the United Nations. It is the successor to the League of Nations Permanent Court of International Justice (PCIJ). It has jurisdiction to hear and decide disputes between UN member states that submit disputes to the ICJ by agreement or that have accepted the compulsory jurisdiction of the ICJ. While human rights questions are of concern in only a minority of the ICJ's cases, its rulings on such questions have a strong influence over international human rights law in general (Wilde 2013). An important decision affecting human rights law, 'Case Concerning Ahmadou Sadio Diallo', is discussed below in the section on the international law of reparations. The ICJ's decisions, in turn, are themselves influenced by the decisions and reports of the HRC and other treaty bodies, as well as the decisions of the regional human rights tribunals and other UN human rights agencies.

2. The Central Role of Residence States and Relevant Elements of the Law of State-to-State Relations

While residence states sometimes take actions to enforce human rights and protect victims of transnational repression, these actions have been wholly insufficient to stem the rising tide of transnational repression to date (Gorokhovskaia and Linzer 2022; Schenkkan and Linzer 2021). Residence states could better meet their obligations by using existing international legal structures to combat this practice, as we suggest below. State-to-state action should be a priority in order to, firstly, institutionalise and normalise the practice of countering transnational repression and, secondly, to raise the costs to offending states. Without the support of their residence state, victims often lack the capacity and resources to pursue claims on their own. Host states can act directly, both through human rights treaty bodies and regional human rights tribunals, and in co-operation with UN agencies. They can also act in co-operation with other host states through diplomatic channels.

Residence states can support and assist resident victims individually by making use of international institutions such as the HRC and regional human rights tribunals. The ICCPR and other human rights treaties and regional human rights tribunals provide procedures for individuals to file claims, including claims for compensation; however, the collection of evidence and preparation of claims can be a difficult process. Documentary evidence may be challenging for private citizens to obtain from government sources. Since governments whose residents are being injured by transnational repression are also themselves injured by the repressing state's illegal interventions into their domestic affairs, however, there is every reason for residence state governments to establish governmental facilities to assist transnational repression victims with claims preparation and otherwise support their efforts.[14]

One of the most difficult tools of transnational repression for states and victims to counter is proxy punishment, i.e. when states punish the families and colleagues of diaspora dissidents to discourage diaspora criticism (see Moss, Michaelsen and Kennedy 2022; Tsourapas this volume; Adamson and Tsourapas 2020). The origin state's proxy punishments are taken against residents of the origin state, as well as against diaspora property located there (as in the cases of land and housing seizures and the freezing of assets). The punishments are typically justified by trumped-up charges under domestic law such as disloyalty, corruption and/or terrorism, which has been legitimated during the ongoing War on Terror (see Roberts, this volume). Residence states are very limited in their ability to directly challenge a foreign state's actions under the residence state's domestic law. Proving that the origin state intends to punish its diaspora critics via the tactic of using false claims is factually difficult. In some instances, the jurisdiction of the courts of the residence state may be challenged and sovereign immunity may be asserted by the origin state.

Nevertheless, the growing practice of proxy punishment and the broader use of arbitrary arrest by repressive states has led human rights advocates to focus on the prohibition of arbitrary arrest and detention; Article 9 of the ICCPR and related international law protections of human rights offer potential remedies.[15] A promising example of multilateral co-operation to confront proxy punishment and related offences by repressive states is a Canadian initiative of February 2021. The Canadian government proposed a Declaration Against Arbitrary Detention in State-to-State Relations, and it issued a call for a response by other affected

---

[14] See, for instance, Anstis and Barnett's (2022) detailed analysis of the obligations of ICCPR state parties that host victims of digital transnational repression. The authors show that host states are obliged not only to refrain from such repression themselves, but also to take affirmative measures to protect residents from repression by origin states.

[15] See, for example, the UN Working Group on Arbitrary Detention (ohchr-wgad@un.org); International Convention on the Protection of all Persons from Enforced Disappearance: https://www.ohchr.org/en/instruments-mechanisms/instruments/international-convention-protection-all-persons-enforced

states as follows: 'By endorsing the declaration, states agree to stand in solidarity against arbitrary arrest, detention or sentencing by other states seeking to exercise leverage over them. Many countries have endorsed and promoted this declaration reaffirming their commitment to its guiding principles and recognizing that their nationals could be vulnerable to this type of treatment.'[16]

Unfortunately, sovereign states differ in their commitment to the treaties to which they have become parties and to the principles of the UN Charter. Victims of transnational repression are present in states that strongly support human rights treaty commitments, as well as in others that are indifferent or hostile to human rights. Victims of transnational repression who reside in states that do not support human rights will likely find little residence-state support for their efforts to invoke international legal commitments to combat transnational repression. In such cases, however, victims may pursue assistance from other sources. Assistance is available directly from UN human rights agencies, and the UN Human Rights Council provides helpful contact information on its website.[17] Several NGOs and private legal counsel are also available to assist in such cases,[18] and national human rights commissions, even in states indifferent to human rights, may also be helpful to victims and their advocates in pursuing claims by this mechanism (Kayaoglu 2021).

A. Confronting Transnational Repression Using the International Law of Reparations

An important potential deterrent to transnational repression by origin states could be vigorous support by residence states of resident victims' right to reparations.[19] A state's obligation to provide reparation for internationally

---

[16] The Canadian call for action can be found at: https://www.international.gc.ca/world-monde/issues_development-enjeux_developpement/human_rights-droits_homme/arbi-trary_detention-detention_arbitraire.aspx?lang=eng

[17] UN Human Rights Council, 'Human Rights Council Complaint Procedure', retrieved 29 June 2022: https://www.ohchr.org/en/hr-bodies/hrc/complaint-procedure/hrc-complaint-procedure-index

[18] See the Center for Civil and Political Rights, 'Individual Communications of the ICCPR', retrieved 30 June 2022: https://ccprcentre.org/individual-communications; The Freedom Initiative, retrieved 2 July 2022: https://thefreedomi.org

[19] For general information on the relation of reparation law to protection of human rights, see the Nuhanovic Foundation website (https://www.nuhanovicfoundation.org/pages/organi-zation/about-us-3). Retrieved 2 July 2022.

wrongful acts, including monetary damages, to both victims and their states of residence, is well established in customary international law. It has also been confirmed in decisions of various human rights and other international tribunals. The right to reparation to victims of human rights violations is founded in the earlier practice of state-to-state claims for reparation for injury to one state's nationals (including corporations) by another state.

In 1928 the Permanent Court of International Justice (PCIJ) (the forerunner of the ICJ), in the case of the *Factory at Chorzow (Germany v. Poland) (Claim for Indemnity) (Merits)*, held that 'it is a principle of international law, and even a general conception of law, that any breach of an engagement involves an obligation to make reparation'.[20] The PCIJ noted that reparations might take the form of 'an indemnity corresponding to the damage which the nationals of the injured state have suffered as a result of the act which is contrary to international law'.[21] The International Law Commission's Articles on State Responsibility, discussed below, provides an authoritative statement of the right to reparation in current international law and its direct applicability to individuals injured, as well as to their state of residence.

Provision for such reparations is provided by the ICCPR and many other human rights treaties, including regional human rights treaties. In cases seeking reparations, international institutions often have ruled that an offending state must cease its violation of an individual's rights and provide monetary compensation for injury. For example, the European Court of Human Rights awarded monetary compensation to Georgia and to some 1,500 Georgian nationals as reparation for violations by Russia of their rights under the European Convention of Human Rights. The Court found that Russia had undertaken a 'coordinated policy of arresting, detaining and expelling Georgian nationals' from Russia in the autumn of 2006. Monetary compensation was awarded both to the state of Georgia and to individual Georgian nationals.[22]

The ICJ has recognised that the scope of diplomatic protection includes protecting individuals from violations of their internationally guaranteed human rights. In the 'Case Concerning Ahmadou Sadio Diallo' brought by

[20] See p. 19: http://www.worldcourts.com/pcij/eng/decisions/1928.09.13_chorzow1.htm

[21] Ibid., pp. 27–8.

[22] Case of *Georgia v. Russia (I)* (Just Satisfaction) January 31, 2019, App.No. 13255/07, available at https://hudoc.echr.coe.int/fre#{%22itemid%22:[%22001-207757%22]}. See also the commentary at 113, the *American Journal of International Law* 581 (2019).

the Republic of Guinea (Guinea) against the Democratic Republic of the Congo (DRC), the Court granted monetary damages to Guinea based upon Diallo's unjustified arrest and detention by the DRC on two occasions, his expulsion from the DRC with less than one day's notice, and his subsequent loss of personal property, which he had accumulated during a period of thirty years living and working in the DRC. In its judgement, the ICJ cited *inter alia* violations of Article 9 of the ICCPR and Article 6 of the African Charter on Human and People's Rights.[23]

In these two recent cases, one before a human rights tribunal and the other before the ICJ (an international court of general subject matter jurisdiction), the international courts held that violations of claimants' human rights required reparations. Neither case involved acts of transnational repression by the defendant states; however, as we have argued, origin states' acts of transnational repression generally involve violations of victims' legally protected human rights such as freedom of speech, privacy, assembly and so forth. There is no reason to doubt that where a court finds that human rights violations are due to acts of transnational repression, the court would also find that an award of reparations would be appropriate. We look more closely at this connection in the next sections.

B. Using the International Law of State Responsibility to Enforce Provisions of the ICCPR

Another potential tool for controlling transnational repression could be enforcement by residence states of origin states' responsibility, using the international law of state responsibility.[24] Doing so would be straightforward

---

[23] 'Case Concerning Ahmadou Sadio Diallo', Judgement of 19 June 2012 International Court of Justice. See Vermeer-Kunzli (2007) for a case analysis and its wider implications for the law of diplomatic protection.

[24] The United Nations International Law Commission (ILC) works to make international law more accessible and coherent, in part by issuing studies and reports on important topics. Such a report on the law of state responsibility was presented to the UN General Assembly by the ILC in 2001. The report has been widely recognised as authoritative by states, and has been widely accepted as authoritative by international courts and tribunals since that time. Draft Articles on State Responsibility and Commentaries can be found in the UN online materials: https://legal.un.org/ilc/texts/instruments/english/commentaries/9_6_2001.pdf

where both residence state and origin state are parties to the ICCPR. The same would be true where both states are parties to other human rights agreements, such as the Convention Against Torture or regional human rights agreements. Article 1 of the Articles of State Responsibility sets out the basic obligation as follows: '. . . every internationally wrongful act of a state entails the international responsibility of that state'. Article 2 defines an internationally wrongful act of a state as one inconsistent with its international obligations. There is no requirement of fault or wrongful intent on the part of the offending state, which alleviates the burden of proving intent for victimised parties. Article 30 requires the responsible state to cease its wrongful conduct and offer assurances of non-repetition. Article 31 requires the responsible state to make full reparation for the injury caused.

Using the ICCPR as an example, when a state party to the ICCPR has performed acts of transnational repression that violate protected human rights of diaspora activists abroad in another ICCPR party state, such as the right to freedom of expression, it should be incumbent upon the residence state to protect its residents by invoking the origin state's responsibility for its wrongful acts and demanding the origin state's cessation and reparation to victims. Arguably, the resident state party to the ICCPR would be liable to the resident victim for reparation if relief could not be secured from the origin state committing the treaty violation.

C. Using the International Law of Diplomatic Protection to Enforce Provisions of the ICCPR

International law has long recognised that a state is entitled to provide protection to its nationals and certain others injured by wrongful acts of foreign states.[25] Like the state responsibility articles, the diplomatic protection articles have been widely accepted by states and international tribunals as authoritatively stating the applicable law. We argue that the law of diplomatic protection

---

[25] In a process like that described above for the law of state responsibility, the International Law Commission adopted Articles on Diplomatic Protection and related commentary, submitting them to the UN General Assembly in 2006. See International Law Commission, Draft Articles on Diplomatic Protection with Commentaries: https://legal.un.org/ilc/texts/instruments/english/commentaries/9_8_2006.pdf

can be an important tool for the use of residence states to protect residents from origin states' acts of transnational repression.

Article 1 defines the term 'diplomatic protection' as the invocation of responsibility by a protecting state against another state that injures the protecting state's national by committing an internationally wrongful act. Article 8 provides for a state to also extend its protection to a stateless person or refugee 'lawfully and habitually resident' in the protecting state.[26] Using these authorities of international law, an ICCPR state party could make a claim against an origin state demanding that the origin state cease its acts of transnational repression, which violate its resident's ICCPR-protected rights and provide reparation to the injured residence state's national or qualifying resident. Such a claim would be based upon the foreign state's acts of transnational repression against the protecting state's resident, which are intended to prevent that resident's exercise of their ICCPR protected rights, such as freedom of opinion and expression.

For example, an ICCPR resident state party could make a state-to-state claim directly against an origin state for violations of its resident's human rights protected by the ICCPR. The claim would be based upon the violation of the victim's ICCPR-protected rights such as freedom of speech, privacy and so forth. Based upon the law of diplomatic protection, we would argue that such claims could be made by a residence state party to the ICCPR, whether or not the origin state is a party to the ICCPR. This is because the residence state party is required by the ICCPR to protect its residents, and thus the origin state practising transnational repression is injuring the residence state by preventing the residence state from honouring its ICCPR obligations. Such failure to protect by the residence state would open the residence state to claims from victims for reparations pursuant to the ICCPR.

Such a claim could be made by a residence state on behalf of a group of resident transnational repression victims targeted by an origin state. The residence state would collect and assert a group of similar claims of illegal action inflicted upon residents of the residence state. Using this tool of international law, diaspora-wide protections against transnational repression could be implemented

---

[26] Diplomatic protection of non-nationals is subject to various conditions, explained in the Diplomatic Protection Articles and commentary, Article 8.

by a residence state. Such group claims, for instance, have been a regular feature of US diplomatic practice through the US Foreign Claims Settlement Commission (FCSC), an element of the US Department of Justice.[27] The FCSC has long operated a number of programmes that analyse and consolidate US nationals' claims of injury caused by foreign states or their agencies. The claims are then adopted (the formal diplomatic term is 'espoused') and asserted by the US government through diplomatic channels against offending foreign states. In co-operation with the Department of State, the FCSC seeks to negotiate lump-sum settlements with the offending state from which US resident victims may be paid.

D. The Requirement of Peaceful Settlement of Disputes

The body of law governing state-to-state relations includes obligations accepted by states as a result of their becoming parties to the United Nations Charter. The Charter is a treaty to which all 193 generally recognised sovereign states are presently parties. We argue that many cases of transnational repression, in effect, give rise to state-to-state disputes subject to Charter Article 33. In most cases, acts of transnational repression by an origin state are considered illegal actions by the residence state. Residence states would be within their rights to demand cessation and reparation for these actions from the origin state. If the origin state does not accept these demands, the residence state could demand that the resulting dispute be resolved peacefully through the provisions of Article 33. This article requires the parties to employ negotiation, mediation, arbitration, judicial settlement or other peaceful means of their choosing. If these means fail, either party may refer the dispute to the UN Security Council or the General Assembly.

Conclusion: Emerging Strategies to Confront Transnational Repression

The impact of transnational repression is serious, even devastating to its victims – but it is also a serious threat to friendly relations among states,

---

[27] Information on the practice of the FCSC and its legal basis may be found in a report of the US Library of Congress, 'The Foreign Claims Settlement Commission of the United States', 29 November 2019.

and therefore to international peace and security. Its use constitutes interference with a resident state's domestic affairs and is a serious infringement of the residence state's sovereignty. Yet transnational repression is increasingly used by repressive origin states to control dissident activities of their diaspora communities (Gorokhovskaia and Linzer 2022).

It is encouraging that a number of states, international institutions and non-governmental organisations are beginning to focus on the problem of transnational repression. The US State Department, for instance, has begun to call out states practising transnational repression in its annual human rights reports. The US federal government has also placed 'Khashoggi Ban' visa restrictions on foreign officials responsible for transnational repression. Such restrictions were first placed in March 2021 on seventy-six officials from Saudi Arabia 'engaged in serious, extraterritorial counter-dissident activities'.[28] In regard to China, the State Department announced the imposition of 'visa restrictions on PRC officials who are believed to be responsible for, or complicit in, policies or actions aimed at repressing religious and spiritual practitioners, members of ethnic minority groups, dissidents, human rights defenders, journalists, labor organizers, civil society organizers, and peaceful protesters in China and beyond' in March 2022.[29] This announcement clearly covers acts of transnational repression aimed at PRC critics and independent civil society members abroad.

Yet, case-by-case criminal prosecutions of individual agents of repressive states under national laws are, by themselves, unlikely to deter repressive states' efforts to control their diaspora communities and target exiled dissidents. Sanctions must be imposed on repressive states themselves, not only on their

---

[28] United States Department of State. 26 February 2021. 'Press Statement: Accountability for Murder of Jamal Khashoggi': https://www.state.gov/accountability-for-the-murder-of-jamal-khashoggi/#:~:text=The%20Khashoggi%20Ban%20allows%20the,%2C%20threaten%2C%20or%20harm%20journalists%2C

[29] United States Department of State. 21 March 2022. 'Press Statement: Promoting Accountability for Transnational Repression Committed by People's Republic of China (PRC) Officials': https://www.state.gov/promoting-accountability-for-transnational-repression-committed-by-peoples-republic-of-china-prc-officials/. See also recent examples of US use of national criminal law to prosecute acts of transnational repression by Iran, China and other origin states in 'United States Indicts Iranian and Chinese Government Agents for Targeting Individuals in the United States', 2022: *American Journal of International Law* 116(1): 179–84.

individual agents operating in foreign territories.[30] Access to international human rights institutions for victims must be facilitated by residence states. As we outline above, residence states should use the international laws of state responsibility, reparation and diplomatic protection to provide their residents with more powerful relief. This would require residence states working with diaspora communities to identify cases of transnational repression and assert claims for cessation and reparations against origin states.

We also suggest the following for countering cases of transnational repression. First, residence states and NGOs should go further by establishing ways to fund victims' individual proceedings before treaty bodies and international human rights tribunals. Second, UN agencies and human rights treaty bodies should also require additional resources, including funding and the employment of qualified staff, to handle an increased volume of cases. Third, the UN High Commissioner for Human Rights should focus on transnational repression as an increasing threat that demands active co-operation among human rights institutions and concerned states. By increasing the financial and reputational costs for repressive state governments employing transnational repression by demanding reparations and imposing penalties such as visa restrictions on repressive states and their agents, residence states can act in concert to deter repressive states. While international law is not a panacea for countering repression and violence, its impact can be substantially increased in the ways suggested in this chapter.

References

Adamson, F. and Tsourapas, G. 2020. 'At home and abroad: Coercion-by-proxy as a tool of transnational repression'. In Schenkkan, N., Linzer, I., Furstenberg, S. and Heathershaw, J. (eds), *Perspectives on 'Everyday' Transnational Repression in an Age of Globalization*. New York: Freedom House, pp. 9–13.

Aljizawi, N. and Anstis, S. 2022. 'The effects of digital transnational repression and the responsibility of host states'. *Lawfare* 27 May. Accessed 18 September 2023. Available at: https://www.lawfaremedia.org/article/effects-digital-transnational-repression-and-responsibility-host-states

---

[30] Anstis and Barnett (2022: 27) provide a set of best practices for ICCPR party states that would be highly effective in confronting repressive states and would also provide assistance to targeted diaspora communities.

Anstis, S. and Barnett, S. 2022. 'Digital transnational repression and host states' obligation to protect against human rights abuses'. *Journal of Human Rights Practice* 14(2): 698–725.

David, V. 2014a. 'Reparations at the Human Rights Committee: Legal basis, practice and challenges'. *Netherlands Quarterly of Human Rights* 32(1): 8–43.

——. 2014b. 'The expanding right to an effective remedy: Common developments at the Human Rights Committee and the Inter-American Court'. *British Journal of American Legal Studies* 3(1): 259–81.

Gorokhovskaia, Y. and Linzer, I. 2022. 'Defending democracy in exile: Policy responses to transnational repression'. Washington, DC: Freedom House, June. Available at: https://freedomhouse.org/sites/default/files/2022-05/Complete_Transnational RepressionReport2022_NEW_0.pdf

Kayaoglu, T. 2021. 'National human rights institutions: A reason for hope in the Middle East and North Africa?' Brookings Doha Center Analysis Paper No. 31. Available at: https://www.brookings.edu/wp-content/uploads/2021/01/ National-Human-Rights-Institutions.A.Reason-for-Hope-in-the-Middle-East-1.pdf

Michaelsen, M. 2017. 'Far away, so close: Transnational activism, digital surveillance and authoritarian control in Iran'. *Surveillance & Society* 15(3/4): 465–70.

Moss, D. M. 2016. 'Transnational repression, diaspora mobilization, and the case of the Arab Spring'. *Social Problems* 63(4): 480–98.

Moss, D. M., Michaelsen, M. and Kennedy, G. 2022. 'Going after the family: Transnational repression and the proxy punishment of Middle Eastern diasporas'. *Global Networks* 22(4): 735–51.

Schenkkan, N. and Linzer, I. 2021. 'Out of sight, not out of reach: The global scale and scope of transnational repression'. Freedom House, February. Available at: https://freedomhouse.org/report/transnational-repression

Shikhelman, V. 2018. 'Access to justice in the United Nations Human Rights Committee'. *Michigan Journal of International Law* 39(3): 453–531.

Wilde, R. 2013. 'Human rights beyond borders at the World Court: The significance of the International Court of Justice's jurisprudence on the extraterritorial application of International Human Rights Law treaties'. *Chinese Journal of International Law* 12(4): 639–77.

CONCLUSION
THE FUTURE OF TRANSNATIONAL
REPRESSION RESEARCH AND POLICY

Dana M. Moss and Saipira Furstenberg

The chapters in this volume advance our understanding of transnational repression in numerous ways. By investigating how authoritarian actors assert illiberal governmentality over their diasporas, we see how acts of transnational repression – which range from forced taxation (Hirt and Mohamed, this volume) and digital surveillance (Michaelsen, this volume) to unlawful renditions (Grossman and Hobbins, this volume) and coercion-by-proxy of families (Tsourapas, this volume) – pose a major threat to democratic freedoms, the rule of law and human rights across the globe.

Transnational repression is not a new phenomenon (Brand 2006; Shain 2005 [1989]). Nevertheless, in the twenty-first century, such practices have been fuelled by the resurgence of authoritarianism, interstate co-operation with authoritarian states, regimes' manipulation of international organisations like Interpol, technological advances and the Global War on Terror waged by the United States and its allies after the terrorist attacks of 11 September 2001. As a result, this problem is not only entrenched, but is increasing in frequency and scope around the world (e.g. Gorokhovskaia et al. 2022). It is no wonder that many diaspora communities feel insecure and helpless to deal with the problem of transnational repression on their own.

However, as Picard and Moss address in Chapter 13 (this volume), transnational repression constitutes an illegal act, and it is imperative that policymakers in host states fulfil their mandates and obligations to combat the practice. Doing so is necessary to protect the rule of law in sovereign territories and strengthen democratic resilience against authoritarian influence. Researchers, legal advocates, educators and university administrators, and civil society members can each play a role in undermining the long reach of globalised authoritarianism. In this chapter, we close by speaking to promising paths forward in transnational repression studies and what advocates can do to help victims of this practice.

Recommendations for Researchers and Universities

The study of transnational repression presents researchers with a number of challenges. For instance, online threats, hacking attempts and acts of proxy punishment can be difficult for investigators to detect and quantify. Diaspora members may be hesitant to discuss their experiences or report them out of fear owing to past traumas incurred from authoritarian repression and host-country discrimination. Anti-regime diasporas may be relatively invisible owing to the threats they face, save for a few outspoken exiles. Furthermore, diaspora members may face pressures to demonstrate loyalty abroad in their personal politics and through their organisational activities.

Yet, as Moss (2022) argues, we cannot assume that diaspora members from authoritarian regimes are apathetic, apolitical or inherently loyal to home-country regimes. It is imperative, therefore, that researchers not only examine transnational repression among diasporas who are willing to speak out, but also among those who are not. Covert regime practices keep people quiet and force them to act 'as if' they are loyal or passive (Wedeen 2015 [1999]), when in fact such communities face impediments of fear and mistrust (Pearlman 2017). This fear may even make the prospect of filling out an anonymous survey a daunting task. Researchers may do well to include diaspora community organisers and brokers in their community-based research, since these individuals are often well positioned to facilitate access, trust and rapport and the provision of testimonies among diaspora circles.

As the recent growth of transnational repression studies and corresponding investigations by think tanks, research groups and journalists illustrates, we now know more than ever before about transnational repression primarily owing to two data-collection methods. The first approach involves interviewing diaspora members, exiles and activists about their experiences with transnational repression. These studies often rely on large numbers of case-based informed testimony to uncover the range of threats facing activists and any patterns in their responses. The second method uses open-source data to track instances of violence that can be quantified, such as murders, attempted assassinations, kidnappings and renditions. Scholars have made enormous strides in compiling original datasets, such as the Central Asian Political Exiles Database (CAPE) and the Authoritarian Actions Abroad Database (AAAD), which document acts of violence committed against diaspora members abroad. Studies have also fruitfully used historical and archival methods to trace the development of transnational repression over time (Brand 2006; Lessa 2022), as well as first-hand observations on the ways that anti-regime activists are threatened by regime loyalists during public events (Moss 2016, 2022).

The above-cited data-collection methods have the potential to shed light on different dimensions of the problem and to counter regime denials of culpability, and such investigatory efforts must continue. Far more research across fields and methodologies is needed, not only to understand how transnational repression threatens diasporas, but also to compare host-country responses, both as enablers of transnational repression and combatants against it. Future work should also tackle how transnational repression intersects with geopolitics, states' migration policies and cultural genocide, racism and Islamophobia, since Muslims remain disproportionately targeted in documented cases (Schenkkan and Linzer 2021).

The growth of research has been bolstered through cross-organisational and cross-national investigations by researchers at Citizen Lab and reporters for *The Guardian* and *The Washington Post*, who have used their expertise to expose the way spyware is used to track dissidents' activities. This research has major geopolitical implications, since this spyware is also used to infiltrate the communications and reveal the whereabouts of political leaders and non-diaspora journalists as well. Moving forward, increased collaboration between journalists, researchers and tech experts will undoubtedly advance our understanding of its practice.

For foreign-born researchers with ties to authoritarian states, norms of academic freedom can conflict with the need to retain access to the home country and protect their families therein. Colleges and universities need to be better informed about these risks to their members. Administrators and department chairs can better direct social-psychological and legal support to their faculty and advise international students appropriately on the risks involved in researching home-country topics. Universities may be able to put systems in place for the safe reporting of incidents of intimidation and interference in campus activities and the classroom environment. At the same time, universities alone should not take on the responsibility of policing these threats internally. It is imperative that outside law enforcement be informed if regime officials are engaged in illegal meddling in student affairs and diaspora organisations through monitoring, financial support, intimidation and threats (Allen-Ebrahimian 2018). Travel warnings and citizenship options are also necessary to protect foreign students like Patrick Zaky, who was imprisoned upon returning home to Egypt due to his research and activism on gender and human rights (see Furstenberg et al., this volume).

Because regimes often control international scholarships and issue migration permissions for students who wish to study abroad, they keep a leash on international student groups to enforce loyalty (Del Sordi 2018). Although media outlets have reported on the Chinese regime's widespread interference in universities promoting free speech on the Uyghurs' plight, Tibet and repression in Hong Kong, for instance, administrators are often unaware of the ways in which students are coerced into expressing loyalty. As universities become more and more dependent on tuition fees from international students, they may be hesitant to challenge the status quo. However, any act of transnational repression taking place on campus constitutes a major violation of the law, the principles of academic freedom and the integrity of university systems. More proactive approaches are needed to inform students about their rights within organisations; to provide anonymous, safe reporting mechanisms for regime interference; and the means to sanction university insiders and outsiders for meddling.

What more can be done? In their study of Middle Eastern diaspora activists facing proxy punishment, Moss, Michaelsen and Kennedy (2022) find that activists and journalists are much more likely to continue exercising their rights when they have *social-psychological* and *legal institutional support*. Those without these kinds of resources are left to bear the heavy social and psychological costs on their own and to self-censor their activities. Such support is vital, therefore, for sustaining faculty and student flourishing and the production of knowledge. Universities should use every tool at their disposal, including legal advocacy, public relations and engagement with policymakers, to protect their faculty and students from such threats.

Recommendations for Receiving States, Policymakers and Civil Society

As several of the chapters in this volume illustrate, a host country's political and economic linkages have a significant impact on its responses to transnational repression by sending states. Quinsaat's research on Filipino-American activism (2019; Chapter 8 of this volume) and Furstenberg et al. (this volume) demonstrate that democracies become complicit in enabling transnational repression by collaborating with autocracies such as the Marcos regime in the Philippines and the Sisi regime in Egypt. Furthermore, Lessa's (2022) impressive book on the Condor Trials in Latin America demonstrates how the US's war on communism led arms of its government to collaborate with dictators in Latin America to track and deport suspected troublemakers across borders. In other circumstances, acts of transnational repression are used as bargaining chips in diplomacy. For instance, although Turkey widely condemned the Khashoggi murder on its soil in 2018, President Erdoğan transferred the investigation of Khashoggi's murder to Saudi Arabia in 2022 to improve bilateral ties. This effectively ended Saudi accountability and has given the regime of Crown Prince Mohammed bin Salman a tacit green light to continue pursuing his opponents abroad.

Host countries must recognise that transnational repression is a matter of national security concern. In combating such illegal acts, governments would do well to openly condemn such practices and sanction offenders, as the US has done by enacting a 'Khashoggi Ban'. As stated in a press release by the US Secretary of State in 2021, this Ban 'allows the State Department to impose visa restrictions on individuals who, acting on behalf of a foreign government, are believed to have been directly engaged in serious, extraterritorial counter-dissident activities, including those that suppress, harass, surveil, threaten, or harm journalists, activists, or other persons perceived to be dissidents for their work, or who engage in such activities with respect to the families or other close associates of such persons' (US Department of State 2022). Some

European countries are also being proactive in expanding asylum and refugee protections (Bocu et al., Chapter 10, this volume) and prosecuting 'refugee espionage', which generally refers to spying undertaken *of* refugees *by* refugees for origin states. While such policies are welcome, they also need to be enforced and supported with funding for training, community-based awareness raising, and language interpretation.[1]

The process of publicly condemning regimes and their members for enacting transnational repression, generally referred to as 'naming-and-shaming', is another important strategy in countering regime repression (Keck and Sikkink 1998). The US State Department, for instance, now includes transnational repression in its annual Human Rights Reports. Doing so alerts regimes that host states are on notice and incorporates transnational repression as a factor in the foreign policymaking process.

Governments could also sanction domestic and international corporations for providing members' personal information to repressive regimes. As Freedom House researchers Gorokhovskaia and Linzer (2022) argue, US State Department reports can be expanded to 'also include information on which companies or countries have provided biometric or facial-recognition data to states using these technologies to violate rights'.[2] Many countries, including Australia, Denmark, Norway and the US, have undertaken new efforts to establish the Export Controls and Human Rights Initiative designed to 'help stem the tide of authoritarian government misuse of technology and promote a positive vision for technologies anchored by democratic values'. These measures are badly needed, as democracies remain on the back foot in regulating and sanctioning the abuse of technology and Internet-based communications.

As discussed by Grossman and Hobbins (Chapter 9, this volume), countries like the United States must also refrain from using Interpol Red Notices as the sole or primary basis for detention and deportation, particularly when issued by regimes known for engaging in transnational repression. While the cross-border collaboration of security agencies is assuredly necessary to pursue

---

[1] US President Joe Biden raised eyebrows by potentially violating its own ban during the visit of Saudi Arabia's Deputy Defence Minister Prince Khalid bin Salman in 2022.

[2] See https://freedomhouse.org/policy-recommendations/transnational-repression, last accessed 5 October 2022.

criminals engaged in human trafficking and sex crimes, for instance, host countries too often act on politically motivated Red Notices based on false accusations. This is despite the fact that the US Department of Justice explicitly prevents the Immigration and Customs Enforcement (ICE) agency from treating a Red Notice as an arrest warrant. Further training is needed so that this practice is halted. Unfortunately, anti-migration policies and popular sentiment – mixed with globalised racism, ethnocentrism and xenophobia – make law enforcement quick to detain and deport without ensuring residents' rights. It is therefore essential that states protect refugees and the rights of asylum seekers, including when such persons are accused of terrorism and corruption by states with egregious human rights records.

The allocation of national security resources by host states towards sanctioning transnational repression is an important way to raise the costs of such acts for regimes. The establishment of tip lines for the safe reporting of transnational repression incidents, such as the one established by the US's Federal Bureau of Investigation in 2022, is a welcome step in that direction. Diaspora community leaders and organisations must be made aware of these resources in order for them to be effective, however. On that note, diaspora and human rights activists should be incorporated and consulted in shaping policy and security responses. Their insights are critically important to tracking transnational repression, identifying perpetrators and informing residents about their rights to free speech and assembly. Civil society advocates could provide at-risk communities with legal support and training on digital security (see Chapter 3), while advocates and state representatives can use international laws as reporting and accountability mechanisms (see Chapter 13). It is only with genuine collaboration and trust-building that diaspora communities will be empowered to speak out about their repression from foreign powers.

As pointed out by Marlies Glasius (2023), the criminal prosecution of transnational repression incidents is very rare. Yet the judicial pronouncement that follows them can provide a point of departure to combat transnational repression and to bring justice to the victims of transnational repression. The standardisation of such judicial practices could potentially bring societal transformations and encourage state actors to fulfil human rights law with greater commitment and integrity. Because threats posed by globalised authoritarianism and transnational repression loom large for the foreseeable future, diaspora members should not be left to deal with the threat of transnational repression on their own. Successfully combating transnational repression will necessarily depend on the co-ordinated efforts of varied institutions and advocates for human rights, academic freedom and democratic values, along with survivors across diaspora communities.

References

Allen-Ebrahimian, B. 2018. 'China's long arm reaches into American campuses'. *Foreign Policy*, 7 March. Accessed at: https://foreignpolicy.com/2018/03/07/ chinas-long-arm-reaches-into-american-campuses-chinese-students-scholars-association-university-communist-party/

Brand, L. 2006. *Citizens Abroad: Emigration and the State in the Middle East and North Africa*. New York: Cambridge University Press.

Del Sordi, A. 2018. 'Sponsoring student mobility for development and authoritarian stability: Kazakhstan's Bolashak Programme'. *Globalizations* 15(2): 215–31.

Glasius, M. 2023. *Authoritarian Practices in a Global Age*. Oxford: Oxford University Press.

Gorokhovskaia, Y. and Linzer, I. 2022. *Defending Democracy in Exile: Policy Responses to Transnational Repression*. June. Washington, DC: Freedom House.

Gorokhovskaia, Y., Schenkkan, N. and Vaughan, G. 2023. *Still Not Safe: Transnational Repression in 2022*. April. Washington, DC: Freedom House.

Jardin, B. 2022. 'Great Wall of Steel: China's global campaign to suppress the Uyghurs': https://www.wilsoncenter.org/book/great-wall-steel. Last accessed 9 June 2023.

Keck, M. E. and Sikkink, K. 1998. *Activists Beyond Borders: Advocacy Networks in International Politics*. Ithaca, NY: Cornell University Press.

Lessa, F. 2022. *The Condor Trials: Transnational Repression and Human Rights in South America*. New Haven, CT: Yale University Press.

Moss, D. M. 2016. 'Transnational repression, diaspora mobilization, and the case of the Arab Spring'. *Social Problems* 63(4): 480–98.

——. 2022. *The Arab Spring Abroad: Diaspora Activism against Authoritarian Regimes*. Cambridge: Cambridge University Press.

Moss, D. M., Michaelsen, M. and Kennedy, G. 2022. 'Going after the family: Transnational repression and the proxy punishment of Middle Eastern diasporas'. *Global Networks* 22(4): 735–51.

Pearlman, W. R. 2017. *We Crossed a Bridge and It Trembled: Voices from Syria*. New York: Custom House.

US Department of State. 2022. Secretary Antony J. Blinken on the Release of the 2021 Country Reports on Human Rights Practices: https://www.state.gov/secretary-antony-j-blinken-on-the-release-of-the-2021-country-reports-on-human-rights-practices/. Last accessed 9 June 2023.

Uyghur Human Rights Project and the Oxus Society for Central Asian Affairs. 2021. 'No space left to run: China's transnational repression of Uyghurs': https://oxussociety.org/wp-content/uploads/2021/06/transnational-repression_final_2021-06-24-1.pdf. Last accessed 9 June 2023.

Wedeen, L. 2015 [1999]. *Ambiguities of Domination: Politics, Rhetoric, and Symbols in Contemporary Syria*. Chicago: University of Chicago Press.

INDEX